MW00333637

How Colonialism
Preempted Modernity in Africa

HOW
COLONIALISM
PREEMPTED MODERNITY
IN AFRICA

Olúfẹ́mi Táíwò

INDIANA UNIVERSITY PRESS

Bloomington and Indianapolis

This book is a publication of

Indiana University Press
601 North Morton Street
Bloomington, IN 47404-3797 USA

www.iupress.indiana.edu

Telephone orders   800-842-6796
Fax orders   812-855-7931
Orders by e-mail   iuporder@indiana.edu

♾ The paper used in this publication meets the minimum requirements of the American National Standard for Information Sciences—Permanence of Paper for Printed Library Materials, ANSI Z39.48-1992.

Manufactured in the United States of America

Library of Congress Cataloging-in-Publication Data

Taiwo, Olufemi.
    How colonialism preempted modernity in Africa / Taiwo Olufemi.
        p. cm.
    Includes bibliographical references and index.
    ISBN 978-0-253-35374-0 (cloth : alk. paper) — ISBN 978-0-253-22130-8 (pbk. : alk. paper)
1. Africa—Civilization—Philosophy. 2. Africa—Colonial influence. 3. Africa—Colonization—History. 4. Europe—Colonies—Africa—History. 5. Colonies—Africa—History. 6. Africa—Politics and government. 7. Missionaries—Africa—History. 8. Democracy—Africa.
9. Capitalism—Africa. I. Title.
    DT14.T35 2009
    325.6—dc22

                                                                                    2009019610

1 2 3 4 5 15 14 13 12 11 10

To
Segun Osoba
Toye Olorode
Dipo Fashina
Teachers, Friends, Comrades

And

John Olubi Sodipo
Sweet are the memories of the just.

The proof is that at present [that is, while colonialism lasted] it is the indigenous peoples of Africa and Asia who are demanding schools, and colonialist Europe which refuses them; that it is the African who is asking for ports and roads, and colonialist Europe which is niggardly on this score; and that it is the colonized man who wants to move forward, and the colonizer who holds things back.

—Aimé Césaire

We claim, in common with the rest of mankind, that taxation without representation is a bad thing, and we are pledged, as all free peoples have had to do, that in our several communities the African shall have that common weapon for the protection and safeguarding of his rights and interests, namely, the franchise. It is desirable, we hold, that by our vote we shall determine by what laws we shall be governed and how the revenues which we help to put together shall be utilized.

Equally do we hold with others that there should be free scope for the members of the community, irrespective of creed or colour, to hold any office under the crown or flag to which a person's merits entitle him or her.

—J. E. Casely Hayford

CONTENTS

ACKNOWLEDGMENTS

For a work that has had as along a gestation as this one, it is quite in order that I have garnered a lot of debts along the way. While the work developed I moved around a lot, and as much as possible, I shall thank my benefactors according to where I met them and where they came to affect the shape or direction of this work.

The oldest antecedent of all the chapters of this book came out of the original project for which I was awarded a Rockefeller Postdoctoral Fellowship at the Africana Studies and Research Center, Cornell University, Ithaca, New York, back in 1990. There I met Kofi Anyidoho. If I could claim nothing else from my stay but Professor Anyidoho's friendship and his interest in and sponsorship of my work ever since, it would have been well worth it. Fortunately, Ithaca was also a place where I was blessed to interact with some old friends and make new ones. I would like to thank David Lyons, whose friendship and mentoring had a greater impact on me than I think he realized. I also thank Anne Adams; Biodun Jeyifo; Jim Turner; Robert Harris, Jr.; Abdul Nanji; and the late Don Ohadike. Yetunde Laniran always managed to save me from the terror of computers and their quirky ways.

In 1991, I moved to the Philosophy Department at Loyola University in Chicago. I was the beneficiary of the kindness and professional support of so many colleagues during the many years I spent there. As the individual acknowledgments in different chapters show, the bulk of the research that has been gathered in this book was done while the department at Loyola served as my home base. My Chicago years were productive but they also were some of the most difficult periods of my life so far, both personally and professionally. I am forever thankful for the support of my Chicago family, who never let me really discover how bad my situation then was until I left and was able to look backward with some detachment. I thank Hugh Miller and his family; David Schweickart, David Ingram, Thomas Sheehan, and the rest of the Heartland Café Sunday morning group; Julie Ward and her husband, Ezio Vailati, "my countryman"; Holly Graff; David Ozar; Ardis Collins; Sue Cunningham; Andrew Cutrofello; Jennifer Parks; the late Hans Seigfried; Ken Thompson; Heidi Malm; Patricia Huntington; Tom Carson; Diane Suter; Cheryl Johnson-Odim and her family; Susan Cavallo; Judith Wittner; Ayana Karanja; Clement Adibe and his family; Chiji Akoma and his family; Charles Mills; Bernard Walker; Leslie Brissette; and Jeanne Huchthausen.

The graduate students who participated in my seminar on Modernity and Colonialism at Loyola University in 1998–1999 deserve mention. Among them, Shannon Shea, who later served as my research assistant, must be cited for special thanks. She was an invaluable assistant and tracked down materials for me at crucial stages in the evolution of my research. Kory Schaff and Katrina Sifferd read earlier versions of chapter 5 and gave me helpful feedback. Colleen Sweeney, Carole Heath, Cynthia Brincat, Carmela Eppright, David Gandolfo, Judy Massey-Dozier, and Lenora Jean Daniels, along with those I just mentioned, are all former graduate students whom I am honored and proud to now call friends.

When I was invited to spend a most fruitful week as a Visiting Distinguished Minority Scholar at the University of Wisconsin-Eau Claire, Professors Tess Onwueme and Obika Gray were incredible hosts. The community there provided the original audience for the precursor of what is now chapter 2. I thank them for providing me with enough activities in one week to try out many new ideas. I also thank Masako Arisawa, then of Menomonee, Wisconsin, now of Kobe, Japan, for her continuing friendship.

I was invited to Bayreuth in 1999, where I served as a Visiting Professor at the Institut für Afrikastudien, Universität Bayreuth. I would like to thank my host, Professor Dr. Dierk Lange and his family; Dr. Peter Probst and his family; and Professor Dr. Ulrich Berner of the Religious Studies Department for their hospitality and generosity. I also thank Gabriele Weisser, Heike Wildemann, Diatou Sylla, Lucia Dogbe, Thorstein Parchent, and Kristin Scherer. Professor Dr. Eckard Breitinger's friendship and generosity remain ever green in my heart. The Nigerian academic community I met in Bayreuth was a welcome surprise and a source of strength and inspiration. I take this opportunity to express my appreciation for the support, encouragement, and friendship of Charles Bodunde, Wole Ogundele, and Onookome Okome. And to the rest of the Nigerian community who welcomed me into their homes, I remain grateful. Part of what they taught me with their stories is reflected in this book. I would like to say to my Bayreuth community that your city and your welcome did a lot more for me than you will ever know.

During my one-year stay at the Carter G. Woodson Institute, University of Virginia, Charlottesville, this book came together, and for that I must thank the incredible good luck that placed me in the midst of one of the most intellectually active communities I have ever participated in. Tejumola Olaniyan, brother, friend, comrade, and original instigator of my venture to UVA, and Mojisola Olaniyan, "de Law," and their family deserve special gratitude. Aà ní tẹ́ lọ́wọ́ ara wa o. Director Reginald Butler and Associate Director Scot French facilitated my work. The core of young scholars, junior postdoctoral fellows, and predoctoral fellows challenged my thinking in more ways than they would permit themselves to believe. Dr. Meta DuEwa Jones, Jemima Pierre, Joseph Hellweg, Mieka Brand, Jeffrey Fleisher, Adrian Hastings, Peter Bwenge, I hope that this reminds you all of what a wonderful time we shared in Charlottesville. I thank Professor Hanan Sabea and Professor George Mentore of the Anthropology Department and Andrew Efemini of the Government Department.

Seattle University has been my home and my place of work since August 2001. I could not have asked for a better place to work and a more positive social setting to operate in. Former dean Wallace Loh led by example and with inspiration, and I will always be grateful for his support and encouragement. I thank the rest of my Seattle University community for your past support: Coreen Painter; Christian Lotz; Burt Hopkins; Paul Kidder; Marc McLeod; Tom Murphy, S.J.; Paulette Kidder; James Risser; Maria Carl; Pat Burke; Marylou Sena; Dan Dombrowski; Mary-Antoinette Smith; Nalini Iyer; Margaret Chon; Kellye Testy; Ron Slye; Hank McGee, Jr.; Gabriella Guttierez y Muhs; Ruth White; Jodi O'Brien; Edwin Weihe; Ed Reed; Jason Wirth; Elizabeth Sikes; Mako Fitts; Gary Perry; Mary Gatliff; Rose Zbiegen; Jo Kirschner; Jeanette Rodriguez; Jacque Ensign; and Kate Reynolds. I look forward to continuing friendship and engagement with all of you. I am grateful to the staff of the Circulation Desk in Lemieux Library at Seattle University for the good humor and efficiency with which they have helped me obtain materials from far and wide. I must single out Saheed Adejumobi, my colleague in the Global African Studies Program and dear àbúrò, for special mention. Although I would hate to put on him any of the responsibility for the ideas expressed in this book, he, more than any other person, has influenced the final shape of this book since he came into it a few years back. Ever forthcoming with links and sources for me, he has made me rethink many parts and look at various sources and has been invaluable in offering advice on so many parts of the book. O kú ọwọ́ọ̀ mi o.

To my extended Nigerian family in Seattle, many thanks for helping make community a reality and for your friendship and support.

I continue to treasure my circle of friends with whom I go back several years. Simeon Ilesanmi, Njoki Kamau, Adetoun Ilumoka, Jacob Olupona, Nkiru Nzegwu, Oyeronke Oyewumi, Akin Adesokan, Adeolu Ademoyo, Idowu Obasa, Dapo Olorunyomi, Kemi Rotimi, Tola Pearce, Sheila Walker, Inka Alasade, Keren Brathwaite, and Susan Babbitt are old friends and worthy interlocutors who with their questions, qualms, doubts (sometimes about my sanity), and even, on occasion, hostility have forced me to articulate the case made in this book with more clarity. Without them this book would not be what it is now. I am forever in their debt, and I thank them for keeping me honest.

I cannot say enough about Adéyínká Táíwò, obìnrin lójọ́ gbogbo (a woman for all time), whose love and support, especially in the darkest days, have been invaluable to me as I have regrouped over the years. *Ọmọ pupa,* I am deeply grateful. To Kayode Táíwò, my perennial "landlord" but, more important, my *igi lẹ́hìn ogbà* in Nigeria, many thanks. *Aà ó ní rátẹ̀hìnkù mọ́ o. Àṣẹ.* May you continue to grow in wisdom.

Dee Mortensen and her assistant at Indiana University Press deserve special thanks for their efforts on behalf of this book and for providing me with a wholesome working experience as they shepherded the manuscript to publication. Kate Babbitt, my copy editor, has made this a better book than when she originally received it. I thank Souleymane Bachir Diagne for a critical intervention at a crucial stage of this book's evolution.

That I am completing the final leg of work on this book in Kingston, Jamaica, is an accident. But that I have the privilege of doing so surrounded by love and support is a testimony to my dear old friend and colleague from our days together as graduate students at Ile-Ife so many moons ago, Ayotunde Bewaji. He and his family have made me welcome for this last half of my sabbatical and have been wonderful in making sure that I am able to meet the challenge of completing this and other works. The staff of the Department of Linguistics, Languages and Philosophy at the University of the West Indies at Mona have been most helpful in ensuring that I accomplished the task with no disruption. I thank them for welcoming me into their community.

To all other friends and well-wishers everywhere whose names I have not mentioned, forgive my lapse. It is not for lack of affection and gratitude.

To all and sundry: *Ire kàbìtì!*

Olúfẹ́mi Táíwò
Kingston, Jamaica
March 2009

How Colonialism
Preempted Modernity in Africa

Introduction
Of Subjectivity and Sociocryonics

Preamble

The work presented in this book and the research on which it is based started innocently, perhaps even obliquely. It was 1989 and the movement that would later morph into the so-called third wave of the transition to democracy in Africa was yet to ignite. For a long time prior to then, I had wondered why the various institutions that we had inherited from or that were bequeathed to us by British colonialism did not work in our land the way they do in the country (and others like it) from which they have come to us. My concerns were quite catholic in scope. But the immediate concern that led me to seek assistance toward a research agenda turned on the career of law in Commonwealth Africa. My motivation for research was summed up in a simple question: Why do African governments almost always win cases involving conflicts between citizens and the state, especially when such conflicts involve human rights? Of course, if you were a Marxist or any of the other varieties of radicalism, including nihilism, that proliferated on the continent then, the answer was simple and straightforward: The system we inherited from or had bequeathed to us by colonialism was only superficially equitable and rigged for justice for all. All the chatter about equality before the law, the law being no respecter of persons, and so on, was just that: chatter. But I could not share those sentiments. In the first place, I thought that instrumentalist theories of law could not deeply explain the law's appeal to even the subaltern classes in modern society and why people, ordinary folk, repeatedly allowed themselves to be "victimized" by the law. Nor was it acceptable to say that subaltern victories were mere sops thrown at them by the ruling classes to pacify them. This would require epistemic competence bordering on clairvoyance on the part of the ruling classes to know what would work and when not to try something that, I am convinced, is not available to anyone, ruler or not.

Meanwhile, to those invested in the British common law system predominant in Commonwealth Africa,[1] the repeated victories of governments could be chalked up to the quirks of the law, the incompetence of lawyers, the timidity of judges or their preferred jurisprudence, and the lawlessness of African executives. Again, I could not persuade myself to accept this alternative explanatory model. Yes, the cited factors may explain part of the riddle, but they themselves are susceptible to deeper etiologies. After all, similar factors had at one time or the other been replicated in Britain and the psychological proclivities involved could not be limited to African operators. It then needs to be explained why these factors turn out the kinds of consequences that they do in Africa. I set out to explore the question and its many answers in three countries: Nigeria, Kenya, and Tanzania. The time frame was roughly the first decade or less after independence. I had thought that I would conclude the research and report it in a series of three country-specific articles for a journal or law review.

As the research progressed, I repeatedly apprehended some commonalities in the experiences of the three countries in spite of their (at least superficially) divergent trajectories in the post-independence period. In spite of their different experiences I discovered that the genealogy of the judiciaries in the three countries went back to the colonial period and did not replicate the emergence of the legal system in the Britain from which they were imported to Africa.[2] I expanded my research to look at what transpired under colonialism. It became clear to me that there was a more complex story to tell than just the career of human rights and judicial behavior in post-independence Nigeria, Kenya, and Tanzania. The essays in this book represent my attempt to tell that story.

The judicatures that I had been studying were part of a complex of institutions that colonialism had introduced to Africa while it lasted. Part of the apologia of Africa's colonizers was that their legacy included the implantation in the colonies of the following concepts:

(1) a democratic mode of governance built on the consent of the governed
(2) a system of governance based on the periodic election of representatives
(3) elected officials who swear to uphold the rule of law
(4) a constitutional regime in which every citizen is equal before the law
(5) a legal system that does not try individuals under retroactive laws
(6) a legal system that does not respect persons based on circumstances of birth or heredity
(7) an assumption that the accused are innocent until proven guilty
(8) trials that are regulated by due process
(9) a system that affirms and upholds human rights, including the right to life, liberty, and all ancillary freedoms

I do not think that many would demur when I assign this complex of ideas, practices, and institutions to what we generally call the legacy of the Enlightenment or modernity. That is, it is a crucial part of colonialists' understanding of colonialism and the narratives of its promoters that it was the vehicle through which Africa and modernity were introduced to each other.

Why Does Modernity Fail to Take Root in Africa?

In this book, I set out to rethink the relationship between colonialism and modernity in Africa.[3] The relationship between colonialism and modernity should once again come under the searchlight in the contemporary period for many reasons. Many problems that afflict various African countries at the present time with differing degrees of intensity are frequently traced to the lingering effects of colonialism. Insofar as colonialism and modernity are used interchangeably in much of the discourse about Africa and its colonial legacy and many of the institutions left behind by colonialism are judged to be modern, it is important to disentangle the two concepts or at least see in exactly what way they have impacted the continent. It is arguable that the key problems that bedevil Africa and are traced back to colonialism can, almost without exception, be conceptualized in terms of Africa's relation to, experience of, and engagement with modernity.

Take law and its vicissitudes in Africa, for one instance. Let us assume for argument's sake that the rule of law and the independent judiciary that it requires to work well are genuine legacies of colonialism in the continent. No one contests the fact that the operation of the law and the experience of Africans with the legal system have not been particularly salubrious. As I said earlier, regardless of which explanation I offer, at some point it will be necessary to deal with the provenance of the legal system in and its necessary attachment to modernity. That is, the municipal legal systems in Commonwealth Africa are of a modern pedigree, which means that as such they are underpinned by some philosophical presuppositions from which they derive their valence and identity. These include the idea of the legal subject, the inviolability without due process of the sovereignty of the subject, the separation of powers in the state, the presumption of innocence and the impartiality of the operators of the system, and the necessity for the judiciary to remain an arbiter between the powerless individual and the all-powerful state. If indeed these are the fountainheads of the institutions colonialism claims to have bequeathed, then we are right to ask why the reality is at such a wide variance with the rhetoric.

The evidence points in the opposite direction. Insofar as the idea of the rule of law is understood as a specifically modern idea, it was not part of the operation of colonialism in Commonwealth Africa. If it then turns out that there is some sense in which we can separate colonialism from modernity and compare the aspects of each with those of the other, we may then be well on our way to a better accounting of why what colonialism claims to have installed in Africa in the shape of modern institutions, ideas, and practices unravels all too often in the post-independence period.

The core idea is to challenge the received wisdom that colonialism facilitated the introduction and installation of modernity in Africa. When I started the work there were few people who even thought that modernity could offer a relevant (much less fecund) explanatory model for analyses of African events. Although times have changed and we have a slew of works that are taking another look at the matter of Africa and modernity, I remain unsatisfied with the state and nature of the scholarship on modernity and colonialism in Africa. First, care is not taken to differentiate between colonialism and modernity.[4] I insist that not only can they be separated, they are indeed historically separate and must be separated for analytical purposes. When they are not separated, a much more severe critique of colonialism on account of its aborting the implantation of modernity in Africa is thereby preempted. What is more, given that modernity has engendered forms of social living that command our approbation in different parts of the world and even in our lands when we have experienced some of its promise, it is not out of place to inquire into what the continent's history might have been like and what its prospects would be were it seriously and under its own steam to embrace what modernity promises.

Moreover, much of the scholarship is apt to treat colonialism as if it were a monolith. This applies not only to analyses of colonialism in Africa but also to our understanding of colonialism globally. Yet even a cursory investigation of the history of colonialism and its philosophical underpinnings will reveal that it does not come in one flavor and that zeroing in on its historicity is crucial to unraveling its differential impact in various countries that experience one or the other form of it. When we identify and work through the implications of different kinds of colonialism it will become clear why Africa's recovery from the ravages of colonialism has been slow to nil while other former colonies have moved on to prosperity that is even enabling them to constitute a new group of alms-givers to Africa's inveterate beggars. Such a process of isolating the specificity of the colonialism that predominated in Africa is our best tool for rebutting the presumption that Africans' congenital inability related to their racial inheritance is what explains Africa's failure to shed the shackles of colonialism.

Not only is it imperative for us to isolate and fully describe the specificity of African colonialism, we also need to resist the urge to collapse the diverse experience of and response to colonialism in different parts of Africa. That is, the widespread practice of talking nebulously about colonialism's impact that does not pay attention to the differentials across the continent in the relative development of material and intellectual culture; the divergent manifestations of African agency in its experience of and response to colonialism among Africa's many peoples and cultures; and the unequal and nonsimultaneous introduction of modernity to various parts of the continent and the degrees of domestication of its principles enacted again by African agency must be eschewed. Needless to say, we must beware of unsupported generalizations informed by a tendency toward homogenization in the discourse about colonialism and modernity in Africa.

To accomplish the foregoing requires us to show not only that colonialism and modernity are separate and separable but also that the relationship between the two is not what conventional wisdom takes it to be. I propose to argue that the only way we can continue to accept this wisdom is if we obscure some key distinctions in the discourse and operation of colonialism. Additionally, if it were indeed true that colonialism midwifed the birth of modernity in Africa, then the career of modernization processes in post-independence Africa ought to have been different. We ought to have had installed in our societies the various markers of modernity's distinctiveness. On the contrary, what we have had have been the superficial markers—skyscrapers, more miles of macadamized roads, more schools, mass consumption, rapid urbanization, and limited industrialization. What is distinctive about modernity is not so much that it builds high technology and creature comforts but that it enjoins modes of being human that have been considered superior to previous and alternative forms in human history. That is, the distinctive marker of modernity is to be found in its politico-philosophical discourses that can be summed up in three key concepts: *subjectivity, reason,* and *progress.*[5] Given that its career, seen in light of its politico-philosophical discourses, has been characterized by failure, a fact that in spite of recent gains in democratization and economic liberalization continues to be reflected in the many books lamenting Africa's awful fate, we must ask why modernity—the essence that modernization processes seek to realize—has not taken hold in the continent.

One possible answer is to say that Africa is hostile to modernity and its presuppositions. That is, that there is something in the African air, water, or soil that makes it inhospitable for modernity to take roots and be firmly implanted there. A related response is to say that Africans are congenitally incapable of working modernity. Neither explanation is plausible. They are racist to boot. But their implausibility does not stem from their racism. The problem is that such explanations tend to ignore history. The genealogy of modernity in Africa predated colonialism. Only if we take colonialism to refer to the entire phenomenon of European adventures in Africa can we sustain the assimilation of modernity to colonialism.[6] Historians have established some differentiations among the ranks of European adventurers in Africa. They have identified three classes of Europeans—missionaries, traders, and administrators—among whose ranks we must include the military adventurers.[7] For the most part, missionaries and traders predated the administrators, and even though traders set up the earliest protocolonial administrations, there is no evidence that missionaries similarly set up administrations for the governance of native peoples. In light of this historical fact, it is necessary to shift the focus away from a monolithic characterization of colonialism to a differentiated understanding of it. That is, we should heed the caution stated above to not generalize on the career of colonialism in the continent.

In addition to their differential roles in Africa's history, the different classes did not all arrive on the continent at the same time. In this work, I have isolated and built the major empirical part of my case around what I take to be the *peculiar* circumstances of Anglophone West Africa. In the aftermath of the initial voyages of the fifteenth century, missionaries and traders alternated in their arrivals, departures, and shifting significance in that region until the nineteenth century, when the administrators made their initial appearance. By the third quarter of that century, administrators had become the dominant class of Europeans in West Africa. What implications may we draw from these empirical factors for our understanding of the impact of the European presence in West Africa?

Fishing for Souls: Making Modern

If we take seriously the differences among the classes of Europeans, we must simultaneously reconceptualize the genealogy of modernity in Africa. I argue that the credit for introducing Africans to modernity must go to the missionaries.[8] Of course, this contradicts the received wisdom that attributes the westernization of Africa and the continent's induction into modernity to colonial administrators. In fact, I go so far as to contend that in their interactions with Africans, the missionaries were the revolutionaries and the administrators were the reactionaries. Once we acknowledge the revolutionary role of missionaries, new analytical possibilities suggest themselves. Modernity is a larger movement than colonialism, and it is the essence that the colonial authorities in different parts of the continent claimed to be implanting in the continent. Missionaries were the first to make the implantation of "civilization," which for so long was indistinguishable from the forms of social living coterminous with modernity, one of the cardinal objectives of their activities in Africa.

But there is an interesting side to the missionary factor in the propagation of modernity in Africa. Although at the beginning of the process the missionaries were mostly white, the complexion of the missionaries quickly changed to incorporate in their ranks Africans themselves. It is not insignificant that the first missionary of this complement to make port in coastal Nigeria, for instance, was Thomas Birch Freeman, a mulatto, and that the person under whose bishopric much of coastal West Africa and huge parts of interior present-day Nigeria were Christianized was Samuel Ajayi Crowther, a recaptive Yorùbá.[9] *I shall argue that the principal agents for the introduction and implementation of modernity in Africa were missionaries and that many of them were themselves Africans.* This fact has implications for some of the central tenets of modernity, especially respecting the centrality of agency or, in philosophical terms, the principle of subjectivity. The promise of self-realization, of the exercise of the privilege of making or marring their lives according to the light of reason guided by their Christian heritage, turned many Africans who accepted the Christian message into proselytizers of their own people. They accepted the Christian message and aspired to make it their own. As a corollary, they sought to remake their societies after the image of modernity.

What I have just described happened specifically in West Africa in the first half of the nineteenth century. It is much discussed in the historical literature, but there is a paucity of philosophical or theoretical analysis that works through the implications of the play of subjectivity in the unfolding of the career of modernity once formal colonialism was clamped on the territory from the later nineteenth century onward. So in a sense, some of the essays included in this collection are attempts to retrieve the contributions of African agents in the discourse and career of modernity in West Africa; other essays are reinterpretive.

West Africa witnessed a second wave of evangelization in the nineteenth century. It was part of the evangelical revival and the humanitarian movement, especially its abolitionist wing.[10] This wave of evangelization was qualitatively different from the earlier one in the fifteenth and sixteenth centuries: it was post-Reformation Christianity. That it was post-Reformation-inflected Christianity that came back to the West African coast in the nineteenth century had implications for the kind of Christianity that was propagated by the new missionaries. Given its predominantly Protestant inflection, the principal tenets of Protestantism—heterodoxy, pluralism, the priesthood of all believers, the centrality of individual conscience and freedom of religion—were in evidence, though not without considerable tension, especially where native religions were concerned.

One could not subscribe to the principle of subjectivity on which the corollary principles of the centrality of the individual conscience and the freedom of the individual to profess or not profess faith are founded and at the same time not take African agency seriously. The missionaries of that period under the official philosophical leadership of Rev. Henry Venn, the long-serving secretary of the Church Mission Society (CMS), held that their aim was to create national churches that, driven by African agency in all its ramifications, would be *self-supporting, self-propagating, and self-governing.*[11]

With all the emphasis on the notion of the self and their solicitous attitude toward African agency one may erroneously conclude that the early-nineteenth-century missionaries thought that Africans were their equals. No; they still thought of their relations with their African converts in hierarchical terms, and they were the superior party. The difference between them and their successors in late nineteenth and twentieth centuries was that they had a benign view of Africans as blighted but by no means any less children of God.[12] Their roots in both the evangelical revival and the humanitarian movement, which was linked to the struggle for the abolition of the slave trade and slavery and in which they had worked with African-descended individuals in leadership positions, meant that they were more likely to think that the Africans' lagging behind the rest of humanity had nothing to do with their nature—they were all God's children—but with the sordid history of enslavement and the general and widespread destruction that it left in its wake. As such, they thought that as a way of expiating their guilt for the fact that their European compatriots had participated in the slave trade and slavery, they owed it to Africans to make them whole again.

As important as it is to remark and work with this cohort's view of Africans, our main focus is on the Africans who were tutored by them. African agency is front and center in the discussion presented in the following chapters. All too often, the overemphasis on the activities of Africa's conquerors translates into a shortchanging of what Africans themselves made of whatever it is that their alien rulers did to and with their subjects. Yet given the centrality of the subject to the philosophical discourse of modernity and the fact that by its very nature the human subject cannot have its subjectivity absolutely eviscerated except in death, it would be strange indeed if Africans were no more than playthings in the hands of alien gods. What this group of Africans did with what they were taught, regardless of what their tutors thought, expected, or wanted to see them do, is the core of the original induction of modernity into Western Africa.

I will show that Africans were diligent and quick learners. When the revolutionary missionaries proclaimed that their aim was to equip Africans to found, run, and support national churches, Africans not only took their words to heart, they set about making themselves worthy of the confidence reposed in them by their tutors. But that was only half of the story. What they learned from the church they took to other areas of life. It is one of subjectivity's quirks that the tutor cannot always determine how the tutored will use the tuition or in what directions the student might choose to express her agency. The African graduates of what I call the missionary school of modernity were no exceptions to this rule. Many (but by no means all) Africans had become sold on the positive features of the new way of life, not the least of which was the metaphysics of the self and the forms of social living that it entailed. The transition to modernity was inaugurated under the direction of native agency in the context of the propagation of Christianity, civilization, and commerce.

The processes that I have just described form the empirical basis for my contentions that modernity predated colonialism in Africa; missionaries midwifed the introduction of modernity to Africa; and modernity was driven by native agency and took place in West Africa and (for the most part) in the Anglophone areas of the region. It might be asked: Why speak of Africa in talking about something restricted to West Africa? And can the conclusion drawn from the West African case be generalized for the rest of the continent?

Working through the contradictions of modernity and colonialism in Anglophone West Africa made me realize that there was only one reason why the contradictions were so acute and their implications so stark: A sizable number of Africans was present who had been inducted into and accepted modernity and its discourses and had become proselytizers to their own people. These individuals wanted to remake their societies along modern lines *before* the imposition of formal colonialism and the ascendancy of the administrator–military adventurer class. It was in the process of making sense of the conundrums generated for the operation of colonialism and modernity in that theatre that I discovered that what happened there—specifically, the philosophical template that informed policy formulation under formal colonialism—is generalizable for the rest of Anglophone Africa, including South Africa. I then proceed to speculate, *not* generalize, on how things might have turned out differently had alternative paths that were indicated not been foreclosed by the colonial authorities. In a sense, then, I am reversing the usual practice of people using Africa as their frame of reference even while they are unmindful of or indifferent to regional variations of the theme they treat. In the present case, I start from a deep exploration of my theme in a specific region. I proceed to invite other scholars to see what this region shares with others and whether the analysis here enables other analysts to see in their respective regions what may be there but has been obscured by their limited inventory of concepts.

Despite my reticence to generalize, the second question on the generalizability of my conclusion remains relevant. Can this conclusion be generalized for the rest of the continent? My simple answer is yes. But that is as far as I am prepared to go. What specific analyses will be needed to flesh out the skeletal yes will have to be offered by other scholars in Francophone, Lusophone, Anglophone, and Islamic Africa. My contention is that using the theoretical template this book offers opens up new vistas for scholarship on Africa, colonialism, and modernity. For example, although I do not do so in this work, there is evidence that the situation in Francophone West Africa, with allowance made for the specificity of domestic French politics and the ebb and flow of the republican idea in France, was strikingly similar to what I have isolated in the Anglophone parts. There is evidence that the motivation for the founding of the four communes in Senegal and their eventual collapse into the later French colonial pattern mirrors the trajectory and fortunes of colonies like Lagos and Freetown in British West Africa. It will require regional works by experts in the area to establish the adequacy of my thesis.

There is one final caveat in this section. My focus here on Christian missionaries as the principal vehicle for introducing modernity to a specific area of Africa does not preclude that there were additional actors in the process. For example, I do think that the career of Samori Toure in the nineteenth century in the area of present-day Guinea may signify a similar path. But this can be established only by research that separates modernity from colonialism and assesses Africa's relations with the former independently of the latter. The focus on missionaries in this work is purely fortuitous, but finding out the qualitative difference in their engagement with West African natives and the specific development of native agency under their initial tutelage deserves the philosophical attention that I have lavished on then.

"Cast not your pearl before swine": The Administrator Cometh

By the third quarter of the nineteenth century, not only was a new cohort of missionaries supplanting the earlier one, the adventurer-administrator class was beginning to assert itself and take the upper hand in the colonies and other dominated territories in West Africa. The difference between the first cohort of Europeans and the latter one must be understood for my argument to succeed. It would be a mistake to think that because the missionaries were desirous of teaching African agents to be autonomous again after the tragedy of slavery and the slave trade there were none among them who held a negative view of Africans and their ability to take charge once again of their own affairs. The difference was that among the original cohort of missionaries the view of Africans as congenitally unable to run their own affairs was present but muted. What was more, given the preponderance of Africans in the ranks of the missionaries and other pastoral workers, any serious doubts about African ability were easily allayed by the proof of African achievements in all segments of the new life, not least of which was being proselytizers to their own people. Thus we can say that even though the Europeans saw themselves as superior, they anchored their superiority not on their racial pedigree but on their cultural or civilizational advancement. As such, they saw themselves as teachers whose success was to be measured by how quickly and well they educated their wards to assume control of their own business and render its tutors superfluous to the running of the lives of the tutored.

We may contrast this model of the possible relationship between superiors and inferiors in a hierarchy with another in which the superior party decides that the inferior are, by their very nature, incapable of progressing beyond a set limit to anything that approaches full autonomy over their lives. Under such a circumstance, the superior commits to giving aid and making the inferior always dependent on such aid, almost in perpetuity. Because the inferior is permanently disabled, its autonomy will forever be impaired. I have labeled the two the *autonomy* and the *aid* models, respectively. The qualitative difference between the first missionary and the later missionary-cum-administrator-adventurer cohort was that the first embraced the *autonomy* model and the second the *aid* model.[13] The difference ultimately turned on the philosophical anthropology that dominated each cohort's attitude toward Africans and their place in the concert of humanity. For the administrators who were the ultimate architects and builders of the colonial structure, the African simply was not part of the human race, and if she was, she was so far down the ladder that she could not be adjudged capable of doing human things without additional evidence.[14] Put differently, for the earlier missionary group, Africans were the same as other human beings but were either unequal with other humans or different from but equal with them. But for the administrator class, Africans were different from and unequal with other human beings. The first group thought that Africans could exercise agency but needed to be taught how best to do so; the second insisted that agency would be too much of a burden for Africans and proceeded to substitute their agency for that of the natives. If the first thought that Africans were one step away from civilization—from human to civilized—the second thought they were two steps removed—from subhuman to human to civilized.

Regardless of one's stance toward modernity, no one denies that the idea of subjectivity is its metaphysical centerpiece and that ideas of the self, the individual, and suchlike are crucial to its constitution. Unfortunately, the idea of the self and its role in the evolution of colonialism and its aftermath in Africa remains largely untheorized. This is only one aspect of the lack of engagement on African scholars' part with the philosophical dimensions of colonialism. By redirecting our focus on these core ideas, we are enabled to come up with better explanations for the abortions that characterized colonialism in Africa. The administrators' views that Africans were not members of the human family were the source of much tension between them and even the missionaries who subscribed to similar views of the humanity of Africans. After all, the missionaries could not escape the quandary of, on one hand, preaching the gospel of the oneness of all humanity in God, and on the other, suggesting that Africans might not apply. In contrast, because the administrators did not deign to answer to any power higher than the Colonial Office in London, they were not caught in any contradiction between their theory and their practice.

The tension between the administrators and their missionary compatriots—and the aims of these two groups were not always the same—was nothing compared to the running battles fought between modern Africans—the erstwhile graduates of the autonomy model—and reactionary administrators who wished to keep Africans in their place; thought little, if anything, of native agency; and generally foisted the aid model on Africans through what I have called *sociocryonics*. Sociocryonics is the ignoble science of cryopreserving social forms, arresting them and denying them and those whose social forms they are the opportunity of deciding what, how, and when to keep any of their social forms. This is where the substitution of European agency had the most devastating consequences. No thanks to this phenomenon, Africans were not allowed to decide *for themselves* what relationship they would have to their existing institutions—social, cultural, political, economic—as well as with those that were newly imported with the advent of Christianity and, in other areas, Islam. Once European administrators adopted sociocryonics as colonial policy, African progress was arrested in the name of preserving (the cryonic moment) what *they*, the rulers, decided was *the* African way of being human. It was euphemistically referred to as "indirect rule"[15] in the political realm.[16] This they did with scant, if any, regard for what Africans themselves thought about what should be the fate of their respective forms of social living.

This is a point that African scholars hardly ever apprehend. The standard story of colonialism is that of the spoilsport who destroyed, distorted, or altered African forms of social living. By extension, any African that took part in or mooted a similar idea of changing or expunging any indigenous institutions along modern lines was, and continues to be, castigated as a running dog of imperialism. In fact, this may explain the positive appraisal that indirect rule and similar policies receive in the literature. I take a different and diametrically opposed view to this widely accepted orientation. The story is amenable to a different telling. First, the standard narrative does not separate modernity from colonialism, and this does not allow its proponents to consider the attempts by Africans inspired by Christianity-inflected modernity to remake their communities without at the same time being dubbed colonialists or allies of the colonialists. Once you fail to separate Africans who were desirous of being modern and lump them together with colonialists who had other fish to fry, the outcome is the false tradition-versus-modernity dichotomy whereby *all* Africans were traditionalists and *all* modernizers were colonialists.

Writing about the debate over modernity in India among its intellectuals, Bhikhu Parekh has identified four different categories of reactions to the phenomenon: traditionalism, modernism, critical modernism, and critical traditionalism.[17] In apprehending divergences among Indian thinkers in their reaction to modernity, scholars recognize that Indians were exercising the autonomy of choosing how they were going to react to the challenge of modernity, which British administrators put before them more directly in ways that were never done in Africa. Some Indians thought that they should embrace everything modern. Others held that India had nothing to learn from modernity that was not already presaged in its indigenous traditions. Yet others contended that indigenous traditions were somewhat defective and could use some leavening with new wisdom from modernity. A final class sought to domesticate modernity by grafting it onto Indian stalks.

Similar categories were replicated among the ranks of African graduates of the missionary school of modernity in the nineteenth century. But one will be hard pressed to find a discussion of what those divergences and their philosophical implications were and how they might educate us at the present time. Philip D. Curtin, too, identified categories like those of Parekh. For him, Africans divided into modernizers and traditionalists. The first category included "Westernizers," "Utopian Modernizers," and "Neo-Traditionalists." The second included "Ordinary Conservatives," "Utopian Reactionaries," and "Defensive Modernizers."[18] Even a perceptive and sympathetic scholar like Curtin who also identified different African attitudes toward modernity—he called it "modernization"—could not find enough African thinkers to anchor his discussion and ended up with a cursory reference to them in his otherwise admirable essay.

What is crucial is that when Africans were inserted or they inserted themselves into the discourse of modernity, they ran the entire gamut of possible reactions. But the most sophisticated among them wanted to marry the best of their indigenous inheritance with the best that the new forms of social living enjoined by modernity had to offer. This is what exercising agency is all about. There are no guarantees that the agent will make choices that will serve her well or that would gladden the hearts of her erstwhile tutors or that she will not turn her agency to less-than-worthwhile pursuits. These are all questions that are irrelevant in an environment where subjectivity is supreme and its manifestation in the world may not be impeded except by the limits set by mortality and the injunctions against causing harm to another. Africans were not only exercising their agency on their own institutions, they were doing the same and could not but do so with modernity itself. The fact that the agent is called upon to make herself—construct and execute her own life plan—must include what to keep of the culture she was born into, what to borrow from other people's traditions, when to expunge any part of her cultural heritage, and so on. For anyone to take away from Africans the privilege, even at the risk of error on their part, of *deciding* for themselves the fate of their forms of social living—indigenous and foreign—is an impermissible interference with autonomy that subverts one of the fundamental tenets of modernity: the principle of subjectivity.[19] Sociocryonics, in this case, was a preemption of African agency.

Not only was African subjectivity prevented from determining its relation to its own indigenous heritage, it was precluded from deciding to embrace and obtain some practice with the new forms of social living presupposed by the new, especially in the political sphere. The consequence was utter failure, especially in the operation of those institutions—economic and political—that define the progress that modernity represents in human history.[20] By their prima facie exclusion from decisions regarding what to do with such modern institutions as liberal democracy, the rule of law, private enterprise, and individualism as a principle of social ordering, Africans were disabled from building their agency to meet the challenges of these new modes of social living and make their peace with them.

Contrast that with what took place in the social spheres, especially Christianity, and how much Africans have domesticated them. No one would deny that the layout of both rural and urban African spaces, the dominant architectural templates, and the details of quotidian living, from colloquial speech to snacks, all exhibit more and more modern characteristics. In spite of all the prattle about communalism, not even the scholars who wax eloquent about their commitment to so-called African values and traditions build their houses or live in spaces that pay any serious attention to those values and traditions. What is worse is that by not paying deliberate attention to the influences that are shaping the evolution of thought and practice in African societies, contemporary Africans end up with spaces and landscapes that are superficially modern but lack the enlivening soul that makes their counterparts in other places such beauties to behold and celebrate.

Even then, I am arguing that although Africans have embraced and domesti-cated modernity in the areas of religion and other social engagements over which they exercised autonomy, the denial of access to practice with liberal democracy and the rule of law explains, in very important respects, why those practices are having a hard time taking root in the continent. Sociocryonics originated in the denial of African subjectivity; it eventuated in the underdevelopment of African agency and failures in the sphere of social and political transformation since independence. Un-fortunately, this model continues to dominate the relationship between Africa and its erstwhile colonizers as well as the rest of the world to date.

Many, especially historians, have documented and analyzed the relationship be-tween the "new elite" of educated Africans and the administrator class of the colo-nizer group.[21] But we need more works that explore colonialism as a philosophical system and analyze the African reactions to it in the context of the philosophical discourse of modernity.[22] Unfortunately, Africans have continued to labor under the twin legacies of a disabled agency and an unrelenting sociocryonics, even in the post-independence era. Evidence of the disabled agency can be discerned in the amnesia of much of the African intelligentsia, outside of the disciplines of history and (pos-sibly) literature, regarding how their forebears engaged with modernity before the imposition of formal colonialism. The amnesia is most acute in philosophy. Yet as I have repeatedly pointed out, the philosophical discourse of modernity, the template from which most of its architectonic is constructed, is the most important of its fea-tures for meaningful and productive engagement. If one cannot name a problem, it is highly unlikely that she will come up with a solution to it, at least not directly. It can be argued that illiteracy about or indifference or hostility toward the philo-sophical discourse may explain the unhappy experience with modernization in the post-independence period across the continent.

On one hand, few have been the attempts on the part of African scholars to come to grips with the decimating impact on African agency of the preemptions that took place under colonialism. This we cannot do until we mine our forebears' writings and debate with them while we at the same time controvert, if not con-tradict, the lies and distortions of their positions concocted by colonial apologists and the truncated history of African ideas that is the tragic legacy of colonialism-inflected education. By extension, the underdevelopment of African agency has con-tributed to the persistence of sociocryonics at the present time. Evidence of the per-sistence abounds in many of the recent accounts of the relationship between Africa and modernity that focus on such "peculiarly African" themes as "witchcraft" and "village."

One does not have to look far for the explanation. First, many Africans were weaned on a diet of treating Africa and African phenomena as if they were sui generis. The result is that many African scholars think that they do wrong if they affirm any similarities between African and other phenomena from other parts of the world, especially those parts that we call the West.[23] Thus we have repeated affirmations of African *difference* and an almost uncritical embrace of ahistoricity in their understanding and explanation of African phenomena. Many feel that to embrace things Western is to abandon African authenticity. It is no less a sociocryonic moment for being popular with African scholars. Second, the task of redesigning African institutions to reflect the march of history and secure for Africans the benefits of modernity has been frustrated by the fear of things Western that was midwifed in the colonial era by sociocryonics and its underlying racism. The African's place in modernity remains a conflicted heritage. We must change this situation.

The Continuing Relevance of Modernity: Bringing Africa back In

I contend that when we think of the history of the relations between Africa and modernity, we must do so in terms of a new periodization: the relationship between Africa and modernity *before* and the same *after* colonialism. This will free us to redeem the explanatory as well as the transformatory possibilities of modernity. Once modernity is adopted as the analytical framework to explain the career of colonialism in Africa, it is possible to augment existing analyses in history, political science, sociology, and anthropology with a critical appraisal that takes a decidedly philosophical turn. This opens up completely new vistas of research that have hitherto been obscured by the neglect of the philosophical dimensions of colonialism.[24] In order for this to happen we need to accept, if only for purposes of argument, some of the professions by colonialists and their philosophers regarding the claim that forms a core part of the self-understanding of colonialism: that it sought to and was desirous of moving "natives," the colonized, along the path of the modern way of life. This claim has different degrees of plausibility attached to it depending on whether or not we are in Anglophone, Francophone, or Lusophone Africa and whether we are looking at conditions in settler enclaves in North, East, and South Africa or in protectorates in West, East, and South Africa or in colonies in West Africa or South Africa.[25]

Had the theorists and practitioners of colonialism adhered to their much-vaunted intention to *transform* the colonies and protectorates into *modern* polities and *socialize* their inhabitants into the *modern way of life*, I would like to argue, the history of the former colonies and protectorates would not be what it has been so far. Various components make up the modern way of life. They include a philosophical anthropology succinctly described by Hegel as "the principle of subjectivity"; a social ontology that respects the relation between the individual and the community and

is manifested in the peculiar bifurcation between the state and civil society; a philosophy of time concerning the relations among the past, the present, and the future;
a social epistemology in which reason plays a central role and knowledge is founded
not on revelation, tradition, or authority but on conformity with reason; and a near-
obsession with the "new" manifest in the near-religious attachment to the idea of
progress. These conjointly make up the subject matter of the philosophical discourse
of modernity.[26] Its complement in politics enjoins a political system built on liberal
democracy and in law a legal system built on the rule of law.

I assume that the modern way of life represents a leap forward in human history
and that the gains it offers, had they been on the table in colonial Africa, would
have made for a better life and more salubrious history than that bequeathed by colonialism as it operated in Africa. This is an acknowledgment that Africans are almost forbidden to make. Yet we must overcome this prima facie hostility to things
modern, especially the philosophical discourse of modernity. Frantz Fanon, Aimé
Césaire, and Amilcar Cabral exemplified in their different ways the kind of critical
embrace of modernity that I wish to advance in this collection. In the essays presented in this book, I take seriously the claim by colonialism and its apologists that
they were desirous of transforming, albeit slowly, colonized Africans and their forms
of social living into their modern equivalents. I am aware that many would dispute
the suggestion that colonialists, especially those that operated in Africa, could have
been part of any positive movement for social transformation. I abjure this dismis-
sive attitude because it is not supported by the historical evidence. There were, as
I show in the book, administrators who took this profession seriously and argued,
even if unsuccessfully, that they and their fellows ought to deliver on this part of
their promise and that that was the only justification for bending the will of Africans under colonial rule. Needless to say, they were not the dominant operators
among the ranks of the colonialists. A more nuanced understanding of colonialism
is one possible path to identifying the roads that were not taken under colonialism
and how it was rendered impossible by its internal contradictions. That is, it would
enable us to strengthen our indictment of colonialism as it transpired in Africa for,
as I show in the essays, it could have unfolded differently with less devastating consequences for its victims.

Insofar as we adopt a monolithic view of the dramatis personae of the colonial
situation we are unlikely to identify, much less explore, the peculiarities of the variety of colonialism that dominated Africa. By separating the particular group of
missionaries that I mentioned above from the rest of the colonizer class while at
the same time placing a premium on native agency as it was conditioned in its encounter with modernity, we can do some new things in our desire to illumine the
sad history of Africa and modernity. In the first place, I show that rather than being the instrument for the introduction and diffusion of modernity into Africa, colonialism indeed aborted Africa's march toward modernity that had been inaugu-

rated under the direction of the revolutionary missionaries of the early nineteenth century, in whose ranks Africans played a major role. Second, I redeem for scholarly attention African contributions to the discourse of modernity and simultaneously indicate ways that current generations of Africans might learn from their forebears in their ongoing struggles with Africa's continuing encounter with modernity. Finally, the essays in this collection are motivated by my effort to understand why Africa and its peoples have borne the burdens of modernity without having enjoyed its benefits, especially those regarding the sovereignty of the individual and absolute respect for her dignity, representative government, and the rule of law. I happen to think that these benefits are worthy of our striving in our efforts to build superior societies in Africa at the present time. Given that the current efforts in Africa toward the implantation of democracy and the rule of law as well as capitalism are best understood as late transitions to modernity, it is incumbent on African intellectuals to take a closer look at what I argue was the first attempt at a transition to modernity by their forebears in West Africa in the nineteenth century. Beyond what lessons we can learn from them, it is time to celebrate their genius and come to a better understanding, modulated by philosophy, of how badly colonialism served Africa.

PART I

COLONIALISM

_1_

Colonialism
A *Philosophical Profile*

I would like to start with a question: What do Canada, the United States, South Korea, Nigeria, India, Australia, and the Republic of South Africa have in common? They are all former colonies. This is not an insignificant fact. In both scholarship and everyday discourse we talk of the original colonies of the United States. American history sets aside a clearly demarcated colonial period. Our talk of the American War of Independence presupposes that at a certain time the relationship between the American colonies and their putative colonial master, the United Kingdom, was one of dependence by the former on the latter. Only if this is the case does it make sense to speak of the United States winning its independence from the United Kingdom. But then we have Canada and Australia as well as many Caribbean countries, including Jamaica, that regard themselves as "former colonies" while at the same time continuing to look up to the queen of the United Kingdom as their head of state. We adjudge all the countries concerned to be independent. Meanwhile, to the extent that India, Nigeria, South Africa, Australia, Canada, and New Zealand are members of the Commonwealth, they are former colonies of the United Kingdom and they all continue to acknowledge the nominal leadership of the queen. Here we come to the limit of the commonality of the countries that we routinely put under the stamp "former colonies." Since the many countries that we often put under that rubric have traversed diverse trajectories both as colonies and former colonies, it is difficult to justify our thinking about them in their sameness, except nominally.

Because whereas Canada, the United States, and Australia are obviously modern states with thriving economies built on intense industrialization (and South Korea, India, and the Republic of South Africa are not far behind), few will say that Nigeria or the rest of the former colonies in Africa either have thriving economies or can be judged modern states. What is more, although Canada, the United States, and Australia have thriving systems of rule of law as well as robust civil societies, in spite of the fact that many African countries are now ostensibly under representative democracies, few will deny that they are nowhere near modern polities. Why is this so?

Colonialism is often cited as the principal cause of Africa's continuing inability to move forward with the rest of the world. African scholars, even though it is increasingly unfashionable to do so, continue to resort to this causal factor more than any other in their diagnoses of Africa's failure. Although I shall argue not just for the relevance of this explanation in the following essays but also its cogency, I believe that circumstances in the current historical conjuncture compel a reconsideration of its foundation. The reason is simple. When the rest of the former colonial world in Asia and Latin America shared Africa's fate, it was very easy, comforting even, to either not see or ignore the defects in this explanatory schema. That is, as long as the former colonies exhibited a uniform picture of grinding poverty, widespread ignorance, and poor health care services—in short, a picture of what used to be called "underdevelopment"—it was hard for challenges to the explanatory orthodoxy of colonialism to gain any traction.[1] This is no longer the case. In the last twenty years or so, we have witnessed the emergence of several former colonies on the world stage as industrial, financial, and even agricultural powerhouses. What is more, a few of those countries were much farther behind some African countries in terms of their potential for success in the development race on the eve of independence.[2] But those countries have not only left their African peers behind, they have become the secondary exporters of investment capital to Africa and exploiters of the continent's resources after the erstwhile colonial powers decided that Africa was not worthy of their precious capital.[3] Given this new reality, it is meet to ask why Africa remains mired in the quicksand of underdevelopment while its fellow sufferers of the recent past have gone on to better lives for their citizens.

The divergences in the career paths of countries that generically are all former colonies give us pause as we establish the etiology of Africa's underdevelopment in colonialism. But these divergences are not the only reason that we need to renew the foundations of our explanatory schema. To the extent that it is correct to speak of the United States, Canada, and Australia as former colonies, it cannot be the case that colonialism per se is a hindrance to the growth of healthy polities in its aftermath. And if this be denied, then we have to say that what the United States and Canada experienced at their founding was either not really colonialism or that it was a different kind of colonialism.

When we turn our focus to Africa, the same is true. We either have to say that there is something peculiar about Africa and its peoples that makes them incapable of breaking the bonds of colonialism-induced underdevelopment or that colonialism may not have been as uniform in its evolution as accepted wisdom seems to have held for so long. The first alternative must be rejected summarily both for its not-so-hidden racist subtext and for the fact that it threatens to continue to view Africa and its phenomena as if they were sui generis. The second alternative forces us to take very seriously the differential experience of colonialism in diverse places that we usually lump together under the rubric of "former colonies" and the qualitative differences in the historical evolution of the phenomenon of colonialism in different places at different times.

In this chapter, I would like to argue that contrary to the dominant ways of looking at the crises of life and thought in Africa in terms of what colonialism did to the continent, it may be more instructive to focus on what colonialism did not do and the consequences of those omissions. But to do this will require a deep philosophical analysis of the idea of colonialism with a view to isolating its historicity. Such an analysis will enable me to circumscribe the specificity of the colonialism that took root in Africa and ascertain to what extent it supports my thesis that it was a bulwark against the efflorescence of modernity in Africa after it was introduced to some areas of the continent in the first half of the nineteenth century.

Others have charted the paths that I propose to take in this book. In the areas of economics and political science there have been very important and, I am convinced, hugely successful efforts to show why colonialism produced different and more deleterious consequences in Africa.[4] What I do here that is different is to take very seriously the historicity of colonialism and explore its philosophical underpinnings. A serious engagement with the philosophical presuppositions is what will enable me to isolate colonialism's peculiar resonance in Africa while at the same time showing how it was riven by internal contradictions. Those contradictions ensured that for colonialism to have delivered what it did for Canada and the United States its executors would have had to negate the very principles of its existence and, by extension, their own being. Yet we shall see that the inevitability paradigm that often characterizes the discourse of colonialism in Africa—things could not have turned out otherwise than they did—is inadequate, if not wrong. The key lies in showing the intimate even if conflicted connection between colonialism and the much larger complex from which it emanated: modernity.

We need to break the connection that is often affirmed between modernity and colonialism. We must reverse the causal line or at least the lexical ordering that seeks to place colonialism before modernity and uses the former to explain the emergence of the latter in the continent. My aim is to offer a more nuanced account of the relationship between modernity and colonialism: one which shows that (1) if one works with an ahistorical conception of colonialism, it will be very difficult, maybe even impossible, to explain the differential impact of colonialism in different places at different times; and (2) if we adopt a historical approach to colonialism, we will find that its modern inflections set in bold relief the peculiarities of the variety that took root in Africa and can therefore give us a more adequate etiology for Africa's evolution in its aftermath. On (2), I will argue that only against the background of the philosophical underpinnings of modernity—the principle of subjectivity, the centrality of reason, and the faith in progress and their socio-institutional appurtenances (the impermissibility of rule that is not based on the consent of the governed and the rule of law, to give just two examples)—can one show what is distinctive about the contradictions of "modern" colonialism. For instance, if it were to have taken seriously its charge to revolutionize the mode of production, it would have had to have built a viable capitalism in the colonies. To foster capitalism would have meant building (or at least not hindering) the capacity of the colonized to compete in the capitalist marketplace, and this could not but detract from the most important rationale for the colonialism that prevailed in much of Africa, whether under the British, the French, or the Portuguese: the pillage and exploitation of the resources of the colonized.

Similar considerations apply in the sociopolitical arena. If the colonial authorities truly believed in the principle of subjectivity and in its applicability to the colonized, then they would have required the consent of the colonized to be governed. But rule by consent could not have been an instance of colonialism. One can envisage a period of educating the colonized to consent following the underdevelopment of agency owing to, say, the natural progression that allows us to bend the will of children in the socialization process or sociohistorical processes when an injured or traumatized people have had their autochthony challenged and damaged, if not impaired. In such a situation it might be a stretch to insist on such a people's autonomy to order their own affairs. We have known of historical instances when a people have asked their neighbors to help them reorganize their polities or sought refuge under another's suzerainty while they strengthened their own capacity for decision-making. In recent times processes similar to this have unfolded in East Timor in the aftermath of Portuguese and Indonesian misrule and the trauma suffered by the Timorese under both. In Africa, kin processes were put in place in Sierra Leone and Liberia after civil wars that were some of the most brutal in human history. When we say that consent could not have been a part of colonialism that predominated in Africa, this should not be understood in absolute terms. This is one way to understand John Stuart Mill's and Karl Marx's insistence that what they termed "Oriental or Asiatic despotism" required an outside jolt to get it and its practitioners out of what they both called its stupor. One can argue that the despotism that Mill recommended for Indians at least had the dubious virtue of preparing its wards for self-rule. No such attitude, we shall argue, was considered or earnestly on offer in Africa.

Additionally, recognizing and embracing the subjectivity of the colonized would have meant allowing the colonized to choose not just whether they wished to be ruled by their colonizer but also what they would like to keep and what to expunge of their customs, institutions, and practices and what to accept or reject of the new customs, institutions, and practices brought by colonialism—and how both of those processes were to be executed. This would have had to have happened at both the empirical and ideational levels. The upshot of all this is that the colonialists were in a quandary that I will be making much of in this work. Because colonialism in Africa was inflected by modernity it had at its very heart a contradiction that it could not resolve without abandoning its very project. If colonialists embraced the peculiar modern commitment to subjectivity, they ought to have cultivated African agency with a view to suiting Africans for the business of social transformation in the modern mode. But had they done so, the legitimacy of their very enterprise would have been undermined. The option that colonialists adopted in the continent ended up subverting modernity rather than enhancing it.[5]

Rather than build African agency in what would have been a nod to subjectivity, colonialists stultified its growth. Instead of allowing Africans to choose from among old and new customs, institutions, and practices, they foisted sociocryonics on the colonies. Sociocryonics is the name I have coined for a situation in which instead of allowing social forms to evolve as they will in the ordinary course of life— emergence, maturation, decline, death, and fresh emergence—under the direction sometimes consciously and most times unconsciously of human agency, humans freeze those forms and preempt their transformation by subordinate others whose social forms they are. In the colonial situation as it obtained in the relevant areas of Africa on which I focus in this book, British colonial authorities not only embraced sociocryonics, it was the bedrock of their attitudes and policies toward Africans who deigned to embrace what modernity had to offer. Indeed, as I shall argue in the next chapter, given that there was evidence of Africans who had embraced modernity with considerable enthusiasm *before* the advent of formal colonialism, the fact that Africans continued to embrace and adapt various social forms—both those of their indigenous inheritance and others that they had borrowed from their tutelage under the missionaries in defiance of British official colonial policy of sociocryonics— testified to the persistent deployment of African subjectivity both during and after colonial rule. I am arguing that colonialists could have chosen differently but that they chose to abort the modern project in Africa. I shall have more to say about these abortions in a moment. Let me, for now, explore the intricacies of the colonialism that will be at the core of our discussion.

Colonialism: A Philosophical Profile

I begin with a characterization of colonialism by Robert Delavignette. According to him,

> Any attempt to define colonization etymologically soon makes the complexity of the subject apparent. The word is usually regarded as being derived from the Latin verb *colĕre*, to cultivate. In his *Histoire des Colonisations*, M. René Sédillot postulates an Indo-European etymology, the root *kwel*, implying the idea of men moving around in order to organize space by occupying the soil. Initially, colonization would thus be the settlement of immigrant cultivators on ground which they have cleared, and all agrarian civilizations would originate in acts of colonization. There can be little doubt that colonization is bound up with fairly large-scale migrations, but it is questionable

whether the object of the latter was always cultivation of the soil. . . . In most cases, colonization takes the form of a political expansion, with the centre of the expansion turning into a metropolis; it becomes a matter of State, and there is a tendency to found an empire based on the principle of linking to the metropolis countries often separated from it even further ethically and sociologically than they are by physical distance. . . . From this point of view, it becomes clear that there is no colonization without a metropolis or mother-country.[6]

Delavignette obviously sees a discontinuity between the two types of colonization. At least he seems to believe that the main form of colonization has to do with a state and the creation of a metropolis-periphery relationship. Before we gloss Delavignette's characterization, let us present another one from V. Y. Mudimbe.

Although generalizations are of course dangerous, *colonialism* and *colonization* basically mean organization, arrangement. The two words derive from the latin word *colère*, meaning to cultivate or to design. Indeed, the historical colonial experience does not and obviously cannot reflect the peaceful connotations of these words. But it can be admitted that the colonists (those settling a region), as well as the colonialists (those exploiting a territory by dominating a local majority) have all tended to organize and transform non-European areas into fundamentally European constructs.[7]

Between them the characterizations by Delavignette and Mudimbe encapsulate the many conundrums that attend the family of concepts that are usually associated in discussions of colonialism: "colonization," "colonialism," "colonialist," "colonist," "colonizer," and "colonized." When Mudimbe hints at some "peaceful connotations of [colonialism and colonization]," he is conceding, even if obliquely, that in their roots the words do not necessarily lend themselves to the negative associations that mark them in our time. Simultaneously, when he talks of "the historical colonial experience," he must be understood to be referring to a specific concatenation of ideas, institutions, and practices that obviates generic readings suggested by the definite article in the noun phrase and that grounds a historicity that circumscribes the particular experience he goes on to describe in his discussion. That is, there must be some significant difference between the colonialism with peaceful connotations and the historical colonial experience that comes in for some criticism in Mudimbe's discussion. This implicit distinction is related to a different, explicit distinction that Mudimbe makes.

Mudimbe cursorily mentions a distinction between colonists and colonialists. What he does not do is go on to explore the implications of the qualitative difference between settlement colonialism (what colonists do) and exploitation colonialism (what colonialists do). Yes, there is a qualitative difference! Only because he paid little attention to this qualitative difference was he able to assert that both colonialisms "tended to organize and transform non-European areas into fundamentally European constructs"; that is, he ended up talking about generic colonialism even though he had apprehended historicized colonialisms. It is not enough blithely to refer to the historicity of colonialism and the multiverse forms it has manifested and outcomes it has yielded. We need to work through the philosophical dimensions of "the historical experience" of colonialism in Africa and the many contradictions that it enfolded. There is no reason to believe that colonists and colonialists the world over are limited to only their European numbers.

Were we to limit ourselves to the implications of exploring the etymological roots of colonialism, we would be forced to conclude that the phenomenon is as old as human settlement itself. But one does not need such a profligate conception to identify differences among several instantiations of the concept of colonization ranging from the Russian colonization of Central Asia to Japanese colonialism in the Korean Peninsula, Indonesia, and Cambodia; Amharic colonialism in the Horn of Africa; and the Moorish conquests in the Iberian Peninsula. Yet much of the contemporary discourse on colonialism makes clear that these other instances of colonialism are not what their authors have in mind. To that extent, Delavignette's distinctions provide us with a more complex foundation from which to proceed.

The colonization that is characterized by "the settlement of immigrant cultivators on ground which they have cleared" gives us what I call colonization$_1$. We find this all over the world, including Africa. But Delavignette quickly linked this general, benign phenomenon to "political expansion." I call this colonization$_2$. It is the colonization that yields the ideas, institutions, and practices that involve a state that eventually serves as the metropolis to a number of satrapies that start out as such but end up wresting their independence from the erstwhile metropolises. It is very easy to see how Canada, Australia, and the United States may be illustrative of colonization$_1$. Their settlement involved large-scale migrations. By itself this type of colonization is unremarkable. It may be the oldest type and probably typified the dispersal of humans across the face of the earth. When we take a historical view of colonization, however, difficult issues lurk.

Colonization$_1$ assumes, most commonly, that the territory under question is unoccupied virgin territory. When it takes place in the context of an empty or sparsely populated world, colonization$_1$ will be unproblematic. When it takes place, however, in a more populated world where every new settlement is likely to require the displacement of earlier settlers, we confront a more complicated situation. Where this is so, even if force is the instrument of a successful takeover, justifications are necessary for such removals of previous settlers as may be necessitated by the latest one. In earlier times when might ruled and the conquered submitted to the will of the conqueror, might was its own justification. Even then, it was never enough to subdue an enemy to prevail in colonization$_1$. Elaborate rituals were invented to aid the acceptance by the displaced of their displacement and various myths developed over time to legitimate what initially was obtained by force. In other situations, the new colonists incorporated so many of the customs, institutions, and practices of the displaced that a new people emerged from the hybridization process. The Hausa-Fulani that emerged from the Sokoto Jihad in Nigeria might be one historical example. In yet others, the new colonists and the displaced would work out an arrangement where the defeated were left to keep their original institutions and practices subject to their acknowledgment of the authority of the newcomers. The latter would submit to a ritual reenactment of the decisive battle that secured their victory as both a nod to the integrity of the culture of the defeated and a reminder to subsequent generations of the grounds of legitimacy of the more recent order. Instances of the sort that I have described can be found in many parts of Africa, especially eastern Yorubaland and Benin in Nigeria. It is a sign of how often African phenomena are treated as sui generis that few obvious colonial situations in Africa among its peoples are described as instances of colonization.[8] I have expanded the range of colonization$_1$ in this case so as to show its global distribution in human history.

However illustrative Canada, Australia, and the United States may be of colonization$_1$, they also depart from it in some quite significant respects. Given that colonization of the areas that later became these nations involved large-scale migrations to lands that were not quite empty or unoccupied, it is meet to comment on their relations with the earlier settlers (colonists) that they found in situ. There were no hints that the new arrivals ever anticipated or, if they did, were interested in any of the arrangements that we reported above. They instead concocted the myth that the lands concerned were "unoccupied" and could therefore offer them new opportunities.[9] They were interested in the land; they wanted no truck with the aboriginal inhabitants. Although the lands were colonized, the native peoples were not. They were marked for extermination. They were like forests to be cleared. Their lands, not they, were candidates for cultivation.

We can now see why it is problematic to adopt a generic view of colonialism, as does Mudimbe. Although it is true to say that, for example, the American colonists were interested in organizing and transforming "non-European areas into fundamentally European constructs," such organizing and transforming activities could *only* refer to their desire to create a European hearth in the North American land. Were we to limit our purview this way, the tragic fate of the aboriginal inhabitants of the land to be transformed and organized would escape us. Additionally, we would miss another important dimension of colonization$_1$ that set apart the European colonization of North America from other instances of colonialism if we failed to recognize the qualitative differences I have been discussing. The colonists/settlers traveled with their citizenship. Given that they are often regarded as extensions of the mother country, it was not an accident that the settlers of the colonies insisted on a reconfiguration of their relations with the metropolis on the same political principles that animated the social organization of the mother country. Only insofar as we consider them in their initial subordinate political position vis-à-vis the mother country can we speak of the United States, Australia, and Canada as former colonies and their settlers as colonized. In their relationship to the lands they expropriated, however, they were colonizers. If the preceding is plausible, then one qualitative difference between Nigeria and Canada, to take one arbitrary pairing, is that they were not colonies in the same way. This leads us to the second type of colonization isolated by Delavignette.

Colonization$_2$ "takes the form of political expansion with the centre of the expansion turning into a metropolis." Although one might say that the colonies morphed into colonization$_2$, that, strictly speaking, would be incorrect. A critical element of this kind of transformation is a development that is distinctive of the era within which this new form of colonization gestated and eventually was born: modernity. Under colonization$_2$, as Delavignette informed us, the emergence of a metropolis-periphery relation turns colonization into "a matter of State, and there is a tendency to found an empire based on the principle of linking to the metropolis countries often separated from it even further ethically and sociologically than they are by physical distance."[10] The critical element here is that political expansion is separated from the creation of new polities under colonization$_1$ that were extensions of the situations in the lands whence the settlers came. By specifying that the new colonies are not merely products of political expansion but are "separated from [the mother country] even further ethically and sociologically than they are by physical distance," we are looking at a qualitatively different emergent reality. Certainly there had been empires that had centers and dominated peripheries in previous eras in human history. The difference is that the kind of colonization that was definitive of the modern era was enhanced by new knowledge that generated technological innovations that were deployed to give birth to a different kind of empire whose colonial adventures shaped and continue to shape our contemporary landscapes and mindscapes. It is this colonialism that owed its origins to the "great maritime discoveries on the eve of the Renaissance" that interests me. This is the colonization that is specifically modern, the colonization of which Mudimbe spoke.

Modern colonialism has some distinctive characteristics. It came in the aftermath of the "discovery" of the Americas, the circumnavigation of the world that included the charting of a new sea route to India and the rest of Asia, and resulted in the domination of the world by Europeans. It was also an era that witnessed the emergence of a new philosophical anthropology respecting what it is and how to be human; a new ontology of time that presaged a different perception/understanding of the relation between humans and the past, present, and future; a new attitude toward nature under which rather than working with nature or propitiating nature, it became an object for subjugation to be brought under control and forced to yield the innermost secrets of its operation; and a new orientation toward knowledge and its production that demoted the authority of tradition and the appeal to authority that it entailed and undermined the legitimacy of revelation as a source of knowledge. Reason became the only authenticating certificate of true knowledge and the experimental method became the primary means of establishing the principles of natural processes. The reign of science had arrived.

In the area of social ordering, the same period heralded a new principle of governance: the principle of consent. The divine ordainment theory under which rulers ruled by the grace of God or sheer might gave way to a new theory of governance under which no one ought to be bound by the dictates of a government she has had no hand in constituting. One consequence of this latter change was the transformation of erstwhile *subjects* of empires into *citizens* of republics who were judged capable of selecting their rulers and by so doing bind themselves to such rulers but who, simultaneously, reserved the right—make that the duty—to remove a government that no longer enjoyed their trust and confidence. As I shall point out in later chapters, these were all epochal changes in Europe that marked the transition from the era of feudalism to that of modernity.

The American Revolution institutionalized the preceding features and represented the most significant herald of the modern age. The French Revolution became the beachhead for the new times in Europe, and Toussaint l'Ouverture and his fellow freedom fighters in Haiti showed that former slaves defined by a total lack of freedom were not any the less enamored of the new ways of being human proclaimed by modernity. In the transition from settlement to state, the American colonies did not claim a discontinuity between their new status and their previous one as British subjects. In fact, they settled the land as British subjects and when they revolted it was in the name of that selfsame citizenship. And that may in part explain the shared identity between the contemporary descendants of the American rebels and those of the Great Britain against which they revolted. In embodying the aforementioned tenets of modernity and becoming societies that rivet the envy of other parts of the world, we tend to forget their colonial beginnings. However, we recall those beginnings in order to show the qualitative differences that we insist mark the later experiences of Africans under colonialism.

As Delavignette points out, the colonies that define the core of our discussion are defined not so much by being parts of a metropolis-periphery relation as by the fact that the periphery, in this case, is often separated from the metropolis less by "physical distance" and more by "ethical and sociological" divergences. In fact, distance could have meant more in previous times. But after the technological innovations of the modern age had been developed, distance came to matter little. This allows us to question, as I do later, why the later acquisitions could not also be absorbed into the preexisting structures of citizenship and politics. The simple answer is the "ethical and sociological distance" between them and their colonizers.

I interpret the colonial enterprise as an integral part of the outward march of modernity from Europe.[11] Hegel's writings provide theoretical support for this interpretation.[12] The irony is that the colonialism that took root in Africa mimicked

Hegel's idea only in South Africa, Algeria, Kenya, and Zimbabwe, where there were attempts to create modern societies in settler enclaves, the most successful being South Africa. According to Hegel, civil society, as it had evolved under capitalism in his day, has an "inner dialectic." This inner dialectic has two moments: on the one hand, there are stupendous achievements in the production of wealth driven by the generalization and expansion of needs in the society and the creation of a division of labor by which there is "subdivision and restriction of particular jobs."[13] One consequence of these twin phenomena is the other moment of the inner dialectic of civil society. At the same time that it creates stupendous wealth, it also brings about a class of people who have no ties to the land but whose labor is superfluous, a situation that increases the possibility of their becoming a rabble. This is the time in the development of civil society when "it becomes apparent that despite an excess of wealth civil society is not rich enough, i.e. its own resources are insufficient to check excessive poverty and the creation of a penurious rabble."[14] The inner dialectic in which there is at one end "the concentration of disproportionate wealth in a few hands"[15] and at the other "excessive poverty and the creation of a penurious rabble" is what drives civil society "or at any rate drives a specific civil society—to push beyond its own limits and seek markets, and so its necessary means of subsistence, in other lands which are either deficient in the goods it has overproduced, or else generally backward in industry, &c."[16]

In this view, a specific civil society might reach a level of production and division of labor at home when expansion possibilities become severely limited, especially in the area of agriculture.[17] When that happens, given that the creation of civil society and industry are intimately connected, the principal motivation of industry, "the passion for gain," "instead of remaining rooted to the soil and the limited circle of civil life with its pleasures and desires, embraces the element of flux, danger, and destruction."[18] It goes out to sea, "the far-flung connecting link [that] affords the means for the colonizing activity—sporadic or systematic—to which the mature civil society is driven and by which it *supplies to a part of its population a return to life on the family basis in a new land and so also supplies itself with a new demand and field for its industry.*"[19] That is, when conditions worsen at home, civil society is driven to found colonies where it may hope to resettle some of its members and make available to them new land in which they may reestablish family life as agriculturists or where it may create new markets for the "goods it has overproduced" or establish new sources of raw materials for its industries. However we think of it, colonization is a moment of an evolving bourgeois society whose principle is dictated by the needs of the colonizer—for new lands, new markets, and so forth—with no consideration for the views, needs, and aims of the colonized.[20] I shall have more to say about this anon. Here is what Hegel said in further explication of his thesis.

Civil society is thus driven to found colonies. Increase of population alone has this effect, but it is due in particular to the appearance of a number of people who cannot secure the satisfaction of their needs by their own labour once production rises above the requirements of consumers. Sporadic colonization is particularly characteristic of Germany. The emigrants withdraw to America or Russia and remain there with no home ties, and so prove useless to their native land. The second and entirely different type of colonization is the systematic; the state undertakes it, is aware of the proper method of carrying it out and regulates it accordingly. This type was common amongst the ancients, particularly the Greeks. . . . In modern times, colonists have not been allowed the same rights as those left at home, and the result of this situation has been wars and finally independence, as may be seen in the history of the English and Spanish colonies. Colonial independence proves to be of the greatest advantage to the mother country, just as the emancipation of slaves turns out to the greatest advantage of the owners.[21]

We can find examples of the kinds of colonization Hegel mentioned in many different parts of the world. But they all share one common trait: They are instances of colonization$_1$. They involved the settlement of large populations of the colonists in the colonies and the settlers continued to see themselves as citizens of their original countries, which they looked upon as their motherland. There also were serious attempts to create polities modeled on those of their original homelands sans whatever they found disagreeable about their motherland. The United States is the most successful of the new colonies; Canada and Australia are not too far behind. Although it is true that the motivation for the creation of colonies in some parts of Africa—South Africa, Zimbabwe, Kenya, and Algeria being the most appropriate examples—was similar to those that Hegel identified, colonization in those places was a hybrid (colonization$_3$) of two types: colonization$_1$ typified by the presence of some settlements and what Delavignette calls "politico-economic colonization" (colonization$_2$), a type that was dedicated primarily to economic exploitation of the natural resources of the "monsoon lands of Asia, and in tropical and equatorial Africa." Colonization$_2$ was the predominant type in Africa, and the inconsistencies and contradictions that marked its justification and operation will occupy us in subsequent chapters. One cannot overemphasize the importance of isolating the specificity of colonization$_2$. Physical distance did not matter in the creation of settlement colonies whose inhabitants remained integral parts of the metropolis. There was no such identity between the colonizer and the colonized in colonization$_2$. The colonized in the latter case were marked by their difference, which was captured in the "ethical and sociological distance" between them and their colonial overlords. These new justifications for the colonial enterprise from the middle of the nineteenth century onward were additional dimensions that Hegel could not have been aware of.

Hegel was no egalitarian. The kind of colonialism that he derived from the evolution of the dialectic of civil society in Europe was colonizer-inflected. What of the colonized? In Hegel's account, the colonized were identical with those that Memmi would later dub "colonizers."[22] This is not surprising because for Hegel the lands that were colonized—that is, settled by Hegel's putative colonized—were at best empty or at worst occupied by creatures who were outside of History's orbit and, therefore, had no legitimate title to or were not worthy of consideration in the fate of the land that they inhabited.[23]

In other epochs, an attitude like Hegel's would not have warranted comment. But this was happening in the modern age. It is part of the self-image of modernity in its political manifestation that it is committed to the ideas of equality, liberty, and fraternity.[24] And it is in the name of exporting these lofty ideals to the "backward" areas of the world that some later colonialists sought to justify their colonial enterprise.[25] If this is true, then one will have to say that the justification is either bogus or was not resolutely meant. Herein is the source of the contradiction that was to typify modernity in its migration to the shores of the peoples that Hegel said did not belong in History. Hegel and multitudes of his successors evince an utter contempt for those who were not part of History's march. So for them there is no inconsistency, much less a contradiction, in, on the one hand, proclaiming the universal equality of *all* humans and, on the other, endorsing the denial of the humanity of millions. I am suggesting that had they taken seriously the universality and humanism presupposed by modernity, they would have been compelled to confront the contradictions that their colonial adventures generated for their theory.

To say this is to put a somewhat positive spin on the colonial enterprise. I do so in full awareness of the risks involved. Indeed, to the extent that we are able to show that colonialism was a phenomenon riddled with several irreconcilable contradictions, we would be able to show how colonialism refuted itself and created grief on native shores. Indeed, many will resist any idea that colonialism could have had any positive impact on Africa. This is a standard element in anticolonial discourse. Yet it is not uncommon for other scholars of Africa, especially historians and political scientists, to offer what they regard as the pluses and minuses of the colonial balance sheet. While my sympathies are with the anticolonialists, I differ with them in their eagerness to deny that colonialism could have followed alternative trajectories in Africa. The key is to identify the immanent determinations of colonialism with a view to showing that it was a phenomenon riddled with several irreconcilable contradictions. Following upon this identification, I will be able to show how colonialism refuted itself and created grief for natives. If we can see the paths not taken, we will at the same time judge colonialism more severely and prevent opponents and supporters alike from continuing to hold on to a one-dimensional view of what kinds of societies it could have fostered in Africa. After all, colonialism built what admittedly are comparatively better societies in the United States, Canada, Australia, and white South Africa while apartheid lasted. Perhaps in coming to a better understanding of the different types of colonialism that took roots in different places, we might come up with better explanations of the extreme divergences that mark the global history of colonialism. To do this, though, we need a more complex, highly differentiated understanding of the colonial movement, an identification of the various strains and stresses among the ranks of the many agents that effected the subjugation of native peoples.[26]

We fast forward to the nineteenth century. The loss of the American colonies redirected the imperial energies of Britain and other colonial powers to Asia and in the aftermath of the abolition of the Atlantic slave trade to Africa. Delavignette has identified "three main directions taken simultaneously by European colonization in the nineteenth century. First, there was colonization by settlement [colonization$_1$], principally in America and Australia. Second, there was politico-economic colonization, mainly in the monsoon lands of Asia, and in tropical and equatorial Africa [colonization$_2$]. Last, there was a mixture of these two kinds of colonization which aimed at combining settlement with exploitation of the native population [colonization$_3$]. This was tried particularly in North and South Africa."[27] The Republic of South Africa, Zimbabwe (formerly Rhodesia), Kenya, and Algeria are instances of colonization$_3$ (see Table 1.1).

I shall not be concerned with colonization$_3$ except when I draw on it to show how the juxtaposition of colonization$_1$ and colonization$_2$ within a single continuous geopolitical space enables us to see the stark differences between them and how spatial location by itself does not compel the choice of one rather than the other or that geography alone could explain colonialism's failure to sponsor modernity in Africa. For the most part, my focus turns on colonization$_2$ in Delavignette's schema. A word of caution here: colonization that is motivated by pillage, rapine, and exploitation of another country and its inhabitants is not a peculiarly modern phenomenon, nor did it take place only under Euro-American direction. Some have suggested that Japanese colonization of the Korean Peninsula took place along similar lines: the Japanese developed agriculture in the territories so as to serve as a kind of breadbasket for the Japanese metropolis.[28] Be that as it may, when colonization$_2$ is placed within the context of the philosophical presuppositions of modernity, the adherence to and institutionalization of which enabled the executors of colonization$_1$ and the settler component of colonization$_3$ to build successful, superior societies, then we have a series of abortions and exclusions that provide a better model for explaining the aftermath of colonialism in Africa.

Given the intimate connection between modernity and the different types of colonization I have identified so far in this chapter, one can draw some implications. If the above distinctions hold, it follows that one may affirm that colonialism can build both exemplary societies and retrograde ones. As the saying goes, it all

Table 1.1

Colonization$_1$	Settlement	Canada, Australia, United States of America
Colonization$_2$	Exploitation	India, Caribbean, Africa
Colonization$_3$	Settlement + Exploitation	South Africa, Kenya, Algeria

depends. It depends on whether one is working with one or the other of the different kinds of colonization described above. Additionally, by historicizing the concept of colonialism and narrowing it down to its modern specificity, we are able to bring out in bold relief the many conundrums and paradoxes that are often remarked in colonial studies with nary an awareness that the ideas involved may not cohere together. For example, when commentators write that Africans in the post-independence period could not run democratic regimes and institutions that had been installed under colonial rule, they must have confused settlement colonialism with exploitation colonialism. What is more, in contexts like South Africa where colonization$_3$ was the norm, it is instructive how the settlement component built solid democratic institutions for the settlers while enveloping the nonsettler native African element in the indignities of colonization$_2$. The fact that solid modern institutions were built on African soil and (for the most part) with African enforcers shows that it is a matter of historical contingency that those salubrious elements were not shared with Africans too. This turn of events becomes even more remarkable when I introduce evidence in later chapters of Africans not merely embracing modern institutions but striving mightily to appropriate those institutions and adapt them to their societies.

The lynchpin in the whole scenario is the historical conjuncture in which colonialism unfolded. Colonial apologists love to proclaim that part of the raison d'être of colonialism was to move the colonized along the path to modernity, to make them embrace "the subtle beauties of Christian forbearance and self-sacrifice," as one of the architects of colonialism put it.[29] Meanwhile, even the colonized often speak and write as if they believe those proclamations. The nationalists among them blame colonialism for tampering with their native culture and introducing "Western" ways that, they argue, are responsible for Africa's current predicament. The radicals argue that colonialism incorporated Africa into the global capitalist system but in a way that stunted Africa's growth. Both sides work on the assumption that colonialism was the vector for ushering Africa into modernity. I argue the opposite.

Colonialism as Philosophical Exclusion

Colonization$_2$ was the dominant form that colonialism took in much of Africa, especially in the British territories outside South Africa and, of course, in those areas of South Africa with predominantly Black populations. Scholars who have written about it agree about its characteristics but few have compared it to other colonizations and analyzed it for its implications and consequences. Even fewer have examined it as a philosophical phenomenon and worked to expose its fundamental presuppositions. An even smaller number have situated it within the discourse of modernity and unearthed the many contradictions lurking in that location. Delavignette was not alone in differentiating among the three colonizations. Albert Demangeon, a French geographer who wrote a glowingly approbative account of British colonialism, also captured the distinction between settlement colonialism and exploitation colonialism.

> British colonization bears everywhere the imprint of the people by whom it has been conducted: energetic, enterprising, practical, and efficient, the race is visible everywhere in its works. But this colonization has not met everywhere with the same geographical conditions, the same problems to be solved, the same peoples to be ruled, or the same resources to be exploited. Sometimes it is applied to hot lands where the European finds it hard to live, and sometimes to temperate countries where he can settle. *Colonies of exploitation and colonies of settlement are therefore two aspects of the colonial work of Great Britain; they are also, as a matter of fact, two original types of civilization.*[30]

Demangeon cannot be accused of being hostile toward British colonialism. In fact, his book is one long celebration of British colonial genius. That is why his articulations serve us nicely in this discussion. He called the two colonizations "two original types of civilization." We already know what type of civilization colonies of settlement exemplified. What of the colonies of exploitation?

> Since the very earliest days of colonization the factor that has given value to colonies in hot countries has been the quantity of costly products that they provide for trade—spices, cotton, tobacco, coffee, tea, cocoa, sugar, rice, oil-seeds, and rubber. Colonial activity takes the form of organizing the production of these commodities under white supervision. But there is another advantage that accrues to the mother country from the possession of these colonies: ever since the day when industrialism took possession of Great Britain she has looked upon her colonies as outlets for her manufactured goods, and it was by seeking for new customers that she enlarged her territorial possessions.[31]

Forget the Marxists, the *dependencistas*, and their fellow travelers. From one of British colonialism's foremost apologists, it is official: colonies of exploitation were coveted for their resources and the primary aim of white colonists was to exploit those resources for the benefit of Britain and for those colonies to serve as closed markets for British manufactures. All other considerations—state-building, the welfare of the natives, the development of the economy, the creation of new societies fashioned along modern lines, putting infrastructure such as railways in place; in short, the civilizing mission—pale into insignificance when placed alongside the need to possess and exploit the land and labor of the colonies under this regime.

Demangeon is not done. It turns out that even in the tropical settlements typified by exploitation there is some differentiation, maybe even a pecking order.

> In seeking to analyze the characteristics of this tropical empire we notice an amazing variety of types of colonial settlement, unequal in extent, different in development, and exploited with varying aims. At the opposite extreme from India, a continent and a world in itself, stand the scattered isles of the Caribbean Sea and the Pacific Ocean, while over against the Antilles, fertile and over-peopled lands, enriched by plantation cultivation, we have the colonies of tropical Africa, living mainly on extensive native cultivation, and in some cases remaining still at the fruit-picking stage of development.[32]

The dig at Africa is obvious in this passage. Among the tropical colonies typified by exploitation, Africa was not even judged ready for exploitation on the same scale as India or the other areas "enriched by plantation cultivation." In the hierarchy of colonies of exploitation, India was put in a category all its own and all other tropical possessions were placed opposite it. Among the latter, Africa was placed at the bottom and, for that reason, could not rate highly or compete with the rest in the race to development, even in the attenuated sense in which one could speak of such in the present context. Needless to say, Africa was not placed at the bottom because it lacked resources. Rather, its peculiar features held Africa back. Here is Demangeon:

> So far as economic development is concerned the African tropical colonies are the reverse of the Antilles. They comprise vast territories in which cultivation has always been carried on in accordance with ancient extensive methods, or even on primitive fruit-picking lines. Apart from Egypt and the islands of Zanzibar and Mauritius, where old trading relations and contact with advanced civilizations were favourable to the plantation system, the colonization of Africa has hardly begun, retarded as it is by the obstacles that the "Dark Continent" opposes to white penetration. These obstacles are as follows: difficulty of communication with the interior; a scanty population, difficult to arouse, and sometimes depressed by a long *régime* of wars, raids, and despotism; the ravages of the tsetse-fly that kills domestic animals and the sleeping sickness that works havoc among men. Tropical Africa has not yet become for the European a sort of black West Indies: it has scarcely risen above the level of native civilization.[33]

So Africa was mired in primitivity, and the fact that it was not yet part of the historical development relay race had little if anything to do with the machinations of its colonizers. That her resources were not developed by colonialism along the lines of parallels drawn from India and the Antilles was to be attributed to Africa's peculiar features that constituted obstacles to historical development. Moreover, Africa was *different* and, hence could not be discussed in the same breath as the rest of the world, even the colonized world. We might then modify the table above ac-

Table 1.2

Colonization$_1$	Settlement	Canada, Australia, United States of America
Colonization$_2$	Exploitation$_1$ Exploitation$_2$	India, Caribbean, Africa
Colonization$_3$	Settlement + Exploitation	South Africa, Kenya, Algeria

cordingly to reflect the difference between one type of exploitation colonialism represented by India and the Caribbean islands and the other type represented by Africa (see Table 1.2).

If what Demangeon described captures, even if slightly, the mindset of those who worked colonialism in tropical African colonies, it stands to reason that alternative paths that might have been available remained unexplored. Furthermore, Demangeon proceeded as if all the lands that he wrote about constituted one monolithic whole, as at the time of his analysis. Nothing could be further from the truth. I shall present evidence in succeeding chapters of Africans who were even willing to concede premises similar to Demangeon's and those of others but who came to different conclusions respecting what colonization should do with, in, to, and for Africa. Where Demangeon saw a limitation, some of those Africans saw challenges; where he saw obstacles to development, they saw an urgent need for accelerated development; where he saw primitivity that was almost typed genetic, they saw historically induced backwardness that owed not the least to the history of Europe's operations in Africa in previous centuries; where he saw an Africa with features that were sui generis, they saw an Africa sharing a common humanity with the rest of the world, exhibiting the same or similar tendencies as those who have shared similar histories of pillage, devastation, and violence. His and similar views that typified the class of Europeans that dominated colonialism in Africa could only conceive of Africa in *stasis*; the Africans whose exertions will dominate my analysis conceived of the continent in *dynamism*.

Even if one were to concede the premises of Demangeon and others like him, it still would not follow that all that colonization could do in those tropical territories was strip them of their resources. How might things have been different? Let us even assume that Demangeon's characterization of Africa was correct. It would require a different mindset to conclude that those features were an inalterable defect rather than a challenge that could be met in the true spirit of modernity. After all, as I shall argue in the next chapter, modern society is meant to be a society that uses knowledge to modify or overcome nature's designs while forcing nature to yield to persistent inquiry its innermost secrets. It would require additional premises that run counter to the main tenets of the modern age in which this colonization unfolded. Were Africans so incorrigible that they could not be tutored to see the benefits of extensive cultivation with scientific knowledge and modern technology? I don't think so. That this course was not followed is what led me to hypothesize that the form of colonialism that predominated in tropical Africa was better construed in terms of what it did not do in Africa. In other words, colonization$_2$, as it unfolded in tropical Africa, was a complex of philosophical exclusions. Isolating and understanding those exclusions will enable us to make better sense of the uneasy relationship between modernity and colonialism in Africa; identify how other paths than those taken were available under colonialism in tropical Africa; understand how contemporary Africa might manage its latest opportunity to turn modernity to its advantage while definitively dismantling the colonial legacy once and for all; and remove Africa from the "different" box in which it and its phenomena continue to be hermetically sealed by scholars in and out of Africa.

The modern era is the era of subjectivity, of the sovereignty of the individual, of no taxation without representation, of knowledge, of progress, of science and technology, and, most of all, of the equality of all human beings and of their entitlement to respect for the dignity of their person and all that pertains to it. These principles had their best efflorescence in settlement colonialism but only on the broken backs of indigenous peoples in the Americas and Africa. The principles form part of the narrative of colonialism in the modern age and they keep intruding into its justificatory strategies when confronted by anticolonial forces within the mother country.[34] These are the same principles in the name of which the modern age claimed superiority to previous eras in human history but for paying lip service to which we can indict colonialism in Africa more strongly. It is therefore not out of place to call colonialism to account for baiting Africans with the promise of a new life and switching on them when it mattered. I shall be arguing that if those who operated colonialism in Africa had meant their modern professions, the history of Africa could have been different. As Demangeon unwittingly pointed out, India and the Antilles were several notches ahead of Africa and the differentials in their respective contemporary situations cannot be separated from the qualitative differences in their experience of colonization. That this is true testifies to my contention that had Africa, too, been looked at differently, the continent might not have ended up in the deep funk it is in today.

Once Africa was encased in the concrete of difference, once the tropical colonies in Africa were determined to be so different that all that pertained to them was sui generis, the road was clear for colonial officials to isolate Africa and exclude it from the general march of progress that modernity was for even the more elevated tropical sites of colonization$_2$. In the rest of this chapter I offer at least five types of exclusion that radically distinguished the variety of colonialism practiced in Africa from that identified with settler colonialism in the United States, Canada, Australia, and white South Africa. They are the exclusion of the "natives" from: (1) participation in the European-inspired movement toward modernity; (2) participation in *citizenship* and its appurtenances that the victory of bourgeoisdom secured for all, including propertyless proletarians in Europe; (3) participation in the modern political and legal systems dominant in the mother countries; (4) acquisition of the forms of social ordering and consciousness prevalent in the mother countries; and (5) the ultimate exclusion, exclusion from membership of *humanity*. I treat them seriatim.[35]

(1) The colonial situation teemed with contradictions. But this phenomenon is only relevant to and has meaning in the modern conjuncture. The first exclusion epitomizes one of the main contradictions in exploitation colonialism. If all that the colonists cared about was rapine of the colonized space in an age that lays claim to the universal equality of all humans and for the principal ideologists of which human nature was improvable through education, the colonizers could not have escaped having to come up with some explanation for why the peoples over whom they ruled did not deserve self-government. If they recognized the entitlement of the ruled to and their capacity for self-government, then colonial rule could have had no legitimacy. As was already pointed out, they could say that they were tutoring the colonized with a view to suiting them for eventual self-government and that colonial rule was merely momentary. Whether or not they were willing to concede self-government, there was also the additional bother posed by the native ways, institutions, and practices of the colonized; in short, the native way of being human. To have recognized the integrity of native ways of being human would have necessitated the prior recognition of native agents as the authors of such ideas and practices and recognition of the integrity of native institutions and the metaphysical templates on which they were constructed. In the British tropical African exploitation colonies, the British invented a wholly new system of governance that, on balance, has attracted a chorus of approbation from commentators, African and non-African alike, the system of indirect rule.

The idea behind indirect rule was that areas that were subject to its sway would continue under the system of governance they had before British colonial overlordship was imposed on them. As it were, their indigenous rulers would continue to rule, presumably with the same sources of legitimation as before colonial overrule. The British colonial authorities would perform for the most part supervisory functions and would intervene only when the principles or dictates of indigenous rule ran contrary to equity and the principles of natural justice. In short, native rulers and native institutions and practices of ruling were interposed between the colonized masses and their British overlords. On the surface, this seems to respect the autonomy of the native and the integrity of their indigenous ruling institutions. What is more, it seemed to enable the British to claim minimum disruption to the rhythm of native life under their stewardship.

Many historians of colonialism consider the system of indirect rule, especially where presumably it succeeded, to be a stroke of genius on the part of its originators, especially Frederick Lugard. On the one hand, it reduced the costs to the British of administering the areas where it was practiced. On the other, it preserved the indigenous modes of governance it found in place. A closer look at the system might suggest a different appraisal. In the first place, it is questionable whether the indigenous modes of governance found in place were kept in place by the colonial authorities. In fact, the evidence is overwhelming that the indigenous institutions were altered, destroyed, and for the most part severely distorted. What is more, many of the institutions that the colonial authorities claimed to have "left in place" were created from whole cloth by the British and their local collaborators. Many Africans could not recognize some of the institutions that were touted as originators or legitimizers of some of the rules by which their affairs were administered.

Suppose, for argument's sake, that the British claim that they left indigenous governance institutions intact was true. New questions are bound to arise. We know what the British overlords wanted to do with the native institutions. What we are often not apprised of or is not even considered by commentators to be worthy of knowing is this: What did the natives want?[36] Again, in the modern era, this issue cannot be elided. In the peculiar circumstances of West Africa that inform the thrust of my work, not only can the question not be elided, it compels a response. By the time formal colonialism was imposed on a large scale on West African territories in the aftermath of the Berlin West Africa Conference of 1884–1885, a corps of Africans tutored in the ways of modernity was already present in the British territories of Freetown, Accra, and Lagos. They did not merely accept its presuppositions, they had commenced on the path to remaking their societies in the modern image. Unless one were to discount the opinions of this and other classes of Africans, it stands to reason that even if other Africans were willing or could be forced to acquiesce in the British plans, the products of the missionary finishing school for the manufacture of Christian modern gentlemen and ladies could not be expected to take things lying down. They did not. It would have been bad enough had the British colonial authorities merely omitted to poll Africans, especially their educated elite, for their preference in matters of choosing institutions of governance. Worse still, they actively opposed and stridently denigrated African views and preferences in these and similar matters.

This brings us to the British justification for preferring what they dubbed indirect rule. The British themselves and many commentators love to cite the preference as a pragmatic response to the exigencies of the colonial situation marked by a chronic shortage of qualified personnel and the dearth of resources to train local people to fill the relevant roles. As in the earlier case, where it was claimed that native governance institutions were left intact, the evidence points toward the contrary. Sacrificing merit to the demands of white supremacy, even when qualified Africans could have been engaged at less cost, the British colonialists imported unqualified Europeans at greater cost. We are right to question the motivation for clamping indirect rule on Africans. This qualm is appropriate only because the modern age is convergent with the "triumph of subjectivity." Discounting African agency, especially when it had merit, was a subversion, not an extension, of the principle of subjectivity in the colonial situation.

This subversion of subjectivity had its counterpart in the colonial attitude toward African social institutions. I would like to argue that this often-celebrated system might in fact have been a pernicious, even if unintended, effort to arrest movement toward genuine epochal transformation in the areas where it took root. Indirect rule was a euphemism for an orchestrated effort to stop Africans from choosing modern forms of life and, by so doing, give the lie to the preconceived British idea that Africans were too primitive to appreciate those modern forms. The resultant effect of this British preference was the deployment of sociocryonics in the African territories.

To show the character of what took place under the cover of indirect rule, let us draw an analogy from similar developments in Western Europe. The transition from feudalism to modernity in some parts of Europe was an example of an epochal transformation. In this process, the emergent burgher class used its burgeoning economic wealth to bankrupt the feudal oligarchies and put Europe's monarchs in its debt. The consequence was the overthrow of the dominance of the monarchies and aristocracies. In places where they survived, the feudal oligarchies and aristocracies were completely and forcibly deprived of salience, both political and economic, reduced to curio exhibits for the titillation of foreign tourists or as relics of past unity in class-divided societies as is the case in, for example, the United Kingdom and Spain. Imagine, for a moment, that the emergent bourgeois classes in Europe had adopted a system of indirect rule in their relations with the crumbling seigneurial system. The consequence would have been that the bourgeois classes would have left the seigneurial system intact and instead of outflanking the manors by establishing cities whose air made people free, they would have administered their polities through the moribund aristocratic class. But this was not what happened. The seigneurial system was smashed up, republics were established, and the regime of capital and its ideological concomitants of *liberté*, *egalité*, and *fraternité* predominated in France and England.

It is worth noting that the histories of countries in which the sort of transitions that took place in France and England never occurred are much more similar to that of Nigeria and other African countries. I refer to late developments in Russia and other countries of the defunct Union of Soviet Socialist Republics, those of Eastern Europe, and until about thirty years ago, Spain and Portugal. In all of them, subjectivity was in play. Spain chose royalty; Portugal did not. Neither did Greece. And in others in which similar transitions took place such as Norway, Sweden, Belgium, and Denmark, they all chose to be and have remained constitutional monarchies with vibrant democracies. Africans were never allowed to choose.

Take Nigeria, for example. Incorporating the indirect rule system meant leaving more or less intact modes of governance that were not necessarily congenial to the development of institutions that are considered some of the most important gains of modernity. The point here is apt to be misunderstood. For those who take a positive view of those indigenous institutions, to deem them uncongenial to the development of modern institutions will be an insult. It is not my intention to give offense to anyone, but I also cannot discount the fact that many of those whose views and preferences rivet our attention had less than approbatory views of the indigenous institutions and practices of their past and sought to remake them in the modern fashion. The point is, regardless of one's position on the relative merits or lack thereof of old and new institutions, the colonized should not be shut out of the processes of deciding what to keep and what to expunge of their mix of institutions and practices. In Europe, new modes of governance were substituted for the moribund feudal oligarchies, whereas in Nigeria, the empirical analogues of these oligarchies were strengthened in the name of indirect rule.[37] The British even sought to extend these modes of governance to places, for example parts of eastern Nigeria, where there were no local antecedents. The so-called commitment to preserving "native" institutions might have merited some approbation had it not been that it proceeded from not so noble motives and was not in consonance with the proclaimed mission of the colonizers to bring "civilization" to the "natives" to whom they stood as guardians. The consequences of this exclusion were deeper still. The next exclusion is one such consequence.

(2) Having excluded the "natives" from "the forward march to modernity" and its concomitants, it would have been incongruous for colonizers to extend citizenship and its attendant benefits to the colonized. They avoided the incongruity. I am arguing that citizenship, as it was articulated in European political theory and defended as one of the gains that the victory of bourgeoisdom secured for even propertyless proletarians in Europe, was not a presence in the colonies. In the colonies, there were citizens, made up of colonial settlers, officials, and their supporting cast, and natives, who could not become denizens of the mother country. Things did not start out this way. When Lagos was taken over, the returnees and recaptives, as residents of the Colony of Lagos, were treated as British subjects, as citizens were then called. In fact, this was also true of Freetown and other colonies on the coast. The citizens demanded and were accorded rights. The situation changed later when the colony was merged with what were designated "protectorates." Gradually, the administrators took away both citizenship and the rights that pertained thereto. For the British, the natives might one day, after long tutelage in the ways of "civilization," become citizens of their own countries to be created through the good offices and benefaction of the British Colonial Office. For the French and the Portuguese, the native could become a citizen of France or Portugal, but only after having become an *evolué* or an *assimilado*. In other words, even for the French and the Portuguese, the native could not immediately be a citizen. Even then, the situation in the French

territories was quite complex.[38] It ebbed and flowed with the undulating fortunes of republicanism in France until about the last quarter of the nineteenth century— specifically after the 1884–1885 conference—when the French too gave up on pre-paring Africans for citizenship and substituted the doctrine of "association" for the "assimilation" that had been driven by republican ideals. From then on there was no difference between the two colonialisms: denying subjectivity and imposing so-ciocryonics became standard. That the imposition of formal colonialism meant the whittling away of rights and forbearances of African moderns was one reason they opposed indirect rule. What I have described in this paragraph refers to the situation that began to obtain after the new regime of colonial administrators took the reins in the territories beginning in the last quarter of the nineteenth century.

Contrast the Nigerian situation with that of Canada or Australia or even the original American colonies and you will find ample confirmation of the argument in this section. British settlers in these places had no trouble traveling with their citizenship. It was not an accident that the American colonists fought for their in-dependence in reaction to what they considered to be affronts to their citizenship by the British monarchy and government. In the case of Nigeria, even returning slaves and freed slaves who came back home via Sierra Leone and who insisted on their rights as British subjects had no success in persuading the British Colonial Of-fice of their entitlement. More ominously, those who persisted in claiming the rights of citizenship got jail and brutalization at the hands of the agents of the colonial state. Also, the colonial nomenclature differed depending on whether it was a settler colony or the sort that proliferated in Africa. Many of the original American colo-nies were styled commonwealths; Canada was styled a dominion. In Africa, there were colonies and protectorates, both designations consistent with the non-self-governing character of the polities concerned.[39]

(3) *Natives* were excluded from citizenship and from the march toward modern institutions. A direct consequence of this exclusion generated a related exclusion. The colonized were excluded from participation in the legal and political systems that dominated the mother countries and were available to those who were *citizens* in the colonies and protectorates. As A. J. Christopher points out:

> Initial occupation and conquest necessitated the exercise of military might, and force or some form of coercion was essential for the maintenance of colonial rule. It was the local administrators who controlled the apparatus of local coercion, dealing with such matters as the police, prisons, law and taxation. Thus in some areas the first evidence of the establishment of the colonial state was the construction of the police station and the prison. Indeed as Jorgensen, J. J. has shown for Uganda, coercion was the domi-nant element in colonial expenditure prior to the First World War. In the ten year pe-riod 1901/2–1910/11 coercion accounted for 33.0 per cent of expenditure as opposed to 2.0 per cent for agriculture, 0.1 per cent for education, and 8.5 per cent for health services. Although expenditure on services rose, the allocation of monies only showed a marked shift towards education as a government provision in the 1950s, when it ac-

counted for 17.4 per cent of Ugandan budgets and coercion only 11.2 per cent. Changing priorities were reflected in the structures built and maintained in the towns and
countryside. Police stations and prisons symbolise the early colonial period, schools
and clinics the late period.[40]

The dominance of coercion in the operation of the colonial state was a consequence of the exclusion of natives from participation in citizenship and its appurtenant practices and institutions. A related consequence was the deliberate invention of a regime of customary law for the natives.[41] Such was the absurdity of much
that the British subsumed under the category "customary law" that many natives
did not find their ways of life in what was touted as the sum of their customs. Of
course, the natives who claimed citizenship rights for themselves were forced to liti-
gate in native courts unless their cause involved a citizen, a euphemism for "European." Meanwhile, when the British deigned to open the jurisdiction of the common law and statutory courts to native participation, magistrates and judges were
mostly appointed from the ranks of civil servants. The phenomenon of police magistrates was widespread in the colonies.[42] This had dire implications for the evolution of modern legal systems in Britain's African territories, especially as it concerned
the core modern tenet of the separation of powers.[43]

(4) Natives, finally, were excluded from participation in forms of social ordering
and acquisition of forms of social consciousness that prevailed in Britain. Well before the imposition of formal colonialism of the particular variety that I have isolated
in this chapter, many Africans, under the aegis of Christian missions, had been exposed to British education and the way of life it enjoined. Some of them, good students that they were, had taken seriously the promise of individualism, the importance of *liberté*, *egalité* and *fraternité*, and had sought to model their personal lives
on this awareness and to bring their communities along on this path.[44] We very well
know who their opponents in this position were: British colonial officials. In some
areas, colonial policies discouraged the breaking down of barriers among national
groups and actively sponsored ethnic organizations.[45] Attempts to form trade unions,
a principal weapon in the emergence of worker consciousness and supra-ethnic solidarity, were frustrated and punished by the colonial state. Socially, to strive to be
modern was regarded as an affliction and many who ventured in that direction got
caught in the kind of bind that Albert Memmi so poignantly described in *The Colonizer and the Colonized*[46] and Frantz Fanon trenchantly analyzed in *Black Skin, White
Masks*.[47] Too "English" for their fellow "natives," too "dependent" for the paternalistic English, those among the colonized who took seriously the promise of new ways
of thinking and new modes of social ordering found themselves in the twilight zone
of acute schizophrenia.

(5) Points (1) through (4) are the inexorable result of the ultimate exclusion
that was simultaneously their basic presupposition: the prior exclusion of Africans
from membership in humanity. The colonial encounter is best understood as an

emanation from arrogance, a swaggering confidence that Europeans exhausted the universe of humanity and that the rest of us have to be dragged willy-nilly to the human universe. For if Africans had been considered human in the first place, it would have been unnecessary to exclude us from the march of history and from the gains that humanity made up till the time of the colonial encounter, especially those regarding respect for persons and human rights. How we periodize this denial of the African's humanity is crucial to the case made here. The denial that concerns us here is a particular legacy of colonialism in its formal aspect. The earlier wave of Europeans that came at the beginning of the nineteenth century, the missionaries, did not evince the same contempt for the African's humanity as did their later cohort, which also included missionaries. As we shall see in the next chapter, the missionaries took the humanity of Africans as given but were concerned to remedy the defects that had afflicted the African character after centuries of slavery and the Atlantic slave trade. As a result they had no difficulty exposing Africans to those aspects of European civilization—modernity—which they thought would enable them to reclaim their legitimate seats at humanity's table. In the next chapter, we shall see what could have been alternative routes that were not taken.[48]

By extension, in the same way that the march toward modernity in Europe made imperative the preservation of monuments, knowledges, and identities that came before, a basic acknowledgment of our humanity might have spared many of the monuments, knowledges, and identities that testified to our human achievements in the period preceding the encounter with Europeans. But this was not what happened. The coming of the Europeans, especially the colonial administrators, and their imperiousness, the subsequent denial of our humanity, conjointly underwrote the devaluation of what was useful in our achievements, the undermining of our collective identities and meaning, the destruction of our indigenous technology and modes of knowledge production, and the withering of our capacity for autochthonous history-making. My argument is that those who were the principal executors of this orgy of destruction—the administrators—never worked seriously, if at all, to put something else in its place.

In the following chapters I develop some themes I have isolated above and work out their implications. I conclude the current chapter by highlighting the significance of the distinctions that I have made. A generic conception of colonialism is apt to obfuscate the issues that are crucial for explaining the contemporary situation in the former African colonies. In themselves, these distinctions have worth as props in a more sophisticated philosophical discourse. Beyond that, if these distinctions bear the weight that I have put on them, they should also have practical consequences. For example, I have made much of the fact that the global colonial system of which the African variety was a mere instantiation is intimately linked to modernity and that many of the conundrums that one encounters in writings about colonialism in Africa can be resolved if the topic is reinserted into the larger

narratives of modernity. This is even more so given that the issue of Africa's relation to, experience of, and engagement with modernity remains topical in our day.
Indeed, a basic motivation for this book is the awareness that modernity is a live
option for Africa today and that the shape of Africa's future will in large part be
determined by what the continent and its masses make of the modern legacy. It
becomes imperative to revivify this discourse, in part because for both opponents
and proponents alike, colonialism was the principal means by which modernity was
introduced to Africa. This has eventuated in a discourse in which the failed career
of modernity in Africa is attributed to the incompetence of Africans at working
its principles and practices. Yet the ideas of Africans who sought to realize modernity in Africa and secure its gains for the continent's peoples hardly, if ever, feature in the discourse on colonialism in Africa. There is an easy explanation for this
absence.

In the discourse of Africa's relations with Europe, Africa is defined by its utter difference from not only Europe but also the rest of humanity. I have argued elsewhere
that the genesis of this manner of looking at Africa is traceable, in part, to the libel authored by G. W. F. Hegel against the continent and its peoples and their heritages in his *Philosophy of History*.[49] There Hegel argued that Africa was not part of
History.[50] From that premise he concluded that the discourse of History must leave
Africa outside its scope. The same mindset that excluded Africa from the march of
history informed the exclusions that I have described in this chapter, and contemporary scholars, African and non-African alike, continue to evince the same orientation in their writings about Africa.

Africans, too, have embraced the metaphysics of difference and they are all too
often overeager to prove to the rest of the world that Africa is so different that any
time African phenomena are to be talked about, new words and concepts must be
fashioned for the purpose. This explains, in part, the fact that except among the
ranks of postcolonial and postmodern scholars much standard scholarship about
Africa does not essay to include African phenomena in the general movement of
world history. Hence, Africa is unrepresented in the discourse of modernity. Indeed,
African scholars often exhibit a reluctance (if not outright hostility) toward taking
seriously the history of modernity and its career in Africa.[51] Although Hegel fore-
grounded this standpoint and supplied the terms of its articulation, contemporary
scholars, Africans and non-Africans alike, have disseminated it and made it standard. I aim to challenge this exclusionary attitude in the rest of the current work. It
is time to reinscribe Africa into the discourse of modernity.

In the chapters that follow, I propose to reinterpret the history of the relationship
between colonialism and modernity in (mainly) West Africa, especially its Anglophone parts. As a consequence of the operations of missionaries, particularly the cohort with roots in the humanitarian movement of the period that spearheaded the
proselytization of Africans in the early part of the nineteenth century, categories of
Africans emerged who were socialized into the tenets of modernity. Some among

them embraced enthusiastically the promise of modernity and subsequently felt un-recognized by their fellow moderns among the colonizers, especially administrators and traders after the imposition of formal colonialism. These are the individuals who would later indict colonialism for failing to live by its own professions. They saw what I am now reporting: that the colonial regime under which they chafed was not being true to some of its professions and was offering them a niggardly package of benefits under the new dispensation. I argue that the disquisitions of these inheri-tors of the Enlightenment legacy, their indictment of their colonizers, their efforts to reconstruct their lives and their societies after the fashion of modernity represent a part of the discourse of modernity that is still omitted from the dominant narra-tives of modernity and its critics. In other words, the existing narratives of moder-nity rarely touch upon the career of the movement in other parts of the world out-side Western Europe and North America. Where the career of modernity in Africa is concerned, the continent continues to suffer from the tradition of placing Afri-cans outside the boundaries of common humanity.

Of course, intellectuals from Asia, Africa, and South America have had to deal with modernity and sift through its consequences. For many, especially in Africa, the fact that colonial oppression and ruthless Christian proselytizing mediated the original introduction of modernity has yielded a legacy of uneasiness or ambivalence about it. This is easily explained. On the one hand, such intellectuals have fashioned themselves, as a consequence of their enculturation, as inheritors of the modern way of life. On the other hand, they are pulled by the need to be true inheritors of their indigenous traditions. Add to this the fact that in many countries seeking to emu-late the new mode of life enjoined by modernity was considered pathological by the colonizer and inauthentic by large segments of the colonized. The exclusion moti-vated by Hegel's libel (which has been enshrined in colonial thought and practice) coupled with the uneasiness of the colonized underwrite the invisibility of the Af-rican contribution to and experience of modernity. I propose to bring these contri-butions to light in the rest of the essays in this collection.

It is important to record Africa's contribution to modernity not merely to show that Africa's relationship to the phenomenon is neither new nor recent but also to show that some of the conundrums that scholars have run into in their study of Africa may be made more comprehensible thereby. Furthermore, if we can remind our contemporaries how our foreparents negotiated their relationship to modernity in the nineteenth century, when many of them were barely removed from the dep-redations of slavery in the New World, we might equip them with better and more effective tools to understand the present situation when modernity is again on our plate. Finally, in making the case for the claim that colonialism subverted moder-nity in the continent, we are enabled to make a stronger indictment of colonialism while simultaneously retrieving what is useful in the legacy of Africa's earlier tran-sition to modernity that was aborted by the imposition of formal colonialism.

_2_

Running Aground on Colonial Shores
The Saga of Modernity and Colonialism

In the previous chapter, I showed how colonialism in Africa was also a system of philosophical exclusions. Dominated as it was by these exclusions, colonialism in Africa unfolded along a particular trajectory that many analysts considered inevitable. But I would like to argue that it is false that colonialism could only have unfolded in Africa in the way that it did. The history of colonialism could have unfolded differently. If we are to reappraise the history of colonialism in Africa, we need to identify the road not taken.[1]

The colonial whole had two moments: the colonizer and the colonized. Each of these entities was itself a unity with several parts. When we speak of the colonizer in Africa, we may mean any one of three possible (but by no means exhaustive) membership categories: missionaries, administrators, and traders.[2] These categories are not exhaustive because there were others in the colonial situation who provided what one might call the support infrastructure for the colonial enterprise: wives of colonial officials and other groups of women,[3] self-employed artisans who migrated to the colonies to seek better fortunes, or adventurers of different sorts who, sometimes at great embarrassment to their fellows in the colonizer class, had a proclivity for "going native"—that is, mixing with the natives and mimicking their ways. Nor should one expect that each category is clearly and sharply delineated from the other. At various times, the membership of one category overlapped with another. What is important is to take seriously the divergences in the colonial situation and how, within what on the whole was a more or less unified world view, there were significant variations that had implications for how the entire enterprise evolved from one time to another. The views of the members of each of these categories were not always convergent; often they were clearly at variance.

It is important to study the various orientations among the different membership categories. What is indisputable is that how colonialism evolved and what its specific contours were were determined by the administrators, among whom must be listed soldiers who led the military expeditions against the native communities and traders, many of whom served as the initial administrators before the home government began to take a more direct interest in the fortunes of the colonies. Different individuals and groups among the colonizers had different opinions about how necessary it was to bring the fruit of civilization to the natives. And the rewards or consequences that each individual or group expected did not necessarily tally with those of the others.

For illustration, traders were interested in finding new markets for their products, new sources of raw materials, and new places to invest in for maximum profits. Some administrators, many of whom started out as adventurers and hired guns for the companies, were motivated by the love of country that made them want to stake out new territories as a way of enhancing the conditions of their citizens and thereby the national prestige of their countries.[4] Missionaries, on the other hand, especially at the beginning, were seized by the injunction to spread the Gospel and harvest native souls.[5] A by-product of this endeavor included disseminating Christian civilization (which by then was indistinguishable from modernity) in native lands.

Hence they set sail. Many ships never reached shore. The cargoes of those that did included not only victuals, navigation equipment, and other items but also substantial ideological war chests, ideational templates for remaking native minds, creating *new* native men and women, and altering the ways of life of those domiciled on native shores. It was this business of social transformation that ultimately unraveled; its abortion is the shipwreck alluded to in the title of this chapter. Had the program of social transformation not come unstuck, the history of Africa might have been different today. And as speculative as this may seem, it is neither idle nor groundless.[6]

It is customary to talk loosely of the westernization of various Africans and the impact of Western values on native culture. However, the reality is much different. The business of transposing modernity to native shores is not an exception. Contrary to the dominant wisdom that laments how Western values have distorted native cultures, the relationship between indigenous cultures and colonialism was a lot more complex. Yes, there was distortion. But there was another dimension under which, in electing to leave indigenous structures "untouched," colonialism managed to damage them. That is, even in its omissions or, as I prefer to call it, in its exclusions, colonialism did a lot more.

Christianity and Colonialism

I contend that colonialism$_2$, British colonialism, never meant to allow the colonized in Africa the option of choosing westernization/modernity/civilization.[7] This is borne out by the consideration of the aims of the three major categories of colonizers: missionaries, administrators, and traders. Of the three, it was the missionaries who, at least until about the third quarter of the nineteenth century, were the most desirous and, in some cases, more aggressive pursuers of the dream of making modern men out of Christian converts and freed slaves. Even after the third quarter of the nineteenth century, the contingent of missionaries that saw possibilities in African subjectivity did not stop cultivating it totally, as we shall find below. True, a newer cohort of European missionaries bought into the period's racist ferment and denigrated African agency. But it is a mistake to talk as if Christianity by that time remained coterminous with the white missionaries who spearheaded the new evangelization movement. It is possible to separate the faith and its professors and to explore the divergences—hermeneutic, political, and theological—in the existing interpretations among the many parties to its dissemination during the period in question. As a creed and a movement, Christianity continued the business of social transformation through the medium of native agency. The political developments in the direction of imposing formal colonial rule—the true moment of colonization₂—did not keep pace with the stupendous results being garnered by native agents in their appropriation of the Christian and modern message. Needless to say, the program of economic transformation that a true transition to modernity would have necessitated never took off: from the standpoint of the dominant administrator class, the colonies were useful only for the natural resources that could be extracted from them. This is why we must develop a different attitude in our assessment of the missionary role in the transition to modernity in Africa.

There are two obstacles to this rethinking of the relationship of colonialism to Christianity. In the first place, many analysts see missionaries as nothing more than the ideological forerunners of colonialism: the recce party that surveyed the landscape and brought an artillery of ideas that softened up the natives for the colonialist infantry that finished the job and ran colonialism until independence. Missionaries are probably the most misunderstood of all the groups in the colonial situation in Africa. The tendency to not distinguish sharply the cleavages within the European communities in Africa has caused even an otherwise sophisticated analyst like Valentin Mudimbe to conflate missionaries and administrators in his discussion of the relationship between the missionaries' goals and those of colonialism. By so doing, he mistook the ingredients of Christian-inflected modernity for "the ideals of colonialism." So did Elísio Macamo when he averred: "Indeed, Christianity was to a large extent an essential element of the colonial project. Africans were brought under colonial rule also on behalf of Christianity as this religion was seen not only as representative of the kind of European civilization Africans were expected to adopt but also as the standard against which their humanity could be measured."[8]

According to Mudimbe, "The more carefully one studies the history of missions in Africa, the more difficult it becomes not to identify it with cultural propaganda, patriotic motivations, and commercial interests, since the missions' program is indeed more complex than the simple transmission of the Christian faith."[9] He presents evidence of the global involvement of Christian missionaries in the post-1492 European conquest of the world, especially as regards the complicity of the papacy in the genesis of Western imperialism. This involvement did not cease with the onset of the Reformation: "The Church's involvement in establishing Western sovereignty was important both before and after the Reformation."[10] In the post-Reformation era, Mudimbe points out, "The scramble for Africa in the nineteenth century took place in an atmosphere of Christian revival: the age of Enlightenment and its criticism of religion had ended."[11] In the specific African theatre of colonialism, Mudimbe, quoting Ogbu Kalu, observes that "of all 'these bearers of the African burden,' the missionary was also paradoxically, the best symbol of the colonial enterprise. He devoted himself sincerely to the ideals of colonialism: the expansion of Civilization, the dissemination of Christianity, and the advance of Progress."[12] Mudimbe's position is representative of many who have considered the career of colonialism and Christianity in Africa. They see a convergence between the aims and methods and ancillary practices of the missionaries and the colonialists whom Mudimbe identified as the missionary, "the explorer[,] and the soldier."[13]

In order for the argument of this chapter to stand, I must cast some doubt on this widespread but facile identification of the purposes of the missionaries with those of the colonialists, whether we take the latter as soldiers and explorers, as Mudimbe did, or as administrators and traders, as I do. I must show either that the purposes of the missionaries and those of other salient groups in the colonial setting were not always convergent or that even when they were convergent, there were different implications for each group depending on their location and the requirements of the primary engagement. I do both in what follows. Additionally, just as I did in the previous chapter, I need to historicize the location of each group; this will reveal that the demographic compositions of the various groups in the colonizer whole were not stable and that the ideas they espoused were not invariant throughout the colonial period. In sum, I present evidence in this chapter that positions such as Mudimbe's may be overly facile.

The second obstacle to my kind of rethinking is that nationalist historiography as well as a widely dispersed anticolonial animus among African intellectuals leads to a plague-on-all-your-houses attitude under which it is almost de rigueur for African scholars to criticize anything colonial and, by association, anything Western. One unfortunate effect of this attitude is that it does not differentiate between what Christianity did and what colonialism wrought, and as a result give short shrift to the ideas and strivings of Africans who accepted Christianity but not colonialism and celebrated what it brought them in terms of forms of social living, being human, and such like. It is part of my hope that the case made here will persuade more scholars to take more seriously the products—ideas, institutions, practices—of African agents regardless of whether or not we agree with them.

I would like to argue that the straight identification of Christianity with colonialism is at best mistaken and at worst just wrong. More often than not, those who base their analysis on such identification manage to conflate many issues that are not only separable but ought to be separated for purposes of clear analysis. Here is a typical example.

> Obviously, the missionary's objectives had to be co-extensive with his country's political and cultural perspectives on colonization, as well as with the Christian view of his mission. With equal enthusiasm, he served as an agent of political empire, a representative of a civilization, and an envoy of God. There is no essential contradiction between these roles. All of them implied the same purpose: the conversion of African minds and space. A. J. Christopher rightly observes that "missionaries, possibly more than members of other branches of the colonial establishment, aimed at the radical transformation of indigenous society. . . . They therefore sought, whether consciously or unconsciously, the destruction of pre-colonial societies and their replacement by new Christian societies in the image of Europe."[14]

I respectfully submit that the ideas that Mudimbe has lumped together in this passage do not cohere easily. But if one takes an ahistorical, generic view of colonialism, such as we saw Mudimbe take in the previous chapter, then any instance of the "cultivation"—from the root of "colonize"—of minds and space will do. To that extent, Mudimbe would be correct in his contention that "there is no essential contradiction between" the different roles associated with the missionary. But once we accept the different kinds of colonialism and their starkly different consequences, it becomes quite problematic to affirm the absence of a contradiction among the missionary's diverse roles. For if my argument in the previous chapter stands regarding the exclusionary nature of the colonialism that predominated in British Africa, then the statement Mudimbe quoted from Christopher must be read as being inconsistent with (if not directly contradictory to) Mudimbe's own submission that the missionary served with equal enthusiasm all the roles he identified. I adduce evidence below to show that while some missionary cohorts sought to create new societies in Africa in the image of Europe, the real colonial authorities—administrators and traders—harbored no such goals. I do not wish to suggest that all missionaries at all times bought into this idea, nor should I be understood as arguing that there were no administrators who were desirous of seeing new forms of social ordering take roots in Africa that derived their inspiration from Europe. But to suggest that there were no tensions between the administrators and the missionaries on this score is mistaken.

Second, only a generalized hostility to Christianity could blind a scholar as well versed as Mudimbe in the history and theology of Christianity to the autonomy and integrity of its discourse and to the fact that only on a sclerotic reading could its meaning be univocal. It is surprising that Mudimbe did not evince any acknowledgment that the debates among different missionary constituencies concerning what to do with the natives whom they sought to convert were not gratuitous. Neither were debates about the constraints the internal requirements of their creed imposed on what they were allowed to do to and with the persons and property of their converts. Hence, I think it is problematic to hold that there is no essential contradiction between "an agent of a political empire" and "an envoy of God." The discussion could use more nuance.

Delavignette described the Christian ideal: "The ontology of Christianity does not distinguish, does not separate its external expansion from its internal life. Colonization is defined by the fact that it presupposes a mother-country, but Christianity does not need a mother-country in the colonial sense of the term. It has the Cross, which is the same everywhere. 'Go and teach all nations.'"[15] There is no doubt that many missionaries fall short of this. Nor do I share any illusion that many or even most of the missionaries accepted the injunction Delavignette quoted. But just as I showed that a particular kind of colonialism was a harbinger of new ways of life for many in some colonies and that modernity-inflected colonialism was not without tensions in terms of the paths available under it, I submit that Christianity also could not, without more evidence, be convergent with colonialism. If the phrase "the Church universal" has any meaning, a Christian who denies the humanity of a prospective convert or that of a fellow Christian must be deemed to have sinned. Similarly, a Christian who privileges his nation as if it were a favorite in God's eyes could in certain contexts be deemed guilty of having blasphemed. That a commitment to the universal kinship of all believers was the gold standard for Christianity is what makes it easy for us to indict missionaries who trifled with it in their relations with the colonized across the globe. By the same token, the debates that continually erupted among various Christian missions about what was the proper attitude to have toward the colonized wherever they were encountered must not be lightly dismissed. I conclude that any attempt to ignore the ambivalences in the Christian position vis-à-vis colonialism is to throw away a line of argument that can be put to good effect in a critique of colonialism.

What is more, looking at the career of Christianity in some of the colonial contexts and some of the models it instituted in its relations with its converts illuminates an alternative path that colonialism could have followed that might have delivered more of the fruits of modernity to those it imperialized in modernity's name. That Christian missionaries are charged to regard all humans as equal both as children of God and in the eyes of God does not mean that the relationship between the missionaries and their wards, their converts, was marked by complete equality or the absence of hierarchy. In the relationship between missionary and convert we see the first and, I contend below, a more promising model of relation between a superordinate group and a subordinate one in a hierarchical context.

Let us turn to Delavignette once more: "Whether one likes it or not, the missionary's mode of life was—and sometimes still is—colonial in style. The missionary was a different kind of colonist."[16] What does it mean to say that even though the missionary shared some traits with colonists he was a different kind of colonist? "The missionary runs the risk of borrowing the colonial officer's acute sense of ownership. 'My colony', says the one; 'My mission', thinks the other. Both regard themselves as landed proprietors, or act as if they were land-owning powers."[17] But there is some difference. While the colonial officer may affirm "his colony" with minimal (if any) unease, few would deny that a parallel sense of ownership does not become a missionary and would be somewhat awkward for him. He is called upon to eschew the lure of patriotism. Nor is he to become a fixture in the land to which he has been sent to missionize: "But he must be cautious in his attachment to the environment to which he has been sent. He is only a man of God on condition that he is not enfeoffed to any form of civilization, western or otherwise. For him, to be anti-colonial would simply be another way of being affected by colonialism. He is the envoy of another world, and both colonialism and anti-colonialism are things of this world."[18]

If the missionary is required to be a permanent exile of the secular world, to subsist in it without becoming of it, what will become of the converts that he secures and of the church that they form? Speaking of the Catholic Church, Delavignette said: "As early as the sixteenth century, the Congregation for the Propagation of the Faith affirmed the supernational character of Christian missions overseas, the need to understand peoples in order to evangelize them, and the need to train a native clergy."[19] It would be very difficult to assimilate this mandate to the kind of imperial ambition that many Christian missionaries later associated themselves with. The injunction "to understand peoples in order to evangelize them" can always be given a sinister interpretation: Learn about them in order all the better to master them. Again, there is no doubt that this mentality dominated the thinking of colonial administrators in British Africa, and it may have motivated a cohort of missionaries that went there. But the force and appeal of this uncharitable interpretation are tempered by the requirement "to train a native clergy." Training a native clergy required a different orientation toward the agency and the capacity of the convert/native to become proficient in the Christian register.

Indeed, one of the surprising results of my research was coming to Delavignette's work and discovering that as far back as the sixteenth century the Catholic Church was directing its missionaries to create native churches. Until then, I thought that such an orientation was an outgrowth of the Protestant commitment to heterodoxy. It became even more interesting when I read Venn's dissertation on Xavier and found that there was more continuity than I ever permitted myself to think between the two traditions. The missionary's task was to identify and suit local agents for the job of creating, sustaining, and propagating the Church in its immediate environs, and his success was to be judged by the ability of the new Church to thrive without the continuing involvement of the missionary. Delavignette wrote, "It is clear that the future of the missions does not lie in the perpetuation of the missions as such, but in the substitution of a native clergy for the missionary clergy and in the elevation of the apostolic prefectures and vicariates into bishoprics. Missionaries are therefore enjoined 'to take in hand the education of the young men by every possible means and method, so as to make them capable of receiving the priesthood', and to establish them in their native countries."[20] If this be colonialism, it must be a different kind of colonialism indeed. I shall argue in what follows that until the eve of independence colonialism₂ *never* shared any of these sentiments regarding the agency of natives and their capability to learn the tropes of modern discourse and operate its appurtenant institutions and practices. On the contrary, the exclusions that came to typify colonialism in Africa emanated directly from the contempt for the humanity of natives that made them ineligible for self-governance of any type.

So far, we have considered evidence of recognition of and respect for native agency and its capabilities from the Catholic Church. But evidence is not lacking for a similar attitude on the part of the Protestant denominations in the evangelization movement of the nineteenth century that Mudimbe singled out in his account of the relationship between Christianity and colonialism. Indeed, the above discussion and the document we alluded to from the Sacred Congregation for the Propagation of the Faith could well be regarded as an early articulation of what Rev. Henry Venn, the foremost theorist and promoter of native agency, would call in the middle decades of the nineteenth century, "euthanasia of mission." By "euthanasia of mission," Venn meant that the success of a missionary was to be measured by how quickly he was able to render himself and his services superfluous to the continuing survival and prosperity of the local church his mission had helped establish. That is, to the extent that the missionary had understood his mission, he would strive to identify, train, and equip his native converts to govern, propagate, and finance their own church as but one part of the Church universal and enable them to keep the kernel of the Gospel even as they adapted other aspects of worship to their local idiom. Venn was very clear about what this manner of missionizing entailed.

In instructions designed to guide missionaries who were to be sent out to distant lands populated by different races, Venn and others enjoined them to "study the national character of the people among whom you labour, and show the utmost respect for national peculiarities"[21] and to be careful that they are not overcome by "long cherished but dormant prejudices" that "will occasionally burst forth,"[22] given that "race distinctions will probably rise in intensity with the progress of the Mission."[23] He also enjoined missionaries, "as soon as converts can be gathered into a Christian congregation," to "*let a native church be organized as a national institution*; . . . Train up the native church to self-dependence and to self-government from the very first stage of a Christian movement."[24] Venn could not have been more definite about how he envisaged the relationship between the missionary and the local church that he might help birth to unfold.

Regarding the ultimate object of a mission, viewed under its ecclesiastical aspect, to be the settlement of a native Church, under native pastors, upon a self-supporting system, it should be borne in mind that the progress of a mission mainly depends upon the training up and the location of native pastors; and that, as it has been happily expressed, "the euthanasia of a mission" takes place when a missionary, surrounded by well-trained native congregations, under native pastors, is able to resign all pastoral work into their hands, and gradually to relax his superintendence over the pastors themselves till it insensibly ceases; and so the mission passes into a settled Christian community. Then the missionary and all missionary agency should be transferred to "the regions beyond".[25]

Certainly one who is hostile to the whole idea of the missionary enterprise can find a way to indict this evidence, which makes it difficult to aver, as did Mudimbe, that "with equal enthusiasm, [the missionary] served as an agent of a political empire, a representative of a civilization, and an envoy of God." Even if Mudimbe were correct, his claim would count against such a missionary only to the extent that he claimed to be acting as a Christian and not as an envoy of a secular authority. At the least, Mudimbe would have to explain what would appear to be inconsistencies in his positions. Moreover, although many missionaries fit Mudimbe's prescription, it is wrong to think that all or most of them did. A principal motivation for my analysis arises from an awareness that during the period of the nineteenth century when the second wave of evangelization made its way to West Africa under the leadership of Henry Venn, some European missionaries took dearly to heart the need to train native agents for the task of uplifting Africans to Christianity and civilization and worked assiduously to realize that objective. Part of my task is to provide evidence of their success and assess their historical significance.

In addition to presenting an overly unidimensional view of Christianity, an unintended consequence of Mudimbe's characterization of the career of the missionary enterprise in Africa is his failure to recognize native agency, much less give it its due. The reason for this failure is easy to isolate. Once one starts with a hostile view of missionary work and neglects the specificity of different locations and the differential play of native agency in each one of them, it is easy to talk as if most of the actors originated from Europe and, by so doing, ignore or downplay the active involvement of native players in the specific theatre of West Africa. My hope is that the discussion that follows will persuade more people to take a look at the products of native agency in the business of the transition to modernity in Africa. It is always possible that the missionary leaders whose reflections I have reported above never meant to conform their actions to the lofty ideals they penned. Be that as it may, once those ideas were put down and Africans had access to them, we cannot ignore what their audience, the African converts, thought of or did with those ideas.

Does this mean that the missionary proponents of native agency thought that they and the natives from among whose ranks they sought converts were equal on all counts? The simple answer is no. In the particular context of Africa that is of interest to us, the relationship between the missionaries who thought highly of native agency and sought to make it the bedrock of evangelization and their native converts was no less hierarchical. Unless we take hierarchy to be bad per se, there is no reason to think that there may not be some hierarchies that may actually redound to the benefit of the subordinate unit in them. I argue that such was the nature of the hierarchical relationship between Vennian missionaries and their native converts.

Hierarchy marks every colonial situation. I do not wish to claim that the formal equality of all human beings in modernity precludes the installation of any hierarchy. But there are two possible models of relationship between two groups where one is superordinate and the other is subordinate. Think of the teaching situation. To assimilate the formal equality of teachers and students as human beings to their equality in the teaching situation is to abort the teaching process. The teacher-student relationship is a hierarchy of merit underwritten by superior expertise. The same situation obtains between a pilot and her passengers. Passengers defer to the pilot because of the skills involved in operating the aircraft and not because she is a superior or better person. By the same token, if parents were to take too seriously their formal equality with their children, they would be preempting the task of child-raising. In all such situations, those with the requisite merit may come to view themselves as superior to others in all other respects and therefore more equal. My position here does not enjoin me to accept such self-delusions. I grant that even hierarchies of merit are often accompanied by or degenerate into supremacist delusions—professionals who think they are gods, parents who abuse their power over their children, teachers who think their students should become their disciples—but they do not have to, nor do they always do. Thus, we should not assume that all hierarchies are inherently bad. The same is true of the colonial situation. In the peculiar situation of an Africa emerging from the depredations of slavery and the Atlantic slave trade that had lasted for at least three centuries, it is to be expected that the people's capacity for the exercise of agency might have been severely impaired. As such, it is not difficult to see how a people so situated might accept a period of tutelage during which their capacity for agency would be restored and strengthened.

I identify two possible models of relationship between two groups where one is superordinate and the other is subordinate. The first is the *autonomy model* whereby the superordinate group is committed to helping the subordinate group become fully capable of running its own affairs again in the shortest time possible. That is, the subordinate group's autonomy or the capacity for autochthony may be lost momentarily. The success of the autonomy model will be measured by how quickly the helping group renders itself irrelevant to the well-being of the helped. The earlier missionaries, under the inspiration of the Rev. Venn, undertook the task of training the African self for the exercise of agency at a later date; that is, they wanted to restore the African's capacity for subjectivity. However, the self, in order to realize its aims, needs resources to build, sustain, and, when necessary, change institutions. Of course there were indigenous institutions in existing African societies, however disturbed, distorted, or attenuated they had become under the ravages of the Atlantic slave trade, but the challenge was to enable Africans to make choices from an informed but autochthonous standpoint.

One other way of assessing the success of the autonomy model was the fate of existing indigenous institutions and of new ones. It is not enough to restore agency; it is more important to allow that agency to manifest itself in the world both as a signal of its capacity to make the world after its image and to accept responsibility for success and failure alike. Thus understood, the autonomy model would allow Africans to determine how they wanted to be either as individuals or as groups. In just the same way, Africans would be allowed to decide what to do with their institutions, old and new. They should be the ultimate determinants of whether or not to keep their old institutions, to change or discard them, or to build new ones de novo or through borrowing (with appropriate modifications), from other societies or epochs. Without such a commitment, the autonomy model means nothing.

Under the *aid model*, on the other hand, the superordinate group takes a dim view of the agency of the subordinate group and of its members' capacity for autonomy. In contrast with the autonomy model, the purveyors of the aid model do not seriously entertain the idea that there could be a time when the subordinate group can be weaned off aid and capably run its own affairs as it wants. The unequal relationship is sustained by substituting aid in lieu of building the subordinate group's capacity. By so doing, the superordinate group substitutes its own agency for that of the subordinate group and proceeds to exercise it on the latter's behalf. Needless to say, the recipients of aid might become quickly addicted to the handouts at the expense of the atrophying of their capacity for autochthony and rest content with becoming human equivalents of pets.

Consider an analogy. If, in the process of socialization, we elect to permanently treat our ward as a child, it is highly unlikely that that person will ever develop the characteristics that we normally associate with agency or autonomy. To the extent that this is the case, it will be unfair of us to castigate the individual for not exhibiting the appropriate agential traits. I would like to suggest that the evisceration of African agency under colonialism$_2$ is one plausible explanation for some of the agency-related failures of the post-independence period. The administrator cohort of the colonial situation that began to hold sway from the third quarter of the nineteenth century and whose apex position in the colonial hierarchy was solidified in the aftermath of the Berlin West Africa Conference of 1884–1885 had a less optimistic view of the Africans' capacity for autonomy. To put it bluntly: They did not think that Africans were a part of the human family, and if they were, they were so far down the human ladder that they were adjudged to be more kin to the lower animals than to humans. We have seen how this mindset determined the choice of colonialism$_2$ as the appropriate model to institute in Africa.

The distinction between these two models anchors my analysis in most of the essays gathered in this book. Generally speaking, in roughly the first two-thirds of the nineteenth century, specifically in British West Africa, working with the autonomy model, Christian missionaries led mostly by the Church Missionary Society and its leader, Rev. Henry Venn, worked to suit African agency for the task of taking control of their affairs once again in the aftermath of the Atlantic slave trade and slavery, guided by Providence. Starting in the last third of the century, administrators, traders, and a new cohort of missionaries who did not share the faith in native agency that underwrote the autonomy model adopted the aid model of the formal colonialism of the same period and, as a consequence, stultified the progress that had been set off and managed to abort the transition to modernity that was under way in the region. This is the basis for my contention that colonialism could have unfolded differently, hierarchy or not, in the region. What follows is the evidence and the argument built on it. I begin with the words of J. F. Ade Ajayi:

> The desire of mid-nineteenth century missionaries to create an African middle class must be emphasized. It was reinforced by the argument that for reasons of climate and of expense, a large part of the missionary staff had to be African. But the aim was often pursued deliberately and for its own sake. "In the history of man," said [an] American pioneer missionary, "there has been no civilization which has not been cemented and sustained in existence by a division of the people into higher, lower and middle classes. We may affirm, indeed, that this constant attendant upon human society—gradation of classes—is indispensable to civilization in any form, however low or high." It was to the lack of this gradation of classes that he traced African backwardness.[26]

The idea of creating a new social order in the societies they evangelized was a recurrent theme for some of the earlier missionaries in the middle of the nineteenth century.[27] As I shall show in what follows, there is ample evidence for this outlook in some accounts of the coming of Christian evangelization in Nigeria for the better part of the nineteenth century. And despite some divergences in their respective analyses of this phase of Nigerian history, the preeminent historians of what is dubbed "the missionary factor" agree that the missionaries, *at least at the outset,* were inclined toward a revolutionary remaking of indigenous societies, especially in southern Nigeria.[28] But later missions ultimately subverted the revolutionary agenda. Throughout the period under review, those who subscribed to the revolutionary agenda were resisted, ridiculed, and at times undermined by the traders and the administrators who eventually formed the colonial hierarchy. The subversion of the agenda of modernization—of the process of institutionalizing modernity and inscribing it in concrete practices and institutions—as well as the insalubrious imposition of various forms of rule that were premised on the African natives' incapacity for modernity are at the core of the shipwreck that modernity suffered in Africa. This had devastating consequences for the subsequent evolution of the peoples and territories concerned.

Some would argue that the consequences would not have been any less devastating had the missionaries had their way and managed to create truly modern structures in the various indigenous societies. They point to the destruction of native ways of life, institutions, and physical structures. I have no difficulty agreeing with this point of view. My difficulty arises from the fact that whatever gains Africans might have made from learning the ropes of the new mode of social living and that might have compensated them in part for the devastation were excluded from reckoning once the program was abandoned. Yet the abandonment of the program did not save Africans from similar devastation as a consequence of the paths that colonialism took in their lands. On the contrary, it has left Africans with the tragic situation in which they have borne the worst burdens of modernity without ever having enjoyed any of the benefits, especially those concerning the rule of law, productive economies, liberal democracy, and some degree of individualism as a principle of social ordering. Indigenous institutions and practices were distorted beyond recognition even as the colonial authorities kept trumpeting their preservation. In the name of protecting the natives from the ravages of modernity, colonialists carefully but effectively shut Africans out of the march of science and technology, new ways of organizing life and thought, and new possibilities of remaking their own communities using whatever new models they might care to appropriate from whatever part of the world they might care to look at. They were subjected to the ravages of the ignoble science of sociocryonics. It is time to look at the paths not chosen in Africa and why they were not chosen and to plot the consequences of these turns for the evolution of life and thought in the continent.

The Missionary Agenda

I begin by providing some evidence of the revolutionary agenda of the earlier missionaries and the convergence of opinion on the character of the missionary agenda in the writings of historians.[29] The earliest recorded contacts with Europeans, at least on the coast of Nigeria, date back to the middle of the fifteenth century.[30] There are reports of feeble attempts at Christianization off and on throughout the period until the nineteenth century. But, as E. A. Ayandele points out, "The introduction of missionary propaganda through the opposite ends of the Nigerian coast, Badagry and Old Calabar, in 1842 and 1846 respectively, altered the above situation and marked a turning point in the political and social evolution of Nigeria. Missionary enterprise turned the white man's activity in Nigeria into a veritable political and social force."[31] It is this crusading, idol-destroying, uncompromising variety of Christianity that I am focusing on in this chapter. It was missionaries of this persuasion who thought and were convinced that, as one of them put it, "the substitution of a civilized authority for the accursed despotism of Pagan and Mohammedan powers is a divine and gracious interposition."[32] As E. A. Ayandele has observed,

> Christian missionaries, fired by the idealism of a faith to which they ascribed, rightly or wrongly, the enlightenment, progress and technological achievements of their countries, *perceived no wisdom in compromising with indigenous customs and institutions*: the new wine of European Christianity had to be put into new bottles. Furthermore missionaries sought to convert individuals, whose soul's relations with God was all that mattered, whilst the unprivileged classes were the object of their solicitude. *They sought the creation of a completely new social order which would wipe away most of the customs and institutions of the old society.*[33]

Ayandele had a much less favorable view of the revolutionary complement of the missionary enterprise. However, even in his hostility he saw clearly that at a certain time in the process of the dissemination of Christianity in Nigeria, the missionaries fancied themselves as harbingers of a distinctively new way of life, of social living, and of being human. The key elements are in the italicized portions of the quotation. The fact that the missionaries were interested in the remaking de novo of native life and that they focused on individuals, especially those at the margins of society rather than rulers, all point to developments that are tied to the discourse of modernity, as I shall later show. J. F. Ade Ajayi had a much more positive view of the missionary enterprise.[34] His discussion offers us the evidence we need to make the case that missionaries sought to move their proselytes along the path that led to modernity.

The wave of evangelization in the period under discussion was distinctive in many ways, the most important of which was that missionaries did not make any serious distinction between Christianity and civilization. In fact, they thought and acted in ways that made one synonymous with the other. Civilization meant capitalism, or commerce, as it was styled.[35] But it also meant a host of other things having to do with social relations, family forms, modes of governance, spatial organization, work ethics and the division of labor, the ontology of time, and the like. (I shall have more to say about these elements anon.) That the missionaries were not merely concerned with saving native souls, the primary object of their religious exertions, but were also seized of the idea of remaking the natives' surroundings and the organization of all aspects of their lives is reflected in the kinds of programs some of them sought to implement in the heady early days of their mission and in the kinds of conflicts and frustrations they encountered in their interactions with natives.

The career of Thomas Fowell Buxton is quite instructive in this respect.[36] According to Ajayi, Buxton argued that "diplomacy in Europe and naval patrols on the

Atlantic" did not suffice to stop the slave trade and that what was needed was to enable Africans to become good in the ways of commerce and civilization so that alternative forms of production would undermine the allure of the slave trade. Buxton wrote in *The African Slave Trade and Its Remedy*: "We must elevate the minds of her people and call forth the resources of her soil. . . . Let missionaries and schoolmasters, the plough and the spade, go together and agriculture will flourish; the avenues to legitimate commerce will be opened; confidence between man and man will be inspired; whilst civilization will advance as the natural effect and Christianity operate as the proximate cause, of this happy change."[37] In further pursuit of this objective "Buxton founded 'the Society for the Extinction of the Slave Trade and for the Civilization of Africa,' with a Journal entitled *The Friend of Africa*, as well as an Agricultural Society."[38]

One may complain about the arrogance that took Africa to be bereft of civilization and sought to endow her with one. In my view, this may be the closest that the missionary enterprise came to embodying the colonial moment. It was as if the African cultural landscape and mindscapes were empty and waiting to be filled with appropriate Christian content from Euroamerican benefactors. That is, this view assumed that Africans were culturally naked. But I have not seen any evidence that the Christian missionaries wanted to take the land and exploit it or exterminate its aboriginal inhabitants. On the contrary, they wanted Africans to operate the land and prosper and to benefit the world by so doing, an approach that is compatible with what I identify as the autonomy model. Even if they did want to be colonizers, we have seen that, at some level, they would have had difficulty declaring such a goal. And we have also seen that hierarchy was ever present. One can point out the paternalism of the attitude that deigns to know what is best for Africa and its inhabitants. However, these criticisms should not blind us to the fact that the opposite attitude, which sees Africans as incapable of internalizing the lessons of civilization and totally unworthy of admission to the hallowed spaces of modern commerce and other practices, is much worse. It is time to consider, if only in strictly counterfactual, what-if terms, what possibilities might have been available to Africans had this professed attitude of the early missionaries been appropriated by their trader and administrator counterparts as well as by other missionary successors.

As part of its belief that the introduction of Christianity was the cure for the ills that its leader and members had diagnosed in Africa, the Society for the Extinction of the Slave Trade and for the Civilization of Africa had a program of civilization whose objectives remain relevant, if not urgent, in Africa even in these opening years of the twenty-first century. It is part of my argument that this program, although it was canvassed by Christians, was singularly secular. More important, it reflected many elements that we have come to identify with modernity and whose absence in many African countries lend credence to the contention that the successors to the missionaries, traders, and administrators, whose policies the missionaries knew were crucial to the achievement of their program, never passionately shared the aims articulated by the missionaries. Here is the program:

- [to] adopt effectual measures for reducing the principal languages of Western and Central Africa into writing;
- prevent or mitigate the prevalence of disease and suffering among the people of Africa;
- encourage practical science in all its various branches;
- investigate the system of drainage best calculated to succeed in a climate so humid and so hot;
- assist in promoting the formation of roads and canals, the manufacture of paper and the use of the printing press;
- afford essential assistance to the natives by furnishing them with useful information as to the best mode of cultivation, as to the productions which command a steady market and by introducing the most approved agricultural implements and seeds. The time may come when the knowledge of the mighty powers of steam might contribute rapidly to promote the improvement and prosperity of that country.[39]

There is nothing spiritual about this program, so it will be difficult to argue that its authors only had Christianization in mind when they framed it. Of course, if they thought that implementing the program did not hold any promise for the advancement of evangelization, it is doubtful that they would have adopted it. But the idea behind their desire to create a secular vehicle for the purpose of advancing their spiritual mission is what makes this adoption more significant. This is how Ajayi put it: "The missionaries placed emphasis on the development of trade because they believed that it would inevitably lead to the formation of such a class who would then themselves begin to carry out the social reforms the missionaries wished to see carried out but would rather not meddle with. Commerce, said [T. J.] Bowen, will aid the 'change in Society which the Gospel seeks.'"[40] For Bowen, commerce was to be the centerpiece of the new society to be constructed. In his estimation, "The extension of civilized commerce to Central Africa, attended, as it would be, by the pure Gospel, could not fail to have a powerful effect on the minds and institutions of the people. The various branches of business called into existence by commerce would require education; and the people would be anxious to obtain it."[41] He was convinced that commerce would lead to "an increase of industry, which, in all climates and states of society, is indispensable to the existence of virtue."[42] He foresaw a time when the growth of commerce would sound the death knell of polygamy.[43]

The missionaries never failed to remind their congregations that *Owó ni kẹ́kẹ́ ìhìnrere* [Money is the bicycle on which the gospel is borne]. It is easy to attribute the focus on commerce to crass materialism. But the missionaries concerned were more sophisticated than that. Commerce was imbricated in a way of life that had many dimensions. In light of contemporary debates about opening the borders of the so-called advanced countries' economies to products from the so-called developing countries, it is significant that in the mid-nineteenth century Bowen tied the development of Central Africa to access to "commerce with the civilized world" as a market for African products. When this happened, Bowen believed, "the introduction of plows, wagons, &c., and the opening of roads, would be a work of real benevolence. The demands of the foreign market would stimulate industry; the supplies brought into the country by foreign traffic, together with education and the Gospel, would create new wants and new aspirations, which would naturally and inevitably lead to the regeneration of society."[44] To that end, the missionaries sought to interpose between themselves and their converts a middle-class complement that was brought up in the arts, crafts, and commerce. This middle-class group would be endowed with appropriate beliefs in the new ways of being human that the new civilization enjoined and would be fired with enthusiasm to rebuild their communities in the modern image.[45] If Ajayi's interpretation is plausible and acceptable, then it is easy to see why the program of Buxton's society may be read as a template for social revolution.[46]

The program of the society was not implemented on anything that approached a grand scale. In the first place, the missionaries who were most seized of the idea did not have the wherewithal to realize the program. They relied on secular authorities, and secular authorities were not as enthusiastic as the missionaries.[47] Yet it is astonishing that Buxton was able to raise a substantial amount of money and mount an expedition up the River Niger in 1841.[48] That is, the program did not stay on paper without any specific attempt to realize it *in concreto*. Quite the contrary, Buxton was able to persuade the British government and some private donors to raise about £100,000 toward creating an advance settlement, the success of which was to inspire others to emulate the way of life it manifested. It is curious that so little has been written about this exciting social experiment in 1841. And this is not the place to examine its social and philosophical implications. But C. C. Ifemesia's concluding remarks to the essay in which he analyzed the course of the experiment bear quoting:

> Whatever were the opinions of Buxton's critics, the British missionaries (especially those of the CMS) never believed that the expedition was a total failure. In support of this view they drew attention to the great amount of information gathered about the Niger valley. They emphasised in particular that something had been learned of the languages of the Niger peoples and that for any work of evangelisation or civilisation to bear fruit, these languages must be reduced to writing. The missionaries carried Buxton's theme of "native agency" to its logical conclusion. If the "deliverance of Africa" was to be wrought by calling forth her own resources, they argued, the human resources should properly take the first place on the African development pro-

gramme. The expedition had demonstrated beyond doubt that the employment of European agency was not feasible; while, on the other hand, the Africans on the Niger
had shown their readiness to learn from their own countrymen. Everything seemed to
point to the necessity of training the indigenous people for the development of their
country, a policy the half-hearted pursuit of which has subsequently led to difficulties
in Nigeria down to our own day.[49]

One point stands out in bold relief in Ifemesia's conclusion: There is a qualitative
difference between what some missionaries thought of native agency and what their
administrator cohort did. It may be time to reexamine at the philosophical level this
difference in the relative standpoints of the various elements of the so-called colonizer class in Africa's colonial possessions.

It is instructive that the British government and the business community judged
the 1841 expedition to be a total failure. Ifemesia tells the story: "On account of the
large number of men lost (53 out of 303), the great amount of public money spent
(nearly £100,000), and the high hopes so suddenly frustrated, the enterprise was
bitterly criticized by the British Parliament, press and public. Buxton was dubbed a
man of visionary ideas and extravagant hopes. Philanthropy was laughed to scorn.
The African Civilisation Society was roundly ridiculed, and a few months after
Webb's return the Society was dissolved. Buxton, its founder, did not long survive
its ending."[50] There is no record of any further attempts at serious social transformation or backing for such in the history of British colonization until the promulgation
of the Colonial Development Act in 1929 and the Colonial Development and Welfare Act of 1940. These laws were not programs of social transformation and were
barely funded.[51] This is a situation where the view one has of native agency matters. It is by no means the case that the negative assessment Ifemesia recorded is the
only plausible one. An alternative assessment would consider some of the successes
of the encounter, especially in the area of gathering scientific data on the flora and
fauna of the area and the ethnographic evidence of the peoples and cultures there.
More important, a positive view of the motivating ideals of the expedition would
have yielded a deeper commitment to figuring out the appropriate material means
to realize them. This did not happen.

Second, the era of the missionaries who saw in the Africans potential candidates
for admission to the middle classes and the modern age (despite opposition from
some of their cohort) ended during the third quarter of the nineteenth century.[52]
This was reflected in the influx into Nigeria of missionaries who insisted that the
natives were not good enough to superintend the evangelization process or be missionaries.[53] They embraced the aid model and sought to manage the affairs of the
local church from England. It was not an accident that this period inaugurated the
proliferation of schisms within the main denominations that saw the emergence of
African independent churches[54] and growing resentment on the part of Africans
toward the overbearing and suffocating embrace of clerical, administrative, and

commercial paternalism that denigrated African agency, if it did not deny it outright. In addition, there was a growing movement in England toward a social Darwinist mentality in which Africans were seen more and more as belonging to the infancy of the human race and therefore needful of European guidance at every step along the way to civilization.[55] Paternalism was not any less present in the program of the Society for the Extinction of the Slave Trade and for the Civilization of Africa earlier in the century. No, it was just that the earlier paternalism, the autonomy model, held that Africans were able and ready to be schooled in the modern ways, whereas the latter variety based on the aid model saw Africans as so far removed that any attempt to realize the program was sure to result in disaster—the destruction of indigenous ways among peoples who were incapable of or unsuited for the acquisition of the new ways. These are crucial issues that had far-reaching consequences for the colonies, consequences that have continued to affect the fortunes of the former colonies.

Finally, the secular authorities—the traders and administrators—on whose material generosity and support the revolutionary missionaries depended increasingly became dominant in the colonial context and began to adopt policies that reflected the view of Africans as infants of the human race for whom accelerated social change was inappropriate, if not dangerous. The commitment to progress both in terms of the improvability of native agency and the substitution of new institutions or the modification of old ones was extirpated from colonial discourse and practice. What is remarkable is that despite these difficulties, the missionaries of the autonomy model garnered stupendous achievements in their implementation of the program Buxton's society outlined. In light of the limited material support of the secular authorities, the occasional hostility of the administrators and traders, and the sheer immensity of the task, we must in hindsight marvel at what the early nineteenth-century missionaries accomplished.

The achievement of these missionaries is often obscured for four reasons:

1) The general tendency among scholars not to make or not to take seriously a distinction among the ranks of the colonizers such as I make in this work
2) The failure of most scholars who do note differences among colonizers to work out the implications of the distinction
3) The failure of many to acknowledge that especially in West Africa, the missionaries that proselytized much of the area looked like their converts—that is, their scholarship subsumes African agency under European agency[56]
4) The fact that many who work in the area adopt a nationalist stance that dismisses the missionaries as misguided do-gooders who inaugurated wholesale destructions of native civilizations and who, for that reason, held a less hostile view of the administrators' embrace of sociocryonics as the template for policymaking in the colonies.

Given that I proceed from the affirmation of distinctions within the colonizer community, the credit for the transition to modernity in West Africa, to the extent that this transition occurred, must go to the missionaries. Because the most important figures in this transition were themselves African, we must set about the task of reconceptualizing the history of modernity in Africa and the mechanisms of interpellating Africans as subjects of the modern age. I proceed to a consideration of some of the achievements of the missionaries that represented points of transition to modernity, or at least a prefiguring of it.

The Missionary Agenda: An Assessment

Take the first item in the program, for instance: creating written scripts for the principal languages of Western and Central Africa. This is one of the greatest achievements of the missionaries in most parts of Africa. In many parts of the continent, the written versions of the local languages are still anchored in the alphabet that was either formulated or inspired by the missionaries.[57] It may cynically be suggested that the primary aim of the missionaries in reducing local languages to writing was not to benefit the locals but to proselytize them. That this was true in the main may not be disputed. But it is not the whole story. Yorùbá literature is very well developed because of its early availability in writing. Nevertheless, it would be crazy to suggest that the spadework done by the missionaries did not provide the basic building blocks of the written languages as we have them today. For example, Samuel Ajayi Crowther, a pioneering scholar and linguist, was a moving spirit in the effort to create a script for Yorùbá. So lasting is the impact of Crowther and his co-workers in this area that the Yorùbá Bible remains more or less the same product that they produced back in the late nineteenth century. And it is only recently that scholars of Yorùbá culture and philosophy have begun to controvert the Christian-inspired usages that characterize colloquial Yorùbá in order to reduce the overweening influence of Christianity in written Yorùbá philosophy.[58]

The importance of the written word and its widespread dissemination in portable forms to constituting the modern age cannot be denied by anyone who is familiar with the revolutionary impact of Martin Luther's decision to make the Bible available to a mass audience and take the interpretation of the Gospel away from the clutches of the clergy. The significance was not lost on Crowther. J. F. Ade Ajayi writes, "When asked to join the 1857 Niger Expedition and begin the Niger Mission, Crowther at the age of over 50 said he would prefer to retire from Niger Expeditions and devote the rest of his life to his work of translations as a legacy to his people."[59] One may detect similar echoes in the following statement by Bowen:

> But our designs and hopes in regard to Africa are not simply to bring as many individuals as possible to the knowledge of Christ. We desire to establish the Gospel in the

hearts and minds and social life of the people, so that truth and righteousness may remain and flourish among them, without the instrumentality of foreign missionaries.
This cannot be done without civilization. To establish the Gospel among any people,
they must have Bibles and therefore must have the art to make them or the money
to buy them. They must read the Bible and this implies instruction. They must have
competent native pastors, and this implies several things which can not exist without
a degree of civilization.[60]

Commenting on the need to meet the contingencies of instructing their proselytes,
Ajayi writes: "Nothing shows the ardour of the pioneering missionaries better than
the effort devoted, within the limited resources of the missions and the ability of
the missionaries, to the study of the principal Nigerian languages, reducing them to
writing, in most cases for the first time."[61] In my opinion, one reason why the missionaries' achievements in this area tend to be belittled is that critics and supporters alike have not considered the wider ramifications of the business of writing and
its associated activities or the fact that many of the activities involved reflected the
development and deployment of African agency.

By itself, writing does not amount to much. The many advantages often claimed
for writing over orality are exaggerated. Once we place it within a wider context,
however, the implications are deep. To consider indigenous languages to be the principal medium of saving native souls is implicitly to assume that although its users
may be heathens, their tongue can be put to the service of the Christian God. More
significant still, this choice of the native tongue is a fundamental recognition of
the agency of the new converts and their compatriots from among whom even more
converts are to be drawn. Add to these elements the fact that the missionaries were
offering a package deal: For the natives to know God, the scripture had to be made
available. For it to be made available it had to be written in local languages and
be manufactured at such a cost that it would remain affordable. Hence, the enterprise
had to be implicated in a system of commerce. Finally, producing written text has
a multiplier effect in creating a support infrastructure made up of printers and their
apprentices, technicians to service the machines, the production of paper and ink,
and so forth. There is evidence that where these infrastructural elements were concerned, the record of the missionaries was unmatched by any of the administrator/
trader regimes that later came to dominate the colonies.

There are other implications that I have not drawn about creating local histories
and creating and consolidating new identities through such histories.[62] To sum up
this section: the missionaries believed that although heathen, Africans were God's
children who were capable of beholding the light of the gospel. To bring this light
to them faster and more successfully, the bearers needed to be indigenes and speak
in local idioms. We shall be exploring the implications for agency later on.

Nowhere did the missionaries acquire a more sterling record than in the area of
education.[63] I do not exaggerate when I say that most Africans who inhabited the

areas where missionaries worked were introduced to modernity through the operation of Christianity and its educational institutions. Thus, for many Africans, the
experience of the new way of life signified by modernity was mediated by Christian
education. Had missionaries only set their sights on enabling the indigenes to read
the Bible in order to understand the word of God, they would not have had to put
in place whole systems of education.[64] But they had other purposes, the most important of which was the creation of a middle class committed to civilization as partak-
ers of its fruits. As part of this grander plan, the school curriculum in different regions included subjects in industrial training and the new ways of life enjoined by
modernity. As Adu Boahen notes, "Besides preaching the gospel, converting people
to Christianity, and translating the Bible into various African languages, these missionary societies promoted agriculture; taught such skills as carpentry, printing, and
tailoring; and promoted trade, literacy, and Western education."[65]

Africans, converts and nonconverts alike, responded with varying levels of enthusiasm. They presented their children for training and by so doing became active participants in sowing the seeds of the future civilization. They contributed labor to build schools. The rich ones donated substantial sums to found and support
schools.[66] They wrote petitions for teachers to be sent to them. By 1859, the first secondary school had been established in Lagos, the first of many such schools to train
the future inheritors and propagators of the new civilization. The first generation to
graduate from the missionary school of modernity included people like Crowther.
The second generation of Africans who graduated from institutions rooted in the
missionary autonomy model of developing native agency were taught or otherwise
educated at, especially, Fourah Bay College in Freetown, Sierra Leone, by members
of Crowther's generation. They went on to expand considerably the program of establishing schools and other institutions either by being sole proprietors or by working with their communities to mobilize support, especially in the provision of land
and labor. For instance, the Kúdẹ̀tì community in Ibadan welcomed the Hinder-
ers, David and Anna, and donated the land on which both a church and school
were built in 1852. Others working through associations formed by the new educated elite in this second generation established schools such as Abẹ́òkúta Grammar School in 1908, Ijebu-Ode Grammar School in 1913, and Ibadan Grammar
School, also in 1913. Each one of these three schools had one connection or the
other with Fourah Bay College, the school that had produced Crowther and where
he had taught at the beginning of his career.[67] Developments were even more spec-
tacular in other areas.[68] These were not isolated cases. They typified the period under discussion. Boahen summed it up well:

> All the missionary societies, Protestant as well as Catholic, founded elementary schools,
> training colleges, and even secondary schools. In West Africa, the CMS, which com-
> menced operations there in 1806, founded the Fourah Bay College as early as 1827, a

secondary school for boys and one for girls in 1842, and by 1841 had twenty-one elementary schools in Sierra Leone. The Wesleyans had also established four elementary schools for girls and twenty for boys in Ghana by 1846; in 1876 they founded their first secondary school, the Wesleyan High School, which developed into the present Mfantsipim School. By 1835, the CMS had 4,000 children in its schools in Madagascar, while by 1894, the Protestant missions had a total enrollment of 137,000 pupils in their schools.[69]

Missionaries cleared new paths in Nigeria and other African countries in other subjects as well; I follow Ajayi in identifying three: architecture, printing, and medicine.[70] In teaching these subjects, the missionaries sought to create a body of artisans and practitioners who would be gainfully employed, develop pride in their expertise, and generally be able to buy as well as read the Bible and live by its injunctions. The introduction of printing enhanced the possibility that the Good News could be widely disseminated. But at the same time it enabled the inauguration, by Henry Townsend, of the "*Iwe-Irohin*, a fortnightly journal in Yoruba giving news of Church and state from near and far, and educating the growing reading public through didactic essays on history and politics."[71] There is hardly a greater testimony to the success of the missionaries in this area than the fact that Nigeria, especially the southern region, where the missionary influence was greatest, has remained home to the most diverse and vibrant print media in the continent. M. J. C. Echeruo's *Victorian Lagos* also testifies to how vibrant the literary culture of Lagos had become by the closing years of the nineteenth century and the opening of the twentieth.[72]

I do not propose to delay the reader with the details of the contributions of the missionaries in the areas of architecture and medicine.[73] Nor have I represented the magnitude of the contributions they made in the field of education, which by far is the area in which their achievements not only were stupendous but, for the most part, defined the boundaries of the indigenous mindscape in ways that the later institutional and other practices of colonialism did not approach. A few passing comments can be made, though. The press is only one consequence. I have already mentioned the creation of local histories and new identities through the facility of writing. Through the church, Africans began to use their theoretical training in music to score native airs and indigenize their Christian inheritance.[74] The consequences are more far-reaching than I think people are willing to admit. Hubert Ogunde, Duro Ladipo, and Kola Ogunmola, the trio of masters of indigenous theatre in Yorubaland and, by extension, Nigeria, all had their starts in drama in the church or church-related institutions.[75] The pioneers of popular music, especially Juju, all cut their teeth learning the intricacies of musical structures in English under Christian inspiration.[76] Tunde King, I. K. Dairo, Tunde Nightingale, Ojoge Daniel, Adeolu Akisanya, Ebenezer Obey, and Sunny Ade are but a few examples.

The same facility, writing, became the idiom in which native protests were articulated. Later on, public letter writers and professional petition writers turned that

instrument on the colonial administration in their agitations against the depredations of colonial rule.[77] I conclude that only by trifling with native agency can we
say that what Africans have done with the legacy of missionary influence does not
matter or should be treated as if it was a mere extension of what the European missionaries intended or, worse, was mere mimicry of their conquerors. The divergence
between European designs and native agency was repeated throughout the history of
colonialism, and I make a lot of it. Whatever their European mentors intended, Africans had their own aims that often were not convergent with those of Europeans.

The Road Not Taken: The Missionary Road to Modernity

What I have said so far surely inclines one to speculate on what might have been
had there been a serious pursuit of the aims articulated in the program of civilization of the Society for the Extinction of the Slave Trade and for the Civilization of
Africa, which represents the most progressive thinking among the missionaries at
the commencement of their task in the beginning of the nineteenth century. It is
meet to ask why the program was never implemented by later missionaries and by
the successor colonial administrations in Nigeria. Few will deny the relevance of the
program to the Africa of the early twenty-first century. I restrict myself to Nigeria.

It is almost cant that Nigeria has nearly 250 ethnic and/or linguistic groups. I
think this is an exaggeration. But there is no doubt that Nigeria is home to numerous
languages. As at this writing, only a few of them have been reduced to writing. The
consequences for educational programs, especially at the primary-school level and
in the area of adult literacy, can be devastating. In the first place, those whose languages have not been reduced to writing will have serious difficulties because their
children will be taught in languages that are not theirs and in which they may not
even be able to operate—instruction is usually done in languages available in written form. Second, the possibility of widely disseminating much-needed information
about agriculture, health, and political activities will be very restricted (radios are
the only available means when written language is not a possibility). One must not
minimize the impact of such limited possibility. These are complex societies spread
over wide spaces that are no longer amenable to old forms of information processing.
Third, and perhaps most important, the country stands to lose significant contributions to its cultural heritage as those who are most versed in the oral traditions
of their people die out and their progeny, having gone to school and become proficient in other languages, know how to use their indigenous languages only for everyday speech. The possibility of such cultures becoming extinct is real.[78] The record
shows that the Bible Society of Nigeria, for instance, has continued to do more in
the area of making the Bible available in more local languages and, by so doing, creating scripts for the languages concerned. The two extant Yorùbá dictionaries remain under the grip of their original Christian inspiration, which has serious conse-

quences for deploying the language in secular studies. Fortunately, the Yorùbá Studies
Association of Nigeria and Yorùbá scholars are correcting this.[79]

One cannot gainsay the relevance of—make that urgent need for—a program to
"prevent or mitigate the prevalence of disease and suffering among the people of Africa" or to "encourage practical science in all its various branches." In many parts of
Nigeria, especially in the south, the church school (primary and secondary) and the
church clinic or hospital were the only social welfare resources available to people
until late in the colonial period, especially the last two decades of colonial rule.[80]
The periodic crises of inadequate food supply and the enduring backwardness of agricultural techniques testify to the continuing relevance of the need to "afford essential assistance to the natives by furnishing them with useful information as to
the best mode of cultivation, as to the productions which command a steady market and by introducing the most approved agricultural implements and seeds," as
the Society for the Extinction of the Slave Trade and for the Civilization of Africa
set out to do.

The failure to implement the program or some equivalent by the successor colonial regimes of traders and administrators that held sway in the colonies lends credence to my thesis that had modernity truly been on the agenda of the colonizers,
the history of Africa would have been different. The modern age, as it has been described and conceptualized by its European ideologists, is noted for placing science
and the rationality it fosters at the center of its intellectual and practical life. Thus
the encouragement of practical science in all its various branches ought to have a
central focus in a truly transformatory colonial administration. The program presaged the introduction of *new* forms of social ordering that might have heralded
large-scale social transformations on the continent. And there is evidence that the
earlier missionaries were not merely concerned with creating institutions and structures of the sort envisaged in the program of the society. In what follows, I would
like to suggest that the other elements of their activities, the less tangible, the less
institutional ones, held more promise of a radical transformation of social living in
both ideological and physical terms than has previously been realized.

As other examples from the twentieth century have shown, it is possible (and it
happens often enough) for a country or society to put in place elements that reflect
the kinds of changes articulated in the program of Buxton's society without necessarily making the transition to modernity. Countries such as Japan, South Korea, and Taiwan have incorporated systems in which all branches of practical science are encouraged, have built roads and canals, have industrialized, and can boast
of skylines that challenge the best that New York and London have to offer. Yet
they have managed to sidestep incorporating some of the intangible components of
modernity—for example, individualism. To the extent that the missionaries sought
to introduce and entrench the intangibles in the structures of social living in Nigeria, we have to adjudge them revolutionaries. The case follows.[81]

The missionaries were convinced that the creation of middle classes was a sine qua non for civilization and that commerce would be the preferred vehicle for creating that class. Christianity was to be the crowning glory of this trinity, the caretaker of the soul, which in Christian philosophical anthropology is the godhead in us. They never lost sight of the importance of creating the kind of material wealth that would enable the middle classes to afford the standard and style of living the new civilization entailed. But they also were aware that their proselytes might just take the money and run—that is, that converts might find the requirements of the new way of life too onerous and therefore seek to appropriate material wealth while shirking from embracing the social ordering entailed by the new creed. Both Ayandele and Ajayi have copious discussions of some of the most intractable divergences between the missionaries and their converts. Other historians allude to them. An examination of some these divergences yields evidence that the missionaries were really interested in a complete makeover of their followers.

Ajayi argues that "what distinguished missionary work in the mid-nineteenth century, what made its social and economic influence go much further than the limited number of converted people was that the missionaries who saw civilization as allied to Christianity attempted more than just a reform of the manners of the converted."[82] For example, it is true that missionaries sought to introduce some of the more pedestrian elements of the culture they traveled with—drinking tea, clothing that met European standards of modesty, and so on. Of greater significance is the fact that "civilization meant to them all that they considered best in their own social manners and customs."[83] Let us examine this claim in light of the markers they set for civilization and the kinds of tensions that characterized their relationships with their converts.

What were those elements that "they considered best in their own social manners and customs"? Ajayi has provided evidence that the missionaries were inflexibly opposed to the institution of polygamy. It was for them an index of all that was wrong with the old ways of being human that Africans, especially their rulers, cherished. Missionaries used a willingness to abandon it to gauge the depth of a convert's commitment to the new way of being human that Christianity and its twin, civilization, presaged. But what was it about the institution of polygamy that aroused such detestation in the missionaries? There is the moral aspect in which having multiple sexual partners must have been odious to the sensibility of Victorian-era parsons and their cohorts. There is no doubt that the moral aspect was important to the missionaries, and they used strong language to convey their abhorrence, especially to the rulers whose attachment to polygamy the missionaries saw as the principal obstacle to their eligibility for baptism. This, as Ajayi points out, could not have been the principal reason why they found the practice so odious. They had little trouble accommodating another morally repugnant practice they encountered, domestic slavery.[84]

Aside from the scriptural condemnation of polygamy and its suspect moral status, the principal reason for the inflexible rejection of polygamy is the following:

> Both for the European missionaries anxiously seeking to reject it, and for the Africans holding tenaciously to it, polygamy was not just a plurality of wives; *it was a symbol of the communal way of life in the family compounds.* . . . Christian missionaries from *an individualistic society,* where whatever folk-culture survived the Reformation and seventeenth-century Puritanism had been virtually destroyed by the Industrial Revolution and the new puritanism of the Evangelical Revival, found life in the family compounds at best incomprehensible, at worst the devil's own institution. Concerned as they were not only to destroy paganism but also to reform the existing social structure in Africa, they were bound, sooner or later, to attack polygamy.[85]

Why did the communal way of life upset the missionaries so much? What are we to understand by Ajayi's suggestion that missionaries came from an individualistic society? Certainly it could not be suggested that there were no individuals in African societies: if nothing else, their members bore individual names! Nor could it be suggested that Europeans in the nineteenth century had no communities: they identified themselves as distinct groups! So there must be something fundamental about the communal structure of African societies that the missionaries found to be radically incompatible with the kind of individualism that they had come to know and cherish. What was it? An adequate answer to these questions requires that we explore the philosophical templates from which the missionaries constructed their notions of "individual," "community," and so on. Exploring the historical phenomena of the nuclear family and individualism that are considered pivotal to the coming of the modern age in Europe will lay bare the presuppositions, or at least some of them, of the philosophical discourse of modernity that formed the foundations of the practice of evangelization and the dissemination of civilization that the missionaries undertook.[86]

Recall what I said in chapter 1 about colonialism being an integral part of the outward movement of modernity from Europe. I propose to argue that the individualistic society and the antagonism to communal life of which Ajayi speaks both relate to one of the defining moments of modernity and that one cannot understand the missionaries' preoccupation with what we might consider petty aspects of native life unless we understand the fundamental disjuncture between the philosophical anthropology they held and the one embraced by the Africans whom they converted or sought to convert.

The nineteenth-century wave of evangelization was the second wave of attempts to Christianize the southern parts of Nigeria. The first attempts were made in the late fifteenth and early sixteenth centuries.[87] They were based on pre-Reformation Christianity and were pretty much limited to the royal courts. The new wave is in-

comprehensible outside of its Reformation provenance. One of the principal rup-
tures with the old Church that the Reformation brought about was the individualiza-
tion of salvation and the inauguration of the priesthood of all believers. However, it
is the secular dimension of this theological transformation that should interest us.

Modernity: A Profile

At the core of modernity is a philosophical anthropology characterized by what
Hegel called *the principle of subjectivity*. According to Hegel, "the principle of the
modern world is freedom of subjectivity, the principle that all the essential factors
present in the intellectual whole are now coming into their right in the course of
their development. Starting from this point of view, we can hardly raise the idle
question: Which is the better form of government, monarchy or democracy? We
may only say that all constitutional forms are one-sided unless they can sustain in
themselves the principle of subjectivity and know how to correspond with a ma-
tured rationality."[88] In further explication of the principle, Hegel says:

> The right of the subject's particularity, his right to be satisfied, or in other words the
> right of subjective freedom, is the pivot and centre of the difference between antiquity
> and modern times. This right in its infinity is given expression in Christianity and
> it has become the universal effective principle of a new form of civilization. Amongst
> the primary shapes which this right assumes are love, romanticism, the quest for the
> eternal salvation of the individual, &c.; next come moral convictions and conscience;
> and, finally, the other forms, some of which come into prominence in what follows
> as the principle of civil society and as moments in the constitution of the state, while
> others appear in the course of history, particularly the history of art, science, and phi-
> losophy.[89]

The principle of subjectivity provides the philosophical inspiration for the companionate marriage and the nuclear family that are considered to be prototypical
of the bourgeois age.[90] Hegel goes on to derive civil society and the state from this
basis. The principle of subjectivity is also the basis of the individualist anthropology
that defines modern times. The centrality of the individual to the dominant forms of
social living in modern society and its associated derivative notions of civic, moral,
and legal responsibility are manifestations of what Hegel celebrates as the triumph of
subjectivity. It is against the background of the preceding comments that we should
try to understand the implacable opposition of the missionaries to polygamy.

In the societies whence the missionaries came or, in the case of the recaptives,
into the ethos of which they had been converted, individualism had to a great extent become the putative principle of social ordering.[91] The missionaries canvassed
a Protestant-inflected Christianity in which, thanks to Martin Luther, salvation was
not a product of communal striving nor could it be obtained vicariously through the

good deeds or faith of any collective entity. Not surprisingly, the new missionizing embraced a plurality of denominations. As Ajayi notes, missionaries focused on individuals as "there was no question of their regarding the community as a unit to be converted. . . . The community [for them] became a pool from which the various fishers of men sought in friendly—or less friendly—rivalry each to attract individual fishes into his own denominational net."[92] In this behavior, missionaries manifested another of the diremptions of modern life identified by Jürgen Habermas: an ontology of separation not only of one individual from another but also of one denomination from another even when they are committed to a common goal. This of course presupposes the permissibility of a plurality of means with each being allowed to prove its mettle in contest with others. This is another key tenet of modernity manifested in the preferences of the missionaries: The notion of competition for and among adherents was not odious to them. Africans would later use the same principles to justify philosophically their separation from the main denominations once it became clear that the later crop of their European counterparts was no longer inclined to recognize African agency and accommodate its role in the enterprise of winning souls. In light of the proliferation of orthodoxies, African Christians would not entertain any suggestions that they were committing heresies or apostasies.[93]

On the metaphysical template just sketched, marriage is construed as a contract between two individuals (forget that until recently, the individuality of women in the modern scheme was a fiction) and the family is supposed to represent a fusion of these two to the total exclusion of all others. Polygyny, the union or cohabitation of one man with more than one woman, amounts to a violation ab initio of this fundamental principle. As one of the missionaries who felt the need to remind his fellows of the doctrine of the Church (Anglican in this case) said, "Christ regarded polygamy as adultery: 'It is written "Let every man have his own wife and let every woman have her own husband."'"[94] Polygamy was rejected on two grounds. The first we have just stated: It violated Christ's injunction. Second, and equally important, it was a symbol of the new convert's failure or refusal to make a complete break with his heathen past. Missionaries, Ajayi reminds us, "tended to regard practically everything in the old society as somehow tainted with heathenism."[95]

There are fewer more significant areas of social life in which to look for commitment to a new form of social living than in the family form. Think of it. If the new converts were seriously to embrace the monogamy, companionate marriage, and romantic love that are at the basis of the bourgeois nuclear family, their behavior would represent a radical severing of links with their societies. It would mean abandoning the extended family, individualizing property holdings, and antagonizing their fellows—a practical turning of one's back on all that had had meaning and consequence for one's life thitherto. This is why I have suggested that the missionaries' insistence on what, on the surface, might have seemed innocuous is indicative of an entire way of life. The theological justification was that salvation is personal. No one person's faith can absolve another; each is answerable only for him or herself.[96]

The secular equivalent of the concern with personal salvation is the incorporation of individualism as the principle of social ordering. Individualism is a cornerstone of modernity, and to the extent that the missionaries were desirous of introducing it into the African context, they intended much more than winning African souls for Christ. They also wanted to see their proselytes live and order their personal lives and social spaces in accordance with what they had come to identify as the preferred form of social living in the culture whence they came. Placed in this larger context, it is easy to see why what they "considered best in their own social manners and customs" was synonymous with a Lebenswelt characteristic of modernity.

The modern way of life encompasses several elements. In addition to the principle of subjectivity and its social concomitant, individualism, other elements of modernity include *the centrality of reason, autonomy of action, liberal democracy, the rule of law, the concept of the open future, and an obsession with novelty.* One can see how different aspects of the missionary enterprise manifested each of these elements of modernity. In affirming the capacity of their converts to not only see the light of Christianity but also become torchbearers to others, the missionaries paid the highest compliment to the rationality of Africans. More important, in seeking to build schools, in insisting that African communities too should become societies of knowledge that were ruled by reason, and in using science to solve the problems of living in what is sometimes a challenging physical environment, the missionaries set out to subvert the belief in tradition, in authority accepted on faith, and instead to substitute modes of knowledge production marked by the experimental method and the dominance of demonstrability.

The preference for autonomy of action is easily seen in the account that I gave of the struggle over how to live in the aftermath of conversion. Where heterodox behavior attracts severe sanctions, it is incomprehensible to talk of autonomy of action. One manifestation of subjectivity is the play of caprice in the lives of individuals—it is a fundamental component of the freedom that subjectivity enjoys in the modern world. It is only fitting that it is in their affirmation of this principle that Africans would later in the nineteenth century and from the beginning of the twentieth create independent churches to challenge the orthodoxies of the established churches. It provided the philosophical template for the anticolonial struggle that was premised on the inadmissibility of rule to which Africans had not consented.[97]

The attempt to create a middle class was linked to the commitment to fostering commerce and introducing new ways of producing and reproducing life in the areas of missionary activity. Success in this area would have meant the emergence or in some cases the promotion of a class of people whose lives would be characterized by mobility (both physical and social) and who did not depend on existing patterns of social rewards and ascription for their position in society.[98] And we have evidence that those who became players in the new economy manifested the best of the open future that modernity promises. Some of them were ex-slaves who became financiers and men of affairs. Others were commoners who in the existing indigenous matrices of social ascription would have been sentenced to positions commensurate with those attached to the circumstances of their birth. That is, their futures would have been foretold in the circumstances of their birth. Modernity subverts this principle in leaving open the possibility of access to office and honor subject to the ability of the individual to make of him or herself what his or her talents and a little luck would permit. Again, when later missionaries from Europe began to subvert this principle, Africans protested loudly that the authorities concerned were being unfair, even dishonest, and were failing to deliver on the promise of modernity that careers would be open to talent.

Finally, the concern with novelty was liberally manifested in the missionary enterprise, beginning with the enterprise itself through the attempt to remake the converts and their lives, their thoughts, and their spaces. Architecture was revolutionized and new trades were introduced, as were new modes of knowledge production, distribution, exchange, and consumption. The processes I have been describing in Africa in the nineteenth century before the partition of the continent and the subsequent imposition of formal colonialism was so widespread that Adu Boahen could declare that on the "eve of colonial conquest,"

> Africa was far from being primitive, static, and asleep or in a Hobbesian state of nature. On all fronts—economic, political, social, and even intellectual—Africa was in a mood of change and revolution, accepting new challenges, showing ability at adaptation and modification, fighting back against racist doctrines, and above all changing its economy and politics to suit the socioeconomic realities of the day. It is also clear from the writings of the scholars that the African never thought of himself as being in any way inferior to the European; instead, he believed that, given time, he would become as progressive as the white. Indeed, by 1880 Africans were full of optimism and felt quite ready to face any challenge that was thrown to them. Above all, they seemed determined to defend their sovereignty and way of life.[99]

I conclude that for the greater part of the nineteenth century, as a consequence of the missionary enterprise, especially under the direction of Africans, the continent was engaged in a transition—of epochal proportions—to modernity.

Formal Empire, or How Modernity Ran Aground on Colonial Shores

In the rest of this discussion, I would like to argue that although the early-nineteenth-century missionaries had introduced elements of modernity to Africans and had committed to making modern subjects out of their African proselytes, from the middle of that century on, a period that witnessed informal empire and, later, formal colonization, their trader and administrator successors either reversed or completely arrested the process. That is, the administrators had no enthusiasm for procuring a genuine transformation of African social formations that in any way resembled the missionary program we saw earlier beyond the changes needed to extract raw materials from the colonies. Consistent with the orientation of colonialism$_2$ presented in chapter 1, those who designed and implemented colonial policies did not consider the colonized Africans worthy or capable of sharing in the culture of modernity, especially those aspects relating to the centrality of reason, the primacy of the subject, and the autonomy of action.[100] Hence, the implantation of modernity was not an item on Britain's colonial agenda. In other words, when the suzerainty of administrators and traders supplanted the authority of the missionaries, the apostles of progress were replaced by the army of regress and stagnation, and optimism about African intellectual and other possibilities gave way to pessimism about and occasionally outright denial of same. Enthusiasm about novelty, especially concerning social forms, was replaced by the ignoble science of sociocryonics, the frozen preservation of outmoded and moribund social forms. It is not surprising that at every point where various elements of modernity could have been incorporated, the administrators took the opposite route. According to Ajayi,

> Just as the boundaries of colonial territories tended to put a brake on historical change, so the colonial regimes themselves tended to ally with the most conservative elements in society and to arrest the normal processes of social and political change. Once conquest had been achieved, it was the submissive chiefs, the custodians of law, order and hallowed custom, rather than the radical educated elite, who became the favored agents of European administration. No colonial regime would have hesitated to ally with the most conservative forces to topple a hostile but progressive and modernist leader. After all, the main preoccupation of those regimes was not to carry out social reform but primarily to control and to maintain law and order so as to facilitate economic exploitation.[101]

I am well aware of the unhappy history of attempts to explain developments in Africa as movements toward modernization. Modernization theorists tend to counterpose what they call traditional societies in Africa to modern Europe and North America. By so doing, they erect all kinds of essences. The consequence is that the historicity of modernity is lost. It is as if Europe has always been modern and the rest of the world has been sunk from time immemorial in the morass of traditionalism. Samir Amin has criticized this as one of the elements of Eurocentrism.[102] Edward Said called it Orientalism, "the ideological construction of a mythical 'Orient,' whose characteristics are treated as immutable traits defined in simple opposition to the characteristics of the 'Occidental' world. The image of this 'opposite' is an essential element of Eurocentrism."[103] What is often forgotten in this dubious dichotomy is that in Europe itself, "modern" was not originally contrasted with a non-European Other. "Modern" was used to distinguish a specific sociohistorical conjuncture whose beginning is usually traced to the closing years of the fifteenth century (1492, to be specific) but for which the most significant watersheds were the Renaissance, the Reformation, the Glorious Revolution, the Enlightenment, the American Revolution, the French Revolution (which has been anointed the imme-diate herald of the modern age), and the Haitian Revolution. Hence, modernity in Europe was contrasted with traditional Europe of the Middle Ages and feudalism.[104]

Once one insists on the historicity of modernity, one is enabled to consider it in its specificity and actually identify its uneven spread throughout Europe.[105] It is simply false to talk as if *all* European countries underwent the transition to moder-nity. Nor did *all* of Europe experience modernity with the same intensity. It is worth noting that those countries in Europe where the logic of the transition to moder-nity was never (or not intensely) relentlessly worked out are more like the countries of Africa than of Europe. Russia, Romania, Spain (until recently), and Portugal, to take a few examples, are more like Nigeria, Kenya, Ethiopia, and Tanzania than they are like Britain or the United States. The commonality they share is their late arrival to the phenomenon of modernity.[106]

My interest here is in the philosophical discourse of modernity and, to a limited extent, its political discourse. There are other discourses of modernity, the most im-portant being the cultural/aesthetic discourse. In *The Philosophical Discourse of Mo-dernity*, Jürgen Habermas has, following Marx, credited Hegel with being "the first philosopher to develop a clear concept of modernity."[107] He writes, "Hegel used the concept of modernity first of all in historical concepts, as an epochal concept: The 'new age' is the 'modern age.' This corresponded to contemporary usage in English and French: 'modern times' or 'temps modernes' denoted around 1800 the three centuries just preceding it. The discovery of the 'new world,' the Renaissance, and the Reformation—these three monumental events around the year 1500 constituted the epochal threshold between modern times and the middle ages."[108] But those who lived through the period did not understand it as the modern period. What we have is a retrospective characterization of a period that in hindsight came to be looked upon as exhibiting some defining features. It was not until the eighteenth century that this "epochal threshold" around 1500 was conceptualized as the be-ginning of the modern era. As Habermas puts it: "The secular concept of moder-nity expresses the conviction that the future has already begun: It is the epoch that lives for the future, that opens itself up to the novelty of the future."[109] The open-ness to the novelty of the future and the openness of the future itself constitute some of the most significant changes brought about by modernity.

One can draw many contrasts between modernity and, say, the feudalism that preceded it in Europe. For example, in premodern Europe the rule of primogeniture was dominant and one's location in the rigid social stratifications of the period was determined by the circumstances of one's birth. Many of Africa's kingdoms and empires included equivalent social circumstances that limited social mobility and determined that one's future was largely determined by one's birth. This was not the case with modernity, where the principle of merit supplants the ascription of status and the future is always waiting to be made, hence its openness. The transition to this new form of social living has implications for everyday life and for the individual's own understanding of her place in it. It imports elements of free will and contingency that traditional Europe or Asia or Africa could not accommodate. The emergence of the concept of careers open to talent, the possibility of breaking free from the shackles of social ascription, and the relentless pursuit of novelty in industry and commerce and in the arts and sciences are each different manifestations of the openness to the novelty of the future. This is how Habermas describes it:

> Modernity's specific orientation toward the future is shaped precisely to the extent that societal modernization tears apart the old European experiential space of the peasants and craftman's lifeworlds, mobilizes it, and devalues it into directives guiding expectations. These traditional experiences of previous generations are then replaced by the kind of experience of progress that lends to our horizon of expectation (till then anchored fixedly in the past) a "historically new quality, constantly subject to being overlaid with utopian conceptions."[110]

The reader may have begun to see the convergences between the changes that the missionaries sought to introduce to the African situation and those that modernity was reputed to have brought in its wake to traditional Europe. I argue that even though the missionaries might not have articulated what they were doing in the language that we are now accustomed to ascribing to modernity, the changes contemplated by the likes of Henry Venn, Fowell Buxton, Thomas Bowen, Samuel Crowther, and James Johnson are indistinguishable from the changes presaged by modernity. In enthusiastically embracing these changes and becoming proselytes to their own people, African converts evidenced a deep understanding of the revolutionary implications of the activities with which they were invited to associate themselves. And when later they saw that their fellow missionaries were beginning to be drags on the progress toward the "historically new quality, constantly subject to being overlaid with utopian conceptions," they broke ranks and cleared their own paths. They refused to be stopped. As is by now obvious, the persistence of the African will, the adamant deployment of African agency in the face of racist subversions and resistance, is a core theme in this discussion. Recognizing it as such and celebrating it as a model worthy of emulation at the present time is a principal motivation for my current effort.

I have shown that the insistence of the missionaries that their converts commit to monogamy was emblematic of a way of life founded philosophically on the principle of subjectivity and sociologically on the principle of individualism. But it was not only in the realm of family forms and marital arrangements that the impact of

such a reordering of life would have been felt. There are other connotations of subjectivity. Habermas has identified four.

> (a) *Individualism*: in the modern world, singularity particularized without limit can
> make good its pretensions; (b) *the right to criticism*: the principle of the modern world
> requires that what anyone is to recognize shall reveal itself to him as something entitled
> to recognition; (c) *autonomy of action*: our responsibility for what we do is a character-
> istic of modern times; (d) finally, *idealistic philosophy* itself: Hegel considers it the work
> of modern times that philosophy grasps the self-conscious (self-knowing) Idea.[111]

To explain the different dimensions of the philosophical concepts of modernity
would take me too far afield. But it should be clear that the various connotations of
subjectivity yield specific practices. For example, in a situation in which the singularity of the individual is denied particular expression in a world of action, (c) will
be impossible to realize. Under (b), the appeal to faith or unquestioned authority
is corroded and the supremacy of knowledge as a precondition for accepting anything is the logical template of modern science. This is a variant of the centrality of
reason. Nor can one expect the niceties of the proceduralism of criminal law and
torts without a presupposition that we may be held responsible only for what we
have done in the world, the object of (c).

But let us for a moment focus on (a). Individualism is the dominant principle of
social ordering in the modern era. It is the manifestation in the social sphere of the
principle of subjectivity. Subjectivity arose from the ashes of antiquity in which community and consensus predominated. The principle of subjectivity, the quintessential principle of modernity, is a principle of division, of differentiation, of diremption.
Its realization required the sundering of the undifferentiated unity of antiquity. Nowhere is this divisive principle better illustrated than in the sphere of life that Hegel (and others since then) called bürgerliche Gesellschaft, or civil society. Samir
Amin has remarked that

> the autonomy of civil society is the first characteristic of the new modern world. This
> autonomy is founded on the separation of political authority and economic life, made
> opaque by the generalization of market relationships. It constitutes the qualitative dif-
> ference between the new capitalist mode and all precapitalist formations. The con-
> cept of autonomous political life and thus of modern democracy and the concept of
> social science result from this autonomy of civil society. For the first time, society ap-
> pears to be governed by laws outside of human or royal will. . . . Secularism is the di-
> rect consequence of this new autonomy of civil society, for entire areas of social life
> are henceforth conceivable independently of one another. The need to satisfy meta-
> physical yearnings is left to individual conscience and religion loses its status as a force
> of formal restraint.[112]

Amin is talking at the level of differentiation of social structures. What he omits to
mention is that the differentiation among individuals was even much deeper or at
least as deep. Individual desires and interests became the dominant motivators of

social action and interaction. Personal responsibility for individual salvation came with the privilege of self-realization that takes no account of the group. Again I quote Hegel:

> The creation of civil society is the achievement of the modern world which has for the first time given all determinations of the Idea their due. . . . In civil society each member is his own end, everything else is nothing to him. But except in contact with others he cannot attain the whole compass of his ends, and therefore these others are means to the end of the particular member. . . . Since particularity is inevitably conditioned by universality, the whole sphere of civil society is the territory of mediation where there is free play for every idiosyncracy, every talent, every accident of birth and fortune, and where waves of every passion gush forth, regulated only by reason glinting through them.[113]

It is the same sphere that Marx called the sphere of unrestricted egoism. But it is also the sphere that calls forth the specification of the limits of each particularity's freedom of action. It is the sphere that calls forth the articulation of rights. And it is not an accident that both Marx and Hegel regarded the French Revolution, which yielded the Declaration of the Rights of Man and Citizen in 1791, as the immediate herald of the modern age.

Let us now relate some of these philosophical musings to the play of colonialism in Nigeria. Recall Hegel's argument that the immediate impulse to colonization arose from the development of civil society in Europe. Additional motivations for the colonial enterprise in Africa included the desire of some of its practitioners to bring the fruits of civilization, which to them was synonymous with modernity, to the natives. That is, an aspect of the self-understanding of colonialism and its ideologists is that its mission was to civilize the colonized and bring the colonized peoples into the modern world from a putative traditional era. If colonial administrators had taken this objective seriously, they would have been the principal initiators of revolutionary transformation of the social forms and individual life experiences of Africans. We would have seen evidence of efforts to move African societies along the path to self-realization and self-determination. Additionally, there would have been concerted attempts to recognize and strengthen African agency with a view to completing the business of creating individuals of the sort the missionaries envisaged. In other words, even though it would still be paternalism, I affirm some positive aspects of the autonomy model in order to show the bankruptcy of the colonial regimes that took charge of African countries in the aftermath of the scramble for and partition of the continent.

In the rest of this chapter, I shall argue that contrary to received wisdom, colonialism *could* have unfolded differently from the way it did in Africa. This in turn is based on an insight by Amilcar Cabral, who argued that "it is part of the historical mission of imperialism to effect revolutionary transformations in the areas where it predominates."[114] Cabral insists that the "historical mission" of imperialism was "the speeding up of the process of development of the productive forces and transformation in the direction of increasing complexity of the characteristics of the mode of production; sharpening class differentiation with the development of the bourgeoisie and intensification of class struggle; and appreciably raising average standard levels in the economic, social and cultural life of the population."[115] Imperialism did this in both North America and Australia and even in South Africa for its white population. It never did so in Africa. Its failure to do so is the shipwreck that is alluded to in the title of this chapter. Paternalism may be bad, but failing to deliver on the promise of even this benign paternalism was crueler. The administrators proclaimed a paternalistic interest in schooling the natives but did not keep their promise. Although the earlier missionary cohort, too, adopted a paternalistic attitude toward their African native converts, they at least created Africans who became the principal apostles of modernity, the new civilization, in Africa's history. Therein lies the difference between colonial administrators and the missionaries whose efforts, even after the initial belief in the agency of the African had attenuated, did not cease. I now proceed to give four examples of how administrators subverted the process of implanting modernity in the colonies.

Individualism

First, the principle of subjectivity and its sociological concomitant, individualism, were not extended to the natives. In the colonial situation, as Frantz Fanon pointed out so poignantly, the native could not be an individual.[116] The native is a type, and all differentiation is erased from native society. One cannot overemphasize this point. In fact, it is curious that it has not received serious attention in the literature. The explanation is very simple. Africans and non-Africans alike believe that African societies are essentially communalistic and are fundamentally reluctant to pollute these waters with any introduction of the bad philosophy of individualism. This is a misplaced identification. It ignores the fact that what needs to be accounted for when we investigate social forms are what type of individualism can be found in various societies, what indigenous nodes of individualist transformations are there to be isolated, and how those nodes were affected by colonialism. What is at issue is not whether there were forms of individualism in any but the most primitive societies but what kind of individualism there is and what role it plays in social ordering. In addition, a blanket condemnation of individualism reinforces a reluctance to identify its presence in African societies, past and present. I abjure such a blanket condemnation. While this is not the place to consider the many sides of individualism, I must insist that its introduction into African societies by the apostles of modernity and its evolution in indigenous societies following upon their own internal dynamics deserve serious scholarly attention that does not preclude condemnation of its deleterious consequences if there have been such.

Given the centrality of the principle of subjectivity and its sociological concomitant—individualism—in the constitution and evolution of modernity and my claim that missionaries believed that it was essential that natives fully embrace their metaphysics of the self in order to be truly converted, the administrators' subversion of individualism is one of the signal failures of colonialism. It is not that the colonial administrators did not recognize any individuality in the colonial situation; the problem is that they recognized the wrong, spurious type of individuality.

I distinguish between two types of individuality. The first is *African individuality*, which presupposes that a set of behavioral orientations is something that is specific and peculiar to "the African." Under this rubric, various ethnic types were created and fostered. Some African groups were dubbed "warlike," others were preselected to be "natural rulers," and so on. Meanwhile, ethnic commingling in urban areas was actively discouraged. Each "tribe," having been constituted as an undifferentiated whole, was expected to act out its assigned characteristics, regardless of what real differences subsisted within those societies and among their members. Ironically, this individuality takes no account of the specific differences that may prevail among individual Africans, and it thus applied across the board to all Africans, whatever their station in life. Many African thinkers have adopted this spurious individuality, and one can find it at the base of theories of African personality inaugurated under the inspiration of Edward Wilmot Blyden in the late nineteenth century and later adopted by thinkers ranging from Kwame Nkrumah to Nnamdi Azikiwe.[117]

The second kind acknowledges and works with the *individuality of Africans*; that is, this theory makes no serious assumptions about what each African is like from the mere (otherwise banal) fact that she is an African. On the contrary, each African is considered in her peculiarities, oddities, and suchlike, an approach that leaves room for the other to be surprised, for good or ill, by the quirks and eccentricities of the individual concerned. This is the only type of individuality that has meaning and is the dominant construal under modernity, the individuality that is fostered and presupposed by modernity. It lies at the root of the principles of meritocracy and achievement. The earlier missionaries epitomized this focus on the self and identified individual talented Africans and made their advancement the object of their solicitude. The same idea was extended to organization within the missionary enterprise. Missionaries wanted to create "self-governing, self-supporting, self-propagating" churches in native communities (in the words of Henry Venn) as a prelude to remaking the material world of the Africans.[118] Where the second type of individuality is deployed, Africans who had accepted the tenets of modernity, who had proceeded to shape their lives and thought patterns à la modernity, would then have extended to them the courtesy of being recognized as *different* from other Africans from whom they themselves had affirmed their difference and had insisted on being recognized as such. It is the kind of individuality that gives full scope to agency and its occasional display as caprice. It is required for adapting foreign influences, domesticating alien ideas, reinventing or recasting indigenous ideas, and stepping forth to take responsibility. Where this is the case, Africans would be presumed to be the best judges of what is good for them, even when they are wrong in their judgment. Such judgment would include what to change in their societies, how to make that change, and what to preserve in African societies and how to so do.

We have seen that in modern terms, individualism is "singularity particularized without limit and making good its pretensions." Hegel insisted that civil society is "the territory of mediation where there is free play for every idiosyncracy, every talent, every accident of birth and fortune, and where waves of every passion gush forth, regulated only by reason glinting through them." In contrast with the first spurious notion of African individuality, the second one deploys a rich tapestry of possibilities, outcomes, personalities, colors, and so on. It is what we find when we examine the debates among Africans and Europeans alike of the first wave of evangelizers concerning African agency, the possibility of a native church, the creation of new men and women who would be the propagators of the new ways of life enjoined by modernity. By the late nineteenth century and the turn of the twentieth, this point of view had been overthrown and supplanted by attitudes that questioned the viability of African agency, placed Africans at the bottom of the human ladder, and proceeded to treat them as if they were children. The consequences that followed were devastating for the efflorescence of African agency.

To start with, both missionaries and administrators of this later provenance convinced themselves that Africans could not be trusted to run their own affairs and substituted Europeans in roles that shaped the lives of Africans.[119] The aid model had become dominant, and the Church of England (in this instance) was well on its way to undoing Venn's legacy. Of course, this approach included no consideration of the individuality of Africans who might break the mold of putative incompetence, who might in fact be geniuses at missionizing and/or administration. Crowther was a shining example; James Johnson was not far behind. And there was Edward Wilmot Blyden, another of Venn's protégés. Their individual achievements meant nothing to the new strain of racist zealotry that became dominant during the period in question. It explains the rubbishing of Crowther's legacy and the humiliation of the man himself.[120] Additionally, Africans were adjudged, *as a bloc*, to be too dull to appreciate the new civilization.[121]

Given the consignment of the African to an undifferentiated individuality, it stands to reason that any attempt by an African to claim the privileges of different, specific, even quirky individuality would be by definition a sign of abnormality. As a consequence, it is deemed out of character for a native to assert his individuality, say, in the total embrace of the modern way of life, either as a product of the rational assessment of it as a superior way of life that is eminently desirable or as a result of an irrational fascination with the modern lifestyle. Such a native is deemed afflicted with a pathological desire to be like the colonizer. She is seen as suffering from a dependency or inferiority complex and with trying to run away from her shadow. She could not exercise the prerogatives of subjectivity, including the capricious embrace of whatever lifestyle engaged her fancy.[122] To be an individual, to choose to be different—in short, to embrace heterodoxy—is to be judged an affliction. Policy formulation, collective punishment, forced identities, and spatial restriction of natives all combined to turn any expression of agency into a crime. The consequences are deeper still, as we will find out presently. Many Africans turned their backs on modernity. Independent churches were founded. Although the emphasis on education increased, in a spate of reactive nationalism many resorted to distorted appropriations of various indigenous practices, some of which they did not quite understand.[123] But even then, they did so evidencing the serious appropriation of modernity that they had made their own.[124]

The Open Future, or How the Color Rule Subverted the Merit Rule

Let us now consider another component of modernity that the administrators subverted: the commitment to an open future. The initial wave of nineteenth-century missionaries was committed to the idea that the notion of the open future applied to their African proselytes. Former slaves and other Africans who converted to Christianity took the idea of modernity quite seriously. Indeed, this is one area where there was a stunning convergence in the ideas of the educated Africans and those of their white counterparts. They bought into the idea that most of their fellow Africans were backward and were sunk in the darkness of heathenism from which they perforce must be liberated by the trinity of Christianity, commerce, and civilization.[125]

Their faith in the possibility of an open future was not groundless. Many of them saw their rescue and subsequent socialization and training as providential occurrences that, among other things, demonstrated the potency of the new metaphysics of time: Their future was not foreordained by their past. This also happened to be a time when many societies in Africa were in turmoil. The old moorings had broken; ancient empires were adrift. Many returnees and recaptives had become captains of industry; they had become gentry and were well educated. What better evidence of the possibility of a different future, of the play of contingency guided by the hand of Providence, than their own journey from obscurity and servitude to prosperity and freedom? They were eager to share the same with less fortunate compatriots. They spoke the language of responsibility, of giving back to their communities, of doing God's work as their way of offering thanks for providential munificence. They wanted to open new vistas for their fellow Africans in the new dispensation.

Furthermore, they figured that they had earned the right to be the guides to the future in their own environment. They had proved themselves worthy by mastering the intricacies of the new modes of social living pertaining to modernity. They had every reason to expect that part of the reward of being such good learners was

that their erstwhile teachers would let them come into their own as teachers of
their own people, that assiduously cultivating the new way would lead to respect
for their agency and autonomy. Above all, they insisted on improving themselves
and their societies. They created schools, they sent their children to prestigious
schools in England, and they trained themselves with a vengeance. They sought to
expand their ranks by not often insisting that beneficiaries of their educational and
apprenticeship schemes should be Christians as a condition of eligibility for participation.[126] All this they did in order to demonstrate and strengthen African agency.
To advance these objectives, they sought the assistance of the various groups of colonizers in the colonial situation: missionaries, traders, and administrators.

The administrators, for the most part, would have none of it.[127] The Africans'
ambitions came up against the administrators' wall of resistance. In clear subversion
of the idea of the open future, administrators reaffirmed the premodern principle of
ascription in which biology and the circumstances of birth determined the future
of the individual regardless of his or her striving. The difference is that in the colonial situation the principle of ascription was based on race. But it operated in exactly the way that the old premodern rules of primogeniture and circumstances of
birth did. In the words of Fyfe, "In colonial Africa, authority was manifested very
simply. White gave orders, black obeyed. A white skin (a skin imputed white) con-
ferred authority. It was an easy rule to understand and enforce, and it upheld colonial authority in Africa for about half a century. Yet some historians seem unwill-
ing to remember it."[128] It didn't matter what the relative qualities of the African and
the European were, they were trumped by the possession of one single quality that
is wholly a product of accident: their skin pigmentation. Because the African could
not shed his skin, he was sentenced by the accident of nature to remain at the bottom of the ladder of the human race.[129] This was a reversion to premodern sensibilities. It was no use for Africans to think of improving themselves. To do so would
be undoing nature's work. Here is the rub: Part of the justification for modernity
was the affirmation of the superiority of reason over nature, the need to bring nature under the governance of reason and subject it to rational manipulation in science. In abandoning reason and upholding nature, the administrators undermined
yet again the implantation of modernity. It also meant an abandonment of the commitment to the improvability of nature and the perfectibility of human nature that
were also tenets of modernity. Africans were excluded on both counts. Here is Fyfe
on this topic:

> Drawing on the mythology of Africa as (in Hegel's words) "the land of childhood,"
> whites could, without compunction, treat Africans as children—but Peter Pan chil-
> dren who can never grow up, a child race. Physiology was brought in to justify this with
> the "suture" theory ([which was] given the credibility of being included in the ninth,
> tenth and eleventh editions of the *Encyclopaedia Britannica*), which claimed that "Ne-
> groes'" brains stopped developing at puberty.[130] But whether or not white people be-

lieved this preposterous theory, they still went on calling grown-up Africans "boys" (house-boy, mission-boy, mine-boy). In francophone Africa, they were addressed as children are with "tu." And one might speculate whether the prevalence of corporal punishment in colonial Africa may not have been partly grounded on the then prevalent adult belief that children (and hence members of a child race) are too stupid to understand anything else.[131]

One direct outcome of the reversion to premodern principles of social ordering was the direct subversion of the merit principle in the colony and the protectorates. As we have pointed out, the open future promised access to social rewards based on merit scored by talent, training, application, and related qualities. Where it is taken seriously, even those who had been slaves but had demonstrated their possession of some talents and a willingness to apply themselves to bettering their situation (even their inheritance, in the view of racist colonialists) could aspire to reach the top without any hindrance arising from the fact that they once were in servitude.[132] If Africans were typified as children permanently, those who strove to demonstrate singular agency and achievement labored in vain. For as far as the administrators were concerned, no amount of education, including from Oxford, Cambridge, Durham, and other top British educational institutions, could wipe away the stigma of the Africans' epidermal inheritance. A white epidermal inheritance was a qualification in itself, and for much of Africa, it often was the only qualification.[133] I quote from Fyfe's succinct characterization of how the color rule subverted the merit rule:

> The system [of indirect rule] introduced into the British protectorates gradually permeated the British West African colonies. As the twentieth century advanced, Africans were deliberately squeezed out of senior government posts. A few outstanding individuals lingered, but as exceptions to a rule that normally restricted authority to whites. Nor was racial stratification confined to the administrative service. The West African Medical Service, constituted in 1902, was restricted to whites: African or Indian doctors, however well qualified, were confined to a subordinate service with lower status and pay scales. However senior, they could not give an order to a white medical officer, however junior.[134]

This was pretty much the pattern in the colonial civil service. One need not dwell on the plethora of modern principles that fell victim to this manner of doing business: efficiency could not have rated a premium; knowledge could not have mattered very much; rationality could not have rated any consideration.[135] Overall, there could not have been any commitment to running a first-class civil service given that unless the administrators possessed a tremendous capacity for self-deception, they must have known that they were lying to themselves every time they affirmed the excellence of their operation. If how the prospective candidate looked was more important than what he could deliver on the job, it stands to reason that there must have been a lot of incompetence in the service. Add to this the fact that Africa was not exactly a plum posting such as India was, and we would not be too

far off the mark if we surmise that a fair percentage of those who sought their fortunes in Africa were of the variety that had limited options at home. These were
the sorts of people who were appointed in place of qualified Africans. On the other
hand, in classifying Africans as one huge undifferentiated blob, colonial administrators foisted *African individuality* on Africans and refused to recognize the *individuality of Africans*. Africans did not fail to apprehend this, and to the discomfort of
the self-righteous administrators, they strenuously and often mischievously pointed
out the contradictions between their official proclamation of the merit principle and
their subversion of that principle in practice.

Novelty, or How Sociocryonics Trumped Progress

Next, I examine the issue of novelty as a constitutive component of modernity.
The near-lunatic obsession with the new is inherent in the ideological term "progress." Modernity is the way of life in which change is embraced for its own sake and
is considered to be good in itself. We witness it every day in a proliferation of scientific experimentation that does not know when to stop. It is what drives capitalist
production, and it reaches its most pedestrian manifestations in the world of advertising. The belief in progress and in its desirability and possibility is at the bottom of
much of the restlessness of the modern age, in which nothing is regarded as settled
and the best always is yet to come. Few inquiries are made into whether progress is
desirable and to question change is to earn the scorn of the apostles of the modern
age, for whom rest is synonymous with decay and death.[136]

The spirit of novelty, the commitment to progress fired the imagination of
nineteenth-century Africans. Africans bought into the new civilization with aplomb.
They fancied themselves as inheritors of a new civilization and sought to rearrange
their mental and physical spaces to reflect their embrace of the new. They built new
houses that sometimes in their opulence were far out of proportion to their surroundings. They adopted new modes of dressing. They were fastidious in their observation
of new social etiquettes concerning food, recreation, music, theatre, and so on.[137]
Despite tensions attendant upon the continuing appeal of polygyny to many of them,
quite a few chose the new forms of family life symbolized by monogamy and companionate marriage and did a fabulous job of implementing them.[138] Furthermore, they
created new forms of political association, the Fanti Confederation and the Ẹgbá
United Board of Management being the most famous.[139] These activities give the
lie to the much-ballyhooed conservatism of the African—another instance of the
imposition of *African individuality* on individual Africans. The evidence pointed in
an opposite direction. Africans are not essentially conservative and if they are, they
are not any more so than other human beings. They were willing to try new things;
they embraced new ways of organizing life. The difference is that they do a lot better and are often more enthusiastic but not any less discriminating when they do
so under their own wings, when such embrace emanates from their own agency; in
short, when they exemplify the autonomy model.

The dynamic of social transformation was disrupted by the intervention of the administrators. For example, as we shall see in chapter 6 below, while both the Fanti Confederation and the Ègbá United Board of Management accommodated chieftaincy institutions, they insisted on incorporating some elective components that minimized ascription in the assigning of offices in their respective governments. They had worked out a creative admixture of the old and the new that allowed elements of indigenous culture that allowed for continuity to be preserved without sacrificing the need for infusing new ideas and creating room for talent outside of traditional pools. They did not proceed on the basis of ignorance or sentiment. Some of them, for example James Africanus Horton, investigated the forms of governance along the West African coast and made recommendations based on his research. Some of his insights were quite prophetic. Ordinarily, one would expect that administrators would nurture these nodes of possible social transformation to full growth. That was not what happened. Indeed, once the erstwhile colonies became minorities in larger units dominated by protectorates, the minimal commitment to government by the consent of the governed gave way to the affirmation of the indispensability of "traditional" structures of governance. Rather than expand the scope of application of new principles, especially those concerning law and politics, the administrators elected to abort them or at least severely restrict their scope.[140]

The assumption that Africans were childlike in nature preempted any consideration of making the living spaces of Africans more livable. Town planning was restricted to areas where the whites lived, and the natives be damned in their quarters. When they were confronted, administrators were quick to point out that putting such lofty ideas and practices before Africans was like casting pearl before swine: Africans, they insisted, were not equipped to appreciate such values. Progress was jettisoned. Sociocryonics was entrenched. It replaced talk of making the fruits of civilization, especially the fruits of progress, available to Africans. All sorts of moribund social and political institutions were given new leases on life, even when modern Africans had better ideas about how to conform them to new realities. It did not matter that in many cases the institutions being foisted on Africans were new fabrications by the colonial authorities and that even when they were indigenous they were being infused with modes of operation that bore no resemblance to their original versions.

The good thing is that Africans never renounced their commitments. But there is no doubt that the rebuff they received from those who had baited them with modern rewards only to switch on them at delivery time had a profound impact on their processing of principles of modernity from that point on. Some of them persisted in their embrace of modernity without qualification. The larger majority began to question the wisdom of an unqualified embrace, and among those many began to take refuge in indigenous African institutions as a kind of nationalist antidote to European supremacist attitudes.[141] Africans backed into sociocryonics: To be an authentic African was to hold on to certain timeless values and preserve as a matter of identity institutions and practices that barely a decade before they were willing to consign to oblivion. This is one of the worst consequences of the administrators' subversion of modernity in the colonies. Such indigenous institutions were accepted uncritically and the arrogance of official power made the possibility of debate less likely for fear that those who deigned to defend the relevance of European-inspired institutions might come off looking like Uncle Toms to their interlocutors.

The same trend has continued in the present. Many in Africa think that accepting any defects in indigenous African institutions and practices will play into the hands of white supremacists who would use such contentions as evidence of the congenital backwardness of Africans. In an atmosphere in which debate is limited or foreclosed about the desirability of choosing certain options in the process of social transformation, it is no surprise that atavistic responses proliferated and that Africans were often frightened off choices that would have redounded to the healthy development of African institutions. The sclerotic state of indigenous African institutions at the present time is a direct result of the imposition of sociocryonics and the abandonment of the commitment to progress. That Africans have been enthusiastic endorsers of sociocryonics does not make it any less odious. Quite the contrary; it makes their choice even more so. Finally, the most important (though not necessarily numerically dominant) group persisted in exercising their agency by critically appropriating modern principles and practices in creative mixture with indigenous ones. The founders of the independent African churches belong to this category, as do the proprietors of schools, the creators of the Reformed Ogboni Fraternity, and composers of African music as well as other Africans engaged in the creative arts.[142] Each of these groups exemplified African agency in response to modernity.

"Character Formation," or the Subversion of the Society of Knowledge

I have already remarked on the missionaries' extensive efforts to create societies of knowledge, efforts that were dominated by native agents. In fact, if colonialism is to be credited with altering or transforming indigenous social formations, the evidence ought to be abundant in the area of knowledge production. One cannot overstress the importance of knowledge to the constitution and identity of modern society. In a different context, Karl Marx characterized the difference between feudal society and modern society in Europe thus: "What took place here was not a political conflict between two parties within the framework of *one* society, but a *conflict between two societies*, a social conflict, which had assumed a political form; *it was the struggle of the old feudal bureaucratic society with modern bourgeois society*, a struggle between the society of *free competition* and *society of the guild system*, between the society of landownership and the industrial society, between the society of faith and the society of knowledge."[143]

If the apologists for colonialism are to be believed, then the colonial period should have been characterized by an aggressive approach to knowledge production, yet no such commitment to knowledge took place under colonialism. Quite the contrary, even the limited progress underwritten by the earlier wave of evangelizers and the enthusiasm of their proselytes was checkmated by the administrators who did not care a hoot for the ability of Africans to adopt a modern way of life. Given that colonialism in Africa was a system of exclusions and was distinguished more by what it excluded from the colonies than by what it included, excluding its wards from participation in the society of knowledge was consistent with its general philosophical foundations.

Let us recall the program of Thomas Fowell Buxton's Society for the Extinction of the Slave Trade and the Civilization of Africa, which was designed to lift Africa out of the quagmire of ignorance and backwardness into which the Atlantic slave trade and slavery had forced it. Even allowing for what might appear to be the practical orientation of much that is in the program, one cannot deny that implementing Buxton's program would more likely conduce to the creation of the society of knowledge that is emblematic of the modern era. It is noteworthy that nowhere in it was there any mention of "character education" or "moral education" or any of the other obfuscations with which colonial administrators elided any serious commitment to furnishing their African charges with the wherewithal to transit to modernity and march in tandem with the rest of humanity on progress's road. On the contrary, colonial administrators took a dim view of the products of missionary education.

In fact, Lord Lugard, the arch-philosopher of empire, was clear in his thinking that what he and others considered to be mistakes in the administration of India would not be repeated in the British possessions in Africa. According to Lugard,

> The impact of European civilization on tropical races has indeed a tendency to undermine that respect for authority which is the basis of social order. The authority of the head, whether of the tribe, the village, or the family, is decreased, and parental discipline is weakened—tendencies which Lord Macdonnell observed, are probably inseparable from that emancipation of thought which results from our educational system and needs the control of scholastic discipline. These tendencies are no doubt largely due to the fact that each generation is advancing intellectually beyond its predecessor, so that "the younger men view with increasing impatience the habits, traditions and ideas of their elders." From this standpoint we may even regard this restlessness as a measure of progress.[144]

India was one place where, he said, such tendencies "became very marked towards the close of the nineteenth century."[145] That such an outcome in India was adjudged unfortunate can be seen in a reference to what he called "the failure of the system of Indian education."

What was at the root of this failure? "'A purely literary type of education was the only one generally provided by Government,' says the Industrial Report of 1919, and the intellectual classes eagerly grasped at the prospect of Government, professional, and clerical employment, with the result that a disproportionate number of persons with a purely literary education were created, and industrial development was arrested."[146] One might conclude that correcting the mistake in India would mean the cultivation of education for industrial development in Africa. That this never happened goes without saying. All one need do is take a look at the contemporary situation in the continent.[147] However, the lament of arrested development was a canard. The real culprit was that literary education was making uppity lads of Indian children and ingrates of the educated classes in their relations with British and other constituted authorities. Here then is the real reason for the suspicious attitude toward "education of the intellect."

> "The people of India have never been so well off, never so wisely cared for, never so secure as they are to-day." Yet the undermining of all authority is rapidly proceeding. Parents complain of the intractability of their boys. The local press preaches sedition, and racial strife is stirred up by misrepresentation and false reports. If "the influence of education for good depends on the qualities of character it is able to evoke," it must be judged to have failed. Its aim, it is alleged, has been to train the intellect, and to gauge the product of the schools by the ability to pass tests in prescribed fields of knowledge, to the neglect of moral discipline and standards of duty. Positive knowledge as tested by competitive examinations has constituted the key to success.[148]

The problem in Africa, as Lugard saw it, was that "the system which had proved so disastrous in India had its counterpart in the Crown colonies and dependencies, and its results were similar. The lessons of India were ignored."[149]

The aim in Africa, according to Lugard and his fellows, was to ensure that the mistake of India was not repeated and where it was being repeated to put an end to it. Hence, colonial education sought to rein in the natives' enthusiasm for heterodoxy, their ability to question the basis of legitimacy of any rule (native rule not excepted), and preempt the installation of the centrality of reason. The overarching concern was with character education. Again, Lugard articulated it best: "My aim has been to urge that these results may best be achieved by placing the formation of character before the training of the intellect, and to make some few suggestions as to how this may be done."[150] The pattern of exclusion that colonialism exhibited precluded from the very beginning any possibility of installing the modern way of life, an element of which would have been a society of knowledge.

It is now time to tie together the many strands of this discussion. As I made clear at its commencement, my concern has been to make the case that there were alternative routes to those taken in the evolution of colonialism in some African countries. Although I have provided historical evidence, where pertinent, to support the core argument, it would be a mistake to ignore the central speculative thrust of the entire project. One cannot overemphasize the importance of speculation in an exercise designed to alert us to possibilities for future organization of life and thought in African countries. Indeed, by calling attention back to those forks in the road where colonialism aborted the implantation of modernity, by showing how things might have turned out and still might turn out should we decide that the picture painted in our speculation is a desirable one, we are better placed to minimize the unnecessary detours, avoid blind alleys, and generally be vigilant about what distortions can once again frustrate the redemption of the promise and benefits of modernity for Africans. Needless to say, the plausibility of what I have just said is dependent on the truth of my claim that modernity is relevant to the understanding of contemporary sociopolitical problems in Africa. Recent and ongoing transitions to democracy and free market economies in Africa are best understood as late transitions to modernity. For this reason, I offer the following remarks as a clarion call to all, especially intellectuals, who by design or by default once again face the task of shaping Africa's future.

Modernity is back on the agenda for Africa. There should be no question about that. The only question is about how Africa and its peoples will negotiate their contemporary encounter with it. In this connection, what is totally uncalled for is a foreclosing of any option in the mistaken belief that modernity has already run its course and that any attempt to argue otherwise is misguided. There is no room for knee-jerk nationalist responses that stigmatize modernity as a Western contraption that is part and parcel of colonialism. I hope to have shown in this chapter that rather than there being any identity between colonialism and modernity, colonialism, as conceptualized and implemented by British administrators, was actually the reason that the transition that was underfoot to modernity was aborted. Nor is it helpful to ask (as it continues to be asked) that Africa come up with its own blueprint for its rebirth if such a call means that Africa must build its own ideational matrices de novo. To ask in this way is to indulge in what someone has dubbed a "do-nothing ideology." But if the call is for African agency to be front, center, and back in deciding what to borrow and how to fit what is borrowed into African conditions, I have absolutely no objection. In fact, what is significant is that it was the colonial administrators' suffocating of native initiative that is part of the litany of failure that we now must replace with a serious, careful, and unsparing engagement with our history and with the history of roads not taken of the sort that I have identified in this work. What this means is that contemporary African intellectuals are called upon more than ever before to take very seriously the history of some of the socioeconomic and political processes that Africa is supposed to institutionalize once more on the road to realizing: liberal democracy, the rule of law, the market economy. The autonomy model must be restored to prominence. Unfortunately, the aid model has so inured itself in the African imagination that even so-called progressives cannot wean themselves from it. Africans must realize that aid can only foster or deepen dependency. No one has ever made a life on welfare.

I am suggesting that the current transitions going on in Africa must not be allowed to fall victim to the absence of knowledge of past attempts to realize the best of modernity for Africa but also knowledge of the development of the ideas and practices in the places from whose experiences we are trying to borrow a leaf. The embrace of liberal democracy beyond its anemic assimilation to periodic elections and multipartyism must be premised on a robust understanding of its evolution in Euroamerica and must be nuanced in such a manner that its redemption in Africa avoids some of the mistakes that others have made. The same must be said of the rule of law, whose philosophical template is often absent from the discussions of African scholars. I am saying, in a nutshell, that current discussions of modernity and its institutional appurtenances are lacking in any fundamental engagement with the philosophical discourse of modernity. For that reason, they are unlikely to result in appropriate recommendations for institutional choices in practice. Needless to say, what I am saying will apply only to those who share my starting point that had the promise of modernity been redeemed for Africa, the history of the continent would not have been one of chaos and devastation, as we have witnessed. Those who do not share this basic orientation are unlikely to be persuaded by my arguments or swayed by my call. But to those who share my conviction, we are called upon to take seriously once again the fundamental tenet of modern society that typifies it as a society of knowledge in which reason is the basic legal tender. Such a course compels us to abjure atheoreticism, to confront what needs to be done without being afraid of being dubbed imperialist lackeys or prostitutes of the West. The materials are already available. What is required is the intellectual resolve to do right by our posterity and ourselves. This is where the sofa bed analogy that I discussed in note 1 of this chapter comes in handy again. There are sofa beds on the continent now. But precisely because we receive them fully assembled, the mindset that attaches to its invention still is not part of our consciousness. In inculcating the modern consciousness that simultaneously fostered the rule of law and the lowly sofa bed we shall be acquiring the mindset that made the sofa bed, rule by consent, and other icons such incredible inventions. The chapters that follow are designed to show the lay of the land and why previous developments were inadequate, maybe even wrong.

_3_

Prophets without Honor
African Apostles of Modernity
in the Nineteenth Century

In the last chapter, I discussed the general philosophical elements of the transition to modernity directed by Africans exercising agency in the nineteenth century and how it was aborted by the administrator class among colonialists. In this chapter, I present what I adjudge to be three representative thinkers of the class of persons whose general orientation I described in the previous chapter. I argue that it is time to recognize their contributions to the history of ideas in Africa, their pioneering roles as modern precursors, and, most important, their prophetic roles.[1] Elsewhere, I have explored the interface between the biblical idea of prophecy and social science predictions. I said there:

> There are three attributes shared by a social scientific model and a jeremiad: descrip-
> tion, explanation, and prediction. In ways that mirror social scientific models, there is
> a description, in a jeremiad, of what is wrong in the community. For example, biblical
> prophets gave stark descriptions of the many sins and transgression prevalent in their
> community, the corruption and debaucheries of the rulers, the absence of righteous-
> ness and upstandingness among their fellows. Secondly, the explanation of the misfor-
> tunes of the community was that the people had strayed from the path of righteousness
> laid out for them by the divine authority. Finally, in the prophecy, there was a warning
> that unless the divine word was heeded, dire consequences would follow. But there is
> at least one clear difference between biblical prophecy and good social science: in so-
> cial scientific models, the "Thus saith the Lord" of a prophecy is replaced with the au-
> thority of analysis, theoretical paradigms, and empirical investigations. Nonetheless,
> in the same way that failure to heed the word of the Lord will mean perdition, so will
> failure to heed the warning in social scientific prophecy lead to social dislocation and
> crisis in the community.[2]

One additional commonality shared by prophecy and social science must be identified. They both often arise from dissent, from heterodoxy, and they usually come
as part of a moral vision that the situation of which the prophecy speaks ought to
be altered.

Why Prophecy? Why Now?

We begin from the present. The entire continent of Africa, not unlike other parts of the world, is at the present time one huge workshop of social experiments in politics, economics, religion, culture, and myriad other areas of life. One frame within which scholars in almost all disciplines interpret contemporary Africa is that of a dichotomy between Africa's much-vaunted attachment (some social scientists say addiction) to tradition and near-congenital aversion to what is generally dubbed "modernization." Those who are familiar with the social science literature in economics, political science, and history will easily recall that in the 1960s and 1970s, African regimes were adjudged successes or failures by how far they had traveled on the road to modernization.[3] Modernization was understood in terms of increasing gross domestic product, total mileage of macadamized roads, and the like. And when the bottom fell out in the 1980s, we were treated to gory accounts of so-called modernization that went too fast, African traditional institutions that were recalcitrant to the changes enjoined by modernization efforts, and so on.[4]

There are two major problems with any attempt to explain phenomena in Africa within the "traditional versus modern" schema. The first problem is conceptual: The means, "modernization," is mistaken for the end, "modernity." This is not a mere verbal point. The end product of all modernization processes must be the transformation of the social organism concerned from a premodern or nonmodern state to a modern one. Properly understood, this means that the organism concerned has had its most dominant institutions infused with modernity, the proper name for the outcome of the process for which modernization is a tool. If this is the case, it is possible to have modernization, understood as the superficial painting of the social fabric with various markers of modernity, without the infusion of the elements that constitute the soul, the identifying characteristics of modernity. Japan and South Korea are the most successful examples of this phenomenon. Taiwan and Hong Kong are not far behind.[5] Relevant here is the distinction I made in the previous chapter between the material aspects of modernity—mass consumption, industrialization, infrastructural development—and its ideological dimensions that I have captured, in part, under the rubric of the philosophical discourse of modernity. Materially, there is not much difference in the landscapes of Japan, South Korea, Taiwan, or Malaysia and those of the United States, Germany, or the United Kingdom. But I doubt that anyone would affirm any sameness in the dominant ideological, political, or philosophical orientations of the two sets of countries. The difference lies in the differential penetration of the philosophical and other discourses of modernity and their institutional analogues in each set of countries.

I suggest that whatever was happening in Africa in the second half of the twentieth century constituted at best inchoate attempts at becoming modern. Yes, Africans were building skyscrapers, yet they were neither producing nor deploying the commensurate knowledge that would procure the appropriate levels of readiness to fight fires in those buildings beyond the lowest floors. Physically, architecture was increasingly oriented toward the nuclear family and forms of social living premised on individualism, yet scholars kept trumpeting Africa's communalism, which translated into their being remiss in producing the kinds of scholarship that would enable Africa not only to make sense of this relative new form of social living but also obtain the best of it for its peoples. The gross domestic product grew exponentially, but governance by consent was off the table for most Africans. When Africans have been accused of failure at being modern, the accusation has always been premised on the mistaken assumption that merely meeting certain economic benchmarks and acquiring contemporary skylines amounted to being modern. If modernity were so defined, one would have to concede the fact of Africa's failure. Given my contention that such phenomena were at best superficially modern and that the more characteristic traits have never been part of either discourse or practice in the continent since the colonial period, the so-called failure cannot be used as evidence of the inability of Africans to be modern. In other words, it boggles the mind to charge Africa with failing at a task that it, in recent times, has not even engaged in: being modern.

The second problem is historical: Most contemporary scholars do not evince any awareness of the rich legacy of past attempts to install modernity in some parts of the continent, most notably English-speaking West Africa. Hence, much of the discourse about Africa and modernity at the present time proceeds as if this is a new problem or there are no antecedent African engagements with modernity. The available historical evidence supports neither standpoint.

As I showed in the last chapter, in the nineteenth century, specifically before the imposition of formal empire on the African continent by various European powers, some parts of Africa were in the beginnings of a transition to modernity. Originally begun under the inspiration of Christianity (and taking this seriously is bound to alter our historiography of Christianity and appraisal of its career in Africa), the movement was taken by the African apostles of modernity beyond the confines of the religious to the larger sphere of the secular.[6] I argue that it is time to honor these prophets and adapt their wisdom to the task that is again before us of moving Africa toward modernity. But we cannot celebrate them if we don't know who they are. Therefore, one modest aim of the present chapter is to introduce these prophets of old Africa.

There is an even deeper reason to embrace them now. It is more insightful, perhaps more correct, to interpret the current experimentation with forms of rule (liberal representative democracy and the rule of law), forms of social living (the ideology of individualism), and forms of economic production (capitalism) in Africa and other parts of the world as late transitions to modernity. I am quite aware that what I say risks being appropriated by social evolutionists who would like to make it appear as if Euroamerica sits at the apex of the human social ladder with the rest of the world climbing up behind them. Anyone who is familiar with the expostulations of Francis Fukuyama and Samuel Huntington will see the point clearly.[7] But we should not refrain from drawing appropriate lessons from history for our own use because some might turn the same results to mischievous ends. It is worth taking the risk involved in this instance because I would like Africa, if its peoples so desire, to engage modernity in a conscious, critical way and embrace or shun it for Africa's own reasons, not out of ignorance or elemental hostility traceable to the conflicted legacy of its career in the continent.

What Modernity?

In this chapter, I work with a very historicized and therefore narrow conception of modernity. The relevant elements of the discourse of modernity in the discussion that follows are the principle of subjectivity and its social concomitant, individualism; the centrality of reason; and the liberal democratic idea of governance by consent. These are the themes that I have selected to illustrate the core ideas of our prophets.

Individualism

The most important of these elements is the idea of individualism. The idea of individualism predated the modern age. My contention is that the notion of the individual that is dominant in the modern age is without precedent, at least in the Euroamerican tradition from which our African prophets extracted it. I also contend that it is under the modern regime that individualism is the preferred principle of social ordering and that almost everything else is understood in terms of how well or ill it serves the interests of the individual. Thus, although it is true that there was some recognition of the individual in premodern epochs, it is in the modern epoch that the individual is not merely supreme. Whatever detracts from the rights of the individual is—precisely for that reason—to be rejected. This notion of the individual took a long time to emerge, but it received one of its most dramatic consecrations in the Protestant Reformation, when the subject—that is, the individual—was made the centerpiece of Christian soteriology. The subject must win eternity for himself, helped of course by grace. One's genealogy, status, and similar attributes count for nothing (or at least theoretically ought to count for nothing) in the allocation of goods, services, or even recognition. The key element is that of individual striving, what the individual makes of herself and whatever talent she is endowed with by nature. Here is the source of the merit principle, the meritocracy that promises rewards to individuals according as they show themselves worthy by developing their talents. One consequence of the focus on the individual in the modern state is that individuals' futures are no longer determined by the circumstances of their birth. Humans can abridge status, class, and other boundaries as long as they are willing to improve themselves enough to fit themselves for whatever station they aspire to occupy.

We saw in the last chapter how at various points the new converts to Christianity and those who proselytized them were at odds in their attitudes toward the form of social living that ought to prevail and that such conflicts centered on the idea of individualism as a principle of social ordering. Meanwhile, some converts took to the new form of social living and sought to remake their societies in its image. Whether it is in their embrace of the rule of reason or the merit principle, some became prophets and exhorted their peoples to change their ways to reflect the new ways of being human.

Our prophets embraced this idea of individualism and made it the cornerstone of their world view. Whatever other influences they would later derive from their African origins and general milieu, they appropriated the idea that if they improved themselves sufficiently they would be rewarded with careers open to talent directly from their engagement with modernity. It is doubtful that they derived their inspiration from indigenous sources. That would have been unlikely, given that they were, in a manner of speaking, exiles from their native communities who had a dim or at least an ambivalent view of their native inheritance. Needless to say, at the core of the individualist orientation is the idea of the person, the self, created by God, saved by grace. In the interim between its creation in sin and its salvation at the end by grace, the self acquires stature by dint of hard work, education, and a little luck. This is the self that is accorded respect and whose well-being is the metric by which to judge forms of social ordering. I am not saying that the kind of rampant individualism that we usually associate with the modern variety would have appealed to any of them. But I definitely would argue that the self of individuals and the collective self of groups were objects of the prophets' concern.

The Centrality of Reason

The second tenet of modernity that is of moment to us is the centrality of reason. Modern society fancies itself as a society of knowledge, one in which the claims of tradition and authority do not mean much and every truth claim must be authenticated by reason. Whoever can show that she has superior knowledge commands our assent and respect. This is contrasted with the premodern situation, where authority was largely unchallenged, tradition reigned supreme, and reason was a handmaiden to revelation. The African prophets adopted this tenet of modernity with aplomb. In their exertions, we can see them working extremely hard to acquire knowledge of not only the new ways of life that their sojourn in the New World of slavery and the slave trade had socialized them into but also the ways of life of their own societies, cultures, and customs. They provided us with our first models of intellectuals under the new dispensation inaugurated by evangelization and colonization. They founded schools. They sent their children to schools in Europe and the United States so that they would use the knowledge and skills acquired there for the betterment of African societies which, they held, could use some accelerated development in light of what they saw as the backwardness of their indigenous societies, no thanks to the deleterious effects of slavery and the slave trade. They desired to create in West Africa modern societies of knowledge run along scientific principles that delivered on the promise of life more abundant presupposed by modernity. They conducted ethnographies, studied their indigenous heritages, wrote local histories, and embraced change, the principle of novelty, with utmost enthusiasm.

Governance by Consent

Finally, I refer to the central tenet of political theory in the modern age that no one ought to acknowledge the authority of or owe an obligation to obey any government in the constitution of which he or she has played no part. That is, no government is legitimate to which the governed have not consented. When the American revolutionaries first used this principle as their rallying cry in 1776, it was the first culmination of a new principle of legitimacy whose philosophical grounds had been foreshadowed in the writings of Thomas Hobbes, John Locke, and Jean-Jacques Rousseau, among others. From that point on, whether it was in the French Revolution, the Haitian Revolution, or the much less abrupt transfer of power from the monarch and the nobility to the House of Commons in Britain, the authority of every ruler by the grace of God or by reason of birth was vulnerable to the challenge posed by the new thinking about who ought to rule when not all can rule. It was this principle that our prophets adopted in their argument that they must be rulers in their own house and that representative government was not a gift to be bestowed on them by the British but a right that they had earned because they were citizens of the empire. Our prophets were so enthusiastic about the doctrine of governance by consent that they sought at different times to remake indigenous modes of governance in accordance with its imperatives. Such was the force of the principle that by the third decade of the twentieth century, "no taxation without representation" was a favorite slogan of leaders of the National Congress of British West Africa.

The Historical Context

In what follows, I shall argue that the African apostles of modernity filled the role of prophets. Their starting point had two dimensions. The first was their experience of having been recaptured from slavers and freed from slavery or descended from such returnees or recaptives. As a result, their appreciation of the liberty promised for all under the modern regime was not merely theoretical. Theirs was an unalloyed disavowal of any and every regime that threatened to undermine liberty. The second was their description of the indigenous Africa to which they had returned. Given the approbation that they bestowed upon their new outlook on life, it is no surprise that they held their native counterparts to be backward, sunk in heathenism, and requiring redemption through the light of Christianity and (modern) civilization. They attributed Africa's backwardness to the ravages of the slave trade and the prevalence of ignorance and superstition. Their preferred solution provides an indication of their moral vision. They insisted that the future prosperity of their land depended on taking the best from modern civilization and combining it with what was best about indigenous practices and fashioning a synthesis that would deliver the promise of Christianity and civilization to their compatriots. They were not mimics; they did not want to be Europeans. (Even if they had wanted to be, as long as they were doing it as expressions of their selfhood, they would be quintessentially modern.) The ones who interest us are those who wanted to create a new synthesis. The best of them displayed confidence and imagination that we, their successors, cannot now claim to have.

Let us rewind to the 1830s. The Atlantic slave trade and slavery had just been abolished. Many slaves—recaptives, as they were called—were being taken by the British Navy from their slavers and returned to Sierra Leone and other parts of West Africa whence they'd been taken. Many were repatriating from the United States and the West Indies or Canada—they were called freedmen. But before their return journeys many of them had undergone some fundamental reorientations, sundry life-changing experiences, the most important of which was that they had become Christians. However, to see this change only in terms of its religious trappings will be inadequate, perhaps mistaken.

At the beginning of the nineteenth century, we saw in the previous chapter, there was a small group of missionaries and politicians as well as other men and women of affairs, especially humanitarians, who believed that the success of their missionizing activities was to be measured by how quickly they were able to render themselves superfluous to the running of the local churches they had helped establish. One might argue that there was a convergence of views concerning the aim of imperial activities among the key sectors of nineteenth-century West Africa: freed slaves who had become socialized into a new lifeworld structured by Christianity; a handful of government officials who felt that the most economical way to build empire was to rely on native agency and who saw their duty as making Africans fit for self-government; and missionaries who saw Africans as blighted children of God (no thanks to slavery) but God's children nonetheless who were capable of redemption and regeneration and who needed only temporary help from their missionary benefactors. Whether or not the government officials meant what they professed and whether or not the missionaries were sincere in their professions, the Africans took the charge seriously and proceeded to make themselves worthy of self-government.

The conjuncture I have described so far provided the context for the phenomena that I discuss in the rest of this chapter.

The most vocal and the most profound missionary at that time was Rev. Henry Venn, who served as the honorary secretary of the Church Mission Society, the spearhead organization for the evangelization activities of the Church of England, from 1841 to 1872. Venn was very clear and forceful in his advocacy of the development of native agency and reposed tremendous confidence in the ability of the agency thus nurtured to remake native society in modern ways. He insisted that the road to Africa's regeneration from the backwardness induced by slavery and the slave trade lay in Africans themselves with help from their allies in Christian civilization. To this end he emphasized that the self-governing, self-propagating, self-supporting native church offered a model that would lead to African recovery in the shortest possible time.

Were we to focus on the implications of building the three selves, we would see the secular reach of what goes on within the religious sphere. Self-support means, first, that there is a self whose capacity to act and whose autonomy to do so must not merely be recognized but respected, celebrated even. And second, support cannot but include the creation of material means to ensure that neither church nor pastor is beggared. Venn took seriously the history of the Church of England and he was willing to extend the capacity for autochthony to the African Church. Only a post-Reformation Christian could articulate the kind of heterodoxy he suggested. Even in our day, the Catholic Church does not allow anything similar. Venn insisted that perpetually feeding the native church through aid from the coffers of the mother church would create a dependent and feeble native church. In his view, the mother church had to equip the native church with the capacity for self-support and had to insist on the latter acquiring such capacity in the shortest time possible. Here we find the distinction that I expounded in the last chapter between the aid model and the autonomy model. Venn (and others who shared his philosophy) wanted a total remaking of the African world, initially under their direction but quickly turned over to Africans themselves, a development that was to be anchored on the other two Cs—commerce and civilization—that they deemed requisite to the achievement of their primary C, Christianity. It is noteworthy that the African churches that broke away from the major European-dominated Protestant denominations thrived, as did the ancillary social services institutions they established—schools, hospitals, nurseries, and so on. We cannot say the same for those sociopolitical agencies that remain tethered to government aid in the colonial period.

To further buttress the claim that the purview of the top visionary of the Church Missionary Society extended to the secular sphere, I refer to a pamphlet Henry Venn wrote and published in 1865. The timing of its publication is not without significance for some of the issues that I examine in subsequent chapters. In the period before the imposition of formal colonialism, British lawmakers and the British executive continually debated the direction of and justification for colonial acquisitions on the West African coast. To that end, as Venn reported, special committees of the House of Commons were formed in 1842 and 1849 "to enquire into the state of British possessions on the West Coast of Africa" and "in the House of Lords in 1850 "to enquire into the policy of maintaining the West African Squadron . . . [and] the commercial and social relations of the British colonies."[8] Venn's pamphlet was designed to inform and appeal to the British government to take seriously its fiduciary responsibilities toward Africans in their climb back from the abyss of slavery and the slave trade. It came with the appointment of yet another House of Commons committee "to enquire into the West African settlements."[9] Venn was concerned to present the committee with some evidence of what had worked—that is, the fruits of missionary labors, especially the role of native agency, in developing West Africa and a clarion call to deepen those advantages in the natives' march to progress.

In his pamphlet Venn adduced evidence to show that British colonies had played a pivotal and positive role in "promoting the civilization of the African races." He was particularly and justly proud of the achievements in Sierra Leone, which, for him, should serve as the beachhead for the civilization of the rest of the West Coast of Africa.

> In Sierra Leone is found a large community of native Christians. Every thing bespeaks an advanced stage of civilization. Elementary English education is universal. Many are highly educated. A large number are prosperous traders, and have accumulated much property. They are eminently a religious people. A Church population of twelve thousand souls supports nine native clergymen. The experienced and intelligent African traveler, Dr. Livingstone, has recorded his testimony to this state of Sierra Leone in the following words, in a published letter to Sir R. Murchison, March 30, 1858:—"Looking at the change effected among the people, and comparing the masses here with what we find at parts along the coast, where the benign influences of Christianity have had no effect, the man, even, who has no nonsense about him, would be obliged to confess that England had done some good by her philanthropy, aye, and an amount of good that will look grand in the eyes of posterity."[10]

Other statements followed, including quite a few from government officials who testified to the progress that had already been made and, most important, celebrated the accomplishments of natives who had exercised agency, especially the vast distances they had covered in so short a time, given the depths from which they had had to climb.

Despite the copious references to positive assessments of native accomplishments from government officials, a section of the pamphlet was devoted to the "Neglect of the Colonial Governments to Educate the Natives, and to Train Them for Government Employment." In it Venn indicted British authorities for not complementing the efforts of the missionaries and, in some cases, failing to provide employment opportunities for qualified natives. Additionally, the government was failing to deliver on its own side of the bargain where the provision of educational opportunities for the natives was concerned.

> In Sierra Leone the education of the whole population has been provided by the Church Missionary and Wesleyan Missionary Societies, and with so much success, that, by the census of 1860, the per-centage of the population under education was 22, whereas in Prussia the per-centage is 16, and in England 13. The elementary schools connected with the Church of England are wholly supported by fees and an endowment created by the exertions of the people themselves. There is a Grammar School, at which Greek and Latin, and mathematics, are taught by a native clergyman, which contains 100 pupils, and is not only self-supporting, but has accumulated a capital of nearly 1000£. . . . By these means the Missionary Societies have raised up a native agency for religious teaching. . . .
>
> The Government contribution to this important and successful system of education has been only one elementary school in Freetown.[11]

Venn did not present this poignant juxtaposition of missionary achievement and government neglect merely to remind the government of its duty to Africans. Rather, it was part of a scolding that, in the wake of the setting up of another House committee in 1865, was to ginger the legislature into performing its oversight of executive policymaking.

My interpretation is supported by the other part of the indictment of British colonial authorities. Missionaries trained the natives to establish and run their own lives and institutions, beginning with their churches. What use is capacity that is trained but is never deployed? The failure to use natives in government departments meant that native capacity for self-government was not being developed and that the government was not availing itself of cheaper alternatives to expensive expatriates who would never be permanently available for local work. Even if one could say that government inactivity was obviated by the strides being taken by missionaries, Venn argued, one could not excuse "the neglect of all the Colonial Governments in one obvious and important duty, namely, the preparation of natives for assisting in departments of the Government. The success of Missionary Societies in raising an agency competent for their work should have induced the Governments to select, and, if necessary, to send home for final education suitable men for their own purposes. Such a native agency would soon have repaid the cost by providing a cheaper and more permanent class of civil servants."[12]

It should by now be obvious that Venn's investment in native agency was not a mere expedient but a deeply held conviction respecting the fortunes of the colonized on the West Coast of Africa. He wanted the West African Squadron to "receive native youths to be trained in navigation under the discipline of a British man-of-war, by which a class of native masters of coasting vessels would be raised up of great service to commerce."[13] To recommit to the development of native agency, to deepen its training of native capacity, to facilitate the creation of a cadre of native civil servants in all areas was the ultimate charge he wished to put before the 1865 Select Committee of the House of Commons.

Venn's charge to the government was not without merit or context. Many in government circles shared with Venn and the humanitarians most of the sentiments regarding the development and deployment of native agency as the quickest and most appropriate tool for the remaking of Africa. For instance, Earl Grey, colonial secretary in Lord Russell's administration from 1846 to 1852, said: "The real interest of this Country is gradually to train the inhabitants of this part of Africa in the arts of civilization and government, until they shall grow into a nation capable of protecting themselves and of managing their own affairs, so that the interference and assistance of the British Authorities may by degrees be less and less required."[14] Perhaps the 1865 committee paid some attention to Venn's admonitions. Witness its resolution of May 1865, which said, inter alia, "that the object of our policy should be to encourage in the natives the exercise of those qualities which may render it possible more and more to transfer to them the administration of all the Governments, with a view to our ultimate withdrawal."[15]

Not minding the bad faith of colonial governments, many Africans took the humanitarian professions of faith in native agency to heart. They set about the task of remaking the African world after the fashion of the world they had been inducted into, the signal values of which they had come to embrace and the fruits of which they were eager to make available to their brothers and sisters who in their estimation were still in the grip of heathenism. It is from among their ranks that the prophets that I am speaking of emerged, fully persuaded that a great future for Africa lay in a critical appropriation of what force and Providence had bestowed on them during their time in the Babylon of New World slavery and the slave trade. According to Ajayi,

> The most important factor in their make-up, however, was that in passing through slavery into freedom they had all been made acutely conscious of the gaps that separated them as a people from the Europeans. And in spite of having been subjected to Europeans or because of it, they wished to be like Europeans. They had all travelled far. A few of them had travelled widely and had seen something of the European world, either in Europe itself, or at secondhand, in Sierra Leone, the West Indies or Latin America. By and large, they all came back desiring to make certain changes come about. . . . They were the first generation of Nigerian nationalists. Their nationalism consisted in their vision of a new social, economic and political order such as would make their country "rank among the civilized nations of the earth."[16]

Ajayi's description requires us to consider these Africans with greater sophistication and sympathy. In assessing the contributions of this group of African thinkers we must resist the urge to see in them glorified "Uncle Toms."[17] All too often in the apologias of colonial administrators, they are represented as persons who suffered from a dependency complex or a near-pathological desire to be "white" or at least "European." I suspect that part of the reason that their reflections have not been taken seriously by African scholars in the contemporary period is connected to the fact that it is this picture of them that is presented to our contemporary minds every time their names come up. The explanation for this is not hard to fathom. By the end of the colonial period, the mode of knowledge production had become thoroughly suffused with the racist-inflected view of Africa as the land of peoples arrested in the infancy of the human race. The memory of African agents embracing and adapting the wisdom of Europe to the specific contours of its own genius had long dimmed. A grand narrative had replaced it in which Africans appeared in modernity only as victims, benighted recipients of Euroamerican generosity, domesticated pets forever dependent on handouts from their owner/benefactors. On the other hand, resisters, nationalists, could not bring themselves to see any positive aspect to the play of modernity that they mistakenly assimilated to colonialism in Africa. Such individuals hardly ever evince awareness of antecedents of modernity in the nineteenth century. The explanation is simple. The aid model had become the sole orthodoxy regarding the options for Africa's future. One consequence is that the figure of somebody like Crowther had declined from the nineteenth-century man of science and man of the cloth to a pitiable, humble, and loyal minion of the Church of England. After all, wasn't he the "slave boy who became Bishop"? Long forgotten till now were his scientific engagements, his explorer credentials, and the centrality of his work to the constitution of Yorùbá literature, language, and identity.

Furthermore, ever since the colonial period and the subsequent hostility that it kindled in nationalistic Africans, Africans who have dared to think that indigenizing the ways of their European oppressors offered a path to serious progress for their own peoples and lands have always attracted the disapprobation of their fellows. Yet to think of our prophets as for the most part desirous of becoming "white" or "European" is to seriously misconstrue what they were about and who they desired to be. Indeed, a close but unprejudiced analysis of their writings and pronouncements will reveal entirely contrary impulses.

The view of the prophets as bad parodies of their European benefactors can sometimes be traced to Europeans' unflattering portrayals of indigenous African practices, institutions, and values, especially when they compared the latter to Africans' newly acquired practices, institutions, and values of European provenance. They are thus spoken of as if they found nothing good in African ways of being human and thought that everything about European ways of being human was good. The problem with this view is that on closer analysis, their standpoints had more nuance than their latter-day critics are aware of or are willing to acknowledge. Our task is to understand where they were coming from, explore their ideas fully rather than as strands taken out of context, and see why they might have appeared as pathological self-haters. I hope that the discussion that follows offers a modest contribution to appreciating their genius.

Unlike the reticence, maybe a profound lack of self-confidence, with which we their progeny now approach modernity and other things "Western," the prophets of old exuded tremendous confidence in their belief that they were destined to be the leaders who would create new forms of social living in Africa by stealing the fire of the "West" and combining it with what was best in their indigenous heritage and doing all this in partnership with Europeans. Thus, we need to investigate their ideas of progress, of the state of Africa during their time, and of how best to fit Africa for its proper place in the concert of humanity.

The Prophets

Samuel Ajayi Crowther

The first of the apostles that I wish to present for rather belated honor is Bishop Samuel Ajayi Crowther (1806–1891). The contributions of Bishop Crowther have usually been processed through religious lenses. He was "the first non-European to be consecrated a Protestant Bishop since the Reformation."[18] The evangelization of much of present-day Nigeria was prosecuted under his direction. This achievement alone would constitute enough justification for celebrating him. But I concur with Ade Ajayi's judgment that we need to probe further to evaluate "the greatness of the man and his achievements." Otherwise, we "fall into the error of the CMS officials who, after the death of Henry Venn in 1872 chose to underestimate Crowther's tenacity of purpose and attachment to basic principles." Ajayi shares Jesse Page's assessment that "he was no fanatic on the subject of a native ministry, but he was a patriot to the core."[19] I would like to add that not only was Crowther a patriot to the core, he was one of the earliest scientists—make that one of the earliest polymaths—to emerge from the modern era in Africa. This aspect of his achievements has not been celebrated.

Let us examine the evidence. Crowther epitomized the man of knowledge par excellence.[20] He was an explorer, a philologist, a theologian, an administrator, an ethnographer, and a multilinguist. In all these activities, he evinced an incredible capacity for observation, a gift for seeing what is valuable in indigenous ways of being human so as to adapt the Christian message accordingly and facilitate the creation of an indigenous Church. This he did in spite of his own conviction that his indigenous African cohort was sunk in heathenism and could only be led forth by the light of the Christian faith and the civilization of which it was an integral part. Misreading him as a quisling of his missionary sponsors is unwarranted. It is the ultimate disrespect for or lack of recognition of native agency. The exercise of native agency does not always translate into approbation for native ways and the rejection of alien ones. Neither does it mean that the native will be cognizant of all her motivations for acting. This is a very human characteristic that is to be found in all cultures. An individual might respond to her native inheritance in different ways, for example. She might conclude that there is nothing of worth in her (in the current case) indigenous African culture. Or she might accept that there is something worthy of embrace that needs to be opened up to new ideas from alien sources. A third possibility is to merge the indigenous and the alien in some new hybrid reality. Finally, she could elect to be an overenthusiastic embracer of things alien or indigenous. The fact that a native falls under one or more of the above categories might be an occasion for some serious criticism, but it should not be a basis for unwarranted name-calling such as has been the case with the judgment by certain scholars of Crowther. But one is unlikely to appreciate fully the man's accomplishments if one is not aware of what road he traveled.

According to Ajayi, the foremost living scholar of Crowther's life and work, he was born in Yorùbáland in about 1806, was rescued by the Naval Squadron in April 1822 off Lagos, and was released in Freetown as a freed slave in July. Ajayi notes that "it is said that he was so eager to learn that he was able to read the New Testament in English within six months."[21] That must have been remarkable enough, and it probably impressed his CMS benefactors. By 1828, he had qualified as a teacher, and in 1837, he published an account of his capture and life as a slave in 1821–1822.[22] He was part of the Niger Expedition in 1841–1842; his journal of that expedition was published as *Journals of Schön and Crowther*.[23] In a recent evaluation of Crowther's achievements, Lamine Sanneh remarked as follows:

> In spite of the hazards and difficulties, Crowther accomplished a surprising amount of work on the Niger, making the most detailed observations and reports of his progress on the banks of the Niger. He was interested in the religious ideas and practices of Africans, and he inquired diligently, listened closely, and depicted as accurately as he could what he observed and heard for himself. He was eager to corroborate, test, and confirm for himself, leaving issues of dispute open to opinion. He avoided rushing to judgment. Thus, although he noted somber aspects of their customs and traditional practices, Crowther was nevertheless enthusiastic about what he learnt of religion among the Ibo people, including their ideas about God (Chukwu, Chineke), ethics, and moral conduct. . . . . The idea that premodern Africa had anticipated in several crucial respects Christian teaching was stated by Crowther with such spontaneous conviction that it marked him as a native mouthpiece, not just as a foreign agent.[24]

Sanneh's assessment illustrates that Crowther exhibited many of the qualities that typify a scientific orientation: the insistence on facts, the suspension of judgment before the facts are in, and so forth. Equally important, he did not prejudge the indigenous culture, and when he was acquainted with the facts, he saw evidence that there were nodes in the native culture onto which Christian ideas could be grafted. Thus, he grasped the possibility of nativizing Christianity and Christianizing indigenous religious antecedents. He was so successful that people now love to hate him for adapting the sophistication of Yorùbá language and religious discourse to the domestication of Christianity. (This was the hallmark of his evangelizing activities for the rest of his life.) And he did so with a scientific mindset that did not permit any unwarranted a priori privileging of either Christian or native religion. Again, I quote Sanneh: "Crowther was not a mere romantic, bowing to native custom and practice. His natural habit of stringent scrutiny of the evidence he never abandoned to nativistic pride, and so he plunged into remote hinterland districts, grateful for what he discovered of encouragement there, certainly, but resolved also to confront what he judged harmful."[25]

Crowther probably did not "grovel" enough in the eyes of the latter generation of white missionaries who succeeded to the leadership of the CMS after Venn's death. They accused Crowther of not being tough enough in his treatment of the heathenish tendencies among the converts under his charge. It was the principal reason they cited for humiliating him and hounding him out of his see. The real reason was to be found elsewhere, though. The late-arriving missionaries were in cahoots with their administrator counterparts in thinking little (if anything at all) of African abilities. But as Andrew Walls points out, "There were some unexpected legacies even from the last sad days. One section of the Niger mission, the one in the Niger Delta, was financially self-supporting. Declining the European takeover, it long maintained a separate existence under Crowther's son, Archdeacon Dandeson Crowther, within the Anglican communion but outside the Church Mission Society."[26]

Crowther's scientific orientation, his commitment to the study of African life and thought as a basis for determining the shape and direction of the native Church, is part of why I insist that it is long overdue to celebrate his genius. And what genius it was! He set about acquiring the necessary tools for the performance of his scientific task.

> When on his return from the Niger Expedition in 1842 he was recommended for ordination, the Bishop of London after interviewing him briefly is reported to have said: "He will do, but polish him up." He was admitted in September 1842 to the CMS Training Institution at Islington. At the May/June examinations, he evidently impressed his examiners. The Regius Professor of Greek at Cambridge said he would like to take his answers on Paley's "Evidences of Christianity" to read to his friends in Trinity College. "If, after hearing that young African's answers, they still contend that he does not possess a logical faculty, they will tempt us to question whether they do not lack certain other faculties of at least equal importance, such as common fairness of judgment and Christian candor." Bishop Bloomfield later remarked: "That man is no mean scholar; his examination papers were capital, and his Latin remarkably good."[27]

Even if one were uncharitably to dismiss the effusive praise of his examiners as so much paternalism toward an unusual African, the rest of his life confirmed not only that the praises were well deserved but that the promise that they all saw in him was fully redeemed.

Having recognized the importance of making native agency the cornerstone of the native Church in Africa, Crowther quickly became a scholar of African indigenous religions and Islam. Most important of all, he became a preeminent philologist of African languages. His achievements in this area cry out for celebration, but at the same time, they suggest that we should study his methodology and his results. Here is the evidence as represented by Ajayi.

> In the 13 years (1844–57) that he was a member of the Yorùbá mission, apart from his evangelical and pastoral work at Igbein, he went up the Niger again in 1854 and 1857, building up the experience he needed for his later career. But the most important aspect of his work in those years was his career as a translator. We tend to take this for granted, but look at the record. He published a few extracts in 1848; the Epistle to the Romans in 1850; Luke, Acts, James and I and II Peter in 1851; Genesis and Matthew in 1853; Exodus and the Psalms in 1854; Proverbs and Ecclesiastes in 1856 and revisions of earlier texts. After 1857, he had to work with others. Thomas King had collaborated with him on Matthew in 1853. In 1857–62, they worked on the Epistles—Philippians, I and II Colossians, I and II Thessalonians, I and II Timothy, Titus, Philemon, Hebrews, John, Jude and Revelations, thus completing the New Testament in 1865. Schön and Gollmer edited these for linguistic consistency and published a revised New Testament in 1865. In 1867, Genesis to Ruth of the Old Testament was published. Others were brought in, probably because of their proficiency in Hebrew—Hinderer, D. O. Williams, Adolphus Mann, etc. By 1889 the whole Bible was available in Yorùbá, though not in a single volume until 1900.[28]

By itself, the achievement of the translation of the Bible into any nonoriginal language would be phenomenal. "The significance of the Yoruba version has not always been observed," Walls notes. "It was not the first translation into an African language; but, insofar as Crowther was the leading influence in its production, it was the first by a native speaker. Early missionary translations naturally relied heavily on native speakers as informants and guides; but in no earlier case was a native speaker able to judge and act on an equal footing with the European."[29] When it is realized that the translation into Yorùbá was being done at the same time as the language itself was being newly rendered into written form, the work becomes even more astonishing. Indeed, beyond the importance of translating the Bible into Yorùbá, the business of creating a Yorùbá script must attract greater significance for it made the language immediately available for other than religious theoretical tasks. It is a mark of how little we know—much less appreciate—of Crowther's philological labors that he is never taught as one of the principal figures of the history of philology—even in Nigeria, where he did the bulk of this work. Nor is he taught to history students in Nigeria, at both high school and college levels, as a pioneer linguist, grammarian, ethnographer, and theologian of no small repute. Nor is he ever acknowledged as an accomplished explorer in the annals of exploration in Africa.

Yet he wrote the earliest grammar and dictionary of the Yorùbá language, *Grammar and Vocabulary of the Yorùbá Language* (London: Seelys, 1852). He also wrote *Vocabulary of the Yorùbá Language: Part I—English and Yorùbá; Part II—Yorùbá and English. To Which Are Prefixed the Grammatical Elements of the Yorùbá Language* (London: CMS, 1843). His labors were not restricted to the Yorùbá language or culture. The following works were also attributed to him: *Isuama-Ibo Primer* (London: CMS, 1860); *Vocabulary of the Ibo Language: Part 2 English-Ibo* (London: Society for Promoting Christian Knowledge, 1883); *The Gospel According to St. John: Translated into Nupe* (London: CMS, 1877); *Nupe Primer* (London: CMS, 1860).

His mettle as an explorer is attested by the following reports that he authored and/or coauthored: *Journals of the Rev. James Frederick Schön and Mr. Samuel Crowther* (London: Frank Cass, 1970); *The Gospel on the Banks of the Niger: Journals and Notices of the Native Missionaries Accompanying the Niger Expedition of 1857–1859 by the Rev. Samuel Crowther and the Rev. John Christopher Taylor* (London: Dawsons of Pall Mall, 1968); *Niger Mission: Bishop Crowther's Report of the Overland Journey from Lokoja to Bida, on the River Niger; and Thence to Lagos, on the Sea Coast, from November 10th, 1871 to February 8th, 1872* (London: CMS, 1872); *Journals and Notices of the Native Missionaries on the River Niger, 1862* (London: CMS, 1863); *The River Niger: A Paper Read before the Royal Geographical Society, June 11th, 1877; and a Brief Account of Missionary Operations Carried on under the Superintendence of Bishop Crowther in the Niger Territory* (London: CMS, 1877); *Journal of an Expedition up the Niger and Tshadda Rivers Undertaken by Macgregor Laird in Connection with the British Government in 1854* (London: CMS, 1855).

The foregoing discussion should give enough foretaste of what is awaiting discovery in the secular exertions of Bishop Crowther. I must not omit to mention that he made all these discoveries in the face of racist opposition from his contemporary and rival, Henry Townsend, and, from 1872 onward, after the death of Henry Venn, a distinctly racist turn both in the CMS and in Europe generally.[30] The latter development eventually led to his removal from service. But as long as he remained in office, he took seriously the promise of knowledge and sought to strengthen the African self with scientific achievements and scholarly rigor. His travelogues were based on commissions. He collected ethnographies and data on native life generally. He was one of the earliest models of the native intellectual who sought to domesticate what Europe had to offer as a means of advancing the interests and welfare of Africans.

We cannot overemphasize the importance of his work in light of the claims I make throughout this book regarding the centrality of reason and the priority of knowledge. He was not satisfied with merely living African while leaving the business of studying Africa to others. He was pivotal in the production and constitution of knowledge about Africans. We need to study the multiplier effects of his exertions on his numerous assistants—translators, interpreters, note-takers, and so on—and the effects of the latter on the creation of a new group of knowledge producers in the African context. Nor should we ignore his offering of new role models of what it was to be an intellectual and the wider impact on successors who furthered the work of knowledge production about, by, and for Africans in a modern key. Most important, he embodied what native agency under the autonomy model could accomplish regardless of the wishes and designs of those who were its tutors, presumptive and literal.

James Africanus Beale Horton

The second of the apostles whose importance I wish to underscore is Dr. James Africanus Beale Horton. Born in Sierra Leone on June 1, 1835, in Gloucester, near Freetown, Horton's parents were originally of Ibo extraction. They were repatriates from Trinidad. He went to school in Sierra Leone and for further studies, beginning in 1855, first at King's College, London, where he trained as a physician, and later at Edinburgh in 1859. "Horton's career [at King's College] was brilliant, and he won prizes in Surgery, Physiology and Comparative Anatomy. His knowledge of Anatomy was amply demonstrated in his book *West African Countries and Peoples, British and Native . . . and a Vindication of the African Race* in which he challenged physical anthropologists who had asserted that the brain of an African was smaller than that of a European and that he was therefore less intelligent."[31] He went on to Edinburgh for further studies and in 1859 he obtained a doctor of medicine (M.D.) degree. He had earlier in 1858 been admitted to membership of the Royal College of Surgeons of England, which qualified him to be a doctor. "He joined the Army Medical Service as an Assistant Staff Surgeon in the West African Service and rose to the rank of Surgeon-Major in 1875, later ranking as Lieutenant-Colonel after twenty years' service and finally retiring on half pay in 1880. He was not the first African doctor, but he was one of the most versatile of his century."[32] He served many tours of duty in different parts of English-speaking West Africa, from Gambia to Ghana.

His initial training as a scientist already makes it easier for us to identify him with the temperament ordinarily associated with doing science. Horton's career was extraordinary enough given his medical and scientific accomplishments. What made his accomplishments even more extraordinary were his writings in government, political theory, ethnography, and sundry other areas. As Nicol remarks, "His knowledge of the classics, history, anthropology, science and medicine was remarkable for a man of any race."[33] An exploration of his prodigious writings in some of these spheres is beyond the scope of the present essay. What I hope to do instead is to present evidence from some of his writings and show how some of his articulations amounted to prophetic insights into times beyond that in which he lived.

Before I do so, I consider one rather unflattering but erroneous assessment of him, his work, and his life by Emmanuel A. Ayandele. Recall that in chapter 2 I referred to the fact that Ayandele apprehended the revolutionary nature of the second wave of evangelization in West Africa. But we chose to go with Ajayi's more nuanced and more sympathetic appraisal. The same animus that made Ayandele excoriate the missionaries that I have presented in this book as heralds of the modern age in Africa informed his review essay on Horton's major work, *West African Countries and Peoples.*[34]

According to Ayandele, in part because Horton was "one of the greatest beneficiaries of British philanthropy" and for that reason "felt a sense of eternal gratitude to Henry Venn and the War Office Education Committee which had been responsible for his training in Britain . . . he was overwhelmed by the marvels of science and technology; Britain became for him the model, its people an embodiment of all that was virtuous, and its government the altruistic benefactor of West African peoples."[35] He called Horton's book "provincial" and claimed that even though Horton "posed as a defender of the African . . . his African was not an uncontaminated one, but transmogrified like himself, who dared not live in the authentic African milieu."[36] Ayandele continues, "The African of Horton's defence and expostulation, then, was deAfricanized like himself, living in the borrowed British milieu of the colony of Sierra Leone."[37] He went on to allege that Horton and others like him saw themselves "as modernizing Africans, and as the class that mattered. . . . Hence the unconcealed contempt and disdain which Horton pours on the pure unlettered African; hence the unconscious levity with which he dismissed the cultural heritage of the continent."[38]

There are more invectives in Ayandele's text. Even a passing familiarity with elementary logic is enough to see through the ad hominem and non sequiturs in the passages quoted above. The vehemence with which he denounces Horton suggests to me that there may be a lot more at stake than what Horton actually wrote. Most of the charges leveled at Horton are absolutely without merit. Horton's only crime, it seems to me, is that he was neither a resister of modernity nor a self-confessed victim of it. By accusing Horton of not daring to live in the authentic African milieu, of being de-Africanized and being contemptuous of "the pure unlettered African"—in short, of not being "an authentic African," Ayandele showed his preference for the administrators' favorite African, an African who was an absolute invention of colonial anthropologists: "the uncontaminated African." From even the limited discussion so far in this book, it should be obvious that I remain unimpressed by such a character and whatever it represents. It is the ultimate nod to sociocryonics that is no less odious for being canvassed by an African and a scholar to boot. In true celebration of African subjectivity, we should expect a full range of heterodox possibilities in the expression of what it is to be African. It is lamentable that one reason that the African engagement with modernity has been unacknowledged, much less discussed, for so long is precisely the point of view that turns the rich multidimensional experience of being African into a sclerotic, unidimensional one of being "an authentic African."

If any evidence be needed that Ayandele's vituperations have no relation to the core of Horton's disquisitions, Ayandele concedes that "irrelevant and unrelated to the aspirations of West Africans in the nineteenth century as this was, [Horton's book] delineated a program that was to become relevant to all of Africa in subsequent generations. Thus, in a sense, Horton was a prophet who discerned the forces that were to determine the future of Africa."[39] The irony was completely lost on Ayandele that by calling Horton a prophet he repudiated the ardent purveyors of sociocryonics for whom he stated a clear preference in his review. In essence, Horton got the future right and Ayandele could not bear to leave the past behind. It is a good time to return to my celebration of Horton.

As a scientist and man of knowledge, Horton's writings were prodigious. In language that anticipated some of the contemporary responses to lingering pseudo-scientific racism, Horton used knowledge and scientific research to refute the racism of his time. It is important to comprehend why the appeal to science is as crucial to racists as it is to anti-racists. Modern society, as I have pointed out, requires that whatever is to be accepted as true must either be capable of demonstrative proof of the type to be found in mathematics (especially algebra) or emanate from empirical investigation (possibly experimentation) supported by facts and figures. Additionally, given that the appeal to tradition and revelatory authority no longer enjoys legitimacy, only the claim that withstands reason's scrutiny is deserving of a thinking person's assent. This was the ground of the modern epoch's denial of legitimacy to both papal and other types of sacerdotal authority and the belief that the authority of royals was bestowed by the grace of God. As a credentialed member of the community in which only the authority of reason and the possession of superior knowledge count, Horton was eager to show that he had the upper hand against the racists of his time. Needless to say, one often is struck by the irony involved in the situation where the self-appointed custodians of reason and scientific rationality are frequently shown to be subverting reason by the so-called nonpossessors of reason when the former, in the face of facts and other proof, continue irrationally to deny the obvious. Consider the following critique by Horton of the alleged inferiority of the Negro race:

It is in the development of the most important organ of the body—the brain, and its investing parieties—that much stress has been laid to prove the simian or apelike character of the Negro race. . . . The skull is, as regards the sutures, intimately connected with the brain; in man, we find that the posterior sutures first close, and the frontal and coronal last, but in the anthropoid ape the contrary is the case. Among the Negro race, at least among the thousands that have come under my notice, the posterior sutures first close, then the frontal and coronal, and the contrary has never been observed by me in even a single instance, not even among Negro idiots; and yet M. Gratiolet and Carl Vogt, without an opportunity of investigating the subject to any extent, have unhesitatingly propagated the most absurd and erroneous doctrine—that the closing of the sutures in the Negro follows the siminious or animal arrangement, differing from that already given as the governing condition in man.[40]

In this passage, Horton was not concerned to excoriate his interlocutor for any charge other than that of being a nonscientist or a false one. Nor was he concerned with the morality of his interlocutors or their ideological predilections. Knowledge and its possession or lack thereof was the only issue as far as he was concerned.[41] He situated himself on the terrain of superior knowledge and commanded assent as such. The fact that he was doing it as an African was at best the icing on the cake of his epistemic supremacy. Even Ayandele could not ignore this fact.[42] In fact, Horton ridiculed his interlocutor, Dr. Knox, as one to whom "race is everything—literature, science, art—in a word civilization depends on it." Knox had gone so far as to say that "with me race or hereditary descent is everything; it stamps the man."[43] It is immediately obvious that Dr. Knox's standpoint is unscientific and not founded on knowledge and, for that reason, unworthy of assent on the part of those for whom the authority of science alone is legitimate. Horton contrasted Dr. Knox's position with his own position, which was based on the practice of science fed by verifiable empirical observation. Surely Knox's claim invited confutation, but his opponents never bothered to offer it. This was exactly the charge that Horton leveled at the recently chartered Royal Anthropological Society.

Of late years a society has been formed in England in imitation of the Anthropological Society of Paris, which might be made of great use to science had it not been for the profound prejudice exhibited against the Negro race in their discussions and in their writings. They again revive the old vexed question of race, which the able researches of Blumenbach, Prichard, Pallas, Hunter, Lacépéde, Quatrefages, Geoffroy St. Hilaire, and many others had, years ago (as it is thought) settled. They placed the structure of the anthropoid apes before them, and then commenced the discussion of a series of ideal structures of the Negro which only exist in their imagination, and thus endeavor to link the Negro with the brute creation. Some of their statements are so barefacedly false, so utterly the subversion of scientific truth, that they serve to exhibit the writers as perfectly ignorant of the subjects of which they treat. The works of Carl Vogt, "Lectures on Man"; of Dr. Hunt, "Negro's Place in Nature"; and of Prunner Bey, "Mémoire sur les Nègres," 1861, contain, in many respects, tissues of the most deceptive statements, calculated to mislead those who are unacquainted with the African race.[44]

Given that his challenge was based on the authority of science and the claim of superior knowledge, it is no surprise that Horton denigrated the ignorance of his interlocutors. As far as he was concerned, he knew what he was talking about; they did not. For that reason, they did not deserve attention. It is noteworthy that in spite of the efforts of thinkers like Horton from Africa and others in Europe and North America, we continue even at the present time to be treated to pseudo-scientific proclamations of the genetic inferiority of peoples of African descent. It is a mark of how little even Africans know of previous scientific refutations of racism by African thinkers that one will be hard put to find contemporary contributions to the debate that show any awareness of the works of Horton in this sphere.

In pursuit of science and of using science for uplifting Africa and its peoples, Horton wrote other scientific works, including "The Medical Topography of the West Coast of Africa, with Sketches of Its Botany" (thesis for the doctorate of medicine, Edinburgh University, 1859) (published with the same title in London, 1859); *Physical and Medical Climate and Meteorology of the West Coast of Africa. With Valuable Hints to Europeans for the Preservation of Health in the Tropics* (London, 1867); *Guinea Worm, or Dracunculus: Its Symptoms and Progress, Causes, Pathological Anatomy, Results, and Radical Cure* (London: 1868) and *The Diseases of Tropical Climates and their Treatment with Hints for the Preservation of Health in the Tropics* (London, 1874). Thomas Fowell Buxton could not have wished for a better exemplar of the realization of part of his program of remedy for the African slave trade. He would have been even more gratified that it was unfolding under the direction of a native agent.

Horton's credentials as a surgeon, medical scientist, and epidemiologist are impeccable by any standards. He applied the same scientific orientation to his study of indigenous systems of governance in West Africa. African forms of governance were not to be embraced or condemned until scholars had obtained a good scientific understanding of them both in terms of their identity and their operating principles, and Horton did his best to study them.[45] As a result, his writings on West African peoples and their customs are even more impressive, given that he was primarily a medical doctor and natural scientist. Simply put, when we shall have devoted to his political philosophical writings the attention that they deserve, we would have to conclude that Horton was also one of the pioneer political philosophers of the modern age in Africa. The dominant theme in his political writings was the fitness of Africans for self-government and their right to be self-governing under the overall suzerainty of the British monarchy. Many mid-nineteenth-century British politicians and humanitarians believed that the best colonialism was one that suited the colonial wards for self-rule in the shortest possible time. These individuals believed in the improvability of human beings through education and could not seriously entertain the idea that Africans would forever be at the bottom rung of the human ladder. However, because morbidity among European expatriates was high, there was a widespread feeling that the human costs of empire might be unjustifiably high. Even so, I think that it is a mistake to hold, as many seem to do, that this exigency was the only or even the principal reason that the possibility of African self-government was seriously entertained in various circles in mid-nineteenth-century Britain and West Africa.

What the motivation was of those who believed in native agency and how sincere they were matters less, though, once we turn our attention to the natives themselves. That is, once we frame the issue in terms of what some segments of the West African population thought of the possibility and desirability of self-government, their capacity for it, and their reaction to the resolution of the House of Commons Select Committee of 1865, we shall find that Africans elected to take their prospects in hand and began to present arguments to urge—perhaps force the hand of—British authorities to extend to them the right of self-governance.

Horton was a principal spokesperson for the movement for self-government. He identified some national groups in West Africa as deserving of the right to govern themselves and argued that they had gone even farther than others along the road to self-governance because they had taken grand initiatives to institute civilized—that is, modern—forms of government in the areas they inhabited. First, he adopted a tactic that presaged contemporary arguments for African genius. He argued that Africa had not always been voiceless in the polylogue of the world's peoples.

> Africa, in ages past, was the nursery of science and literature; from thence they were taught in Greece and Rome, so that it was said that the ancient Greeks represented their favourite goddess of wisdom—Minerva—as an African princess. Pilgrimages were made to Africa in search of knowledge by such eminent men as Solon, Plato, Pythagoras; and several came to listen to the instructions of the African Euclid, who was at the head of the most celebrated mathematical school in the world and who flourished 300 years before the birth of Christ.[46]

He went on to argue for the Africanness of ancient Egyptian civilization. It is a mark of the resilience of global white supremacy that later writers such as Cheikh Anta Diop and Martin Bernal fought the same battles in the last half of the twentieth century with almost the same language and facts against the propagation of lies about the African past. Horton concluded: "And why should not the same race who governed Egypt, attacked the most famous and flourishing city—Rome, who had her churches, her Universities, and her repositories of learning and science, once more stand on their legs and endeavour to raise their characters in the scale of the civilised world?"[47] If it is the case that "nations rise and fall; the once flourishing and civilized degenerates into a semi-barbarous state; and those who have lived in utter barbarism, after a lapse of time become the standing nation," then Africa's time was bound to come again. And he argued that he had detected the nodes of such renaissance in some areas of West Africa in all spheres of human achievement. Using knowledge of the African past, he argued for the historicity of the African experience as a basis for future prosperity.

I now turn to his specific reflections on government. At the present time, many who speak of the dismal prospects of liberal bourgeois democracy in Africa attribute those prospects to the recalcitrance of African traditions to the tenets of modernity. Yet in the nineteenth century, in West Africa, there were serious and far-reaching experiments in modern liberal democratic government. In fact, Horton argued that the incorporation of modern governance could be used in part to attenuate the illegitimacy of an otherwise unjustifiable colonialism. His example was the British annexation of Lagos in 1861. He lauded the Fanti Confederation, which between 1868 and 1871 wrote for itself one of the earliest instances of a modern constitution anywhere in the world. It has been suggested that that constitution was inspired by Horton's work, *West African Countries and Peoples, British and Native. With the Requirements Necessary for Establishing That Self-Government Recommended by the Committee of the House of Commons 1865; and a Vindication of the African Race* (London, 1868).[48] However that may be, what stands out is that Horton took a decidedly modern view of the appropriate mode of governance for Africa. For example, he embraced the core tenet of modernity with regard to political legitimacy: No one ought to obey any government to which he/she has not consented and in the constitution of which she/he has not had any hand. The most direct way of indicating this consent is through the vote. Hence, the electoral principle is the cornerstone of political legitimacy in the modern age. It was the political theoretical foundation of the demand for self-government by many in nineteenth-century West Africa.

In his consideration of what sort of government should be adopted by "the political union of the various kings in the kingdom of Fantee under one political head," Horton recommended the electoral principle. "A man should be chosen either by universal suffrage, or appointed by the Governor, and sanctioned and received by all the kings and chiefs, and crowned as King of Fantee. He should be a man of great sagacity, good common sense, not easily influenced by party spirit, of a kind and generous disposition, a man of good education, and who had done good service to the Coast government."[49] Meanwhile, in his discussion of what mode of governance was appropriate for Accra, he recommended a republican government.

If this place must ultimately be left to govern itself, a republican form of government should be chosen. An educated native gentleman, of high character and good common sense, who has the welfare of his country at heart . . . should be selected by the Government as a candidate for the presidency, and offered for the votes of the populace in the various districts; and, when once elected, he must be regarded as supreme in everything, and the natural referee in all their quarrels and differences. He should be assisted by counsellors chosen by the people as their representatives. The term of office of the president should not be less than eight years, and he should be eligible for re-election.[50]

Whether he was writing about Sierra Leone, Gambia, or Lagos and Abẹ́òkúta, he was unwavering in his insistence that the only legitimate government was one that received its sanction from the consent of the people expressed through the vote. His inclusion, at some points, of selection of governors should be treated as mere bows in the direction of the reality of a people who were momentarily humbled by various historical forces and whose elevation was a matter of time and of the hard work of those—the British—who had come to lend the Africans a hand in finding their feet once again.

Second, there was no room in his theory for ascription. For him, the circumstances of one's birth did not mean anything, inheritance ranked nil, and tradition was of no moment. Eligibility for office had to be earned—the merit principle—and even then it was necessary that the people offer their electoral stamp of approval. This explains his enthusiastic approval of the experiments in new modes of governance that were under way during his life in the Gold Coast—the Fanti Confederation—and Abẹ́òkúta—the Ẹ̀gbá United Board of Management.[51]

In his appeal to the British colonial authorities to support the Fanti Confederation, his justification makes clear his conception of modern government and his conviction that what the Fanti were doing amounted to the incorporation of a new order in governance.

> It is on this ground that there is now a loud cry for a *codex constitutionuum* for the Confederation from the Government of the Coast. It is essential so that every branch of the Government should have its power and limits well-defined [anticipations of separation of powers and limits on government by the rights of the people], protecting it against aggression, and "ascertaining the purposes for which the Government exists," and the rights which are guaranteed to it; securing its rights in the various provinces, and restraining it from exercising function which would endanger liberty and justice [obviously, a stated preference for liberty]. The present drooping state of the Confederation can say with great truth, *novus rerum nascitur ordo*—a new order of things is generated.[52]

Horton had a positive view of the new political order in which there was separation of powers, limits on the reach of the government, and protection of the liberty of citizens. He clearly wanted the new order to be embraced in some fashion. The idea that the Fanti confederates were harbingers of a new order, a new way of being human motivated much of the writings of the nineteenth-century apostles. In this, they were quintessentially modern. A good part of their claim to novelty is to be found in the idea of the self that they not only embraced but also embodied.

Rev. S. R. B. Attoh-Ahuma

Another of the apostles was very clear about what the idea of the modern self entailed. I refer to Rev. S. R. B. Attoh-Ahuma. I conclude this discussion with a brief look at some of his reflections. Attoh-Ahuma's book *The Gold Coast Nation and National Consciousness* is a collection of columns he wrote for the *Gold Coast Leader*. I was intrigued by the author's foreword to the collection, part of which I quote:

> The Author indulges the hope that the principles therein set forth, and the sentiments to which he gives so inadequate an expression, may *influence* for good, not his

contemporaries only, but also—and especially—the members of the rising generation, whose birthright, privilege, duty, destiny and honour it is to usher in an era of Backward Movement, which to all cultured West Africans is synonymous with the highest conception of progress and advancement. Intelligent Retrogression is the only Progression that will save our beloved country. This may sound a perfect paradox, but it is nevertheless, the truth; and if all educated West Africans could be forced by moral suasion and personal conviction to realize that "Back to the Land" signifies a step forward, that "Back to the Simple Life" of our progenitors expresses a burning wish to advance, that the desire to rid ourselves of foreign accretions and excrescences is an indispensable condition of National Resurrection and National Prosperity, we should feel ourselves amply rewarded.[53]

What sense is one to make of this strange foreword and its core phrases—"Backward Movement," "Intelligent Retrogression"—which, on the face of it, suggest the opposite of progress? It is even stranger that those locutions describe the sine qua nons of progress. It is easy to read into the foreword the ruminations, perhaps even fears, of a wistful conservative in the grip of nostalgia for a lost world. Yet when one reads the essays that make up the collection, one finds that the author's deployment of what he called "a perfect paradox" is not meant to be taken at face value. Much of his conservatism was directed at his bid to prove that the peoples of the Gold Coast, regardless of their ethnic affiliations, did constitute a nation and deserved to be accorded all the dignity and respect due such entities, especially in the context of nineteenth-century debates about nationalism.[54] We should not discount the importance of the changed context in which Attoh-Ahuma was writing. He wrote after the rejection of educated natives by their white tutors. The mid-century optimism about and enthusiasm for the partnership with the British had given way to skepticism, even hostility toward British suzerainty. Needless to say, he was reacting to doubts about and often outright denials of African capability by the newly dominant administrator class in the colonial territories.

But Ahuma was also concerned to combat the excesses of those who thought that their salvation lay in absolute mimicry of European ways. In his view, the options for Africans were not limited to total opposition to or mimicry of the European ways of being human. What he advocated was the creative appropriation of indigenous culture and its use as the pivot of the construction of modern societies that would borrow whatever was useful from its European-inspired legacy.[55] The man who seemed to be looking backward wrote on progress and the importance of the individual in language that conceded nothing to modern conceptions of both terms. Quite the contrary, he called on youth to make self-improvement their vocation, patriotism their cause, and the advancement of Africa their mission. To do all these things he asked youth to take individualism seriously, pursue knowledge, and build the African nation.

In an essay titled, significantly, "I Am: I Can: An Appeal to the Rising Generation," Ahuma wrote: "The first essential prerequisite in the voyage of the discov-

ery of ourselves as a people is the consciousness of ourselves. 'I AM' is the keynote
to all the harmonies and concords of individual advancement and power. Not 'I
AM' simply as a psychological abstraction, but the realization of the living personality and all that it denotes and connotes. The first person singular of the verb To
Be is, after all, the most formidable word in the vocabulary of human thought and
progress."[56] He argued that the individual who affirms "I AM" is the bedrock of all
progress and development.

> "I AM" and to know it, is the head and fount of all true and genuine success in life. It
> is the fount from which bubble those graces and virtues which minister to the growth
> of a nation's vitality and productivity. The horse, the elephant, and the greyhound
> cannot testify to such consciousness; science may, in its ultimate deductions, credit
> them with the possession of intuitive faculties marvellously akin to the perfection of
> instincts on the borderland of human psychology, but the creatures can never know
> that they know. To save the country, to develop its resources, to maintain its rights and
> privileges, and to advance its interests in all directions without bungling and blunder-
> ing and against fearful odds, our young men must "see visions" and "multiply visions";
> and this is impossible of accomplishment unless they *know themselves*.[57]

The charge to "know oneself" as the starting point for making an individual fit
for her duty to her community or humanity was a singsong in the nineteenth century. Some of its philosophical antecedents are traceable to the philosophy of self-
love and the theory of moral sentiments of the eighteenth century. Some of its most
famous proponents were Adam Smith, J. B. Hutcheson, Joseph Butler, David Hume,
and the poet Alexander Pope. Not unexpectedly, therefore, the essay contained references to Aristotle, Tennyson, Byron, Galileo, Bunyan, Sir Walter Raleigh, Bee-
thoven, and Thomas Edison. Ahuma wanted young people to cultivate their individuality, to steel themselves each in his own uniqueness for the task of serving
humanity. One plausible way of construing Ahuma's "perfect paradox," then, is to
see it as a charge to Africans not to take comfort in blind imitation but to appropriate the wisdom of others and that of their own ancestors through the arduous
task of making such wisdom their own. To do so they needed to acquire knowledge
of themselves, their heritage, other people's wisdom and follies, and so on. In other
words, they needed to make of themselves worthy residents of the society of knowledge. Horton, in a similar charge to youth said:

> [The Youth] should make it their ruling principle to concentrate their mental powers,
> their powers of observation, reasoning, and memory, on the primary objects of their
> engagement. "Never to observe without a thought; never reason to confident conclu-
> sions without a sufficiency of certainly verified facts; never to acquire facts without
> submitting them to the test of reasoning and, when occasion offers, to the test of ex-
> perience, as it has been conclusively remarked that observation without thought is a
> hasty observation, and the experience derived from it wasted; and if we reason without
> a sufficiency or verification of facts we shall reason into error; and if we remember

without comparison the result will be that we shall be a vast storehouse of inconsequential knowledge."[58]

The commitment to creating a society of knowledge in West Africa and deploying there the habits of science was a common thread running through the ideas of Crowther, Horton, and Ahuma. This thread was by no means restricted to them, but it set the stage for their incessant criticism of the new imperialism that later replaced the erstwhile colonialism that I have identified. Under the latter, the aid model was supreme, and its consequences were grim for the development of the society of knowledge that had been the rallying cry of our prophets.

We have evidence that Attoh-Ahuma was not only familiar with some of the thinkers he named in his essays, he appropriated, in a creative if unsystematic way, some of the ideas that we associate with some of the leading philosophers of the Enlightenment. Having cited Alexander Pope's declaration that "The proper study of mankind is man," Ahuma went on to expound upon Pope's idea: "The proper study of each man is himself—body, spirit, soul, the cultivation of self-knowledge first, self-reverence leading naturally and inevitably to self-control. The whole being must be *educated*—the power of mind and body guided by power of will—far and away more excellent than mere literary knowledge and worldly success—the divinity that is in man driven forth for man and country and God."[59] Ahuma challenged the individual who was called to know himself as a precondition for knowing other things to undertake this pursuit of knowledge both for its own sake and for the sake of the African nation.

Ahuma was exercised by the fate of the continent that he and others thought of as a nation. In so thinking they anticipated not only the Pan-African movement that was inaugurated by the Trinidadian Henry Sylvestre Williams in 1900 but also the idea of continental unity and the union government that Kwame Nkrumah would make famous in the 1950s and 1960s. Although I cannot make the case here, Ahuma's idea of nation is part of a nineteenth-century intellectual ferment that gave us the unification of Italy and the unification of Germany in spite of the presence of many traditions of particularism in their respective territories. Ahuma did not think that the presence of diverse traditions of particularism that prevailed in the coastal areas of Ghana precluded the inhabitants thereof from forming a nation.

In spite therefore of the dogmas and *ipse dixits* of those wiseacres who would fain deny to us, as a people, the inalienable heritage of nationality, we dare affirm, with sanctity of reason and with the emphasis of conviction, that—WE ARE A NATION. It may be "a miserable, mangled, tortured, twisted tertium quid," or to quote a higher authority, a Nation "scattered and peeled . . . a Nation meted out and trodden down," but still a Nation. If we were not, it was time to invent one; for any series of States in the same locality, however extensive, may at any time be merged into a nation. We have a nation, and what is more, we have a Past—"though ungraced in story." We own a Political Constitution, a concentric system of government, of one Race, born and bred upon our own soil. With the Akan language one can cover a seaboard 350 miles in extent, and an area of 105,000 square miles, more or less. The so-called languages may perhaps be simply regarded as so many dialects, often mere Provincialisms.[60]

He challenged his contemporaries to embrace this idea of nation and begin to develop the appropriate structures of consciousness that would enable them bring their nation to glory. He inveighed against "the residual anomaly of tribal exclusiveness [that] has the regrettable tendency of evolving unhappy antagonisms against those called of and qualified by God to harmonise the disorganised interests of our country. . . . We are in sore need as Africans of an expansive horizon, an outlook upon life and life's duties that is as broad as the heavens."[61] As was the case with Horton, Ahuma too believed that Africa had been hard done by by the ravages of slavery and the slave trade as well as other historical calamities. Hence he too referred to a time when "Europe looked to Africa for new ideas, for fresh inspirations, and the saying was perpetuated and handed down from generation to generation, *Semper aliquid novi ex Africa*—There is always something new from Africa."[62] The challenge before him and others as he saw it was as follows:

> The most difficult problem of our times is how to think so that Africa may regain her lost Paradise. How to think the thoughts that galvanize and electrify into life souls that are asleep unconscious of their destiny; How to think the thoughts that produce, multiply, divide and circulate for the general good—the thoughts that make crooked places straight, that pulverize gates of brass and cut in sunder all bars of iron—the power that gives friends and foes alike the treasuries of darkness and hidden riches of secret places—the Art that brings National Evangels, binding up broken and despairing hearts, proclaiming liberty and freedom to the captives, and the opening of the Prison to them that are bound or have bound themselves.[63]

It is for the advancement of this African nation, expansively conceived, that the pursuit of knowledge and the development of individuals are requisite. Whether in their agitation for self-government or the establishment of tertiary institutions, Ahuma and his contemporaries felt that Africa could not afford to waste any more time in the race for progress and enlightenment given that there were people like them who already were the harbingers of the brave new future that modernity represented. It is in looking at what the administrator thought of and did with this class of Africans that we can begin to see how badly administrator-inflected colonialism disserved Africa and its inhabitants.

Crowther, Horton, Ahuma, and several others were all part of a ferment in the nineteenth century made up of those who stood for the primacy of native agency, the capacity of Africans for self-government, and the recognition by the rest of humanity of the resurgence of Africa in the aftermath of the debacle of the slave trade and slavery, all within the boundaries of a deep faith in the promise of modernity, especially regarding liberty, equality, and fraternity.[64] If in reading this essay others are challenged to begin to delve into their legacy and situate them properly as precursors for African intellectual discourse at the present time, its modest aim will have been more than achieved. In the next chapter, I shall be considering the philosophical reflections of the arch-philosopher of British colonialism in Africa, and we shall see how his racist predilections aborted the promise of modernity that the thinkers discussed in this chapter insisted should be redeemed for Africans. Indeed, such redemption they took to be the only possible justification for what to them was an interim period of governance without consent.

_4_

Reading the Colonizer's Mind
Lord Lugard and the Philosophical Foundations of British Colonialism

Of the two components of the colonial whole, the colonized and the colonizer, much attention has been directed at the situation of the colonized. Few attempts have been made to go behind the mind of the colonizer. Of course, I am aware of historical studies, biographies, and such like that do. However, the pickings are very slim when it comes to examinations of the ideas that inform colonial practice.[1] It is time to take seriously the other component of the colonial totality: the colonizer. After all, as both Frantz Fanon and Albert Memmi so eloquently tell us in their works, there would have been no colonized had there been no colonizer. This acclaimed symbiosis between the colonizer and the colonized underscores the inadequacy of not taking seriously the need to unearth the motivations behind the colonizer's activity.

The colonizer is itself a whole with several determinations. Albert Memmi identifies three such determinations: "a colonial, a colonizer and the colonialist."[2] Fanon, too, never failed to point out the many demographic and other groupings in the ranks of the colonizer. For our purposes, though, I focus on other possible determinations of the colonizer whole as identified in chapter 2: missionaries, administrators, and traders. The man whose views are analyzed in this chapter belongs to the second category. The character of colonialism and its principal lineaments were fashioned by administrators, and this is why it is important for us to make sense of their views and, where available, their justifications for them. Additionally, acquainting ourselves with those views might enable us to make better sense of the policy options discernible in the practice of colonialism. It is an unargued assumption of this chapter that those views had such consequences. However odious the views held by the colonizers, however much they discomfit us, we ignore them only at our own peril insofar as they had consequences for colonial practice.

We saw in chapter 2 that the early missionaries did quite well in implementing various items on their program of civilization. Unfortunately, their administrator and trader successors never implemented this program on any scale. One may cite

the dynamics of the evangelizing missions themselves and their relative penurious-
ness to explain the absence of implementation on a grand scale, but one must consider the machinations of the other constituents of the colonizer component of the
colonial totality: traders and administrators. Traders wanted new markets and new
sources for raw materials, and in their search for both aided the missionaries for a
time in the latter's quest for native souls. They let missionaries travel on their ships,
and from time to time they shared stations and victuals with itinerant preachers.
But this class of colonizers is not the focus of my interest here, for missionaries and
traders both ultimately yielded to the last arrivals to the colonies: administrators.
The rest of this chapter is devoted to the examination of the philosophical assumptions that informed the practice of the administrators. Let us sum up the discussion
so far.

Strange as it may seem, in Britain's African colonies, the missionaries were the
progressives, and the administrators—soldiers, residents, hired guns—were the reactionaries. The missionaries were not only the ones who felt it their duty to bring
the native to civilization, they were also the ones who were willing to put in place
some of the most important institutions for filtrating modernity into the colonies.
So it is easy to see why they were the ones who insisted that the Africans had to
abandon their old ways in their entirety and embrace the new ways. I should not be
misunderstood; I know that this approach was fraught with danger for the Africans'
engagement with modernity. Yet I also must insist that the revolutionary nature of
the missionary enterprise stands out in sharp contrast to the reactionary conservative nature of the administrators' enterprise. I can cite several indices. Christianity[3]
recruited from the outcasts, the marginal elements; the administrators' favored recruits were mostly of chiefly provenance.[4] Christianity wanted to wipe the slate
clean, to implant new forms of social living, new ways of being human, new ways of
seeing the world and of naming it; administrators inaugurated sociocryonics with
its attendant consequence of preserving or shaping existing institutions, regardless
of their state of health or relevance, to serve their limited needs for low-cost empire-
building. Christianity had an expansive view of its mission—the implantation of
civilization; administrators had a narrow view of their mission—to do whatever
would redound to the glory of the motherland and the profit margins of those who
funded their activities. Most important of all, missionaries were willing to commit
the resources required; administrators were content with doing the minimum.[5] If my
thesis is plausible, then there is some warrant for investigating the enabling views of
the administrators.

In the rest of this chapter, I examine one such set of enabling views held by a
man whose career as an imperialist and colonizer few could match—Frederick Deal-
try Lugard, later Lord Lugard. He worked in India, East Africa, and West Africa.
It was in West Africa that he became the principal philosopher of empire. His philosophy was distilled from his practical engagement with the exigencies of empire-

building, first as a hired gun deployed by commercial interests to stymie the east-
ward advance of the French in West Africa at the end of the nineteenth century
and later as the administrator who amalgamated the components of what is now
Nigeria through becoming a peer and elder statesman of empire until his death in
1945. His service alone qualifies him for scholarly interest, but his attempt to provide some philosophical justification for colonization and his authorship of the theoretical guidebook for the practice of colonial administration are what qualify him for
philosophical treatment.

I propose to analyze critically his two major theoretical works. The first is *Political Memoranda*, which has been described by one of the principal administrators
whose own practice was built on the book:

> Granted the inherent difficulty in separating the influence of the model [of indirect
> rule] outside Nigeria from the book which embodied the whole system down to details
> of routing, the importance of *Political Memoranda* lies not in their use as a blueprint of
> British colonial policy but in a considerable measure as a highly rewarding illustration
> of Lugard's own perfectionist view of Nigerian administration in practice. To this ex-
> tent alone, granted Lugard's respected place among the proconsuls of empire, *Political
> Memoranda* may be consulted as an index to colonial thinking.[6]

The second work is *The Dual Mandate in British Tropical Africa*, which was published in 1922. In it, Lugard describes his object thus:

> The object which I have had in view in setting down these notes on administration
> in British tropical Africa is twofold. In the first place, I have hoped to put before those
> who are interested in the development of that part of the British Empire beyond the
> seas for which Great Britain is directly responsible, an outline of the system under
> which those responsibilities have originated and are being discharged, and some idea
> of the nature of the problems confronting the local administrator. In the second place,
> in discussing these problems I have ventured to make some few suggestions, as the re-
> sult of experience, in the hope that they may be found worthy of consideration by the
> "men on the spot"—in so far as the varying circumstances of our Crown colonies and
> protectorates may render them in any degree applicable.[7]

It is easy to construe the first text solely as a handbook of administration, and
it is often so construed. But interspersed with the book's plethora of administrative
and policy guidelines are numerous and wide-ranging summations of principles behind and justifications for specific administrative choices and the reasons why alternative paths were shunned. It is possible to tease out of these reflections and guidelines some of the philosophical views that provided the background and justifications
for colonial practice. In the case of the second text, the author set out to provide a
philosophical justification for British colonialism. The title itself is a shorthand description of what he took to be the charge that the British had in colonizing Africa.
The "dual mandate" refers to the responsibility that it had pleased God and history

to bequeath to Great Britain, to make available to Europeans and the rest of humanity the riches and resources of Africa, which "lay wasted and ungarnered . . . because the natives did not know their use and value. Millions of tons of oil-nuts, for instance, grew wild without the labour of man, and lay rotting in the forests. Who can deny the right of the hungry people of Europe to utilise the wasted bounties of nature, or that the task of developing these resources was, as Mr. Chamberlain expressed it, a 'trust for civilisation' and for the benefit of mankind?"[8] There are few clearer statements of colonization$_2$. On the other hand, Great Britain needed to bring the light of civilization to the blighted heathenish peoples of the "Dark Continent": "As Roman imperialism laid the foundations of modern civilisation, and led the wild barbarians of these islands [Britain, that is] along the path of progress, so in Africa to-day we are repaying the debt, and bringing to the dark places of the earth, the abode of barbarism and cruelty, the torch of culture and progress, while ministering to the material needs of our own civilisation."[9] Apparently this idea was not original. The epigraphs in the frontispiece of the book are: "'It will be the high task of all My governments to superintend and assist the development of these countries . . . for the benefit of the inhabitants and the general welfare of mankind.' [HIS MAJESTY THE KING.]" "'The wellbeing and development of peoples not yet able to stand by themselves, form a sacred Trust of Civilisation.' [*Covenant of League, Art. 22*]" "'We develop new territory as Trustees for Civilisation, for the Commerce of the World.' [JOSEPH CHAMBERLAIN]" What Lugard did in the text was present a case for these sentiments and write a full-blown justification of colonialism as he had worked it out from what seemed to be a ferment of opinion in the late nineteenth and early twentieth centuries.

My task in this chapter is to present in as coherent and integrated manner as I can the philosophy of colonialism that inheres in these texts, but before I do, it is important to lay out in some detail the circumstances of Lugard's departure for Africa, what sorts of views he had about Africans when he arrived, and how those views were altered or reinforced by his experiences in Africa and of Africans. I consider these earlier views important because I argue that the policy options that he adopted and the practice of colonialism that he embraced were influenced by them, if not directly determined by them. That is, the administrative structures that were deemed suitable for the natives in Africa (outside the constraints of limited resources) and the types of institutional practices that were considered appropriate to impose on the natives were profoundly affected by Lugard and his cohorts' ontological commitments and philosophical predilections. This is one situation where it truly can be said that ideas have consequences. In the conclusion of the chapter, I submit that an exploration of the formative views of the colonizers is apt to shed some light on why some of the institutions that are the legacy of colonialism do not behave the way we expect them to based on our view of their operations in the lands from which we copied them.

Bound for Africa: Formative Views

Lugard's initial departure for Africa took place in inauspicious circumstances. He had been extremely ill, so, as he put it, "finding myself unfit to discharge purely routine duties satisfactorily, I applied to be placed on temporary half-pay, and this course was permitted to me on the recommendation of a medical board. The question then was, what should I do? What I felt I needed was active hard work—rather than rest—-in order to recover from the strain."[10] What hard work did he find? He went in search of adventure: "So with fifty sovereigns in my belt, and with practically no outfit at all except my favourite little .450 rifle,—which had done me service already in many countries, for some years,—I got on board the first passing ship, as a second-class passenger, and sailed I knew not whither."[11] Although it was true that he knew not whither he sailed, there was little doubt that he wanted to see action and, to this end, was on offer as a hired gun. The ship he boarded sailed for Naples, which suited him well. He wanted to join the Italians for military service, but the Italians refused to give him a commission. He had a fallback position: "My hope was, that I might embark in some useful undertaking in Africa, if possible in connection with the suppression of the slave trade."[12] So Lugard the hired gun was available for service to the Italians, who were engaged in an imperialist dance of death with Emperor Menelik of Ethiopia at about this time, culminating in their defeat at Adowa in 1896. Failing that, he was available to anyone who would use his service to suppress the slave trade. This seeming ambivalence between wanting to push back the imperial frontiers, British or Italian, and at the same time feeling morally indignant at the traffic in human beings was to characterize Lugard's entire career in Africa. For this reason, it is important to not fall into the trap of dismissing him all too easily as an arch-imperialist scoundrel. I have no doubt that he meant his protestations of interest in and desire to rescue the African from the infamy of slavery, but this desire was based on an evolutionistic characterization of the African as belonging to the infancy of the human race. He brought this characterization with him to the continent, and it remained largely unchanged through his many tours of duty in Africa, the only exception being his selection of the Fulani in northern Nigeria as belonging at least to the pubescence of the human race. What were the elements of this characterization of the African that provided him with an ontological template from which the architectonic of colonialism was constructed?

Lugard can speak for himself. After his arrival on the East African coast in the first quarter of 1888, he sailed south to Zanzibar and later to Mozambique. He was on his way to the interior in the area of present-day Malawi in order thereby to cut at its root the Arab-run slave trade on the East African littoral. "On board the *Dunkeld* I met for the first time a South African 'gold prospector.' . . . He told me success in African travel depended entirely on prompt and resolute action. He begged me to remember his words—'On the first signs of insolence,' he said, 'or even of familiarity, kick them under the jaw (when sitting) or in the stomach. In worse cases shoot, and shoot straight, *at once*. Your life in Africa depends on such prompt measures!'"[13] Lugard did not need to be taught this lesson again, for his views about the relative ranks and merits of natives and of Europeans, especially of the British variety, were already well formed before he went to Africa. In the same book, he retold with relish the story of an earlier incident, the elements of which show that what the South African prospector told him could only have reinforced, not shaped his own views.

> Before leaving Mozambique an unfortunate incident occurred. An Indian Moham-medan trader had brought some goods on board for shipment. The officer of the ves-sel had been working for many hours in the heat transferring cargo, and had sat down for a few minutes to rest. The trader demanded in an insolent manner that he should immediately rise and attend to him. He declined and the native then made some gross remarks in Hindustani, which I understood, but the officer did not. Extremely indig-nant at such an affront, I asked him if he could tamely submit to be thus insulted by a native? He replied that if he resented it, he would be "run in" and would lose his ship; that the Portuguese authorities encouraged such action, and were absolutely sure to take the part of the native against an Englishman, and the British India Company would hear no excuses. I, however, had no ship to lose, and I cared not for the Portu-guese authorities. I therefore told the Buniah, in Hindustani, that had he used one-half the insolence to me that I had heard him use towards the ship's officer, he would have had cause to regret it. Thereupon he included me. Not liking to strike a native with my fist, I gave him a heavy box on the ear. He seemed inclined to show fight, for he was a strong-built man, but received another similar cuff, which effectually silenced him, but unfortunately broke a bone in my hand, spraining also my thumb and wrist against his cast-iron head.[14]

Let us examine this passage for some of the pointers to Lugard's view of what na-tives are. First, what gave offense was that this native had been insolent to a white man. In the second place, when he, the native, had the good fortune of being shown the error of his ways by a more cultured European, he did not have the good sense to step back and apologize; quite the contrary. Fortunately for the native and for his education in civilization, a good teacher and an adult was present who would not flinch from cracking the whip to teach him how to behave properly. But behaving "properly" was not a matter of not being rude to anybody or treating everyone with respect. Rather, it was one of knowing one's place and its duties. In this instance, it was out of place for a native to speak insolently to his superior, the white man. This idea that the peoples of the world were organized in a hierarchy that the white man sits atop is the lynchpin of the world view with which Lugard arrived on native shores. The South African's admonition was a mere reminder, not a fresh disclosure, of how the African was viewed from the perspective of a late-nineteenth-century white man. For Lugard, as for his contemporaries, the African belonged (if he be-longed to the race at all) to the infancy of the human race. Worse still, he was a savage, an animal who was able to mimic humans. Throughout his career, Lugard never abandoned this view of the African.

He was equally unwavering in his detestation of the traffic in human slaves. Si-multaneously, however, he cautioned against undue haste in emancipating African slaves because, according to him, it might do more harm than good. He excoriated his fellow Europeans for their hypocrisy in condemning the Arab slave trader when they themselves had engaged in similar activities for so long. He argued that they had "a duty of expiation to perform towards the African."[15] Yet this belief did not stop him from issuing the following caution:

> In our efforts to perform this duty, we must recollect how the African has been wedded to slavery through centuries on centuries, so that it has become the product, as it were, of the blood-stained soil of the land. . . . The nature of the African, moreover, is not of that stamp which chafes at the yoke, like the nations of Teutonic blood. Let us ac-cept all this, and clear the ground of all high-coloured nonsense—of "kingly hearts" beating in the bosoms of slaves, and so forth; and taking the African as he is—as cen-turies of wrongs have made him—apply ourselves to raise him to a higher level.[16]

The theme of the African's natural suitability for bondage, for being ruled, con-tinued to dominate Lugard's thought until the end of his life. Witness the following entry of September 10, 1888, in which Lugard quoted himself from his own diary:

> These savages do not think or act as we do. They are, in truth, like "dumb driven cattle." With the slave caravan they suffer uncomplainingly starvation, the scourge, and all the painted horrors of so many writers. They meet a European *safari*, and they hide in the jungle and rejoin the Slavers. Like cattle, they will face any misery but dread the unknown. They are brought on by us—fed, clothed, and spoken kindly to; they bolt. Why? . . . I think, however, it is merely the dumb brute's instinct to wander which makes them go. The long, hot, dusty march, &c., is a bore. They wander off as cattle do, regardless of stall and food, of danger from lions, of danger of a cruel master, in-stead of a kind one. The very immediate present is the only thought, and sooner than march tomorrow to the unknown, they slip off to-day, and follow the caged bird's in-stinct, and, like it, they perish in their ill-advised liberty; but, who blames the fool-ish bird?
>
> I have copied the passage *verbatim*, though it is somewhat lengthy, and perhaps those who read it will begin to understand that the African must be treated differ-ently from the European with centuries of culture to his making, and that coercion is sometimes necessary for their own good.[17]

In addition to the repeated characterization of the African as a savage who was closer to the lower animals than the higher races, he continually regarded and de-scribed Africans as belonging to the infancy of the human race. To Lugard, they exhibited a childlike nature characterized by innocence, a lack of appreciation of danger, a basic lack of understanding of and concern for the future, and a penchant for leading a carefree existence marked by sexual abandon and unbounded happiness.

> The happiness of these people is quite phenomenal. Nothing seems to distress them for long, and ties of love and affection sit lightly upon them. Their intellects are not strong enough to enable them to suffer acutely from *anticipation* of evil, nor to *realise* danger till it is actually before them. Hence they live a careless, happy life, laughing incessantly all day, dancing all night; supremely happy, if meat is abundant; able to endure hunger like the beasts of the field, if food is not to be got; plucky, because believing themselves invulnerable by reason of their *dawa*; undisturbed by hopes and fears of a hereafter; rarely subject to those ills that flesh is heir to—headaches, toothaches, and their kindred woes—by reason of their strong animal physique. Such are the Manganja, and with some minor alterations in detail, such is the typical savage of Africa.[18]

Elsewhere, he stated:

> The African holds the position of a late-born child in the family of nations, and must as yet be schooled in the discipline of the nursery. He is neither the intelligent ideal crying out for instruction, and capable of appreciating the subtle beauties of Christian forbearance and self-sacrifice, which some well-meaning missionary literature would lead us to suppose; nor yet, on the other hand, is he universally a rampant cannibal, predestined by Providence to the yoke of the slave, and fitted for nothing better, as I have elsewhere seen him depicted. I hold rather with Longfellow's beautiful lines—

> > "In all ages
> > Every human heart is human;
> > That in even savage bosoms
> > There are longings, yearnings, strivings
> > For the good they comprehend not.
> > That the feeble hands and helpless,
> > Groping blindly in the darkness,
> > Touch God's right hand in that darkness."

> That is to say, that there is in him, like the rest of us, both good and bad, and that the innate good is capable of being developed by culture.[19]

Once again, we confront the insistence that while the African might be way down on the human ladder, she is not completely off it. On the road to becoming more human, what she needs is guidance and tutelage by advanced humanity, of which the British were the most advanced. Several implications can be drawn from this premise. In the first place, the metaphor of the child and the requirement of "the discipline of the nursery" were aptly chosen. In exactly the same way that it would be irresponsible for parents to let their children grow any way they wish, it would be irresponsible of civilized races not to take the African in tow and lead him carefully and firmly to civilization (through all the social equivalent stages of pubescence, adolescence, to adulthood). Additionally, the discipline of the nursery sometimes requires its enforcer to be rough with his ward. Third, we do not ordinarily put before children complex social rules or expect them in infancy to comprehend the principles that enable and justify those rules. We do not hold children responsible for many of their actions, and we therefore exclude them from much of responsibility discourse.

> For the rest, if we are in earnest in our efforts to benefit the slaves, we must be content to accept, as a part of the task, the natural apathy of the people, and their indifference to a yoke, which to us would be terribly galling. We must realise that the ties between husband and wife are often of the loosest kind; that a greater affection is said to exist between man and man than between the sexes (as is often seen among the lower animals); that mothers, and more especially fathers, do not feel so intense a love for their children as Europeans generally do, and hence ruthless separation from relatives or family, though it may involve some grief, cannot be said to be so terrible an ordeal as we should imagine by analogy with our own feelings; that when once these ties are ruptured, and the slave transported miles from his own home, he has no resource in himself, no object in the recovery of his freedom and thus his master's house is his sole refuge. His apathetic and submissive nature adapts itself to his surroundings, and he often ceases to desire to be free.[20]

If indeed Africans were the children of the human race, they could not be held accountable in the same way that adults are accountable, and it would be a mistake to try to put before them in their childhood the "subtle beauties of Christian forbearance and self-sacrifice." After all, in good Christian ethics, it is unbecoming to cast pearls before swine! This attitude, which cautioned against putting the pearls of civilization before the unschooled African swine, dictated Lugard's opposition to the activities of many Christian missionaries in the nineteenth century, activities that to him were instances of inappropriate pearl-casting. That is to say that in Lugard's estimation, much of what I celebrated in the last two chapters as evidence of the African's capacity to learn to be modern and of her missionary teacher's effort to improve her agency were misbegotten both in conception and execution. Indeed, he never accepted that the products of missionary education were anything but double bastards, both in their own indigenous heritage and in the European inheritance that many of them so enthusiastically embraced and sought to domesticate.

Lugard's complaints about the missionaries were not groundless. In the early to mid-nineteenth century, many missionaries not only thought that Africans were capable of doing exactly what Lugard held they could not do—that is, "appreciate the subtle beauties of Christian forbearance and self-sacrifice"—but also went ahead to create ministries with Africans playing principal roles. They held that if the progress of evangelization was to accelerate, Africans had to be sought and trained to perform the task. Most controversially, perhaps, they held that Africans were ready for the fruits of modern civilization and its attendant opportunities. Lugard would have none of it. He did share the missionaries' belief that the African was part of the human family, but he did not share their view that the African had marched in tandem with the rest of humanity and might therefore be in a position to appropriate quickly the fruits of civilization.

> One word as regards missionaries themselves. The essential point in dealing with Africans is to establish a respect for the European. Upon this—the prestige of the white man—depends his influence, often his very existence, in Africa. . . . In my opinion—at any rate with reference to Africa—it is the greatest possible mistake to suppose that a European can acquire a greater influence by adopting the mode of life of the natives. In effect, it is to lower himself to their plane, instead of elevating them to his. The sacrifice involved is wholly unappreciated, and the motive would be held by the savage to be poverty and lack of social status in his own country. The whole influence of the European in Africa is gained by this assertion of a superiority which commands the respect and excites the emulation of the savage. To forego this vantage-ground is to lose influence for good. I may add, that the loss of prestige consequent on what I should term the humiliation of the European affects not merely the missionary himself, but is subversive of all efforts for secular administration, and may even invite insult, which may lead to disaster and bloodshed.[21]

What I have done in the preceding section is present Lugard in his own words from the time of his first landing in Africa. His views did not change much, if at all, throughout his tenure in Africa till his death in 1945. When he arrived in Africa, Lugard was a bearer of the following interrelated views:

(1) The human race is organized into a hierarchy of races. Each race had its own genius and a nature appertaining to it. But these geniuses were not coordinate. On the contrary, the hierarchy of human groups mimicked an evolutionary ladder in which some races were at the top and others were at the bottom, with any number of others on the intervening rungs. Whatever Lugard's views about other races, one thing is clear from the passages previously cited: For him, the European was at the top of the hierarchy and the African was at the bottom. But because this is an evolutionary structure, the European exhibited what was best about what humanity could become and had become up till that time. Simultaneously, to the extent that the European represented the measure of the best possible, he was also a lawgiver to mankind beneath him. The more removed from the European and the more unlike him you were, the closer you were to animals and the less human you were. But there was hope: You could become more like the European if you had the good fortune of being colonized or imperialized by him and you learned your lessons well on how to be human. If, on the other hand, you had the misfortune of being imperialized by a slightly less inferior race—for example, the Arab—it would take you longer to cover that distance between your animal-like existence and the God-like existence of the European.

(2) The African world was not a human world. It was a world peopled by "primitive savages" who, though they had human hearts beating in them, would require wholesale makeovers before they could be seated as full members of the comity of humans. By the same token, the European who found himself charged with the onerous but honorable responsibility of rescuing the African from the thrall of savagery had to watch out for any signs in him or his cohort of slipping back into the infancy of the race, resist any atavistic tendencies, separate himself mentally and physically from the natives, and at the same time execute his responsibility. The African world had to be made livable for the European—humanized, as it were—and those areas that were made livable needed to have a cordon sanitaire erected around them to make sure that they were not infested, polluted, or otherwise muddied by the disease-carrying primitive savage. This idea of the animal and natural character of the African world would later have grievous but widespread implications for colonial policies about the spatial organization of the colonies and protectorates.

(3) As a result of the first and second views, the relation of the European and the African in the colonial world could not be direct or immediate; it was always to be indirect and mediate. For example, given the first view, the African first had to move away from the depredations of his animal nature before he could be suited to appreciate the "subtle beauties of Christian forbearance and self-sacrifice." As nonselves, Africans had to become selves before they could become Christians. As children, they had to grow and mature before they could be admitted as members of the adult community. Given the second view, it would be foolish to install the principles of liberty, equality, and fraternity in a world populated by savages. Thus, the only logical procedure was to hold off on the introduction of these principles until one was sure the savage is humanized and could therefore make sense of them. This combination of philosophical anthropology and social ontology had serious consequences for the evolution of colonial structures and ideologies.

In light of the preceding philosophical predilections, we should be less surprised that Lugard authored the kinds of policies that are to be found in the *Political Memoranda* or that he chose the options that he did in the African colonies where he worked. In the next section, I present and examine the policy options that Lugard chose and the types of administrative mechanisms that he deemed suitable for the Africans in his charge. Of course, I take care to show that, contrary to the apologias of his biographer, Margery Perham, or of Anthony Kirk-Greene, one of the men who operated the system that he set up and shared his mindset about the African, alternate paths in the colonies could have been chosen but were not. What were the policy options that were chosen in the colony? It is time to introduce the *Political Memoranda*.

Racism as Administration: *Political Memoranda*

The subtitle of *Political Memoranda* is *Revision of Instructions to Political Officers on Subjects Chiefly Political & Administrative*. As a handbook, it has little interest for those of us who are not administrators, but because the instructions come with explanations of and justifications for particular policy choices as well as several observations and ruminations on the nature of the African native, indigenous institutions, and so forth, we may use the book as Kirk-Greene has suggested—"an index to colonial thinking." The book has thirteen memoranda: "(1) Duties of Political Officers and Miscellaneous Subjects; (2) Books, Returns and Office Records; (3) Judicial and Legal; (4) Education; (5) Taxation; (6) Slavery—Forced Labour, etc.; (7) The Use of Armed Force; (8) Native Courts; (9) Native Administration; (10) Lands; (11) Townships; (12) Goods and Vessels in Transit; (13) Forestry."[22] To consider each of these topics in their several subsections would be impractical, so instead I have chosen the ones that, in my estimation, illustrate the general frame in which colonial policies were formulated or reflect the combination of philosophical anthropology and social ontology I have identified as the template from which the architecture of the colony was constructed—in particular, memoranda 1, 3, 4, 8, and 9.

The first memorandum contains a restatement of the aim of British colonialism as it pertained to the natives. According to Lugard, political officers—residents and district officers and their subordinates, administrative officers—were the executors of the aim and objectives of British colonialism, stated as follows: "3. The British role here is to bring to the country all the gains of civilization by applied science (whether in the development of material resources, or the eradication of disease, &c.), *with as little interference as possible with Native customs and modes of thought*."[23] The italicized portion points up the ambivalence that I already identified in Lugard's attitude toward Africans. How, on one hand, is the country to get "all the gains of civilisation by applied science" and, on the other, escape with as little interference as possible with native customs and modes of thought? This recommendation is more curious still when it is recalled that Lugard regarded Africans and their native customs and modes of thought as being out of the loop of civilization; he called them savages. I submit that in light of the philosophical anthropology and social ontology that governed his views, one-half of these twin objectives could not have been seriously meant. That is, the resolution of the apparent paradox was to ignore the injunction to bring all the gains of civilization to the natives and thus to leave them little improved. The sociocryonic moment trumped that of progress. The justification for this choice is easy to find.

Recall that (in Lugard's ontology) primitive savages populated the colony. Among them, however, some had climbed higher than others on the evolutionary ladder.

Hence, Lugard identified "advanced tribes" and "backward tribes" in the colony.[24] This is yet another instance in which African individuality is privileged over the individuality of Africans, of typification over the multiple representations of what it is to be African. Advanced tribes were those that had hierarchies, atop which sat chiefs or similar functionaries. Backward tribes lacked this simple marker. "Applied science" was to be done in accordance with the relative standing of the tribes concerned in the hierarchy of races, a standing that was itself determined by how well or ill the social organization of the tribe mirrored the example of the advanced British. So groups that had chieftaincy systems were judged "advanced" and those that did not were judged "backward."

Even among those judged "advanced," the closer their institutions and practices were to those of the British, the more approval Lugard extended to them—hence, his almost irrational identification of the Fulani as the most gifted rulers among the peoples of Nigeria and his consideration of the Yorùbá as not as good. Given this schema it should not be surprising that Lugard worked hard to extend the administrative reach of native Fulani authorities to areas of Northern Nigeria that had successfully resisted the Fulani encroachment on their territories. Where there were no chiefs, the political officer was literally invited to invent them. "If there is no Chief who exercises authority beyond his own village, [the political officer] will encourage any village Chief of influence and character to control a group of villages, with a view to making him Chief of a district later if he shows ability for the charge."[25] This was being done in Nigeria, a place where at the time there were large pockets of modern-inflected lifestyles and communities. What if there were individuals or groups within the relevant area who did not care to live under the rule of chiefs or who had been exposed—however that came about—to other forms of rule that gave them more say in the administration of their community's affairs or their own lives and wanted those? In the specific situation of Northern Nigeria, many communities had become Christian and/or had within them heterogeneous populations and heterodox beliefs. But it was not only with reference to native administration that the preference for "as little interference as possible with Native Customs and modes of thought" trumped the requirement "to bring to the country all the gains of civilization." I would like to suggest that this was so in all the areas of activity in the colony and protectorates of Nigeria.

For example, like Memo 1, Memo 9, "Native Administration," was virtually a blueprint for restoring the Fulani aristocracy in Northern Nigeria after the British had militarily vanquished them. "The cardinal principle upon which the Administration of Northern Nigeria was based was what has been commonly called 'Indirect Rule.' viz., rule through the Native chiefs, who are regarded as an integral part of the machinery of Government, with well defined powers and functions recognised by Government and by law, and not dependent on the caprice of an Executive Officer."[26] The policy of indirect rule is usually celebrated as evidence of Lugard's genius. For many, the preservation of indigenous modes of governance was symptomatic of Lugard's appreciation of native administrative and political development. For others, the savings to the British colonial treasury that accrued from not having to employ regular and modern trained civil servants meant that the colonial adventure could proceed on the cheap. I take a different view of the practice. Contrary to received wisdom, especially among African scholars, I argue that the reason that the option of using modern trained civil servants was foreclosed was that the natives— savages that they were—were not deserving of such benefits of applied science and in any case were not ready for institutions of governance founded on the principles of accountability, meritocracy, and strict adherence to rules and procedures.[27] Only a government founded on the latter principles could have brought the gains of civilization to the country. That was what, in part, the installation of modernity was in Europe and, incidentally, in India under British colonialism. Lugard stated the policy as follows:

> The *de facto* rulers who after the British conquest of Northern Nigerian had been reinstated or appointed to the various Emirates, and all other *de facto* Chiefs who had been recognised by Government, were to be supported in every way and their authority upheld. Already in Memo. 1 it had been laid down that it was the duty of a Resident to rule through the Chiefs, to endeavour to educate them in the duties of rulers, to seek their co-operation and to maintain their prestige.
>
> It was laid down, however, that no independent or revolted Pagan tribes were to be included in the jurisdiction of a Moslem ruler without the express sanction of the Governor.
>
> The Native Chiefs thus recognised were not to be regarded as independent rulers. They were the delegates of the Governor whose representative was the Resident. The Central Government reserved to itself the sole right to raise and control armed forces, to impose taxation of any kind, to make laws and to dispose of such lands as are, under Native law and custom, vested in the paramount power. These limitations were specifically set out in the letter of appointment under which each Chief of the higher grades held his office.[28]

It is only on a generous interpretation of these directives that one can hold that Lugard was preserving native institutions. In the first place, it should be obvious that the rulers who were kept in place were not kept in place on terms that reflected their preeminence in the preconquest days. The basis of legitimacy had been profoundly altered. No matter what survived in ritual and ceremony of their previous basis of legitimacy, the fact that what made them rulers in the new dispensation was a piece of paper—the "letter of appointment"—meant that it was more important for them to be in the governor's favor even as they fell or remained out of their people's favor. They had become "civil servants" of sorts interposed between the British resident or political officer and the people over whom the latter ruled. That the native chiefs were not to be regarded as "independent rulers" and owed their appointment to the administrative fiat of the British governor or his representatives was made clear by the fact that the British issued "letters of appointment" that stated the terms of their appointment. One may therefore conclude that instead of seizing the opportunity of the defeat of the erstwhile absolute and paramount rulers to put in place new forms of administration based on modern principles, as had happened in Europe, Lugard chose to revivify modes of governance that were well on their way to withering.

Moreover, to have sought to create a modern bureaucracy peopled with beneficiaries of meritocracy, of careers open to talent, would have violated one of the cardinal principles of Lugard's philosophy: that the natives were not ready for the twentieth century and that a direct relationship with natives would have meant extending to them the benefits and courtesies of citizenship. Hence, the philosophical anthropology that dominated his view of the natives precluded the option of bringing to the latter all the benefits of civilization. This conclusion is supported by the following prescription: "Subject to these limitations it was the declared policy of the Government to restore to the Chiefs the prestige and authority which they had lost by the British conquest, or forfeited by their own previous mal-administration. I was not myself very hopeful of far-reaching reform among the men who had for a lifetime been used to other methods, and who would necessarily chafe under the restraints imposed by British rule and the curtailment of their despotic power."[29] And a consistent Lugard offered the following justifications for the policy: "The obvious folly of 'attempting any drastic reform which would cause a dislocation of methods which, however faulty, have the sanction of traditional usage, and are acquiesced in by the people, until we had an increased knowledge both of Moslem methods of rule and of Native law and custom.'"[30] As long as Lugard restricted his purview to Muslim Northern Nigeria and one went along with the suggestion that the society was characterized by the unanimity that made them be one with their rulers, there might not be any problem. One cannot say the same for the other areas of the country for which Lugard would later be responsible and to which he sought to extend the system.[31] At every point at which the imperative of bringing all the gains of civilization to the natives dictated severe reorganization of native life and practices, the weight of Lugard's evolutionary thinking led him in the opposite direction of preserving institutions and practices, some of which frankly were moribund. He chose sociocryonics instead.

Even more noteworthy was the record of decisive movements in the area of law away from substituting new forms of social ordering and away from implementing new institutions and practices that would have ensured for the natives all the gains of civilization. Doubtless one of the most significant gains heralded by modernity was the triumph of the rule of law. Under it, formal equality before the law was guaranteed, even if only in theory, to different classes whose relative social power may have varied widely. By the same token, given that the law is supposed to be no respecter of persons, those who laid down the law were not exempt from the strictures of the laws they made. Finally, modernity marked the triumph of process whereby rules and adherence to them are considered the ultimate hallmarks of a good municipal legal system. Ordinarily, one would have thought that the colonial authorities would have made haste to induct the people into the system of law that is usually considered one of the jewels in the crown of modernity.

But what did Lugard do? There were two types of courts in the colony: British courts and native courts. In the British courts, the governing laws were "the Common Law, and the doctrines of Equity (administered concurrently), and the Statutes of general application, which were in force in England on January 1st, 1900. This is modified by the proviso that British Courts shall in Civil causes affecting Natives (and even non-Natives in their contractual relations with Natives) recognise Native Law and Custom when not repugnant to natural justice and humanity or incompatible with any Ordinance, especially in matters relating to marriage, land and inheritance."[32] On the face of it, British principles of justice provided the benchmark for the administration of justice system in colonial Nigeria, and this benchmark at least in theory applied to the second category of courts—native courts. "The fundamental law in the Native Moslem Courts of Nigeria is the Maliki Code of Mohammedan Law, and in the Native Pagan Courts it is the local Native law and custom. Both are subject to the proviso that all judgments and sentences must not be repugnant to natural justice and humanity, or to any Ordinance of Nigeria. In Criminal Cases, however, the penalties awarded are not strictly limited by the Criminal Code."[33] The reader should note the exception at the end of this passage because once again it illustrates the divergence I have pointed out between the stated aim of bringing to the natives all the gains of civilization and the failure to put in place the types of institutional mechanisms that would enable the attainment of this aim.

On one hand, native law and custom would be recognized only as long as it did not conflict with the benchmark set by British notions of natural justice and humanity. On the other, the same principle was not to apply in criminal cases. Why this inconsistency? Again, the answer is to be found in the philosophical anthropology that supplied the background for Lugard's views. If Africans were closer to animals than they were to humans, they were sure to be impervious to the logic of arguments but amenable to the logic of the prod. In Memo 3, Lugard wrote: "Under British rule the principle of reprisal and mutilation has of course been abolished, and imprisonment has become the commonest penalty. Flogging for theft and other offences for which it cannot be inflicted in a British Court is not, however, illegal in Native Court. It used to be common in Native Court returns to find that the sentence for theft (mutilation being illegal) was 'to return value of articles stolen.' Native judges should be told that this is an insufficient sentence and that a punishment should always be added to restitution."[34]

It is curious that flogging, which was dehumanizing enough to be restricted in British criminal cases, was not judged to breach the requirement of conformity to natural justice and humanity but that Lugard considered levying accused persons the equivalent value in lieu of articles stolen, humane as it obviously is, to be inadequate. This exception in criminal cases is merely an instance of Lugard's general refusal to extend to the natives the benefits of civilization that he took to be one of the principal justifications of British colonialism in Nigeria. This particular refusal— that is, the refusal to implant new legal systems—is significant in other ways.

Few would deny that law in its dirigiste dimensions is a vital instrument for orienting people's behavior. And it is equally true that one of the most definitive achievements of modernity was the installation of the rule of law as the principal mode of rule in civilized societies. Even in the Britain of Lugard's time, the king had become a constitutional monarch, and British subjects did not take kindly to anyone trifling with their hard-won rights under the rule of law. This was why many of the remedies that Lugard wrote into his memoranda would have been considered ultra vires under a regime guided by the rule of law. It was not that Lugard did not try to replicate some of the institutions that entitled Britain to regard herself as law-giver to the rest of the world. There were so-called "British courts," as already pointed out. In those courts, at the apex of which was the Supreme Court, formalities and procedures were standard. They included representation by counsel, and the native elite were particularly enthusiastic about the opportunity to embarrass the colonial authorities using the instrumentality of law.[35] Although the operation of the British courts did not follow the standards set by their originals in Britain, they at least aspired to do so until Lugard set them back with so-called court reforms in 1914. Here, the native courts are most interesting because, as usual, they provide us with another example of the institutional face of what Lugard thought of the natives in his charge.

Native courts were set up for two reasons. First, the dearth of personnel trained in British law and practices made it impossible to establish British courts for the entire territory. Second, making British law available to all within the territory would have made it impossible for colonial authorities to prevent natives from raising uncomfortable questions about the legitimacy of British rule. To be sure, this was what happened with the native products of missionary-inspired "Western" education. In light of Lugard's evolutionist predilections, it should be obvious why, using the first reason as a shibboleth, he would settle on native courts that would be palpably inferior to the British courts and would be kept so. Let us bear in mind that the principles that made the rule of law such an enticing ideal include the following: equality of all before the law, those who make law are not above it, meticulous adherence to procedure and rule-following, and so on. What do we find in the native courts, though?

The jurisdiction of the native courts was restricted to natives, except in criminal cases and in those cases involving natives who were "not ordinarily subject to Native Courts": "The practice and procedure of Native Courts is in accordance with Native Law and Custom, and *no unnecessary formalities may be introduced.* . . . No legal practitioners may appear in a Native Court."[36] I have already mentioned that forms of punishment that would be unacceptable under British law were to be allowed under native law and custom. Lugard reinforced the injunction not to introduce unnecessary formalities in his description of how to keep native court clerks in check: "Members [of native courts] will be taught that the clerk's self-asserted knowledge of procedure and of English law is of no account in the eyes of Government, *which sets no value on forms and procedure,* which will be simplified as much as possible. It will be impressed upon them that *a knowledge of English law is valueless since the Court administers Native law only.*"[37] One must resist the temptation to regard the italicized sentiments in the passages quoted as mere pragmatic cautions. In the general context of Lugard's thought regarding what was suitable for Africans, given their retarded development, these sentiments meant that he held any attempt to introduce the intricacies of forms and procedure to a people who were not ready for them as a recipe for disaster for all concerned.[38] He not only restricted the jurisdiction of the Supreme Court as part of his court reforms in 1914 but also eliminated representation by counsel—to prosecute or defend—from the provincial courts he created. This was a significant step backward, especially in the western part of Nigeria, where the legal profession was growing.[39]

Why discourage natives, especially those who had benefited from missionary education, from trying, if they saw any value in the new mode of life to which they had been introduced, to incorporate into the operation of the native courts forms and procedures that they might have learned from English practices? The argument about means or costs is less persuasive given that Lugard himself states: "It has occurred to me that in many centres in the Southern Provinces, where there are mission schools, an intelligent youth of the local population who had learned to read and write would possibly be the best selection as Native Court clerk, and would be less likely to attempt to domineer over the Court. The Resident, Ọ̀yọ́, reports that the experiment has been a success."[40] If there were such nodes for possible transformation of social forms in the legal area, it was a disservice to discourage their development. In affirming that the natives were not ready for forms and procedure, in terms reminiscent of his earlier insistence that the Africans were incapable of comprehending the "subtle beauties of Christian forbearance and self-sacrifice," Lugard arrested the growth of African institutions in directions that might have made Africans beneficiaries of "all the gains of civilisation."

Even more curious, the native law and custom that the native courts were charged with enforcing was hardly recognizable to many people who were supposed to be bound by it. Indeed, for the most part, the native law was whatever the relevant chief said it was if he was able to persuade the resident to take his word for it. And as we have seen, in areas without chiefs, the colonial authorities created "warrant chiefs." In other cases, many natives were bitten by the bug of modernity and fancied themselves worthy of British citizenship and claimed it but were forced to submit to the jurisdiction of native courts that they considered beneath their dignity. In fact, Lugard fought a running battle with educated natives who thought that they were the advance brigade of the new civilization in their communities. Although he made use of them when it served his purposes—for appointments, for example, as court clerks—he always saw them as bad parodies of Europeans who had become sundered from their moorings in native soils. He saw them as people who thought that they could run before they had learned to crawl.

In light of the foregoing, it is fair to conclude that the tension between the twin injunctions to bring to the natives "all the gains of civilisation" but to interfere with native customs and modes of thought as little as possible was resolved in favor of the latter. The problem, though, was that the latter option came too late for some parts of the country, specifically certain areas of southern Nigeria, where modernity under the tutelage of Christianity had already made serious inroads on both the landscape and the mindscape of the natives domiciled there. In addition to Christianity, the principal medium through which this reordering of native life was effected was education, for it was a part of the educational agenda of the missionaries to create a native middle class equipped with the wherewithal to read, make, and buy the Bible and generally to afford the type and standard of life that would set them apart from their lower classes. By the time Lugard was standardizing the administrative procedures represented in *Political Memoranda*, the areas of western Nigeria—especially Lagos, Abẹ́òkúta, and Ibadan—and Eastern Nigeria—especially Onitsha, Calabar, and Port Harcourt—were home to a coterie of professionals in law, medicine, the building trades, the press, and education who fancied themselves as deserving of equal treatment with Europeans simply because they had proved their mettle as participants in the new dispensation. So how did education, given its importance, fare in *Political Memoranda*?

In Memo 4, Lugard described the principles of an educational policy thus:

> The primary function of education should in my judgment be to fit the ordinary individual to fill a useful part in his environment with happiness to himself, and to ensure that the exceptional individual shall use his abilities for the advancement of the community, and not to its detriment, or to the subversion of constituted authority. We are to-day beginning to realise our failure in this respect both in India and in West Africa. If the local Press may be taken as a criterion of the feelings of the educated communities in all the West African Colonies we must admit that education has not brought them happiness and contentment. It should be the ideal of a sound educational policy

to exchange this hostility for an attitude of friendly co-operation, and to train a generation which shall be able to achieve ideals of its own without a slavish imitation of Europeans, and be proud of a nationality with its own definite sphere of public work and its own future.[41]

This passage encapsulates Lugard's attitude toward the education of his native charges. No one can argue with the first part of his articulation of the principles of education that informed his policy. One can even go along with his insistence that education should suit its recipients to work for the advancement of their communities or that it should not be training in subversion. Furthermore, one must not ignore the influence of the strictly hierarchical society from which Lugard came on his need to prevent subversion of constituted authority. But these cautions cannot explain his hostility to the educated African's insistence that he and his people deserve all the gains of civilization and that they should have a say in constituting the authority that bound them. What Lugard did not disclose was the fact that the running battles he fought with the new educated elite in the southern parts of Nigeria turned on their justifiable horror at the extension to the south of the practice of indirect rule, which in reality was the northern native administration system writ large. They also protested vigorously his court reforms of 1914 and their implications for the southern elites' understanding of what direction their progress should take. Against this background, Lugard's injunctions take on a more sinister coloration.

Why denounce Africans who saw value in the new ways of life as engaging in "slavish imitation of Europeans"? And in any case, if that was what they wished to do, in true Millian spirit, they should have had their way. If it was important to get the native elites to substitute an attitude of friendly cooperation toward colonial authorities, as was the case with the northern native authorities or with chiefs in many areas of the south, why not address the grievances of the elites and, given their predisposition to accept English ways of life, use them as the principal medium for the evolution of colonial rule? This was not what happened. Lugard's policies represented a clear retrogression from the advances that had been made thanks to missionary education. For instance, whereas the missionaries sought to transform local languages to writing in order to facilitate literacy so the natives could read the Bible (even though they continued to teach English to their native wards), Lugard took the opposite tack:

In the South, and perhaps in some districts in the North, English must be the common language, and though, as Lord Kimberley said, instruction in English must, of necessity, at first be given through the medium of the vernacular, Government encouragement should not be enlisted to stimulate or preserve the use of these Native tongues. The acquisition of sufficient knowledge of the vernacular to enable the British and Native Staff to teach English or Hausa presents difficulty, and is a cause of delay, but as their use will be confined to the simplest instruction given in the lowest classes, complete mastery of them will not be required. Only one vernacular (other than Hausa) will be used in any school.[42]

It is strange that, on one hand, indirect rule is pledged to the preservation of native modes of life and thought but, on the other, "Native tongues" were slated to wither on the vine.

Stranger still was Lugard's failure to celebrate the unruliness of the beneficiaries of missionary education. If Lugard was right, they had become exactly what the missionaries thought and desired that they would be: iconoclasts and rebels against the old ways of doing things. We must trace Lugard's hostility toward this group to his evolutionist orientation, according to which Africans were not yet ready for freedom or reason. Thus, he championed the type of education that was driven by the nitty-gritty requirements of servicing the colonial system, not the type that would open the minds of its recipients to new ways of being human or make them question, with a view to improvement, age-old customs. For example, he held that purely secular education was ill suited to the level of development of Africans:

> The examples of India and China, as well as of Africa, appear to demonstrate that purely secular education, and even moral instruction divorced from religious sanction, among races who have not the atmosphere which centuries of Christian ethical standards have produced in Europe, infallibly produces a class of young men and women who lack reverence alike for their parents, their social superiors, their employers, or the Government. They lack self-restraint and control, and they lack the foundation on which the best work is based, whether of public usefulness or private effort. . . . It remains more than doubtful how far the African is capable of being restrained by moral precepts divorced from the incentive of religious sanctions, and I am impressed with the belief that the African boy requires every force which can be brought to bear if his natural proclivities are to be overcome, and he is to learn self-control and discipline.[43]

Hence, he supported religious instruction in schools. Here again, we confront another inconsistency. Earlier, we were told in *The Rise of Our East African Empire* that the African was not yet at the stage where he could appreciate the subtle beauties of Christian forbearance and self-sacrifice. So how could the same African learn Christian morality? With this question, I conclude my discussion of the policy options articulated in *Political Memoranda* and the philosophical justification for them.

Ideas Have Consequences

I have argued throughout this chapter that when Lugard arrived on the African continent, he came with preconceptions about the African that ruled his policy choices in his role as an influential administrator in Nigeria. As a result of the play of these views, the tension in his characterization of the dual mandate component regarding the duty the British owed to Africans was resolved in a specific way that shortchanged Africans. Recall Lugard's declaration that "the British role here is to bring to the country all the gains of civilisation by applied science (whether in the development of material resources, or the eradication of disease, &c.), with as little interference as possible with Native customs and modes of thought."[44] I have suggested that it would have been impossible to bring to the country all the gains of civilization without simultaneously interfering heavily with native customs and modes of thought, more so if we consider how he was already convinced that the native customs and modes of thought barely rose above the level of the lower animals. It is right to conclude that even though the opportunity was available to effect a total transformation of native life using the template of modernity, à la Christian missionaries of the early nineteenth century, Lugard either held back or went in the opposite direction. Colonial racism explains this unfortunate choice. What is left for us to do is to explore, albeit briefly, the philosophical grounds that Lugard gave for the choices that he made in what is considered his theoretical magnum opus: *The Dual Mandate in British Tropical Africa.*

Throughout the entire period that he served as an administrator in Nigeria, Lugard fought a running battle with a certain category of natives: the Western-educated elite made up mostly of returning slaves and indigenous converts to Christianity. He made few policy choices that did not attract complaint, criticism, or condemnation from this group of natives. Incidentally, most of the members of this group were to be found in the southern parts of Nigeria. Lugard and his cohort fully reciprocated their hostility. His reaction to them contrasted sharply with his fawning disposition toward the Muslim rulers of the northern parts who had been defeated by the British. Lugard's favoring of northern Muslim rulers over southern Christians was somewhat counterintuitive.

One would have thought that Lugard would have felt a closer kinship with those who not only had accepted the new civilization but had gone to great lengths to become good at it and to become proselytizers on behalf of the new mode of social living represented by Christianity and capitalism. One can make a strong case for affirming this close kinship between Lugard and the Christianized native elite. Those who have studied this group of natives in the period before the dominance of the administrator-colonizer have made clear that the educated elite shared many of the philosophical justifications of the missionizing and civilizing activities of the Europeans. This attitude was most pronounced among the returned slaves who, although they condemned slavery, sought to explain their initial capture as evidence of the hand of Providence that had chosen them to be recipients of the Gospel and the new civilization that they adjudged superior to the civilization from which they had been taken in captivity. As a result of their education in the ways of being hu-

man in the modern sense—which, as I have argued, was coterminous with being
Christian—they fancied themselves as the inheritors of the new civilization. They
thought that the basis of the legitimacy of both the missionizing activities of the
evangelists and the imperializing activities of the administrators was to be found in
their claim that they were the purveyors and embodiments of a superior civilization.
Having been baptized and having acquired the other trappings of the new way of
life epitomized by Christianity and capitalism—education, lifestyle, family forms,
speaking English, and so on—they were persuaded that they deserved to enjoy the
privileges and benefits appurtenant to these acquisitions. Hence, they demanded
that they be treated as British subjects, as citizens of the British Empire were then
called. That meant creating in Nigeria the appropriate equivalents of modern British institutions, and they were willing to put their money where their mouths were.
As both Ade Ajayi and Ayandele document, the late nineteenth and early twentieth centuries witnessed serious efforts by this new elite to recreate as best they
could the institutional forms of social living that they felt were required by their new
cultural acquisition. They created schools; they set up hospitals, publishing houses,
and presses; and they built magnificent structures that have remained monuments
to their assiduous embrace of this new way of being human.

In addition to Ajayi's and Ayandele's works, a significant source of information
about this category and their achievements in one location—Lagos—is Michael
J. C. Echeruo, *Victorian Lagos: Aspects of Nineteenth Century Lagos Life*.[45] In this
work, the author attempted to "reconstruct the patterns of life and thought in Lagos during the second half of the 19th century, as reflected in the Lagos Press of that
period."[46] I present some evidence from this source because the picture the press presents to us might offer a plausible approximation to what life was like during the stage
of Nigeria's history before Lugard wrote his works. According to Echeruo, this segment of the elite in western Nigeria was very small indeed, making up about "only
a tenth of the entire population."[47] But it is not their number that makes them important to us, it is what they represented.

> These Lagosians were usually very conversant with events in Europe and America, es-
> pecially with the progress and consequences of the American Civil War. They main-
> tained close contact with friends and other descendants of rescued slaves on the West
> African Coast. They had high hopes for themselves and for the Africa they were go-
> ing to help civilize. They felt deep obligations to the hinterland, and yet considered
> the civilizing influence of British power sufficiently beneficial to justify the gradual
> control which Britain was gaining over Yorubaland. They wanted good education for
> their children, and fought to have Government subsidy for schools; they wanted their
> children to be "refined," and so they frequently sent them to England. These children
> had to be in the smart circles of Lagos, so they went into the right professions—law,
> medicine and the Arts. Educated Lagosians wanted to associate themselves with the
> usual recreations of a sophisticated Europe, and so went to the Races, to Fancy Dress
> balls, to the Gymkhana games, and to cricket. In the evenings, they went for "brisk

walks" or for "short rides." On such occasions, (as an advertisement reminded them), they called first on "their friend, the hairdresser. Everything will be done to your taste and profit and you will come again PRO BONO PUBLICO."[48]

It was not only in the area of everyday expressions that these new converts sought to display their new adherence. Of greater significance to our discussion is what Echeruo has identified as "the intellectual context" of Victorian Lagos. This community was riven with tension between its "instinctive and deep-felt attachment to Yorubaland and to Yoruba life" and the fact that most of its members "had grown up in foreign lands—in Sierra Leone, in Cuba or in Brazil." The latter fact, according to Echeruo, placed them "at some advantage over their own people because of the opportunity that expatriation and education had indirectly offered them to acquire some of the characteristics of European civilization."[49] As inheritors of such characteristics, "they became, as it were, brokers for the new civilization and the new culture; the propagators of a 'higher' morality, a new way of life and a novel affluence."[50] Fierce debates were waged within the community concerning what the possibilities were of the African adopting European ways of being human and the consequences thereof:

> It is not difficult to identify the source of this disorientation. The educated Lagosian of the century was a typical creature of the times. His philosophers were Spenser and Darwin; his idea of progress was inseparable from the Victorian idea of evolutionary development. Where Europe, especially Germany and England, troubled itself about the future of civilization and of the chosen races, Lagosians sought to fit their community into a system which Europe had set up for its own convenience. In this scheme, their society was primitive, undeveloped. Accordingly they continued to see themselves in a pattern of world history reconstructed from the Darwinian hypothesis.[51]

Echeruo then presents evidence from the editorials and debates in the Lagos press of the day of the widespread acceptance of the Darwinian hypothesis concerning the place of the African on the ladder of evolution. The debate then turned on what the African had to do to secure a place on the "Progress Express" then hurtling toward the twentieth century. He concludes: "The Lagosian of the period thus saw Africa as a continent yet to evolve into something. He saw the customs, morals and institutions of his people as desperately in need of improvement through the use of good (probably European) models. And no effort should be spared in his search for these models and in his application of the whole self to understanding them."[52] Echeruo gives us a specific picture of the tendency that I described in chapter 2. It enables us to move from the macrosocial to the particular and show how principles were particularized in single contexts. Similar examples could be presented from Accra, Freetown, and Calabar.[53]

Here is a convenient point to get back to Lugard. On what can be deemed one of the most important philosophical points of Lugard's scheme—the African's need of tutelage in the ways of the new civilization—there was a remarkable convergence between his views and those of the educated elite in Lagos. So why did Lugard not see these gentlemen as the main agents with or through whom to bring all the gains of civilization to the natives? However we look at it, using them made the most sense: They met the requirement of using native agents; they were schooled in the language and ways of the white man; even if they were not proficient yet, the fact that they already had the appropriate foundations in place meant that it would require just an intensification of the way of life they had come to know and to adore; and they already saw themselves as "brokers for the new civilization and the new culture." The failure of European colonizers to entrust this task to them was inconsistent with the colonizers' declared aim. This refusal to recruit native talent but instead to hire unqualified Europeans at higher cost caused *The Mirror* to "remark, quite bitterly that 'one of England's noble objects in acquiring possessions in Africa, is to train the natives for self-government. Yes! we are trained with a vengeance, and strained into poverty, to be left ruined at last. . . . The Colony is overburdened with needless European officials, and it cannot further withstand the strain.'"[54] Why did Lugard not see this kinship, and if he did, why did he not celebrate it and put the Western-educated local elite in charge of the administration of the colony? I can provide a very simple answer.

Although there was convergence between Lugard's view and the view of the local elite, there was a crucial divergence between them: *each placed the African on a different rung of the ladder of evolution*. For Lugard, the African had barely, if at all, emerged from the ranks of the lower animals and was at best still in the infancy of the human race. For the repatriates, their lives represented proof of the educability of the African and of the fact that he was willing, able, and ready to assume the task of joining the rest of humanity in the race to progress. One should not accuse them of self-deception on this issue. After all, the evangelization of the southern parts of Nigeria had been accomplished under the superintendence of one of them: Bishop Samuel Ajayi Crowther. Here, then, we find the most powerful demonstration of the power of the philosophical anthropology and social ontology Lugard formulated before he went to Africa. Even though the reality in southern Nigeria was completely different from his perceptions, his pretensions to science failed the supreme test of any decent empirical science: the priority of facts over theory. That is why he would write *The Dual Mandate* without feeling any need to change any of the formulations he had as early as his first contact with Africa in the closing years of the nineteenth century. The hold of racism on Lugard's mind was so strong that whole passages of *The Rise* were worked into *The Dual Mandate* virtually unchanged. In some other respects, *The Dual Mandate* even amplified some of the themes he emphasized in earlier works. It also helps explain some of the policy choices he made and described in the *Political Memoranda*. For example, it turns out that his preference for the Fulani as rulers had nothing to do with their genius for administration. They were preselected because they were light-skinned.

But for the most part the progressive communities adopted and owed their advance to the adoption of, an alien monotheistic religion, which brought with it a written language and a foreign culture. It is to the creed of Islam that this political and social influence has in the past alone been due. *It has been the more potent as a creative and regenerating force, because it brought with it an admixture of Aryan or Hamitic blood, and the races which introduced it settled in the country and became identified with its inhabitants. They possessed greater powers of social organisation than the negro aborigines, and may therefore claim to be of a superior race-type.*

In West Africa the conquests of the Arabs and Berbers from the north-east introduced the creed of Islam in the belt bordering the southern edge of the Sahara early in the eighth century. The modern history of the advanced communities of Hausaland and Bornu in Nigeria "may be said to date from the period at which they accepted the Moslem religion, though the purer black races had established their domination over the inferior, and ruled by force of superior intelligence and cultivation long before that time." They founded kingdoms which, in the zenith of their prosperity, rivalled the civilisation of Europe of that day. Their descendants, the Fulani, still form the dominant caste, and rule the Moslem States of Nigeria.[55]

This backhanded compliment to the Fulani and Hausa rested on their (s)kinship to the Aryan or Hamitic stock. If they looked like Aryans as a result of the admixture of Aryan or Hamitic blood with their original types, they should automatically share the latter's genius for administration and conquest. Given Lugard's a priori designation of the "negro" stock as closer to the animals, the more "this stock" demonstrated their capacity to assimilate the new way of life presaged by Europeans, the more they appeared to be irredeemable pathologies. It turns out that the animus directed at the repatriates and other natives who enthusiastically embraced modern European civilization arose not from their inability to wear the garb of civilization well but from an a priori assumption that modern natives were misbegotten. Here is how he described them: "The Europeanised African differs not merely in mental outlook from the other groups, but also in physique. Doctors and dentists tell us that he has become less fertile, more susceptible to lung-trouble and to other diseases, and to defective dentition—disabilities which have probably arisen from in-breeding among a very limited class, and to the adoption of European dress, which writers in the native press say is enervating and inimical to the health of the African."[56]

For corroborating evidence, he looked to the United States, where there were more "Europeanised" Africans.[57] He acknowledged the progress that blacks had made in the United States, but he attributed it to their living in close proximity to and tutelage under white Americans. Even then, he misconstrued W. E. B. Du Bois's contention that Blacks in the United States should not desire to be other than themselves. As for the insistence of Europeanized Africans that they were the natural brokers between their people and the new civilization, he argued that "however strong a sympathy we may feel for the aspirations of these African progressives, sane coun-

sellors will advise them to recognise their present limitations."[58] It is remarkable that
he wrote this passage at a time when the Pan-African movement was afoot and the
National Congress of British West Africa was already agitating for the extension of
the rights of citizenship to West Africans.

If as late as 1922 Lugard remained unyielding in his perception of the African as
mired still in the infancy of the human race and as yet having a long road to join
the ranks of humanity, I think I am justified in my insistence on the centrality of
this view as an explanation of his policy choices in the colony. Reason dictated that
he should have made common cause with the repatriates, and his failure to do so is
evidence of how his racism trumped the declared aim of one-half of the dual mandate: that of moving the natives along the path to civilization or bringing all the
gains of civilization to them. Finally, in preferring to preserve old institutions even
when reason dictated the substitution of modern ones, Lugard substituted the ignoble science of sociocryonics, for the genuine science of social transformation that
would have ushered in, with all their attendant strains and stresses, new ways of
being human for Africans who found value in them. By embracing sociocryonics,
Lugard distorted the old institutions for his own ends or bastardized them beyond
recognition. Simultaneously, he deprived Africans of the opportunity to engage critically with their own culture for the purposes of moving it along, expunging those
elements that had outlived their usefulness, keeping in altered forms those that remained relevant, and generally borrowing from other cultures whenever they felt
the need for new forms that their indigenous structures lacked. Such critical engagement would have been the ultimate demonstration of self-government and would
at the same time have been closer to the normal evolution of all human societies
when they are not forced artificially to keep a world that in certain cases would be
well lost.

PART II

THE AFTERMATH

_5_

The Legal Legacy
Twilight before Dawn

In an era dominated by the strident polemical lucubrations of postmodernism, it is risky, to say the least, to argue for the relevance of modernity, specifically its political discourse, to an understanding of some contemporary phenomena. In the earlier chapters I argued that contrary to the claims of some of its apologists and those of its principal theorists, colonialism was a bulwark against the transition to modernity in Anglophone Africa.[1] This chapter explains the first of the preemptions that colonialism procured in the colonies: that concerning the introduction of modern legal systems into Africa. One component of the modern way of life as manifested in the legal system is the ideal of the rule of law. Subsumed under this ideal are two assumptions regarding the moral autonomy of each person: the capacity to have her own conception of the good life and the right to realize it so long as she does not impair another person's right to the same; and the impermissibility of affirming the supremacy of any particular conception of the good life over others. Both principles combine to deny to the modern state any right to force upon its citizens its conception of the good life. In the area of politics, these two principles yield liberal democracy in its many forms and in law; they are manifested in the institutionalization of the rule of law. These are the fundamental elements of the political discourse of modernity that failed to take hold in Africa and that I propose to use as a part of the explanation for the many problems that scholars have identified in the municipal legal systems in some African countries. This chapter focuses on law; the next one takes up politics.

As independence dawned, almost all African countries proclaimed their commitment to the rule of law and established, if they did not inherit, judiciaries that (in form at least) were quintessentially modern. But these institutions are modern in appearance only. Even if we concede that colonialism introduced some elements of the rule of law and its political twin of liberalism into African countries, it quickly orphaned them in ways that shed more light on why the ideals and practices failed to develop in the post-independence period. Although African countries possess judiciaries with a full complement of judges, solicitors, advocates, and other officials, the record does not permit us to conclude that the law rules in them. This is so in spite of the fact that the forms of legal discourse are properly "legal."

There is a repeated disjuncture between the appearance of the indigenization of modern legal systems and the reality of constant failures on the part of those who operate and direct these systems to deliver on their promise. Such failures are manifested in an inability and/or an unwillingness of the executive arms of government in African countries to uphold the rule of law and submit themselves to its demands and in the inability and/or unwillingness of judiciaries to see themselves as the citizens' main bulwark against state "power's all-intrusive claims."[2] Concrete illustrations of the failures are found in the fact that African governments rarely, if ever, lose cases in court, especially cases involving individuals and the abridgment of rights whose preservation and defense are integral, even defining, features of modernity. In cases involving conflicts between the rights of citizens and the claims of the state, judges behave more often like civil servants than like "oracles" of the law. The executive branch meanwhile behaves in ways that are inconsistent with the minimal requirements of a modern polity of respect for the law and respect for the autonomy of persons, the proverbial right to be let alone![3] On the rare occasions when they lose cases, governments try to tamper with the judiciary, up to and including removing "errant" judges without cause;[4] indulging in blatant intervention to corral judges' cooperation in the subversion of justice—nocturnal visits, threats, and so forth; and ostracizing judges to show displeasure with their failure to cooperate. Some executives have even contemplated abolishing the legal profession, tout court.[5]

Why is this so? Or, put differently: On the one hand, why is it that African governments insist that all institutions of governance must subserve their interests, often narrowly defined? On the other hand, why do judges in African countries either fail to see that they are impaneled to ensure that citizens are protected from the all-intrusive claims of the modern state or refuse to see themselves as the impartial arbiters that the modern state interposes between itself and those under its sovereignty? These questions encapsulate the most salient features of the problems manifest in the legal order of post-independence Anglophone African countries. This chapter seeks to identify the roots of the problems and provide an explanation for why they persist. Current experiments in multiparty democracy and renewed commitments to the rule of law should not deceive us into believing that the problems are resolved or that change is abroad in the direction of greater observance of the rule of law, although there is no doubt that elective governments provide the minimum conditions for beginning to incorporate the rule of law into the fabric of social living.[6]

I argue that one plausible and adequate explanation for the crisis of the legal order can be found in the failure of African polities to consummate the project of modernity. In the rest of the discussion, I shall describe the nature of the crisis in the legal system, summarize some of the ways that commentators have tried to explain the crisis and point out the limitations of some of their approaches, and explain the elements of the political discourse of modernity appropriate to the understanding of the crisis. Finally, I show why this is a deeper and better explanation than some others that I examine in this discussion.

The Nature of the Problems in the Modern Legal System

Apologists for colonialism and their opponents share a fundamental attitude toward colonialism that calls for critical attention. Both accept the view that colonialism implanted new legal systems in African countries. The claim should not be lightly dismissed, and some empirical support for it exists. Indeed, constitutionalism is often taken to be one of the principal legacies of colonial rule.[7] At the dawn of independence, very detailed provisions were made for almost all Anglophone African countries to entrench human rights in the constitutions that heralded independence and statehood.[8] In addition, many of the constitutions contained provisions for the judicial review of legislative and executive actions and the exercise of judicial power by the courts on behalf of citizens' rights against encroachment by the state through declarations of rights, mandamus, certiorari, and habeas corpus.

According to B. O. Nwabueze, "Constitutionalism recognizes the necessity for government but insists upon a limitation being placed upon its powers. It connotes in essence therefore a 'limitation on government; it is the antithesis of arbitrary rule; its opposite is despotic government, the government of will instead of law.'"[9] The defining feature of constitutional government is whether or not it imposes limitations on the powers of the government. It is not enough for constitutionalism that there is a constitution or that it is written or unwritten. The constitution must provide for "judicial restraint upon the executive agencies of government."[10] It is to ensure that there is judicial restraint that these various mechanisms have been institutionalized in the constitution. They are embodied in the phenomenon of judicial power. Nwabueze has identified seven attributes of judicial power. They are:

1) The existence of a dispute between two or more parties about some existing legal right; an act, e.g. a contract or an industrial award, that only creates new rights by which future conduct is to be regulated cannot therefore be judicial
2) A compulsory jurisdiction at the instance of a party to inquire into the dispute
3) A power to determine authoritatively (i.e. conclusively) the facts of the dispute
4) A power to determine authoritatively the law relevant to the dispute
5) A decision arrived at by the application of the relevant law to the facts, and which, by declaring the rights in question *finally* disposes of the whole dispute
6) A final determination that binds the parties in the dispute
7) A power to enforce compliance with or obedience to the decision[11]

All the post-independence African constitutions vested judicial power in the judiciary. For many of them, specifically Nigeria in its first post-independence constitution, "in vesting the judicial powers of the Federation in the courts (section 6) there was no restriction except where the Constitution specifically excluded some matters from being justiciable. Section 6 (6)(a) extends, notwithstanding anything to the contrary in the Constitution, to all inherent powers and sanctions of a court of law."[12] The same was true of Kenya and Tanzania.[13] It is arguable that in terms of formal or statutory instruments, the judiciaries in Commonwealth Africa are well supplied to act in behalf of the protection of the individual and of groups from power's all-intrusive claims.[14] The problem, though, is that in the studies that have been done of the judiciary and its performance in African countries, there is a disjuncture between the availability of judicial instruments to protect citizens' rights and the reluctance of judges (if not on occasion their outright refusal) to deploy these instruments in the service of justice. Every assessment of the performance of the judiciary in these countries, both in the immediate post-independence period and at the present time, ends with a gloomy picture of judicial complicity in the subversion of citizens' rights. Here are a few examples of such assessments.[15]

I begin with Gaius Ezejiofor's analysis of the judiciary in the Nigerian First Republic of 1960 to 1966. Ezejiofor has argued that "among the causes of the crises which ultimately led to the collapse of the First Republic was the failure of the courts to interpret the Constitution fearlessly, impartially and liberally."[16] One consequence of the reluctance of the courts to interpret the Constitution "fearlessly, impartially and liberally" was that individuals were reluctant to go to law to resolve cases or to have their rights declared, affirmed, and protected. Again, Ezejiofor:

> The reluctance to go to the courts is explainable largely by the restrictive way in which the courts dealt with the cases that came before them. And this explains the sharp decline in the number of reported constitutional cases after 1962. Only one statute was declared void for being *ultra vires* the Legislature (*Balewa v Doherty* [1961] 1 All N.L.R. 604) that enacted it and only a statute, a section of a statute and an action taken under a statute were read down for contravening the human rights or other provisions of the Constitution. The judges probably feared that an active interventionist policy of interpreting the Constitution in a liberal spirit would lead to open confrontation with the politicians and the consequent weakening of judicial authority. Consequently most of them were anxious to render decisions favourable to the Government and its supporters. Indeed they behaved as if it was their duty to adopt challenged measures of the authorities as valid and to find arguments to justify them.[17]

The language of Ezejiofor's description of the behavior of the judges in the immediate post-independence era in Nigeria is quite significant.[18] Their behavior anticipated many of the problems associated with the operation of the modern legal inheritances of the former colonies. He identified "an active interventionist policy of interpreting the Constitution in a liberal spirit" that, he said, risked an open confrontation with politicians and later with military usurpers of power in various countries. The judges apparently feared that they might or could not win this confrontation and that the result might be a weakening of the judiciary. The judges' fears were not groundless.

The judges' fears arise from the peculiar location of the judiciary in the modern state. In the first place, the judiciary does not have its own instrument for enforcing its directives. It must rely on the executive organs of the state for such enforcement. As Alexander Hamilton long ago observed, "The judiciary . . . has no influence over either the sword or the purse; no direction either of the strength or of the wealth of the society; and can take no active resolution whatever. It may truly be said to have neither FORCE nor WILL, but merely judgment; and must ultimately depend upon the aid of the executive arm even for the efficacy of its judgment."[19] In addition, in the countries concerned, very limited efforts were made to guarantee the financial independence of the judiciary such that it could be responsible for its own finances, and this continues to be the case. In other words, the judiciary lacks control over its own funds. It depends on the executive and the legislature and is forced to rely on its moral authority and the good faith and commitment to justice of those who have control of the purse and the sword. In his examination of the vicissitudes of judicial power in Nigeria, P. Nnaemeka-Agu has identified the numerous ways— what he calls "factors militating against exercise of judicial power"—in which the power of the judiciary is attenuated in practice, irrespective of whatever constitutional and other provisions exist to the contrary. These include lawless attorneys-general and state governors and police officers who "openly [defy] or refuse to enforce Court orders."

> But what of the "housing" of the Judiciary in the Constitution? As if the above disabilities which militate against the free exercise of judicial power are not enough, the Constitution—in appropriate metaphor—has given independence to the Judiciary with one hand and taken it away with another.[20] For, after the hallowed provisions for separation of powers in Part II of Chapter I, it proceeds in sections 140 and 178 to create Judicial Service Commissions, at the Federal and State levels, which are structurally under the thumb of the Executive and *de facto* open to political pressure. *The Judicial Service Commission is simply one of the Federal or State Executive Bodies, as the case may be.*[21]

Meanwhile, however morally upright the operators of the judiciary may be, it is important that what moral authority they might possess be widely recognized and prized by the majority or at least the most dominant segments of the population they serve. It is only in such a situation that a clamorous and insistent citizenry that will not sit idly by or feel powerless in the face of executive lawlessness or legislative overreaching reinforces the moral authority of the courts. In other words, a fundamental requirement for strengthening the judges' resolve to do right, besides their own moral strengths, is the availability of a strong civil society. The situations I have just described are not peculiar to African countries. They are typical of any legal system closely associated with modernity. So by itself, the judiciary's lack of the above capacities does not mean that the institution is forever sentenced to groveling before the executive of the modern state.

An active interventionist interpretive policy ordinarily ought not to lead to confrontation with the executive branch. It is part of the judges' vocation to take the law in new directions, anticipate new possibilities, and, on occasion, act as savants in deciphering "the intimations of their political traditions," to use Michael Oakeshott's felicitous phrase.[22] That such a policy is rendered synonymous with confrontation is one of the oddities of African polities. Even if the risk were real, as I acknowledged above, it is not obvious that the alternative is necessarily a policy of supine, unquestioning acceptance of executive behavior. But the situation was much worse in the Nigerian First Republic. Because, if we are to believe Ezejiofor, it was not just that the judges were willing to accept the behavior of the executive (which would be bad enough); in Ezejiofor's estimation, they on occasion actively subverted justice when "they behaved as if it was their duty to adopt challenged measures of the authorities as valid and to find arguments to justify them." When this happens, the judge abandons all pretense of neutrality between the citizen and the state and becomes one of the weapons in the hands of what is often a vengeful state armed with a monopoly of power against citizens who are absolutely bereft of it.

Ezejiofor is not alone in remarking this aspect of judicial behavior in Africa. Nwabueze came to a similar conclusion from a survey of judicial performance in various African countries. "The picture that emerges . . . is one of inadequate performance by the courts in the Commonwealth, especially those in Commonwealth African countries, of their role in government. It is particularly noteworthy that in many of the Commonwealth African countries e.g. Zambia, Kenya, Tanzania and Botswana, no statute has ever been declared unconstitutional by the courts. In Nigeria, in spite of its federal set-up, only twice has the sanction of constitutional invalidity been visited on a statute."[23]

What happened in Nigeria was remarkable, for the country was a federation at the time. The regional judiciaries were quasi-autonomous. That there was such convergence as the data reveal calls for explanation. Nwabueze argues that the judiciary jeopardized its legitimating function by undermining the legitimacy of governmental measures and diminishing public confidence in its own integrity.

The point here is not that every one of the decisions handed down by the Nigerian Supreme Court between 1960 and 1965 was necessarily wrong in law, but that they should all have gone in favour of the Government was remarkable, and naturally created the impression of political bias. People began to feel, rightly or wrongly, that the justice administered in the courts was influenced by extra-legal considerations, by political or sectional interests; that it was intended not to uphold the law, but to repress interests opposed to the Government. The situation was all the more lamentable because most of the decisions concerned individual civil liberties. . . . It began to look as if the courts were actively aiding the politicians in the persecution of opponents and in the perversion of the Constitution. Confidence in their ability to decide political issues impartially was consequently undermined, and the position was eventually reached where there was a general disinclination to take political complaints to them. To go to court on such matters was felt to be a vain effort; from past experience, a decision in favour of the Government was considered a foregone conclusion.[24]

The courts began to lose their moral authority. People stopped believing that it was worth their while to go to court because it appeared to them that the court was already captive to unseemly partisanship. Some of the conditions Nwabueze described suggest a much deeper malaise than the judges' fear of executive thuggery. It is a cliché of legal discourse that it is not enough for justice to be done; it must be seen to have been done. In any legal system, most people who go to law know that having their day in court and having a fair trial of their cause is the most that justice under law promises. They understand that having their day in court means that they might lose. This is especially true in the modern state, where the process is more important than the outcome. Insofar as people see that the most elementary rules and procedures have been observed and that good-faith efforts have been made to adhere to them, it is unlikely that they will raise questions about the justice of the disposition of their cause. Thus, it is important that the judiciary determinedly discharge the duty minimally to appear impartial and, from time to time, to endeavor to be impartial in the adjudication of cases.

The commitment to impartiality is important for yet another reason. The judiciary, unlike the executive, does not control the machinery of enforcement. A good part of its power is derived from its moral authority, which is purchased with the goodwill of the people and their trust in its integrity. This is its ultimate weapon in any conflict with the executive.[25] When it fails to enjoy the confidence of the people, the judiciary is even more vulnerable to the predations of executive lawlessness and legislative overreaching. No judiciary can afford a situation in which people come to feel that going to court is a vain effort, especially on matters concerning civil liberties, the protection of which is one of the fundaments of the modern state. For when that happens, the judiciary becomes dispensable, almost irrelevant. Worse still, in case of the Nigerian First Republic, the perception was not merely that the courts were merely failing to protect the rights of the people; they were perceived as actively perverting and subverting the Constitution. The courts, no less than the government, became the object of popular hostility and contempt. I am sure that this point was not lost on the politicians who wanted no formal obstacles to their grab of total power.[26]

To sum up this section: We have in the immediate post-independence period in some African countries a combination of circumstances that, on one hand, militated against the implantation of the rule of law and, on the other, was a product of the absence of the rule of law to begin with. This convergence was not fortuitous.

It was the product of processes that predated independence that had virtually ensured that those who would take the reins of power after independence would lack the wherewithal to make sense of the requirements of the rule of law and be their stout defenders. We had politicians who did not care for the niceties of modern political philosophy, of which the rule of law is an integral part, and judges who were not too clear on the concepts of impartiality, proceduralism, respect for persons, and what their office entailed in terms of protecting citizens from the excesses of the state. Both groups lacked the concomitant temperament that alone could have obviated whatever proclivities there might have been to subvert the relevant institutions.

It is easy to look at current efforts at democratization and conclude that all is well. We should resist such a temptation. Many of the current transitions to democracy in Africa are showing a similar severe lack of clarity about the rule of law and its entailments in the behavior of judges, legislators, and executives alike. For example, in spite of the introduction of multiparty democracy and the embrace of periodic elections, we still have evidence that the independence of the judiciary does not agitate either scholars or politicians and that politicians continue to use the instruments of the state to intimidate opponents. Daniel Arap Moi's long rule and that of his successor, Mwai Kibaki, in Kenya; Gnassingbe Eyadema's rule in Togo, which was terminated by his death and the rigged succession by his son; and Robert Mugabe's long rule in Zimbabwe despite multiparty elections in these countries over the course of the last decade, all attest to the need for caution in our assessment.

Explanations of the Situation

Most commentators on the legal system have focused, however inchoately, on the jurisprudence that informs the behavior of African judges. The explanation has two aspects: (1) the debate about judicial passivity versus judicial activism and; (b) the debate about legal positivism versus its many oppositions. Under (a), it is said that many judges who embrace a passive attitude tend to adopt a literalist approach to the interpretation of the law. For them, their role does not go beyond that of declaring what the law is without making any overt commitment to what the law ought to be or inquiring into whether it is good or bad law.[27] Nor do they think that it is part of their duty to second-guess the intent of the lawmakers by reading into it what they, the judges, think the legislators were trying to do beyond what is stated in the letter of the law. Elias put the case with characteristic forcefulness. Commenting on a case in which a Sierra Leonean chief justice struck down a constitutional amendment for "not being reasonably justifiable in a democratic society," Elias wrote:

> This bold decision must be one of the very few in which a court in an African Commonwealth country has expressly disallowed legislation on the ground that it was not rea-

sonably justifiable in a democratic society. It seems strange, however, that the learned Chief Justice had chosen to overrule legislation, not on the basis of its procedural and substantive validity as enjoined in the relevant section of the Constitution, but on that of its objective or moral validity. By so doing, the learned Chief Justice would seem to have opened himself to the charge of going beyond his task of mere interpretation of the Constitution provisions, so that he himself could be said to have exceeded his judicial powers as much as Parliament has exceeded its own by passing *ultra vires* legislation. . . . Fortunately, however, the Sierra Leone Court of Appeal reversed the Supreme Court by re-stating the proper function of the courts as being limited to an examination of the procedural and substantive validity of the legislation. It is not the business of the courts to preoccupy themselves with moral considerations or the rightness or wrongness of the legislative policy of Parliament.[28]

For adherents of activism, on the other hand, the law is open-textured and is imbricated in a mode of life that makes it susceptible to considerations of policy and politics. For this reason, the law is sometimes unclear in its direction to the judge. At other times, the law or the case invites considerations of policy and politics. In such circumstances the judge must not be reluctant to go beyond the letter of the law when it is likely that issues of policy and general welfare are involved. Putting the case for activism in no less forceful a manner, Akinola Aguda wrote:

> [Judges should] disentangle themselves from the cocoon of conservatism which many of them have woven around themselves by their training in British Universities, or in Nigerian Universities, Faculties of Law manned by those trained in the former. They must break loose from what some of them consider to be maximum prison into which Austinian positivism has confined them. They must gallop quickly into the light of economic and social justice and into innovative judicial interpretative processes designed to lead to the same and in order to justify their very existence which has the responsibility and the mandate of their people to lead them to their Cana[a]n of redemption. Austinian positivism has blinded many of our law men from seeing or possibly acknowledging the evils that have been perpetrated in the name of the law by generations of our political leaders. For too long have many of our judges given unqualified support to the Leviathan ruler but we cannot afford that they should carry that support to the 21st century.[29]

For several years now, the legal scene in Nigeria has been dominated by an intense debate among academic lawyers and judges of the high courts and the Supreme Court about the issue of judicial activism.[30]

Under (b), some subscribers contend that African judges tend to adhere to analytical or legal positivism. They suggest that such an attitude makes judges more likely to take the law as it is and not be concerned with any questions as to the goodness or badness of it. Nwabueze has argued that positivism has been the bane of African judicial behavior because it has inclined judges to not ask questions about the morality of the laws they are called upon to interpret. According to Nwabueze,

"Granted that the courts in Commonwealth Africa have had limited opportunity to participate in government, their performance in the cases that have come before them has been unsatisfactory. The primary reason seems to be the inherited common law attitude towards the judicial function; it is an attitude that requires literalness and analytical positivism in the interpretation of the law, enforces a narrowness of outlook towards problems presented for decision, and discourages creative activism."[31] Although I share Nwabueze's sentiment concerning the dominance of some variant of legal positivism in African judicial thinking and the role it plays in the acquiescence of judges to executive thuggery, I do not believe that legal positivism per se determines such behavior. There are different kinds of legal positivism.[32] Some are more amenable to complicity with executive lawlessness. Others are motivated by a commitment to law reform and thus provide what amounts to an opening for a reform-minded, activist judge to fill the law's silences with progressive interstitial judicial law-making.[33]

Others have acknowledged the forces against which judges were compelled to operate in the period after independence. Much is made of the overbearing attitudes of the executive branch in various African countries. I may add that African judges did not and still do not have the kind of guarantee of tenure that is ordinarily presupposed in jurisdictions where the independence of the judiciary is justly celebrated. The many constitutional provisions regarding the independence of the judiciary and the security of tenure of judges and other judicial officials are more often observed in their breach.[34] Again, while I am in sympathy with those who cite the extrajudicial constraints on judges' freedom of action, it is not part of my aim here to dwell on the impact of those constraints, although I recognize how pernicious their impact has been and can be in specific cases. Such a focus is unwarranted in the present exercise because Africans are not unique in their experience of the constraints. The main ones dealing with the absence of control over the sword and the purse are not peculiar to the African situation. Whatever differences there may be between the United States, for instance, and African countries, concerning formal guarantees of the independence of the judiciary are of degree.[35] What is important is not so much that there are constraints but how the process of institution-building proceeds in a particular society, the mettle of the individuals who are called upon to read the tea leaves of social practices—in this case, those of the law, and how timid or intrepid they are in pushing the limits of the permissible in their operation of the system. We shall find later that this group of factors has not been sufficiently canvassed in the literature on the legal systems in African countries.

There is an additional reason why I think that some of the explanations above are inadequate. I am convinced that they themselves are susceptible of deeper explanations. For instance, when we accuse judges of passivity, we can ask further why judges make this choice. What predisposes judges to passivity? The same question may be asked of activism. It is obvious that the choices are no less present for judges in the countries in which the ideal of the rule of law is better realized. They too choose according to various principles and predispositions of the sort that I shall be analyzing below.

Furthermore, we tend to valorize judicial activism and condemn judicial passivity. I am assuming for present purposes that these terms are easily understood. Having said that, beyond its ideological appeal, judicial activism is neither obviously just nor is it obviously right to be an activist judge.[36] Simultaneously, a proclivity toward judicial passivity may issue from clearly noble and well-founded political, ideological, and even moral principles.[37] Indeed, what made the picture that Nwabueze painted about the Nigerian First Republic more dismal was that "it began to look as if the courts were actively aiding the politicians in the persecution of opponents and in the perversion of the Constitution." That kind of activism is pernicious in extremis. We cannot ever discount the possibility of this perverse kind of activism. Given that the will of the judge is always a factor in the adjudication process, she still needs to assess the facts with her own light, however limited it may be. If the light shines brightly, we have a visionary judge who plays prophet and leads society to possibilities within the law that may not be obvious to others. If not, we have an apparatchik. If it is absent, we have a judge who will do wrong regardless of what the executive does. An activist judge in the service of the executive's interests is much worse than one who sleepwalks to the same end. An activist judge may actively subvert human rights, and there have been cases where activist judges have done so. An activist judge in the mold of the late chief judge of Lagos State, Nigeria, who averred that the executive is akin to the *kábíyèsí* (the monarch in the indigenous Yorùbá mode of governance whose word was law and who, it was presumed, could not be questioned) will be a disaster for litigants who are seeking a declaration from the court that their rights have been infringed upon by the executive.

Meanwhile, even when activism is supposedly done on behalf of good policies, it will not be any less problematic. It may instantiate exactly the kind of judicial lawmaking that usurps the legislative prerogative. Finally, although activism requires imagination of the sort that engenders creative and novel interpretations of the law, their novelty does not render them inconsistent with the rest of the law or the sway of its institutional history.[38] This is the only way for the judge concerned to avoid the charge of whimsical lawmaking. We find this type of imagination at work in the Supreme Court of India, where, in cognizance of the peculiarities of the Indian situation, the court has created novel instances of *locus standi* called "epistolary jurisdiction" and of litigation under the name "social action litigation."[39] For these reasons, I do not think that we will get far in explaining the failures of the legal system by espousing judicial activism and excoriating judicial passivity or vice versa.

When we cite the repressive tendencies of the executive, we must also explain why such tendencies are prevalent in Africa. In other words, we must ask and answer the question Why was/is democracy such an unattractive option for African rulers? These are the sorts of questions that debates about legal positivism or judicial passivity or activism do not illuminate. We must look more closely into the political history of the relevant countries and see to what extent the attitudes of both judges and executives have been conditioned (determined, in some cases) by the dominant political theories and forms of political socialization found in them. To that extent, what follows is meant as a complement to the many other explanations for failures in the legal system already abroad in the field. Given the complexity of the situation in which legal systems do not work the way they are supposed to, no purpose will be served by advancing monocausal theories, however insightful they might be. What I do next is to supply a theoretical model with which to read the political histories and forms of political socialization to be found within the polities whose legal systems engage our critical attention. The aim, ultimately, is to explain the forms of judicial behavior that are symptomatic of the problems we see in the legal system and lay bare their causes as a propaedeutic to modifying them.

The Relevance of the Political Discourse of Modernity

The beginning of wisdom in unraveling why the promise of the rule of law has not been redeemed in African countries is to acknowledge the provenance of the legal systems domiciled in them. Such an acknowledgment forces us to pay attention to the enabling circumstances in the birthplace of the legal traditions that African polities supposedly mimic. The origins of the judiciaries that are domiciled in the African countries are an integral part of the movement of modernity. That is, the legal systems introduced by British colonialism to Commonwealth African countries are a component of the modern way of life. As such, they are infused with the modes of discourse, institutions, and epistemologies that are elements of modernity. In Britain, the original country from which the legal system was appropriated and introduced to our environment, the legal system emerged as a single element, among several others, in a movement toward epochal social transformation from feudalism to capitalism, from the Middle Ages to the modern age. The transformation had multiple facets: philosophical, economic, political, legal, religious, social, and so on. The legal system did not emerge in isolation from these other elements, although they did not all evolve at the same time. The victory of the legal system was part of the triumph of a way of life that was all-encompassing in its effects. As a result, the legal system has organic roots in the society whose members' behavior it regulates, directs, or punishes, as the case may be. The basic assumptions of the legal system are in symbiosis with other areas of life and are shared by all and sundry in the society.

What I have described above is absent in the African situation. There, the legal system was not introduced as part of a program of general social transformation. It was not the outgrowth of a system of interrelated organic institutions. Quite the contrary, it originated as a tool, a weapon in the arsenal of the colonial authorities for the singular purpose of keeping the colonies and protectorates safe for the colonizers and the natives in their place. It was a part of the coercive institutions fabricated by the colonial state to secure its rule over unruly "natives." As such, there was no interest on the part of those responsible for its introduction to plant the whole seed from which a fully grown plant might have been cultivated. Nor was there any chance that an organic system could have been replicated in the dependencies for logical and practical reasons, some of which I have expounded in earlier chapters. The colonizers were left with a stalk that was grafted onto local receptacles from which they and we have expected a full plant to emerge. Little or no effort was expended to prepare the local receptacles for a successful graft.

To use a different analogy, the best that we could expect given the circumstances of the introduction of the modern legal system into our countries was that the transplantation of the legal organ into the local bodies would not suffer rejection. For that to have succeeded, it was necessary that there be readily available huge amounts of social "cyclosporin"[40] to ensure that the chances of rejection by the host body of the foreign tissue of the modern legal system were minimized. As I have argued in the preceding chapters, some African communities did not lack the requisite social "cyclosporin," even if it was in short supply. The appropriate course would have been to see to the multiplication of this vital ingredient through successful social organ transplantation. Allowing native agency to embrace and make its own these preferences would have provided a possible organic node. That is, the ranks of those who were orphaned by the policy choices made by administrators, as I discussed in chapter 2, ought instead to have been expanded. No such expansion took place under administrator-inflected colonialism. As a consequence, the legal system was always a hostile, foreign presence in the organic life of the colonies and protectorates. Unfortunately, perhaps ominously, not much has happened since independence to reconcile the legal system to its African milieu.[41]

Additionally, it is arguable that there was no intention on the part of the British to introduce a modern legal system. Such a conclusion follows from their insistence, from the third quarter of the nineteenth century on, that Africans were unfit for any large-scale genuine transformation of their social formations and their belief that putting the niceties of modernity before the African was like casting pearls before swine. The administrators and their clerical cohort, given their attitude, regarded the centrality of reason, the primacy of the subject, and autonomy of action as foreign to the African world and potentially productive of harmful consequences were they to be implanted in that world. The failure of the legal system, of which the judiciary's failure is the most dramatic example, may be traced to the failure to consummate the project of modernity in Africa. This is the core claim of this chapter. But why trace the problems and failings of the legal system to the career of modernity in the former colonies?

There are two reasons. First, I have argued that an aspect of the self-understanding of colonial ideologists is that colonialism's mission was to civilize the colonized and bring them into the concert of the modern world from a putative traditional era. We all too often either do not take their profession seriously enough or accept it too uncritically. I have elected to take the profession seriously in order thereby to show that had the colonialists meant it, they would have done for Africa what they did for the United States, Australia, Canada, and white South Africa. The possible impact of institutionalizing what is presupposed by their profession is better appreciated when we consider what it might have meant for ideas such as habeas corpus, the presumption of innocence until proved guilty, the restraints on the modern state because it enjoys a monopoly of power, and the like.

Second, an explanation in terms of modernity is not only apt to yield more fruitful insights into the reasons for the failures I have spoken of thus far, it also enables us to reintegrate African countries into the philosophy of world history contra the twin apologias of Eurocentrists who try to deny the significance of the European impact for African development and Afrocentrists who are so concerned with emphasizing Africa's difference from the rest of the world that they are wont to ignore what their countries share with other peoples and fail to draw appropriate comparative lessons. The importance of the latter mode of proceeding cannot be overemphasized, because while the apostles of difference remain oblivious to similarities, the phenomena of social ossification and negative appropriation of foreign influences in all areas are taking a huge toll on African lives and thought. At a time when there is a renewed interest in liberal democracy and the rule of law in Africa as an integral part of ongoing global processes, the success or otherwise of the new experiments cannot but be seriously affected by how sedulously we cultivate the concomitant temperaments and nurture the appurtenant institutions. Given my insistence that ongoing transitions to democracy and market economy are best understood as late transitions to modernity, Africa's latest chance at modernity must not be frittered away at the altar of ignorance about what needs be done if Africans are to become beneficiaries of a way of life whose burdens they have borne more than any other people.

In chapter 2, I examined in considerable detail the philosophical discourse of modernity. I identified there various elements that form the core of modernity. In this section, I shall be concerned with the institutionalization of the philosophical discourse of modernity in law. Of significance here is how well or ill the law and the legal system that the British bequeathed to their African colonies embody the philosophical presuppositions that enable us to identify them as instances of a certain kind and partly explain their operation and success in Britain, Canada, and Australia and their astounding failures in Africa. We cannot do this unless we know what these presuppositions are and what role they played and continue to play in the operation of the municipal legal systems that form the source of contemporary African legal systems. Again, I start with the principle of subjectivity.

According to Hegel, "the principle of the modern world is freedom of subjectivity." The sociological variant of this principle is individualism. In liberal political theory, the basic justification for the existence of civil society is the individual who is the object of protection from the state. In Hegel's estimation, the individual is not only at the core of the modern legal system but is also the object of all the protection that the system offers. At the heart of the modern legal system as it has evolved in Britain and other Euroamerican countries, of which the legal systems in African countries are instances, lies the *legal subject*.

Let us recall the other four connotations of subjectivity identified by Habermas. They are: "(a) *individualism*: in the modern world, singularity particularized without limit can make good its pretensions; (b) *the right to criticism*: the principle of the modern world requires that what anyone is to recognize shall reveal itself to him as something entitled to recognition; (c) *autonomy of action*: our responsibility for what we do is a characteristic of modern times; (d) finally, *idealistic philosophy* itself: Hegel considers it the work of modern times that philosophy grasps the self-conscious (self-knowing) Idea."[42] A core tenet of individualism understood as a principle of social ordering is that what is prefigured in (a) involves allowing the individual the freedom to realize herself in the world without prior restraints that would preselect, without any ascertainment of an individual's preferences, a conception of the good life and how to obtain it for her. This is the general philosophical presupposition at the root of the political theory of liberalism in which the individual is regarded as prima facie sovereign and presumed to be the best judge of how he or she should lead his or her life.

Of course, the question arises how political authority can be founded in a community of heterodox individuals and what the normative foundations of such authority would be. In its various permutations, the consent theory of obligation under which no one ought to be bound by an authority to which she has not given her consent—the abiding core of contract theories—builds on the presumption of the sovereignty of the individual.[43] The individual comes to the world fully constituted as a being deserving of respect for her sovereignty from her fellows, and the protection of the individual in the enjoyment of this right is held to be the principal raison d'être of the state. The rule of law in its barest form is nothing other than the deployment of the instrumentality of law in securing the sovereignty of the individual and the conditions for the exercise of same by all without exception. The insistence that the right be enjoyed by all without regard to circumstances of birth, fortune, or differences in individual merit is the basis of the commitment to the formal equality of all in all areas of life. Hence, the cardinal principle of modern law concerning the equality of all before the law is intimately connected to the general philosophical orientation that all human beings are equal and that no person is more equal than others.

Moreover, the individual, the legal subject, is counterposed to the modern state. In the philosophical disquisitions of liberal theorists, the relationship between the individual and the state is an inherently unequal one in which the puny individual is confronted by a state that enjoys the monopoly of power and violence. How the state comes to be so constituted is the object of much of the political sociology that undergirds much of liberal political theory, beginning with Thomas Hobbes through John Locke and Jean-Jacques Rousseau to John Rawls and Robert Nozick.[44] According to liberal theorists, left to their own designs, human beings will always seek to get the better of their fellows. But the individual is unable by his own designs alone to fend off such predation, given his limited powers. A combination of the individual's inability and the danger from his neighbors makes it necessary to install a power to which all shall surrender their right to self-government and, by extension, to self-help in redressing wrongs perpetrated against them. In place of self-help, the common power is deployed to restrain human beings from preying on their fellows. Yet this power cannot run itself nor can we do without interposing human agency in its operation. The question then becomes How can we ensure that the natural human tendency to prey on their fellows will not get the better of those who are charged with wielding the common power? How can we know that they will not turn it to the service of themselves and their cohort? There is no guarantee that this will not be the case. To prevent such an outcome, the rule of law is brought in to preempt the rule of man and power is hemmed in with myriad restrictions about the relationship between the state and the sovereignty of the individuals that make it up, institute it, and consent to its authority.

The rule of law has neither been present throughout history nor distributed globally so that we could say that the principle and its institutional manifestations occur in all cultures. As it is meant to be enshrined in the legal systems domiciled in African countries, the rule of law is embedded in a singular history traceable to the dawn of the modern epoch in Europe. The failure to acknowledge these historical roots has contributed in no small measure to the failures that I am concerned to explain. The rule of law as a pillar of the modern state and the protections afforded the individual in the modern politico-legal scheme are neither products of the good nature of Euroamerican rulers in the past nor inexorable historical developments. People fought for these practices to become commonplace, and they came into being at specific historical junctures. The American Revolution was the first institutionalization of the philosophical discourse of modernity in 1776. The French Revolution in 1789 and its Declaration of the Rights of Man and Citizen in 1791 made the distinction between civil society and the state a recognizably structural one and inserted a wall around the individual that the state may not breach without a serious reason. In insisting that the purview of the liberty under the law proclaimed by the French Revolution extended to them, too, the protagonists of the Haitian Revolution thereby inscribed themselves as co-authors of this historical movement. And England, the home of the Magna Carta, began from the Act of Settlement of 1701 the process that saw the increasing bourgeoisification of power in the country that culminated in the twentieth century in the supremacy of the House of Commons as the principal legislative organ of the British people.

The individual who is the centerpiece of modern political theory and the object of serious protection in the modern state is itself a product of history. I alluded briefly to this history in chapter 2, dating it from the fifteenth century.[45] It remains only to outline the peculiar realization of the individual in the realm of law. Essential to the notion of the sovereignty of the individual is the ability of the individual to form and hold conceptions of the good life and the means to realize them. The individual must be free to act in the world to realize her conception of the good life. The freedom to act is judged the basic position of the human being in the world. But it is precisely in acting that the individual is likely to come up against the exercise of the same freedom by other individuals. When conflicts arise from the respective exercises of freedom by sovereign individuals, the law and the state are called upon to moderate, arbitrate, and adjudicate such conflicts, making sure that social relations are so calibrated that each individual exercises as much freedom as is compatible with equal freedom for others. Whenever there are infringements, the state steps in to exact appropriate consequences from the transgressor. But the state may not make laws that preempt action or punish actions that are contemplated but not yet been carried out. The state is prohibited from administering "punishment for thought."

Once the subject acts, she is held responsible for her actions. The notion of responsibility involved here is peculiarly modern.[46] It involves associated ideas about the nature and causes of action, the issue of whether or not the actor could or ought to have foreseen the consequences of his action, the prior knowledge that what he was about to do was an *actus prohibita,* and so forth. But for all the preceding conditions to be met and for liability to ensue, what is alleged must not be an accident, an occurrence over which the individual had no control or that could not have been said to emanate from her intention to bring the said action about. In other words, the individual must have his wits about him, as it were, before he can be held liable for the consequences of acting—indeed, for him to be deemed to have acted at all. This is the philosophical foundation of the requirements of mens rea and actus reus. But none of these elements should be assumed to have been established from looking at the action alone. Inquiries must be held as to whether the actus was reus and the appropriate mens was rea, that the consequences were foreseeable, and so forth. Hence, there is a presumption that anyone accused of committing an infraction is innocent until proven otherwise. Given the modern state's monopoly of power and the ever-present possibility that it may be turned to the advantage of faction, one cannot overstress the importance of the presumption of innocence for preserving the sovereignty of the individual, who remains ever-vulnerable to false accusation and suchlike malfeasance on the part of power-holders.

Let us sum up the discussion so far. Freedom is taken to be the basic mode of being of the individual in the modern state. As a free entity, the individual may not be prevented from acting. She can only be held responsible for the actions that she has willed into being and she must know beforehand that consequences of her actions will attract sanctions. Within these boundaries, the individual is the lord of his domain, a private zone that is forbidden to the government and to other individuals unless the owner of the zone consents accordingly. Simultaneously, the rule of law was invented to take care of the contingency of human behavior and the many ways that it is likely to be deployed to secure undue advantage, especially in the relationship between those who wield power in the modern state and those who are subject to it. Here then are two pillars on which the legal system of the modern state rests: (1) the sovereignty of the individual and the attendant confidence in her ability to have, hold, and seek to realize her conception of the good life; and (2) the impermissibility of the state to decide how the individual should lead her life and its prima facie exclusion from most areas of private life save for ensuring that this right is not used by anyone to deny others the benefit of enjoying the same right.

So far I have looked at the constitution of the legal subject and how and why she is surrounded by multiple protections in the modern state. The state itself was remade in some serious ways in the wake of the modern age. The philosophers of the modern age, especially in the area of political theory, were quite aware of the abuses associated with the absolutism of feudal rulers, whose excesses formed part of the inspiration for the modern age. They knew, because they fought against, the arbitrariness of will, the concentration of power in one person or a group of persons, the weight of tradition and the rigidity of social location, and so forth that were the hallmarks of premodern social formations. The weight of history coupled with the negative philosophical anthropology presented earlier led them to seek ways to create institutions that would diffuse power and that would put no one person or faction in a position to order the destiny of the rest merely by seizing control of a single institution in which all power is concentrated. That is the historical genesis of the doctrine of separation of powers, theorized in considerable detail by Baron de Montesquieu and first given institutional representation in the American polity that remains the best example of the principle to date.[47]

In the United States, sovereignty resides in the people. The representatives the people elect may therefore appear to be the embodiment of popular sovereignty. But the executive, the president, is elected by the votes of every eligible American voter, a situation that gives him a national constituency as opposed to the miniature constituencies of members of the legislature. Yet despite this, the president is not supreme. Meanwhile, the judiciary has interpreted the judicial power vested in it by the Constitution to include the power to inquire into whether or not the president or Congress has followed the letter and spirit of the Constitution in enacting laws; this is the power of judicial review. The upshot is that each arm of the government is set up as a check on the others to prevent a slide into arbitrariness or absolutism in matters concerning their relations and, more important, in their dealings with the individual citizen, whose welfare and ability to lead her life as she wishes is the raison d'être of the state.[48] Thus, the courts are set up and charged with the responsibility of ensuring that the rights of the individual have not been infringed upon, that the state has not overreached itself in its relations with its constituents, and that when it has done so, it has done so either legitimately or with good reason or mistakenly but in good faith. Rules are crucial, and proceduralism is one of the principal concomitants of the formal equality of all that undergirds life in the modern state.

In its institutional manifestations, the rule of law enjoins strict adherence to rules laid down beforehand and to fairness in the promulgation, administration, and enforcement of law. It places the onus on the state or its agents to show that their exercise of power is in line with the procedures laid down. It requires that departures from this principle be supported by very good reasons or are mistakes committed in good faith. It leaves the individual free to act in the world and bear responsibility for consequences that are traceable to her actions. It arms the individual with the presumption of innocence until a properly constituted tribunal has determined that she is guilty after thorough investigation and impartial trial. It also invests the individual's personal space with sanctity such that the state or its agents may not enter unless they have been permitted by the individual concerned or have convinced a proper tribunal that an entry is warranted, in which case their entry will be facilitated by a properly executed warrant. It leaves the individual free to go before a tribunal and ask that the tribunal declare that her rights have been violated, compel the state to perform some task that she deems necessary to her enjoyment of her rights, or refrain from performing some task that she deems inimical to the exercise of her sovereignty.

It follows that if the modern legal system such as we have inherited it in Africa is about anything, it is about protecting the individual and the groups they belong to from unwarranted interferences with the enjoyment of their individuality in its infinite permutations by their fellows or their governors. This system must be judged by how well or ill it redeems its implicit promise for African legal subjects. Otherwise its operators must show either that the ideals that animate the legal system are irrelevant in the African context or that the benefits it promises are not good enough for Africans or Africans do not deserve them or that if its underlying principles were embraced in Africa, it would generate dysfunctional results for social relations and individual strivings. Until then, the metric by which we determine how well or ill African judiciaries are doing will continue to be that supplied by the underpinning philosophical principles and the historical experience of the modern legal system.

With the aid of the above elucidation I can now proceed to state the case for the relevance of the political discourse of modernity in making sense of the problems and failures associated with the operation of the modern legal system in African countries. I hope that I have shown that the legal system in Euroamerica was one element in a whole complex of transformations that typified the transition to modernity. Outside of the larger matrix within which are inscribed the principles of the modern legal system, we cannot make adequate sense of that system's many quirky procedures and formal commitments. It is true that African municipal legal systems have their origin in the modern legal systems of Euroamerica. But it bears restating, because although all assert it, most either do not realize the fuller implications for the operation of the legal system or think that it follows that the legal systems in African countries operate like their Euroamerican originals and that whatever is missing is to be ascribed to the hostile soil of African culture and life, the inability of African operators to handle the tasks the system requires, and so on. I beg to differ with these sentiments.

Although the British legal system is supposed to be the template from which the legal systems of Africa were constructed, I would like to argue that the African version was a branch that was grafted onto a plant that was never prepared to receive the new piece. Given African history, it would be too much to expect that without a huge settler component, the invading British could have engineered a complete social transformation in Africa of the sort that took place in Europe and was replicated in the settler colonies. Nevertheless, as I showed in chapter 2, before the imposition of formal colonialism (of which the legal system was an integral part), a transition to modernity that was spearheaded by African converts to Christianity was already under way in some parts of Africa. The problem, though, was that African converts were not the people who handled the transplantation of the legal system. Had they been the agents of the introduction of the legal system, it might have emerged as an aspect of their generally favorable estimation of the new way of life enjoined by modernity and other things might have followed as a consequence. No such evolution took place.

The transplantation that took place might have had better success had those under whose direction it evolved trusted the capacity of Africans to learn and domesticate new modes of life and encouraged the continual practice of having the state acknowledge and respect their individual sovereignty, the rule of law, and all the other characteristics of the modern politico-legal system described above—that is, if they had adopted the autonomy model. Sadly, that did not happen. Especially with regard to the relations between the state and the individual, the colonial state banished almost all niceties of the modern legal system from its dealings with Africans. Africans never had the privilege of enjoying the practice of the rule of law— much less have their turn at its practice—during the colonial period, including the immediate period before independence. If it is true that practice makes perfect, then all those who have argued and continue to argue that the failure of the rule of law in Africa is proof that the African environment is not conducive to its flourishing are mistaken in their analyses. Unfortunately, even in the post-independence period, analysts have not taken seriously the factor of history and have continued to write as if the African is congenitally incapable of living modern in law and politics. It is a way of thinking that has persisted in spite of the fact that we have many references in the literature of history, political theory, and law to the fact that the colonial state was not particularly interested in installing a modern politico-legal system in Africa. Such references are often too cursory and they indicate that their authors have not come to a significant awareness of the magnitude of the process that they often reduce to throwaway status in their writings.

Are we back with the old bugaboo of blaming the failures of Africans on their colonizers and not holding Africans themselves responsible for some of the failures? No, that is furthest from my intentions. The problem is that we have moved from one extreme of blaming everything on colonialism to a new one of not blaming anything on it. Neither alternative is acceptable. My purpose is to show how the absences, abortions, and preemptions that characterized the colonial period have not been sufficiently theorized in the post-independence period by intellectuals. The result is that all too often appropriate answers are left unexplored and the continuing nationalist problematic that frames African intellectual endeavors, first as a reaction to colonial denials and now as an almost knee-jerk reaction to global racism, does not allow African scholars to take in hand the heritage of modernity which, I argue, is now part of the constitution of their identity. Even if it were not, to the extent that some (myself included) believe that the way of life enjoined by modernity is superior to that bequeathed to the continent by colonialism and to many aspects of the continent's own premodern inheritances, it behooves scholars to explore ways that the promise of modernity might be redeemed for their fellow citizens.

Thus, I am putting the legacy of colonialism back on the agenda not as a way to restore to respectability the dodge of responsibility that has been justly discredited by generations of African scholars and leaders but as a way of reminding everyone of what might usefully be appropriated from the colonial heritage that would serve to redeem the promise of modernity for Africans. If the sorry history of failures and disappointments that has occasioned my retrospective is not to be repeated, we must acknowledge the provenance of our modern institutions, commit to learning well the intricacies of their operations in the countries of their birth, and creatively adapt their best possibilities for our posterity and ourselves. How much is the need just adumbrated recognized in the literature about law and its institutional manifestations in Africa at the present time? Unfortunately, I am afraid, very little. Here is why.

As is the case in the United Kingdom, from which the bulk of the laws of the African legal systems is derived, most of their legislation is framed in terms of the individual and her protection from other individuals and from the state. After African countries achieved independence and assumed republican status, they continued to enact laws that were couched in terms of the rights, privileges, and responsibilities of the legal subject of modern law, even though these polities no longer subscribed to the authority of British precedents. A cursory look at the constitutions of African states also reveals an overarching concern with the legal subject. Given the overwhelming presence of the legal subject in the legal system in Africa, one must remark the equally overwhelming absence of concern with the legal subject in the discourse about law among African jurists, lawyers, political theorists, sociologists, and philosophers. Even our most sophisticated scholars and jurists such as A. O. Obilade, Akinola Aguda, Chukwudifu Oputa, Kayode Eso, Yash Ghai, Issa Shivji, and Benno Ndulu can be faulted on this score. Although there are repeated references in the literature to the individual, the philosophical dimensions of this concept and their implications for legal theory and practice are hardly ever apprehended, much less discussed. Needless to say, the fault cannot solely be that of legal scholars. African philosophers have been painfully remiss in making available to their intellectual communities relevant discourses about the core tenets of modernity and their careers in the African context.

Legal discourse in African countries is burdened by an overarching technicism in which there is an unending concentration on the mechanics of promulgating law, on the various writs, and on a strict but narrow focus on the technicalities of the law. This should not come as a surprise, because lawyers conduct much of the discourse. Lawyers and judges rarely know or read philosophers who write about the law.[49] Such is the weight of the attention to technicalities that it seems that if one does not possess "registrable" qualifications—that is, if one is not a lawyer—she cannot be deemed to know what the law is about or to have anything useful to contribute to the understanding (much less the development) of law and its discourse. But if what I have said in this chapter holds even partly true, then a very important element is missing from the discourse about law in Africa. The discourse does not evince a robust sense of the larger context of the historical and philosophical underpinnings from whence it originated. There is a marked lack of awareness of the symbiotic connection between the central concepts of the legal system and the associated ideas from political philosophy (governance by consent), the history of philosophy, and even the philosophy of mind (intention), metaphysics (the ideas of the self and causality), and epistemology (foreseeability and knowledge). Much of the discussion of the shortcomings of the legal system turns on particular cases, executive lawlessness, judicial timidity, and professional incompetence without deep engagement with why these factors (which are by no means peculiar to the African environment) do not have the same consequences in other societies as they have in ours or why they do not wreak similar havoc in the lands from which we have copied the legal system.

Why are rules more often observed in their breach in African polities, especially by those sworn to uphold them or charged with interpreting and enforcing them? Why are African constitutions often not worth the paper that they are written on?[50] Why do we have the obvious paradox inherent in the fact that the constitution of the most powerful country in the world, which has the most robust protections for individual rights and whose people enjoy freedom that often borders on license, is a mere few pages long and the Constitution of Kenya at independence had a section on human rights that is longer than the U.S. Constitution yet did not invest the citizens of Kenya with anything that resembles respect for their rights as individuals and as citizens? These are not insignificant qualms. As we have seen, the modern legal system is built on a basic philosophical disposition that is suspicious of power and of the state in which it is vested. Such healthy suspicion of government and the state is absent from the discourse about law in Africa.[51] Indeed, one is often confronted with the ugly spectacle of jurists who have studied the violence that the state has visited on its citizens through illegal detentions, unwarranted long periods of remand before trial, and the like asking the same state to do something about the victims of its original cruelty, intended or not.[52]

Although one repeatedly runs into the inevitable references to individuals, I have yet to come across a single treatise on law written by an African jurist in the Anglophone countries on the theme of the legal subject. Nor are there discussions of why the modern legal system evolved the way it did in Euroamerica beyond the ritual retelling of how the rule of law had its origins in the Magna Carta.[53] The discovery of the individual, the emergence of the self as a fully constituted subject without organic connections to any but itself (a discovery in the Euroamerican tradition originally made by René Descartes), and the development of Cartesian themes in Hobbes and others of the contractarian tradition do not form part of the training or the world view of even our most distinguished jurists. A fuller explanation for the failure of the modern legal system to deliver on its promise to Africans must include reference to the fact that most of its operators—legislators, executive, judges, jurists, lawyers, prison officers, police officers, and so forth—have little or no training in the intricacies of twentieth-century modern discourse and as a result do not possess anything that approaches a deep appreciation of the progress the achievements of liberal political theory represent for humankind.[54] There is no recognition of the sovereignty of the individual. The interminable recitation in various textbooks and discussions of the human rights guaranteed by different constitutions is no substitute for very deep examinations of what those guarantees mean in terms of the individual's ability to have, hold, and seek to realize conceptions of the good life, to not be disturbed in the enjoyment of his solitude if he so desires, and, most important of all, to have his fellow citizens rise up in his defense when law enforcement agents turn themselves into judge, jury, and executioner for whatever infractions he may have committed.[55]

I conclude that what we have in African countries are modern legal institutions in shell alone, totally shorn of the philosophical soul that enlivens them and makes them such a quantum leap in the march of humanity toward the best life for humans. The inattention to the larger context, I argue, is a direct result of the manner in which the legal system was incorporated under the colonial regime. The administrators who were fully in charge by the time of the introduction of the legal system into the colonies and protectorates could not afford to midwife the full development of a modern legal system because it would have led to the undermining of their claim to rule in the colonies. Thus, just as we found in chapter 2 in the case of the other components of modernity, they aborted the transition to modernity in the area of law. As a result, the law and the legal system were introduced in their hostile incarnations alone—as tools for pacifying the natives and keeping them in their place. Right at its inception, the legal system in the colonies was afflicted with a terminal case of sclerosis from which it has yet to recover. On all the points requisite for the emergence of a truly modern system of law, the colonial administrators went in the opposite direction.

Sowing the Wind: Aborting the Transplantation of a Modern Legal System

Individual Rights and the Colonial Legal System

In chapter 2, I pointed out that the principle of subjectivity is central to the constitution of the modern subject, and we saw above that its legal manifestation is the legal subject. If the colonial administration did not recognize the basic and unqualified humanity of the natives, the very prerequisite for the possibility of subjectivity, it should come as no surprise that there was no attempt whatsoever in the colonial period to develop the idea of the legal subject and make it the centerpiece of the legal system. For the latter to have been the case, natives would have had to have been constituted as citizens.[56] To ensure that that did not happen, colonialists created a different category of colonies for Africans: protectorates. This is one situation where there is more to a name than its nominal function. In the cases of Canada and the United States, the colonists traveled from Britain with their citizenship intact. Thus, in the lands of their sojourn, even as they created new structures of governance, they did so using the model that they were accustomed to in the mother country, in the name and under the legitimacy of the home institutions, and as physically separate but otherwise integral parts of their homelands. As a result, they discharged their civic duties to the motherland. When the United States seceded from Britain it did so in the name of the selfsame principles of citizenship, political legitimacy, and obligation that obtained in Britain. I have restated these points because they show that there is no incompatibility (much less contradiction) between being a citizen of a colony and enjoying the rights pertaining to citizenship of the suzerain power that

rules over one. There is evidence that colonies in Africa, too, started out with subjects who were citizens and that many of their inhabitants regardless of their epidermal inheritance had well-grounded expectations that they were candidates for full
citizenship of the colonizing power. Although the numbers were few and the eligibility requirements were onerous, France and Portugal admitted many Africans to
citizenship and full participation in the French and Portuguese polities.[57]

In the British colonies, however, a quick separation was made between colonies
such as Freetown and Lagos and what were styled "protectorates." At the beginning,
the inhabitants of the colonies were treated like British subjects: they enjoyed some
of the rights, duties, and prerogatives of citizenship. But the much larger areas over
which Britain ruled were called protectorates. Protectorates were so designated because such territories were to be left under the "rule" of native potentates and because
their inhabitants (regardless of their preferences) could not choose to be treated as
British subjects (citizens) even if they were otherwise no different from the residents
of the colonies. Besides the politico-legal legerdemain associated with protectorates,
all that being a protectorate entailed was that the ruler accepted British overlordship
and would not enter into arrangements with any other European imperial country.
In reality, though, protectorates were designed to enhance the installation of sociocryonics. It turned out that the inhabitants were being shielded from change and
what British administrators judged to be the deleterious effects of the ongoing transition to modernity. In short, protectorates were bulwarks against social transformation. The inhabitants of protectorates were judged to be beyond the pale of British
citizenship for no other reason than their being characterized as subhuman, non-
human, or inferior humans who would need first to reach the status of human beings before they could aspire to that of citizen and holder of rights.

The distinction between colony and protectorate was the foundation of the dual
system of law and politics that was typical of Africa's British colonies and which, I
shall argue, is the principal reason that a modern legal system, regardless of appearances, cannot be counted as a legacy of colonialism in Africa. The dualism went by
different names, but its practical and institutional manifestations were always the
same: common law versus customary law, modern law versus traditional law, regular
courts versus native courts, citizens versus subjects, and so on. One system of law
and its remedies was available to those who were designated human and deserving
of respect due to legal subjects. Those who fell within this category, in line with the
level of development of legal theory and practice in England, could invoke any of
the remedies arising out of the capacity for subjectivity, such as habeas corpus, mandamus, and certiorari. They had no fear of arbitrary arrests and they could expect
not to be judged guilty of having performed an act unless the mens was rea and the
actus was reus.

Another system of "law" (and, one is tempted to add, its chronic lack of remedies) was available to those who were deemed inferior humans and hence not de-

serving of the respect due legal subjects. They were left at the mercy of their native/ indigenous modes of governing and resolving disputes. The justification was that nothing should be done to destroy native institutions and that Africans were best ruled through their own institutions.[58] On the surface, the arrangement looked good enough. Few would deny the importance of preserving indigenous institutions. Because the missionary program of the early to mid-nineteenth century placed native agency at the core of social transformation, one might obtain the mistaken impression that the administrators too were desirous of preserving native institutions in order to allow room for the activation of native agency. Had the administrators shared the missionaries' motivation, they would have left room for native agents to choose to be governed differently. They did not do that. The administrators' motivation was quite different from that of the earlier missionaries. The missionaries wanted natives to remake their societies, and they did not preclude natives from eligibility for full participation in the new ways of living and being human. The administrators, in contrast, would not allow native agency that sought to make the modern way of life its own and redeem the promise of the new. They denied Africans the freedom to choose any element of the good life of a modern flavor. To start with, Africans could not be individuals, and without recognition of individuals there can be no legal subjects.

It is important to point out that the way that I have chosen to describe the two systems of law in the protectorates is not often found in the literature.[59] I attribute this to the fact that analysts have not taken seriously the idea of the legal subject and the peculiarly modern metaphysical template from which it is fashioned. Yet there is a convergence in the literature about the inferior nature of the "legal system" in the protectorates and the fact that it has ill served the people for whom it was meant. The reason is easily located once we grant the adequacy of my earlier description of what a protectorate was. Here are some of the assessments in the literature.

According to Ghai and McAuslan, "The basic point which must be kept in mind in the ensuing discussion is that a protectorate is, in the eyes of English law, a foreign country, and its inhabitants are not therefore British subjects. This applies to a colonial protectorate as much as to a protected state, and it does not matter that the system of government is indistinguishable from that of a colony."[60] Although this description occurs quite often in the literature on African law and politics and analysts often try to describe its consequences, few endeavor to explore its centrality to the organization of political and legal systems in the African colonies. Fewer still tie some of the unsavory consequences to the implications, theoretical and practical, derivable from this division.

By defining Africans as less than or not fully human and their space as other than a colony of expatriate denizens or of surrogate citizens of the mother country, colonial administrators paved the road for the kinds of subversion of principles, failure to adhere to procedures, and outright violence that characterized their behavior in their design and operation of supposedly modern politico-legal institutions in the African context. Had administrators construed Africans and their spaces differently, different consequences would have followed. There are significant grounds for my confidence in the probability of a different outcome. Canada, Australia, and South Africa became successful liberal democracies and rule of law countries for their white inhabitants precisely because their colonial status did not preclude their settlers from enjoying citizenship rights. Even in India, where there was no settler colony, the results were not too dissimilar because Indians were not prima facie precluded from choosing modern institutions and from having serious practice in them and they were not forced to keep the maharajahs and other native rulers. The consequences of stymieing the choices of Africans and disabling the agency of natives were inexorable.

In a discussion of some historical antecedents of human rights in Nigeria, M. A. Ajomo observed: "None of [Nigeria's] pre-independence constitutions was designed with any formal or conscious objective to safeguard human rights. Indeed, it would have been most interesting to see how a constitution with human rights provisions would have been fashioned at a time when under inter-temporal law, slavery, forced labour, racial discrimination and restriction of movement were legitimate instruments in the hands of colonial administrators not only in Nigeria, but all over Africa."[61]

B. O. Nwabueze, commenting on what he calls "political justice" in the post-independence era, writes:

> The view that the objectives and values of the state should be a factor in judicial decision is of course not new in Commonwealth Africa. The idea of "political justice" was an accepted technique of British colonial administration in Africa. An important objective of the colonial state was the subjugation and exploitation of the colonial peoples, and law and the courts were a vital instrument in the pursuit of that objective. The courts were there to enforce the law as well as the extra-legal objectives and policies of the colonial government. The courts of the administrative officers were especially active in this. Unfettered by the principle of strict legalism, they administered a kind of "political justice," which was thought to be pre-eminently conducive to an orderly and paternalistic administration of a backward people. But the "political justice" of the colonial courts was often in disregard of the law. . . . It was also on the ground of disregard of the law that "political justice" was criticised by the more progressive colonial administrators.[62]

The standpoint from which the law became an instrument for the "subjugation and exploitation of the colonial peoples" and under which the courts helped "to enforce the extra-legal objectives and policies of the colonial government" was not limited to the operation of the courts. It was extended, with unfortunate results, to the establishment of the legal profession in the colonies. I cite evidence from Fauz Twaib's study of the legal profession in Tanzania. According to Twaib, "Colonial administrative policy deliberately kept the [legal] profession, in terms of participation, and dispensation, within clearly defined limits. It was intended that the profession cater only to the needs of Europeans and other foreigners."[63]

Although the dual system typified the colonies in Africa, some colonial officials, especially those that served in the judicial arm (such as it was) apprehended the incongruity of the practice they were engaged in with the theory they had imbibed in their training. Some took seriously the "civilizing mission" argument and contended that the British owed it to Africans to school them through the practice of legalism and adherence to the rule of law in the ways of modern living. Others were driven by purely professional concerns, including the lawyer's vocation for strict adherence to rules and unflinching commitment to legality. But the dominant segment of colonial administrators saw no contradiction, inconsistency, incongruity, or wrong in the routine subversion, distortion, or abandonment of the rule of law and the most basic requirements of legality in the colony. We see here the force of presuppositions. Unless and until administrators were willing to acknowledge or could be persuaded that their African wards were in significant respects like themselves, there was no way that they could believe that they were wronging Africans who, after all, were not citizens. The responses of administrators to charges that they were not upholding the principles of civilization in the colonies almost without exception came down to their exclusion of Africans from the human universe.

The reaction of administrators in Tanganyika when some members of the judicial arm challenged the exclusion of lawyers from native courts and the lack of requirement that colonial officers who sat as magistrates in native courts be lawyers or have training in the law is instructive. I quote from Twaib:

> The following exchanges, for example, took place between Alison Russel, then Chief Justice of Tanganyika, and Sir Philip Mitchell, then Governor, on proposals to simplify procedural rules in Native Courts. The Chief Justice considered the proposals as having been motivated by the conscious or unconscious intention on the part of administrative officers to rid themselves of the labour of trying cases according to definite rules of procedure, rather than the desire "to relieve illiterate native of embarrassment." He further wrote: "I submit for consideration of Your Excellency that . . . there are no doubt some administrative officers who look back regretfully to the days of Livingstone under his tree or James Martin marching up from the coast: days when, unencumbered by stationery, undistressed by the labour of keeping a record and untroubled by the thought that somebody might want to read it, decisions were given offhand and out of the head; and so on to the next *shauri* [case]. This method of disposing of cases is no doubt extremely prompt and agreeable. But everyone who has tried cases knows how often a quiet perusal of a well-kept record influences a judgment."
>
> The Governor's response was a complete disapproval of the Chief Justice's views. He retorted: "Livingstone under his mango tree probably got a good deal nearer to the truth and to justice than a Judge on the bench in Dar es Salaam." Thus, the administration considered legally qualified Judges, magistrates, and advocates as anathema to the native's notion of justice.[64]

A different governor, Sir George Taubman Goldie, this time in Nigeria, expressed a similar sentiment about why there should be a similar dualism:

> Even an imperfect and tyrannical native African judicial administration, if its extreme excesses were controlled by European supervision[,] would be in the early stages, productive of far less discomfort to its subjects than well-intentioned, but ill-directed effort of European Magistrates, often young and headstrong, and most invariably gifted with sympathy and introspective powers. If the welfare of the native is to be considered, if dangerous revolts are to be obviated, the general principles of ruling on African principles through native rulers must be followed for the present.[65]

The choice of the so-called native option was made without any consultation whatsoever with Africans, especially the new class of modern Africans, graduates of the missionary school of modernization. Africans were not consulted to ascertain their preference. Of course, the graduates of missionary enterprise resolutely resisted the sociocryonic option.

Few administrators expressed qualms about their decision to exclude Africans from the purview of modern law in which rights were central and the sovereignty of the individual sacrosanct, especially about the impact such exclusion would have on the development of modern institutions in Africa. In many of the areas where they meant to rule via African institutions, the communities concerned were not as homogeneous as the administrators pretended they were. Aside from the fact that in some areas there were cities where individuals belonging to different ethnicities and nationalities lived, it required a stretch of the imagination to suggest that they could all be accommodated under one undifferentiated African customary law. One could say that a qualified recognition of this fact probably explained the policy of encouraging different ethnic and national groups to live apart even when they occupied the same town or city. The problem, though, is that in other areas there were large numbers of natives who had signed on to the way of life enjoined by Christian-inflected modernity and who insisted that they had earned the right to be recognized as modern citizens and treated as such. But, in part because of what I referred to in chapter 2 as the foisting of African individuality on individual Africans, administrators forced this group of Africans into the category of "native" sans differentiation.

Finally, the policy of apparent preference for ruling through African institutions was a sham because in almost every case, the British mounted punitive expeditions against any African ruler that sought to affirm her or his independence or any African people that had their own ideas about what their institutions were or how they were meant to operate when those ideas were at variance with those of the governor and his cohort. Africans who embraced modernity were judged inauthentic. It turns out, then, that "rule through African institutions" was a ruse for distorting or abolishing African institutions and practices or generally preempting any attempts by Africans to lay hold of new institutions, practices, and ways of life and indigenize them. The net effect was to leave Africans bereft of the benefits of the new while simultaneously arresting the evolution of indigenous institutions powered by native agency. It was sociocryonics par excellence. The consequences have continued to reverberate in and stalk the African context to the present.

Once Africans were ruled ineligible for the benefits of modern institutions, the native courts and the "for-Africans-only" legal system worked against preparing Africans for the successful implantation of a modern legal system. The African half of the dual legal system was marked by disregard for the law, disdain for procedure, abjuring of technical rules, inattention to consistency, and sheer failure to recognize the integrity due the person of the native. Where the modern legal system was anchored on individual responsibility, the colonial legal system was suffused with laws requiring collective responsibility; where the modern legal system allowed the manifestation of subjective will in action without undue restriction, the colonial legal system hemmed in native subjective will with myriad restrictions including, especially, spatial ones; where the modern legal system was founded upon respect for the integrity of the person, the colonial legal system legitimized or required forced labor that was, at bottom, a denial of subjectivity; where the modern legal system sought to cloak itself in legitimacy founded on the consent of the governed through the latter having a say in the constitution of their government, the colonial legal system made it a felony—sedition—for those who asked that they not be ruled by a government in the constitution of which they had had no say; where the modern legal system had a built-in presumption of innocence for an accused, the colonial legal system had a built-in presumption of guilt until proven innocent for native accused because, according to the image of the native that dominated the thinking of the colonial administrators, Africans were congenital liars.

Why did those who claimed to induct their wards into a civilized way of life and lift them out of what they considered to be the morass of heathenism and savagery so willingly turn away from the path dictated by their aim? Why did it come so easily to them to not embrace earnestly the task of delivering on the promise of civilization to African natives, in this case in the area of law? The answer is so simple and is often so casually mentioned in most writings that it is almost a scandal that little or no attempt has been made to place it at the root of the preemption of the project of modernity in Africa: Modern law is built on the metaphysical template of the self and the necessity to protect it from the predation of other selves either in their individual capacities or organized in groups. If the African could not be a self, then it follows that he or she could not be a participant in the system built around the self and could not be eligible for its benefits in law or in politics, in economics or in culture. It is only by tracing the nonperformance of colonial administrators that we are enabled to make sense of why otherwise humane, even noble individuals who kept trumpeting their concern for the welfare of Africans would at the same time put in place institutions and practices that subverted the promise. Ghai and McAuslan have well and starkly described the consequences of their preference:

Thus neither the lawyers nor the politicians [at the time of the Scramble for Africa] saw the function of the law as standing impartially between two sides, or even leaning in favour of the weaker side, but as making the way smooth for the stronger. Was it impolitic to annex African protectorates? This did not matter; the law was sufficiently flexible to ensure full governmental powers in a protectorate. Was it politic to break agreements with African rulers? It did not matter; the law would permit an Act of State to be pleaded which would avoid the embarrassment of having to justify one's action in court. It may be unrealistic to expect lawyers to have acted any differently, but then it is also unrealistic and not a little hypocritical to suggest that one of the main benefits of British colonialism was the introduction of the Rule of Law into Africa, for if that concept means anything, it means that the law should help the weak and control the strong, and not *vice versa*. From the African point of view the English law introduced into East Africa was one of the main weapons used for colonial domination, and in several important fields remained so for most of the colonial period, only changing when Africans began to gain political power. The role of the received law then from the beginning of the colonial period in Kenya was to be a tool at the disposal of the dominant political and economic groups.[66]

The ugly reality that was inaugurated at the commencement of the era of formal colonialism and that Ghai and McAuslan have described not only marked the evolution of colonialism; its consequences are still very much present with us today. I shall now explore how the ugly reality was institutionalized in practice.

Separation of Powers

The metaphysics of modernity is one of diremption, of separation beginning with a philosophical anthropology that conceives of individuals as being naturally separate one from another and needing to negotiate the terms of their association in the motley groups within which they are forced to lead their lives. The same metaphysics undergirds the many separations within the modern environment: state and civil society, public and private spheres, state and church, politics and law, and so on. The same inspiration lies behind the doctrine of the separation of powers by which modern society separates the legislative from the executive arm of government and both from the judiciary. The separation of powers is motivated by a philosophical outlook that holds that human beings are vulnerable to corruption by power and can be tempted to subvert power to partisanship. The pioneer thinkers of modernity had strong historical grounds for their suspicious attitude toward human nature, having had to fight their way out of the thrall of monarchical or ecclesiastical absolutism in which spiritual and temporal as well as legislative, executive, and judicial powers were combined in one person or small group of persons. The separation of the judiciary is important for an additional but related reason.

The formal equality of all persons in the modern polity requires that all be equal under the law and that preferences of station or of birth not be allowed to tilt the scales of justice. Additionally, the principle that the judge/adjudicator should be

different from and impartial to the accuser and the accused is calculated to ensure that power-wielders do not use it to judge unfairly or wrongly those they may
have accused without cause. It is the fundamental basis of the independence of the
judiciary and for the judiciary's insulation from executive or legislative interference.
It is also why the judiciary is insulated in numerous ways from legislative or executive overreaching. Simultaneously, those who serve in the judiciary are required to
aspire to a capacity for impartiality that borders on the superhuman, especially in
light of the negative philosophical anthropology that is part of the theoretical foundation of the modern social ordering. It is obvious that judges often fall short of
the requisite threshold in the discharge of their functions. They are not judged by
their failure. Indeed, that the failures are so few in a good legal system is testimony
to how much judges strive to attain the threshold. Judges who demonstrate the capacity for impartiality in spite of the proclivities of human nature are judged good.
To the extent that we take seriously the oft-repeated claim that part of the legacy
of colonialism is the installation of a modern legal system in African countries, we
must consider how the colonial administrators did with respect to the doctrine of
separation of powers that is an absolute fundament for the independence of the judiciary.

There is no doubt that colonial administrators worked with and installed separation in African colonies. But, alas, it was the wrong kind of separation. They rig-
idly separated the natives from the colonizers, hence the dual legal system. They also
separated natives from one another, not in order to foster the modern individualist
principle of social ordering but instead to preempt them from forming new identities through their work (trade unions), civic associations based on mutual interests across ethnic/regional lines (political parties), and novel supranational identities overlaying the traditions of particularism (citizenship). This was not the kind of
separation called for by the new mode of social living that colonial tutelage claimed
or that it ought to have heralded in Africa.

The appropriate separation would have seen the colonial authorities inaugurat-
ing (at the very least) institutions and practices that would have represented nodes
for future transformation to modern legal systems. Lest I be accused of not taking
a realistic view of the conditions in the colonies and protectorates in Africa from
the beginning through much of the colonial period, which were marked by chronic
shortages of relevant trained personnel, I would like to submit that the difficulty is
often exaggerated and that many (including African) scholars who advance it give
the impression that the road taken by the administrators was the only one available or the best among possible several others. In light of the discussion in previous chapters, I contend that had there been a different view of Africans and their
agency, other possible roads might have been considered and the problems that are
now virtually shibboleths would have attracted answers other than those that were
provided.

Doubtless at the commencement of the colonial period, the enterprise suffered from chronic shortage of personnel in all areas, including the judiciary. This was neither unexpected nor extraordinary. It was the same situation that the British confronted in colonial America, colonial Canada, Australia, and South Africa. Anyone familiar with the history of the original thirteen colonies of the United States also knows that their judicial or other organs of government were not staffed from the onset by the best of men or by qualified ones. This, however, did not lead colonialists to make the same choices that were made in Africa. So what were the possible options in Africa that were not considered?

One option was to increase the number of British personnel. That was not feasible simply because where Africa was concerned, successive British administrations (not to mention public opinion) were determined to enjoy the benefits of empire without having to pay for it. When we add to that the unattractiveness of West Africa for Britons and its quickly acquired notoriety as the white man's grave, it is easy to see why the ranks of British administrators could not be expanded considerably. Another option would have been to recruit local personnel and train them. The advantages of this option should be obvious. For instance, the lasting success of missionary work is traceable to its embrace and cultivation of native agency at its inception.[67] No large-scale social transformation can be effected without the mediation of native agents except in situations where the native presence is completely devastated and the territory peopled with the foreign conquering population. By deploying and taking advantage of natives, the colonial administrators would have put in place agents of social transformation who were unlikely to be stinting, once persuaded of the desirability of the new way of life, in their commitment to and prosecution of the task of remaking their society in all aspects. It was an option that recommended itself much more strongly because there were individuals in some colonies and protectorates in West Africa who had been inducted into modernity as a result of their conversion to and acceptance of Christianity. This is not to say that they were candidates who were ready or able to go; quite the contrary. I am saying merely that some of them had gone to great lengths to train themselves in the modern way of life and had, in some cases, become apostles of the new to their fellows and that these individuals constituted a pool from which possible personnel could have been drawn for training. At various times throughout the colonial period, the option was exercised but never in a way that would have helped along the task of social transformation. It was done only at the level of keeping the administrative wheel grinding along. The explanation for not going farther is not hard to find.

The imposition of a spurious African individuality and its complex of negative associations meant that no distinction could be made between Africans who were desirous of change and those who wished to preserve the status quo. Had the alternative path of recognizing differences among African ranks been chosen, the initial merging of powers would have been a mere stop on the way to a full-fledged modern

legal system. But later developments would have tended to increase the separation
of powers, and the judiciary would likely have been staffed by natives who were taking the initiative of training themselves for service in that sector. Administrators in
the judicial arm who thought that Africans deserved a modern legal system, whatever their rationale, reminded their colleagues at various junctures of the importance of putting in place structures that were consonant with the new way of life
and reminded them that introducing these structures was part of their justification
for exercising rule over the natives without the latter's consent. For this group of administrators, the problems in the way of installing a modern legal system were of a
practical kind. Insofar as the will was there, they reasoned, there were alternatives
that were not being pursued. More important, they thought that movement should
be in the direction of increasing the separation of powers and ensuring the independence of the judiciary.

I cite one example that is not atypical of the kind of debates that took place between the administrative and the judicial arms of the colonial administration in
Kenya. According to Ghai and McAuslan, a commission of inquiry was set up in
1933 to look into the administration of justice in Kenya, Uganda, and Tanganyika
in criminal matters. The commission concluded: "The machinery of the administration of justice as apparently set up by law in these territories does not work, and
as at present constituted cannot work."[68] According to the authors, the commission
condemned the operative "administrative conception of the function of the courts"
and "rejected the administrative approach *tout court*."[69] It is significant that three of
the five members of the commission were lawyers and were unsparing in their condemnation of the turning of what was meant to be an impartial arbiter into an administrative tool for keeping natives in their place. It is instructive that the commission concluded "that while administrative officers must for some time be retained
as magistrates, their powers should be reduced, the High Courts' valuable powers of
revision of criminal cases must be retained, more judges should be appointed to the
High Court so that there could be more circuits and the aim should be to replace
administrative officers with legally qualified professional magistrates."[70]

It is of further interest to us that the commission and administrative officers di-
verged on the subject of technicalities. Administrative officers insisted that when
high court judges reversed convictions because of technicalities, they let people go
free "who were clearly guilty." This was a curious thing to say. Under the modern
system, trials were to be impartial and findings were to be based on evidence and
guided by rules clearly formulated to show that the guilt of the accused had been established by reason and beyond reasonable doubt. On what basis might an administrator challenge the outcome of such trials or the nullification of outcomes that did
not hew strictly to such procedure? Obviously, such administrators must have felt
that their summary say-so should have sufficed. Meanwhile, the commission insisted
that process was no less important than outcome and that where injustice had been

done, it needed to be redressed and that this was not just a matter of technicalities. They insisted that "convictions were only quashed on serious irregularities."[71]

The terms used to describe the differences between two arms of the colonial administration hold fecund implications for my thesis. The lawyers do not have to be construed as having a more positive view of Africans: They probably held the views they canvassed only because they were following the dictates of the morality of duty enjoined by their profession. But some may have shared the views of the missionaries that we encountered in chapter 2 and believed as did the latter that they were duty bound to induct Africans into the modern way of life. Hence they called for a gradual program of increasing professionalization of the judiciary to move it closer and closer to the British ideal as the practical problems of staffing were solved.

Administrators challenged the assumptions on which the commission's conclusions were based. The chief native commissioner faulted the commission's assumption that what had been inducted into Kenya was "a British system of justice." What had been in place since 1907 instead was "a different system for Kenya suited to local conditions in which magistrates were given powers and required to exercise them 'without undue regard to technicalities.' . . . The administration of justice to the Africans had been entrusted to those who knew about them because only with their background knowledge could magistrates get at the truth."[72] Ghai and McAuslan conclude that the difference between the commission and its administrator-critics "represented a fundamental division of attitudes as to the nature and function of courts and law enforcement."[73]

Administrators did not try to pretend that what they were operating was an empirical analogue of the British legal system. The legal system was "an essential part of native administration" whose sole function was "overriding necessity to maintain law and order." They contended that such subversions were necessitated by the need to attend to "the welfare of society as a whole" and the fact that "until order and respect for order had been established, law and justice were irrelevant and obstructive. Force, not justice, was respected and the courts must be used for the first objective before they could be used for the second."[74] This was not unlike Lugard's insistence that the African was only amenable to the logic of the prod.

The standpoint of these administrators was "anathema to the judiciary and most lawyers." For them, their point of view was convergent with that of the Bushe Commission,[75] which had stated that "it is the duty of the Government to civilize and maintain peace and good order and this can only be done by the introduction of British conceptions of wrong-doing." As far as the commissioners were concerned, "the duty to civilize and the introduction of a British judicial system are correlated, and the fundamentals of this system were the need for the judge to comply with the law, the notion of individual criminal responsibility, and a procedure which would prevent one innocent person from being convicted even if it meant that nine guilty men went free."[76]

Similar divergences of opinion had emerged in Nigeria in 1914 when Lugard introduced court reforms that involved setting up provincial courts from which lawyers were excluded and from which appeals lay to the governor. These courts were violently opposed by lawyers in Nigeria (of whom there were quite a few) and by the body of modern enlightened opinion that saw the reforms as retrograde and a destruction of the gains that had been made in southern Nigeria on the road to developing modern politico-legal institutions in the colony. Here is Omoniyi Adewoye's description of the reaction of African lawyers to Lugard's judicial reorganization.

> Then there were the lawyers. The African barrister, after his experience at the English Inns of Court, came back to his country ignorant of the laws and customs of his own people, but "thoroughly imbued with English manners and beliefs." Far from being upholders of African ways of life, African barristers stood out clearly as "opponents of things African." What was more, their professional role in the protectorate was only to direct the eyes of the masses deliberately away from the Resident and the chiefs and towards the Supreme Court as "the only seat of authority." Every case taken out of the hands of the chiefs and away from the provincial court "is another step upwards in their progress towards attaining political power," because of the importance attached in popular estimation to the exercise of judicial powers. It was the chief secretary to the government, H.M.M. Moore, who clinched the argument by saying that unbridled exercise of jurisdiction by the Supreme Court in the protectorate "can only end in the political supremacy of the lawyer over these communities."[77]

What causative factors explained the success of lawyers and the interest of the new African elite to make the modern heritage their own? Again, Adewoye bears quoting at length:

> In considering the roots of litigation in Southern Nigeria one should not fail to mention the growth of individualism. The factors that contributed to this development are connected with the imposition of colonial rule itself: the opening up of the country to the outside world, western education, missionary influence, the new money-oriented economy, foreign travel and the like. These various factors imbued the people with new values, sometimes out of tune with the traditional mores. Among the educated Africans in particular, there was a heightened consciousness of the individual's worth and, by the same token, a decreasing emphasis, in varying degrees, on kinship ties and obligations. With individualism went feelings of independence and personal freedom. The individual resorted to the court if he felt his rights were being encroached upon—thanks to the over-arching British colonial umbrella under which such rights could be enforced. This was the sociological environment in which the British-established courts had been operating in Southern Nigeria before 1914. Surely, one cannot ignore it in judging the wisdom or otherwise of the direction of the judicial reforms of 1914.[78]

In almost every case, the goal of fitting the colonies with a modern legal system lost out to the point of view of administrators and the elements of a modern legal system were not put in place until after independence. Unfortunately, African countries have not seen fit since independence to explore the modern legacy in economics, law, and politics—a move that would enable them to realize the magnitude of damage done by colonialism. The consequence of the victory of the administrators' view of law, construed as law in the service of order, of justice as political justice, of the legal system as a subordinate arm of the executive, was that throughout the colonial period until the eve of independence, the doctrine of separation of powers was meaningless and the impotence of the judiciary vis-à-vis the administration was continually underscored.

By now it should be more clear why the legal system evolved the way it did in the colonial period. Once the debate about what type of legal system was suitable for the African was resolved in favor of the colonial legal system, the choice of means was severely constrained. In such a setting the means that would have led to the emergence of a modern legal system, for example those identified by the commission discussed by Ghai and McAuslan above, did not attract the attention of the administrators. Even when such personnel were available, colonial authorities refused to recruit them in part because the colonial purpose was different and the color bar subverted the recruitment of qualified Africans or the training of new recruits. Finally, in imposing the system of indirect rule, colonial authorities chose sociocryonics over progress. It would have been bad enough if we understood it simply as preserving antiquity and its salience in the lives of ordinary Africans. It was worse because it did not allow the natives to choose what was to be preserved, it distorted the institutions that it pretended to preserve, and it manufactured other institutions de novo and ascribed them to the natives.

The greater percentage of the population was excluded from modern jurisdictions, and where there were no customary laws, administrators invented them: Witness the warrant chiefs in Igboland.[79] Omoniyi Adewoye is the leading historian of the legal profession in Nigeria. In a paper titled "100 Years of the Legal Profession in Nigeria," he observed that in colonial Nigeria, "the inferior position of judges vis-a-vis the Executive had become an accepted fact by 1910."[80] He further averred: "The (colonial) judiciary also left another legacy: the habit of judicial self-restraint underlain by a certain desire to safeguard the interest of the Executive. . . . Nor was the administration of justice devoid of political and other extraneous considerations, especially where fundamental issues of power, authority, prestige or major economic interests of the colonial regime were involved. The courts were thus used without regard for any fine points of law and procedure to deal with cases of alleged slave-trading and economic sabotage."[81] He concluded: "The exigencies of the colonial situation precluded putting into operation the English notion of judicial independence."[82] For instance, most of the judges were administrators. Adewoye was able to find only one exception to this rule—that of George Graham Paul, who served from 1933 to 1939.

Throughout the colonial period, the administrators who held sway did nothing to introduce the separation of powers or to put in place the foundations for the independence of the judiciary. Sharing his thoughts on the historical evolution of the Nigerian judiciary at a conference in 1986, Justice Ayo Irikefe, then chief justice of Nigeria, said:

> During and after our British colonial experience, the courts in this country were run as an extended arm of the executive sector of government. What we had was [a] Judicial Department as opposed to a National or State Judiciary. The British needed the courts in order to enforce pax Britannica while at the end of their rule it was considered both necessary and expedient by those who replaced the British that law and order should continue to be enforced through the existing courts. Thus it was that with effect from 1960, the courts in the country were left to function as they had done in the past as a department of the executive arm of government. Many citizens, lawyers included, stated from time to time that the judiciary was the third arm of the government.[83]

Justice Karibi-Whyte expressed similar sentiments when he remarked: "Like the preceding era, and to a considerable extent during the struggle for political independence, the Judiciary was dependent in all aspects of its functions upon guidance from without. The Judiciary was not separate from the Executive. It was in fact a department of and controlled by the Executive branch of the Government."[84] The turning of judges into civil servants, the inferiorization of the judiciary, the substitution of politics for merit in the staffing of the judiciary, and related defects that have been identified in the post-independence judiciaries of Africa are continuous with processes that originated in the operations of the colonial administration. One does not have to commit to the view that the situation in the colony inexorably determined the processes that unfolded after independence. Nevertheless, one cannot escape the fact that as an order of practical reason, law requires consistent practice and constant activity for its operators to become proficient at operating it. To the extent that the colonial finishing school in law was an education in arbitrariness, subversion of procedure, and plain illegalities committed by those who were supposed to guide the implantation of the rule of law, one must not discount the causal impact of colonial education on the processes of institution formation and construction of legal consciousness in the post-independence era. I shall have more to say about this anon. It is time to consider the last element of the preemption of modernity in the area of law under colonialism: the rule of law.

Rule of Law

The rule of law places limits on the state's power to interfere with the individual. Since in the eyes of the colonial administrators Africans could not be individuals, there could be no subjects that deserved protection under the rubric of the rule of law. Here we find the origins of the nonrecognition of the legal subject that continues to dominate theory and practice in contemporary African legal systems. Africans must perforce remain members of "tribes" even when many sought to have their individuality outside of tribal boundaries recognized. In the area of criminal law, the notion of personal responsibility barely resonated in colonial administrative policies. Whole villages were sacked for transgressions committed by individuals if those individuals could not be immediately apprehended. Family members, friends, even townspeople were detained if the authorities could not identify a specific wrongdoer or if the suspect could not be found. White administrators used the instrumentality of law to punish their African subordinates for what would at best have been civil infractions.

Echoing sentiments that I cited earlier from Ajomo, in the chapter of their work titled "Human Rights and Public Order," Ghai and McAuslan wrote:

Human Rights, as defined and protected in the Universal Declaration of Human Rights, the European Convention on Human Rights and the Bills of Rights in the Constitutions of many countries, had little place in the colonial regime established in Kenya. . . . The colonial administration established and maintained by means of law a governmental and social system characterized by authoritarianism, and racial discrimination in such vital fields as the administration of justice, the development of representative institutions, and agrarian administration.[85]

In the name of excluding "unnecessary technicalities," administrators made no effort to socialize Africans into the respect for procedure and principled adjudication that are the hallmarks of the rule of law. By turning judges into civil servants, colonialism kindled in those who were therein schooled an attitude that made them think in civil servants' terms and see themselves as protectors of the government against the citizen rather than (at the very least) as impartial arbiters between the citizen and the state or, more appropriately, as bulwarks for the protection of the citizen from overreaching by the state. Administrators, concomitantly, were armed with wide discretionary powers supported by ouster clauses in constitutions that denuded substantive provisions of power through the insertion of exceptions designed to empower the state. Such clauses barred such judicial organs as existed from exercising any review or adjudication powers over the administrators and their actions.[86]

Because lawyers were excluded in the native courts, the development of the legal profession was deliberately stunted and the merit principle was subverted. Native lawyers, even though they were well qualified, could not practice on behalf of white clients, and since they were excluded from native courts, they had little incentive to study law and aspire to practice it in the colonies. As a result, colonial policies prevented another crucial component of the modern legal system—the existence of a vigorous, well-educated, and experienced bar—from developing. The bar that managed to develop did so in spite of the colonial administration, thanks to the dogged pertinacity of natives.

The government of the colonies was a government of men and (occasionally) women, not of law. It was absolute. To ask questions about the legitimacy of its rule was to risk a charge of sedition, a criminalization of discourse about public matters insofar as they related to colonial rule. As a government instituted to keep down the natives the government was captive to faction—white administrators, settlers, and so forth—and thus was not an institution constituted to ensure that legal subjects were protected in the enjoyment of their solitudes, free to have, hold, and seek to realize their own conceptions of the good life.

What I have described so far in the last few sections lasted in African countries for the entire length of the colonial period. Then, suddenly, quite abruptly, in all the countries without exception, on the very eve of independence, the niceties of the rule of law were written and enshrined in the constitutions by which the territories were to be governed after independence. It is crucial to stress the suddenness and abruptness of the shift that was inaugurated at independence. Only by so doing can we make better sense of the failures in the post-independence period. Institutions and their operators had been steeped in coercion, arbitrariness, and a view of the law as an extension of the government and a means of keeping down those opposed to or otherwise ill-disposed toward the government. It was these individuals who were expected overnight to make a complete turnaround to embrace proceduralism, strict legalism, respect for the individual, and protection of individuals from the government's overreaching. I am surprised that others have apprehended the phenomena that I too have described but have failed to see how drastic a change this would have meant and why the likelihood of success was close to nil.

Reaping the Whirlwind

Almost everyone who has cared to examine the performance of African judiciaries in the post-independence period has commented on their inability to deliver on the promise of the rule of law and of serving as the citizens' bulwark against "power's all-intrusive claims." I have already cited some explanations from some writers as to why this has been the case. I can summarize with the aid of a few views the general terms of the indictment of African judiciaries. Borrowing Mark Twain's satirical remark about the United States ("In our country we have those three unspeakable precious things—freedom of speech, freedom of conscience, and the prudence never to practice either"), Justice Chukwudifu Oputa, one of Nigeria's most profound jurists, said: "In the same way, in [Nigeria], we [mouth] the independence of the Judiciary, we proclaim it in theory, we provide for it in our Constitution but in practice we exercise 'the prudence' never to grant the Judiciary true and *de facto* independence from Executive violence and Executive control, *due mainly from our not understanding the place and the role of the Court.*"[87] After describing the dismal reality of a systematic undermining of the judiciary, beginning with its chronic underfunding and financial vulnerability, Oputa concluded: "After considering all these and more, I came to the sorry conclusion that our people do not understand and they do not appreciate the place and role of the Judiciary in our society. . . . It will be pointless to preach the independence of the Judiciary to those who do not understand what the Judiciary is all about."[88] Here the judge is talking about the attitude of the executive toward the judiciary.[89] Twaib reached a similar judgment concerning the same relationship in Tanzania. "The above instances are illustrative of the inability to appreciate the constitutional division of functions which vests upon the Judiciary and other bodies of dispute settlement the power and right to determine matters concerning the rights and duties of citizens. It can only be hoped that as the country moves further towards constitutionalism and democracy, there would be greater respect by the executive and legislative arms of the State for principles of human rights, the Rule of Law and the role of the legal process."[90]

The executive constitutes one tier of the problem. Another tier is that made up of judges themselves. After reviewing some of the cases concerning human rights in the post-independence Supreme Court of Nigeria, Justice Karibi-Whyte observed:

> In coming to these decisions the ordinary rules of construction of statutes were applied. The provisions construed were regarded as indeed they were, ordinary statutes of the imperial Parliament or the local legislature as the case may be. *No special emphasis was laid on the fact that the liberty of the citizen was involved and that in such cases any benefit of doubt in a decision between the executive and the citizen should be given to the citizen.* The court in construing the provisions of such statutes should in all cases, lean towards the liberty of the subject but careful not going beyond the natural construction of the statute. The question that was being asked in all cases was what Parliament meant by the words used? *It did not appear that there was at any time any anxiety to safeguard the liberty of the subject.*[91]

We do not need to posit executive interference in the decisions Justice Karibi-Whyte criticized. What he is pointing to is the basic predisposition of the judges involved not to take seriously the notion of the legal subject whose liberty and sovereignty over self the modern state was constituted to protect. Those judges were not seized of the idea that freedom is the natural state of being human and that it is those who wish to abridge that freedom who must justify themselves. That the judges never even bothered to show that they were involved in some balancing act between the demands of public order and those of safeguarding the liberty of the subject is proof that these ideas did not resonate with them.

We now come to the third tier, formed by the society within which the various organs of government operate and whose members are bound by the laws formulated, enforced, and interpreted by the former. Ought we to expect from them a different attitude that would appreciate the liberty of the subject and defend same as well as the independence of the judiciary that is a requirement for its existence?

Concerning Kenya, Ghai and McAuslan answer our question thus: "Executive discretion unfettered by law was, to some extent controlled by political means as far
as Europeans were concerned through their system of cooperative administration,
but such a system did not apply to Africans for most of the colonial period. Thus
Africans in Kenya came to political awareness within a legal system whose rhetoric
praised equality and justice but whose practice sharply distinguished between those
with, and those without, power, wealth and influence."[92] "Such an inheritance,"
they conclude, "cannot but breed cynicism and a lack of respect for the processes
of the law. The law is seen solely as being a tool of the wielders of power who use it
as they think fit, legalizing their own illegal exercises of power, and attempting to
prevent the acquisition of power by, and the development of, the powerless."[93] The
people had not had any experience of their lives being governed by due process, of
the law respecting them in their individual uniqueness, of the state being restrained
by law, of those who had power being forced to exercise it within the limits set by
law, and so on. It would thus have been too much to expect them to be at the bar-
ricades safeguarding the rule of law in the immediate post-independence period.

I conclude that the parlous state of human rights theory and practice, the unsuccessful transplantation of the rule of law and its institutional appurtenances in
Africa in the post-independence period, must be regarded as the sordid harvest of
the whirlwind that was sown by colonialism. Mine is not a garden variety of invok-
ing the colonial bogeyman to explain Africa's failure. But we cannot say that because we must not blame colonialism for everything that has gone wrong with Africa, we may not blame it for anything at all. Without a serious, adequate, maybe
even correct explanation of how we got to where we now are, it is unlikely that we
will identify the correct way out of the present quandaries.

Various analysts have cited, inter alia, the following reasons why the judiciary has
turned out the way that it has in Africa:

> (1) African judges tend to embrace analytical positivism, especially of the Austinian
> variety, which predisposes them to see no evil, hear no evil, and speak no evil of the
> laws they are called upon to interpret and adjudicate which, in turn, explains their
> proclivity toward judicial passivity.
> (2) The intellectual quality of judicial appointees is poor.
> (3) The system that they are called upon to operate did not grow organically out of
> the traditions and values of African societies, as they had been in the older democ-
> racies.[94]

Without doubt, (1) through (3) must form part of a complete explanation for why
the rule of law has not taken roots in Africa. But as they stand, some of them explain little and themselves require further explanations. For instance, the chief justice who presided over the cases Karibi-Whyte and Nwabueze and Ezejiofor criticized was none other than Adetokunbo Ademola, and the attorney general who

advised the government when some of those same cases came up was none other than Taslim Elias.[95] It is out of the question to accuse either one of those jurists of poor intellectual endowments. So we are right to ask why neither of them displayed "any anxiety to safeguard the liberty of the subject." Nor can we accept the explanation that the legal system is foreign to Africa. Unless we were to suggest that Africans are naturally incapable of learning new ways of doing things or have a natural disposition away from the rule of law and democracy, we must look for the historical roots of the problem and show how the historical circumstances that I described in the last section have combined to produce the mess we are in.

Law is an order of practical reason. Although it has a nature peculiar to it, it is a product of human reason that is ultimately discovered, articulated, and institutionalized through the medium of human practice. The countries that are usually held up as models of rule of law polities each have histories of arbitrary rule, monarchical despotism, slavery and lynching, aristocratic oppression, and other forms of misrule by humans. Nor did modern law come into being fully constituted. The discovery of the individual that undergirds modern law and the development of the complex protections now erected around this individual are themselves products of history. In this evolutionary process the development of the law has been shaped by judges (some of whom have been savants of their societies) who have succeeded in anticipating the possibilities lurking within their politico-legal traditions and writing judgments that drew out the intimations of those traditions. Some of them were minorities when they initially articulated their anticipations as dissents, only to have their views become later the correct and majority opinion.[96] Brilliant advocates and legal draftsmen and women have also done their own part in putting flesh on the law's skeleton through effective and imaginative lawyering, thereby enabling judges and legislators alike to make and interpret laws in ways that enhance the objective of the modern state as well as help move the polity closer to whatever is best in its traditions. Finally, I must mention ordinary people who take seriously the profession by their rulers and their ideologists of the equality of all before the law, of the entitlement of prince and pauper alike to equal protection of the law, and who, as a consequence, insist that their rulers play by the rules announced beforehand, respecting their entitlements and forbearances under the ambit of the law. They sue, they challenge, they protest, they vote their rulers out of office. All that I have just adumbrated could not have obtained without a matrix of common and shared meaning that binds the disparate groups in society together: the philosophy and ideology of modernity.

For Africans to replicate the processes iterated above, they too would have had to have constant practice of the sort I have identified. Given that colonialism was the medium through which the key politico-legal institutions were introduced to Africans, it follows that any adequate explanation of why those institutions have not worked in Africa must investigate how colonialism operated and guided their careers while it lasted. Where the latter is concerned, the record is one of repeated abortions. The institutions were set up without their animating spirits and only on the eve of independence were desperate efforts made to decree into existence African sophistication at manipulating them. The chronic lack of practice meant that the operators of the institutions were bereft of the appropriate mindset. Their mindset was of the type that went with the arbitrariness, coercion, and disrespect for rules that they had developed as a consequence of their practice within the colonial system.

The impact on the people was more devastating. Given the underdevelopment of civil society in the colonies, it should be no surprise that the electorate in those countries have never had any say in who was elevated to the bench, low or high; it has always been done by the executive with perfunctory consultation with the bar association or the occasional vetting by the legislature where appropriate. Until recently, there was little or no debate about the performance of the judiciary in Nigeria, and I have yet to hear of a protest by the public, even the informed segments of it, when judges have been victims of humiliation or violence or intimidation by the executive and others. The populace expresses no outrage at the fact that judges are scandalously underpaid and that they do not have appropriate resources to work with. In such circumstances, the system is unlikely to attract reasonably qualified candidates to the bench, much less attract lawyers with sterling qualities. Finally, the citizenry does not rise in stout defense of judicial independence because deep down everyone, even those who are supposed to know better, either does not understand the idea of independence or does not think it is necessary or actually think that it is dangerous. For others, judges are civil servants who are mere mouthpieces of the government. Others are convinced, for the most part wrongly, that judges are complicit in setting criminals free on "technicalities" or that only those who have extrajudicial lines of communication with the judge either through bribery or shared membership in secret societies, social clubs, or political parties win their cases. In sum, a combination of factors that originated in the colonial era but has persisted in the post-independence period has served to ensure that modern legal theory and practice has not had the same resonance in Africa as it has in the countries from which it was imported. Aberrant judicial behavior, executive thuggery, and legislative overreaching are merely symptoms of this deeply embedded malaise, which is traceable to the abortions created by colonialism.

After independence, what was called for was a radical reconstitution of the institutions bequeathed by colonialism. Of course, given the underdevelopment of those institutions under colonialism, the reader is right to ask where the resources for the required reconstitution would have come from. Needless to say, the strengths of the various countries were not the same respecting the presence of segments of their population who might have served as the nucleus for this movement. West African countries were better placed than East African ones, for reasons described in chapter 2. But other factors were at work that preempted the necessary transitions. This is where we must place the responsibility for not putting the issue of modernity on the agenda in the newly independent countries on the shoulders of intellectuals. It is why I am asking that the latest opportunity to redeem the promise of a transition to modernity for Africa not be frittered away on the altar of blind but irrelevant and unproductive nationalism or sheer intellectual indolence. My hope is that works such as the present one will contribute to this rebuilding process.

_6_

Two Modern
African Constitutions

In the last chapter, I argued that in accounting for the failure of a rule of law regime to take root in Africa, we must resist the temptation, however alluring it may be, to blame African cultures or any so-called defects in "the African character or personality." Nor should we continue to accept blithely the widely held idea that there is something about Africa or its inhabitants that predisposes them to hostility toward the modern rule of law regime. If the story of African openness and receptivity toward the modern legal system is true, it is no less true of their orientation toward the modern political system, which was founded on the same metaphysical template of modernity. I would like to present evidence that in some areas of West Africa in the nineteenth century, Africans were prosecuting a transition to modernity in matters of politics and the appropriation of modern political forms that included, significantly, the embrace of liberalism, especially as regards representative democracy founded on the principle of consent as the basis of political legitimacy. They sought to remake some of their polities along the lines suggested by modernity in its political manifestation.

When administrators took over in the aftermath of the Berlin West Africa Conference of 1884–1885, their principal concern was to dismantle the embryonic modern forms of political organization already set up by the natives because in their eyes such institutions were an affront to their racist sensibilities. Their reaction made perfect sense. Colonial rule of the variety that dominated in Africa could not have been established on the basis of the consent of the colonized. How does one tell another "Please give us your consent to rape and loot your country"? Moreover, had the colonial authorities allowed the idea to be disseminated that no one should submit to the dictates of a government to which he or she has not consented or had a hand in constituting, it is obvious that the very basis of colonial rule would have been severely compromised. In electing to preserve their rule at all costs and in refusing to school their colonial subjects in the ways of modern politics, the colonizers stunted, even aborted, the growth of a tradition of responsible and responsive government in the erstwhile colonies. I submit that we are still paying for those abortions.

The political manifestation of modernity is to be found first in liberalism and only later in liberal representative democracy. It is often forgotten that many Western countries had long been liberal before they became democratic.[1] What defined liberalism in its political aspect was its introduction of the doctrine that rulers were not emplaced by the grace of God and divine right. Rather, they were rulers by the consent of the governed and the latter's willingness to surrender their individual sovereignty over their selves to an external body that they had had a hand in incorporating. But liberalism was beginning to fray at the edges as a result of internal changes in the seventeenth and eighteenth centuries. I shall not go into the details of the historical evolution of the transitions it underwent. But the revolutionary implications of these changes marked an epochal division between the feudal past and the modern present. Not all societies can be fitted into the feudal-modern grid, and the lines of division would necessarily be different and be differently realized from one society to another. How those lines were realized in West Africa needs to be spelled out.

African theorists of the nineteenth century acknowledged their debts to their conquerors. They may have been mistaken in their identification of the antecedents of the principle of political governance to which they subscribed. But we should not read back into the past our current nationalist predilections. We should address those thinkers in their historical specificity. The embrace of the principles of political modernity were no less revolutionary in West Africa than they were in Europe inasmuch as heredity ruled for some of the African polities. By accepting our African intellectual precursors' embrace of modernity as their starting point, we can make more sense of their departure from that standard later when, shunned by the racist colonialist class, they embraced what some have called "reactive nationalism" by the end of the nineteenth century and through the twentieth.[2]

Beginning with the final abolition of slavery in the British Empire in 1833, the earlier settling of Sierra Leone in 1787, and the second wave of Christian evangelization, many Africans had been inducted into the way of life enjoined by modernity and had taken to it with considerable aplomb. They spoke English, they attended British and American universities, and they comported themselves in ways that they felt were consonant with modern requirements. As a consequence, they insisted that the British extend to them the privileges, immunities, and forbearances appurtenant to their modern inheritance. One of the key areas in which Africans were determined to incorporate the new things that they had learned and assimilated into their way of life was the arena of politics—more specifically, the sphere of political experimentation with constitution-making.

The flurry of political experimentation with constitution-making in the third quarter of the nineteenth century is the ferment from which arose the two constitutions that I wish to discuss in this chapter. It is crucial to point out that in various parts of Africa during the nineteenth century there were large-scale experiments in forms of social living that manifested themselves in the agglomeration of erstwhile smaller states or even city-states into larger political units that were more often than not quite heterogeneous in their populations. In many parts, too, either under the inspiration of Islam or the new movements of Christian evangelization, individual Africans were engaged in differing levels of research and other investigations into indigenous forms of social living with a view to reconfiguring them to respond to new challenges. New large states were being put into place by the likes of Ahmed Baba, Samori Toure, Usman Dan Fodio, Emperor Menelik, and others. The erstwhile Ọ̀yọ́ Empire was crumbling and Ìbàdàn and Abẹ́òkúta in Yorùbá country were evolving novel forms of political organization. The Mfecane movement in South and Central Africa had already yielded a unified Zulu Empire that was not homogeneous. Lobengula was putting together the Ndebele kingdom that would prove such a formidable opponent to British imperial designs in southern Africa. The fact that I focus on just two experiments in constitution-making in nineteenth-century Africa does not mean that there were not others that might engage the attention of interested scholars.

By themselves, constitutions are important. They are theoretical and programmatic statements of a society's view of itself, what it wishes to be, what type of human is expected to inhabit it. The nineteenth-century constitutions I consider persuade me that their framers were aware of and motivated by similar considerations. Moreover, during the same time period scholars and writers were busy working on how Africa might take advantage of its insalubrious history of relations with white people to reconfigure their societies.[3] As participants in the modern moral economy and intellectual discourse, these intellectual productions deserve recognition and serious scholarly attention.

Why is it important to resurrect these constitutions now? In themselves, the experiments are worthy of scholarly attention; they are even more so as embodiments of African genius. In addition, I write in an era when people, scholars, politicians, and others, including many Africans, have come to believe the lie that something in the African air, soil, and water makes the continent a hostile environment for liberal democracy to take root, much less thrive. It is incumbent on those of us who know otherwise to challenge ourselves to take a closer look and begin the archeological work necessary to put before contemporary Africans the legacy of African contributions to and appropriations of the political discourse of modernity for both pedagogical and practical purposes. Finally, at a time when Africa has another chance to make the transition to modernity in a more organized and positive way, it is crucial that we inquire into what our forebears did with a similar opportunity before colonialists scuttled their aspirations and effectively dismantled their experiments.

The Fanti Constitution

The Prelude

In December 1867, the Fanti states on Ghana's coast (then called the Gold Coast) came together and resolved to bind themselves together under a constitution. Historians are divided about what led to the coming together of the Fanti states at that time. According to David Kimble, "The immediate occasion was the exchange of certain Gold Coast forts between the British and the Dutch in 1868. This was partly designed to facilitate the British imposition of customs duties; but when the treaty came into force, the pattern of mercantile penetration and colonial influence which had grown up over the centuries was, for no good reason in African eyes, changed overnight almost beyond recognition."[4] A case can be made for this line of explanation. In the first place, the Fanti states that were transferred to Dutch control were not consulted before the exchange was made. As Kimble pointed out, "By the time they were assembled, the exchange had come into effect, which meant that some of them were, strictly speaking, already under Dutch protection. They refused to accept this—especially as they had not previously been consulted—and were stimulated into proclaiming their solidarity."[5] One ground on which the Fanti states objected was the British failure to consult with them before they were transferred like so many objects to another putative owner. They viewed this mode of proceeding as an affront to their right to and capacity for self-government. I shall have more to say about this in a moment.

They had yet another objection to the transfer. Kimble put it well. "The second main objection was to the methods of Dutch administration; it was believed that they were hostile to many forms of social progress: 'No missionary is permitted to live amongst them, nor are there any schools worth noticing for the benefit of the rising generation.'"[6] The significance of this objection cannot be overstated. As we will see presently, in the nineteenth century, the issue of social progress and African attitudes toward it played a fundamental role in Africans' choice of allies and, occasionally, overlords. It is no surprise that considerations of social progress featured prominently in Fanti reactions to their unsolicited transfer to another authority.

There are additional genealogies for the Fanti Confederation. Some historians have argued that the ever-present threat to Fanti territorial integrity and sovereignty posed by the Asante kingdom provided another impetus for the constitution. But the Asante threat was nothing new, so we need to have some additional factor that made it more salient than it had been before1867. The Fanti felt more vulnerable in light of the report of the Select Committee on Africa (West Coast) of the British House of Commons in 1865 that had contained language that could have been construed as presaging an imminent British withdrawal from colonial adventures on the West African coast.[7] J. F. Ade Ajayi describes it thus: "When it appeared from a Parliamentary Report in 1865 that the British Government might withdraw from parts of the 'informal empire' in West Africa, the Christian party around the Castle, felt obliged to intervene more directly in the politics of the [Fanti] states. Perhaps this was mostly to protect their commercial interests in the face of continued threats from Asante expansion."[8]

As important as the Asante might have been, the fact that they were a recurring threat and that it required an additional trigger to move the Fanti to action must lead us away from the suggestion that the threat itself could be a satisfactory causal explanation for the confederacy. And what Ajayi says in the next sentence in the passage quoted above is instructive in this respect. "The writings of Africanus Horton, however, show that the mission-educated elite saw [the Parliamentary Report of 1865] as an opportunity to demonstrate the benefits of their Christian education to improve on the politics of the non-literate traditional chiefs. The aim was to create new structures of enlightened government in which the authority of traditional rulers would blend with the expertise of educated Christians."[9] Ajayi's line of analysis is the one that I propose to follow in the rest of this chapter. That is, I shall interpret the emergence of the confederation and its founding instrument as being in part motivated by the desire of the new Christian educated component of the Fanti elite to reconfigure their modes of governance in light of the new civilization they had embraced.

By the same token, I shall attribute more causal efficacy to the 1865 parliamentary report than some, for example Francis Agbodeka, are willing to ascribe to it. Agbodeka has protested the assumption "without careful analysis," according to him, "that the movement for Fanti self-government derived from the report of the 1865 parliamentary committee that recommended British withdrawal from the greater part of the coast of Western Africa."[10] But Agbodeka did concede that "this suggestion gives us only part of the picture," another part being attributable to "the Anglo-Dutch interchange of forts in 1868."[11] It does not follow from the fact that one identifies both the report and the exchange as elements of a causal matrix that one cannot at the same time agree with Agbodeka's conclusion, after a thorough study of the event, that the roots of the confederacy must be traced much deeper into Fanti history and the history of their contacts with various European overlords on the coast. Indeed, my analysis represents a full development of the line of argument anticipated by both Ajayi and Agbodeka. My argument is premised on the belief that native agency is the most effective explanation for the emergence and operation of the confederacy. It is a mark of the centrality of native agency that the various imperial authorities on the coast did their best to stigmatize the confederacy as the handiwork of a few disgruntled and opportunistic "half-educated" Africans who were duping the "traditional chiefs" into going along with their nefarious scheme to oust British imperial rule and substitute their own.

It may well be true that "the upsurge of protest among the coastal states—especially the Fanti states—had much deeper causes, born of the very traditions and ancient practices of the people."[12] There has always been a strong democratic bent among the Fanti, a fact that explains the occurrence in their polities of what Agbodeka called "an almost endless process of fragmentation of authority." Hence, he concluded, "this breaking up of large centralized states into small traditional areas has been an important feature of the democratic movement on the Gold Coast."[13] Despite the long-standing tendency toward democratic governance Agbodeka identified, one can argue that the kind of democratic process the educated Fanti who crafted the constitution of the confederacy envisioned was nothing like the old Fanti prototype. In fact, both supporters of the confederation and their opponents as well as commentators are agreed that what the confederation aspired to was unheralded in Fanti history or that of any other community on the coast up to that time. The radicalism of their proposals provoked the most vehement opposition from the imperial authorities, who went to sometimes absurd lengths to impugn the character of the principal architects of the programme.[14] I, too, interpret the Fanti Confederation as one of the earliest and most sophisticated attempts to remake the political world of an African people along the lines enjoined by political modernity. For our purpose, the immediate occasions for the coming together of the principal actors in the movement that led to the confederacy were in part the Dutch-British exchange of territories in 1864 and in part the *Report from the Select Committee on Africa (Western Coast)* on British imperial activities in 1865.

It is worth recalling that from 1833, when Britain abolished slavery and made the slave trade illegal, a ferment continued about what to do to ensure that others did not continue to prosper from the human traffic and about what to do to make abolition worthwhile for the erstwhile participants in the trade in Africa, especially on the continent's west coast. The humanitarians continued to be a moral and a political force, a fact that was demonstrated by Fowell Buxton's success at forcing the Whig ministry under Palmerston to back the 1841 Niger Expedition.[15] In addition, opinion was divided about what to do with the freed slaves, especially the returnees. Finally, Britain already had a variety of presences on the West African coast ranging from settler colonies such as Sierra Leone, whose inhabitants were regarded as British subjects, to protectorate agreements with various local potentates all along the coast.

Many had come to believe that the involvement with the slave trade was a sin, or at least an unfortunate misunderstanding. They wanted Britain to make amends and make Africans whole again in recompense for British complicity in the centuries-long brutalization of the African. Some thought that such remediation had to include direct colonization and administration. Others believed that Britain should do its best to train natives to prepare them to govern themselves along modern lines in the shortest time possible. For the latter group, ruling others without their consent was permissible as long as the goal was to act as tutors to the native peoples in the interim while they learned the ropes of modern living. Politicians were caught up in this debate concerning what the British government's African policy should be in the aftermath of the abolition of the slave trade and slavery throughout the empire, and the 1865 report was a product of this ferment.

The key resolution of the report was as follows: "That all further extension of territory or assumption of Government, or new treaties offering any protection to native tribes, would be inexpedient; and that the object of our policy should be to encourage in the natives the exercise of those qualities which may render it possible for us more and more to transfer to them the administration of all Governments with a view to our ultimate withdrawal from all, except, probably, Sierra Leone."[16] Historians have often interpreted this resolution as evidence of British reluctance to play the imperial game and indulge the propensity for full colonization on the pattern of Australia or Canada. That might well have been the case. But little, if anything, rides on what was on the mind of the British government at that time. Whatever British politicians might have had in mind probably had a limiting impact on what Africans could do. But it would be implausible to argue that within whatever limits might have been set by British official policy, Africans were without options about how they would construe the intent of this resolution.

Both in politics and religion, mid-nineteenth-century Britain was the scene of significant debates about what to do with the territories and peoples that were coming under British suzerainty. As important as those debates were among British politicians, humanitarians, missionaries, academics, and so on,[17] to concentrate on them as the sole or principal determinants of events on the West African coast would tantamount to an ignoring, if not an outright denial, of native agency in the relevant places. For even as the British were debating among themselves as to the fate of their African possessions, Africans were also engaged in parallel debates, in both politics and religion, about what they were going to do with the opportunity offered them by their socialization into the modern way of life. Africans who fancied themselves inheritors of the new way of living sought to reflect that reality in the organization of their daily lives. Some of them adopted Christian ways uncritically. Others sought to preserve what was best about indigenous forms of social living while improving those with insights borrowed from the new inheritance bequeathed to them by Christianization. Still others resisted any attempt to import foreign elements— political, religious, or cultural—into the ways of life their ancestors had embraced from time immemorial.[18] In short, coastal West Africa, especially areas that had come under Christian sway in the nineteenth century, was a complex place indeed, and any sound description of its mindscape must be necessarily complex.

The educated Fanti who spearheaded the organizing of the Fanti Confederation and were the principal authors of its constitution belonged, for the most part, to the group of Africans who were desirous of remaking their societies in light of modern Christian civilization. That did not mean that they were sundered from the indigenous forms of social living. Their purpose was to establish governance on new principles that combined the best of the old with the best of the new. Their preference for the new made them revolutionaries. It was out of that desire and their ability to tap into the democratic tradition of which Agbodeka spoke earlier that the Fanti Confederation and its constitution emerged in 1868. In their letter submitting what they called the Mankessim Constitution to the governor-in-chief in November 1871, the chiefs gave their reason for binding together:

We have united together for the express purpose of furthering the interests of our country.

In the Constitution it will be observed that we contemplate means for the social improvement of our subjects and people, the growth of education and industrial pursuits, and, in short, every good which British philanthropy may have designed for the good of the Gold Coast, but which we think it impossible for it at present to do for the country at large.[19]

They repeated the same motivation in the preamble to the constitution itself:

To all whom it may concern.

Whereas we, the undersigned kings and chiefs of Fanti, have taken into consideration the deplorable state of our peoples and subjects in the interior of the Gold Coast, and whereas we are of opinion that unity and concord among ourselves would conduce to our mutual well-being, and promote and advance the social and political condition of our peoples and subjects, who are in a state of degradation, without the means of education and of carrying on proper industry, we, the said kings and chiefs, after having duly discussed and considered the subject at meetings held at Mankessim on the 16th day of October last and following days, have unanimously resolved and agreed upon the articles hereinafter named.[20]

Elements of both the letter of presentation to the governor-in-chief and the preamble to the constitution echo some of the objectives of Thomas Fowell Buxton's Society for the Extinction of the Slave Trade and for the Civilization of Africa. The references to progress, education, and industrial pursuits all bespeak eminently modern themes. Their allusion to "every good which British philanthropy may have designed for the good of the Gold Coast" was consistent with the general ferment that existed in Britain and West Africa in the nineteenth century. They hinted at their realization of the limits of philanthropy and sought to take responsibility for their own well-being with minimal assistance. They believed that their capacity for citizenship as British subjects and the British recognition of this capacity was part of every good intended for them, and their decision to assume responsibility was one way they wished to demonstrate that capacity. Conversely, they did not believe that they were giving anything precious away of their national pride in acknowledging that their subjects and peoples were in a state of degradation.

The Constitution

It is time to present the constitution. In what follows, I explore the constitution in some detail taking adequate care to point out the modern inspiration for the text and how it represented one of the most exciting social experiments of the nineteenth century. Many items showed the struggle of its framers to marry the best of the native with the most promising of the alien. Thus, it cannot be true that they were unoriginal imitators of things European.

I propose to examine the Fanti constitution under various headings. First, I shall argue that even though one can identify deep democratic roots in Fanti tradition and political culture, the democratic form that motivated the framers and that they sought to realize was of a foreign pedigree. Second, although some might be tempted to suggest that the Fanti framers parodied European ways or that they wanted a wholesale rejection of the ways of their forebears, I shall argue that their objective was a remaking of their polity that preserved the best of their indigenous modes of governance and injected new content into those modes, thereby recreating them. Finally, I shall argue that the framers bought into the idea of what Christopher Lasch, borrowing from Nathaniel Hawthorne, has called "the true and only heaven"—the idea of progress as both a motivator and measure of desirable forms of social living. I aim to reinscribe the Fanti leaders' efforts into the history of one of the central ideas of modernity—progress.

Embracing Governance by Consent

From the very beginning the Fanti framers left no one in doubt about their commitment to the electoral principle as a mechanism for choosing who ought to rule in their community. This principle, which is founded on the modern philosophy that no one ought to be bound by the dictates of a government to which he or she has not consented, is a quintessential element of modern political theory and practice. This principle was quickly announced in the constitution.

> ARTICLE 4.—That there shall be elected a president, vice-president, secretary, under-secretary, treasurer, and assistant treasurer.
> ARTICLE 5.—That the president be elected from the body of kings, and be proclaimed king-president of the Fanti Confederation.

One might argue that nothing in these articles appears to depart from what might have been the practice within the various Fanti states of the confederation. After all, Agbodeka has reminded us, a penchant for democracy explained the infinite fragmentation of polities and political authority in Fantiland. Such an argument is wont to miss out on the fundamental shift some of the provisions of the constitution represented. To start with, at the time the constitution was drafted, not all Fanti paramountcies were subject to the electoral principle; in some of them, the principle of hereditary succession held sway. But in the new dispensation the framers envisioned, the electoral principle would be put in place in all regions of the proposed confederation.

In addition, in setting up what it regarded as the legislature of the new confederation, appropriately dubbed the Representative Assembly of the Fanti Confederation, the constitution provided for separation of powers, however rudimentary, among the legislature, the executive, and the judiciary that it anticipated creating. The members of the representative assembly, even though they were local chiefs themselves, were to stand for election every three years (Article 18). Those who were to serve in the executive that the constitution envisaged were also to have three-year tenures. What was perhaps most radical of all, under Article 38, the ministry and executive council was charged with the duty of determining "according to the majority of votes of the people, the succession to the stool of any king or chief." In other words, they managed to write into the constitution a provision that even if it had been practiced by a few Fanti states, would, with time, have turned all kingships and chieftaincies into elected offices.

But the framers were not done with entrenching the electoral principle into all areas of the political system. Article 41 provided that "all laws, bills, regulations, ordinances, &c., be carried by the majority of votes in the Representative Assembly or Executive Council, in the latter the vice-president possessing a casting vote." They did not stop there. The same principle was enshrined in the description of the duties of the national assembly:

ARTICLE 42.—That it be the duty of the National Assembly, held in October of each year—
Section 1. To elect from the body of kings the president for the ensuing year, and to re-elect, as often as may appear to it fit and proper, the outgoing president. . . .
Section 3. To place on the stool, in cases of disputed succession thereto, the person elected by the executive council, with the concurrence of the principal inhabitants of the town, croom or district.

The Fanti framers did not adopt the electoral principle for mere pragmatic purposes, nor were they providing sops to British public opinion, especially that segment of it that believed that Africans were incapable of absorbing the best that modern life had to offer, although they were doubtless mindful of that segment of public opinion. The more plausible explanation for their choice must be premised on their belief that self-government was best and that they were capable of it. In addition, they did not defend self-government on the basis of reverting to indigenous forms of governance, with which many of them had problems and to which quite a handful had serious objections. No, their aim was to prove themselves worthy of self-government and able to run it.

Given their deep approbation of the modern form of government founded on consent, it is easy to see why they were concerned to put in place structures—beginning with a constitution—that would enhance a quick and smooth transition to modern government founded on the electoral principle. This point has been well remarked by historians. According to David Kimble, "The immediate object of [appointing a single king for the Fanti] was strategic. Lacking a leader, the Fantis lacked discipline and organization to fight their own battles; with one, they could concentrate a large force at short notice at any given point of attack from their powerful neighbours. But the long-term aim was to pave the way for self-government."[21] That the aim was self-government was not lost on the imperial officials on the ground. Ussher, who was the British representative in Accra at that time, continually remarked this point and it was at the root of his extreme antipathy toward the educated elite. As Agbodeka reported, Ussher "thought that it was unfortunate that apart from the effort towards a closer union among the tribes 'another and less creditable movement has been secretly at work, and threatens at this crisis entirely to undermine British influence.' He thought it was the educated Africans who took the initiative, and who were giving out 'that the time has come to govern themselves, and to throw off our rule; retaining us here as advisors only.' "[22] Ussher's apprehension is consistent with my presupposition that the autonomy model was the one that the framers were working with.

Meanwhile, during the earlier protest by the Fanti under King Aggrey of Cape Coast that Agbodeka regarded as the precursor of the movement toward confederation, Aggrey's "argument all along had been that British jurisdiction depended on the 'distinct consent' of the chiefs and people without which any claims of Cape Coast Castle over any portion of the 'Protectorate' could not be valid."[23] Kimble, too, has noted that the desire for self-government was especially prominent among the ranks of the educated natives and that by 1868

> some of them were ready to look beyond the horizons of the village or tribe towards a possible wider unity; but thanks to the attitude of the Administration, they were becoming increasingly dissatisfied with the political direction of the British, and their influence upon the Chiefs was exerted accordingly. The need to help the Chiefs to draw up "some measures for our self-government and our self-defence" was being strongly canvassed during 1868, and a general invitation was issued from Mankessim to all "Friends and Countrymen" to assemble for discussion.[24]

From the above, it can be seen that Agbodeka inadequately attributed the movement for self-government to "traditional democratic practice" of the Fanti. The phenomenon involved was a new way of conceptualizing governance, and the changes that educated natives were canvassing in the late nineteenth century were profound. If they had been isolated changes, then one could argue that they were no more than the protest movement of local potentates striving and possibly conniving to win back power they had lost to the Dutch and the British. But they were not isolated changes.

ANTICIPATING SEPARATION OF POWERS

I have suggested that the educated natives sought to remake indigenous society after the image of modernity. They took seriously the principle of separation of powers in the distribution of functions in the governance structure anticipated in the constitution. The representative assembly was designed to serve as the legislative arm of the polity to be established. It and the rest of the polity were to be headed by the king-president (an intriguing designation in itself), who was to be chosen from among the ranks of the existing Fanti paramountcies. To that extent, Article 5 sought to preserve an important pylon of indigenous rule as it occurred among the Fanti: the enthronement of a king. Article 6 provided for the creation of "the ministry" to be comprised of "the vice-president, secretary and under-secretary, treasurer, and assistant treasurer." In Article 38, these officeholders were charged collectively with the duty of serving as the executive council of the confederation. Their functions included, among others specified in Sections 1 through 9 of that article, the following:

Section 1. To advise the king-president in all State matters.

Section 2. To see that all laws, bills, ordinances, resolutions, &c., passed by the Representative Assembly, after receiving the sanction of the king-president, are carried into effect with as little delay as possible.

Section 3. To examine carefully the financial condition of the Confederation.

Section 4. To hear, try, and determine all important appeal cases brought before it by the undersecretary, option being allowed any party or parties dissatisfied with the decision thereof to appeal to the British Courts, on application from which the minutes of the proceedings therewith will be forwarded.

Articles 30 through 35 specified the duties of the various members of the ministry. I need not go into any more details concerning them here. Section 4 anticipated the creation of a judiciary since it provided for the executive to serve as "the final court of appeal of the Confederation" (Article 34, Section 3) with further appeal to the British courts. The constitution provided for the establishment of a legal system in Article 29, which stated "that provincial assessors be appointed in each province or district, who shall perform certain judicial functions, and attend to the internal management thereof." Article 36 specified the duty of the provincial assessors:

Section 1. To hold courts in the districts to which they are appointed, with the assistance of the king or principal chief.

Section 2. To transmit to the secretary a statement of all cases tried during each month, showing the decisions arrived at thereon according to a form hereafter to be prescribed by the Executive Council.

Section 3. To keep an account of the summonses, writs, &c., issued during the month, showing the costs and fees thereon, as well as all fines imposed by them.

These provisions anticipated a future judicial system. The provisions may be rudimentary, but they do contain the seed of a judiciary. Of especial importance are the provisions regarding keeping records of writs and books of accounts showing costs, fees, and fines. The importance of record-keeping for purposes of accountability cannot be overstressed. The same goes for a legal system built on stare decisis.

One might argue that the principle of separation of powers is somewhat subverted by the provision that made the executive council the final court of appeal of the Fanti Confederation. Such an objection ignores the fact that the ranks of the educated natives at that time were quite thin. Given their numbers, their plans must strike us as extremely audacious and ambitious. In any case, I am talking of a historical period when even Britain, which the Fanti wished to emulate, was still wrestling with the whole issue of what the balance of power would be between the House of Lords and the House of Commons, not to mention its continuing practice of making the House of Lords the ultimate court of appeal of the British judicial system. In any case, how genuine their intentions were would have been better measured if they had been able to operate the constitution for several years, a situation that would have afforded the opportunity to see whether or not they continued to evolve toward ever-increasing refinement of the principles of modern administration that, I argue, motivated them. Unfortunately, the British imperial authorities aborted the experiment. In embracing the principle of separation of powers and essaying to institutionalize it in the construction of their administrative organs, even if in a rudimentary way, the Fanti framers buttress my claim that this was an experiment in modern constitution-making in Africa.

BLENDING THE OLD AND THE NEW

We have further evidence of the radical nature of the changes envisaged by the Mankessim Constitution. I have argued that in remaking their society the constitution framers did not desire to abandon all previous forms of political administration within the Fanti territory and that they preserved indigenous institutions as much as possible. But the radicalism of their proposals can be seen in various provisions of the constitution. I have discussed the ministry and its functions. Article 6 provided "that the vice-president, secretary and under-secretary, treasurer, and assistant treasurer, who shall constitute the ministry, be *men of education and position*."[25] Although it is easy to attribute this last requirement to sheer jobbery, such an interpretation should be resisted. Had they not mandated that men of education and position would run the ministry and the new judiciary they sought to install, there would have been little or no improvement on the practices of governance found in Fanti culture from time immemorial. Such conservation would in turn have foreclosed the possibility of reordering Fanti political culture in light of new modes of social living. The commitment to creating a new political culture is clearly stated in the hierarchy they strove to install in the relationship between the old forms of authority and the new one they wished to found. At all levels, they did not anticipate that the new men of education and position would be mere executors of the wishes of kings and potentates who derived their authority and legitimacy from the old indigenous institutions, nor were they merely to play glorified secretaries to existing monarchs and other local rulers. On the contrary, they provided for a radical reversal of roles in the relationship between the new and the old.

In the first place, Article 15 provided "that the National Assembly shall appoint an educated man to represent the king-president, and act as vice-president of the Confederation; and that the vice-president shall preside over all meetings convened by the secretary." Second, in a provision that, I think, anticipated the incorporation of a constitutional monarchy, Article 18 stated "that the king-president shall not have the power to pass any, or originate any, laws, resolutions, ordinances, bills, &c., nor create any office or appointment, excepting by, and under the advice of, the ministry." Third, in the judicial sphere, provincial assessors were "to hold courts in the districts to which they are appointed, with the assistance of the king or principal chief." Taken together, these provisions have the effect of replacing the old chiefly authority with the authority of the new government headed by the new men of education and position. The chiefs would survive but as nominal heads of polities in which real power would devolve upon the educated class, who in turn would derive their legitimacy from the consent of the governed as expressed through the instrumentality of the vote.

Agbodeka probably missed the point when he averred that "the constitution under which the government was established appears to be the same as the traditional setup, providing for a King at the top, supported by counciliors (kings, elders, etc.) and then by a National Assembly made up of representatives of the *oman* from the various territories and including the counciliors and the king-president."[26] That the revolutionary implications of the scheme proposed by these new men of education and position were not lost on the British imperial authorities could be ascertained from the vehemence and (sometimes) crudity with which the latter opposed and ultimately scuttled the Fanti experiment. Kimble has pointed out in his summary of the reaction of the acting administrator, Salmon, that "the worst feature was the way in which all power was to be taken from the Chiefs and placed in the hands of the 'Ministry,' composed of young men of doubtful respectability and scanty means."[27] The proposed constitution would have altered the distribution of legislative power, executive competence, and judicial authority. Chiefs and kings were to become advisors to courts that would be presided over by educated administrators. No laws were to originate from or with the king-president. Why anyone would insist that much of the original authority of indigenous Fanti potentates would survive in the new dispensation is hard to fathom. Scholars and commentators may miss the many subtle ways in which the authors of the Fanti Confederation were insinuating revolutionary changes into the structures of governance, but the point was not lost on

British administrators. What is scandalous is that few have captured the sophistication and profundity of the Mankessim Constitution and acknowledged its place in the annals of modern constitutional experiments in all the perorations about the saga of modernity and Africa.

Leading in the Name of Progress

Why did the new educated men think that they were best suited to be the rulers in the new dispensation they were urging on their fellow Fanti? Recall what was said above about their embrace of one of the principal tenets of modernity: the idea of progress. They accepted that idea as both motivator and metric of desirable forms of social living. This is one aspect of their legacy that bears close attention in the contemporary situation. The motif of progress is present throughout the constitution. One can also find that motif generously deployed in the writings of the educated native throughout the nineteenth century in much of West Africa. This group, made up mostly of repatriated slaves and freedmen but not limited to them, accepted that the Africa they inhabited was backward and that if the continent was going to move forward with the rest of enlightened humanity, it had to follow the light represented in the trinity of Christianity, commerce, and civilization.[28] In addition to their concerns about security and self-government, a principal aim and motivation of the confederation as stated in one of their preparatory documents was "for [the] express purpose of improving the interior & developing [the] resources of country."[29] The new elite made up of self-styled men of education and position saw themselves as harbingers of new ways of being human that promised accelerated progress toward development for their backward brethren. It was on the basis of their advanced standing in the army of civilization that they claimed the moral right to be leaders of their polities.[30] In light of this moral claim, we can make better sense of their proposed reordering of the structures of authority in the Fanti polity derived from alternative foundations for legitimacy. The theme of progress and development was quickly foreshadowed in the constitution and the pragmatic provisions of the document made clear their fundamental commitment to moving their country along rapidly on the highway to progress.

I refer again to the preamble-like statement that opens the constitution, which acknowledged that the Fanti were "peoples and subjects in a state of degradation, without industry" who desired to remedy that deplorable situation by banding together and fitting themselves for the task of development. Article 8 of the constitution clearly articulated the aim.

ARTICLE 8.—That it be the object of the Confederation—

Section 1. To promote friendly intercourse between all the kings and chiefs of Fanti, and to unite them for offensive and defensive purposes against their common enemy.

Section 2. To direct the labours of the Confederation towards the improvement of the country at large.

Section 3. To make good and substantial roads throughout all the interior districts included in the Confederation.

Section 4. To erect school-houses and establish schools for the education of all children within the Confederation, and to obtain the service of efficient schoolmasters.

Section 5. To promote agricultural and industrial pursuits, and to endeavour to introduce such new plants as may hereafter become sources of profitable commerce to the country.

Section 6. To develop and facilitate the working of the mineral and other resources of the country.

Having diagnosed what they regarded as the main ills of their country, they were united in the view that progress as articulated above was the panacea and that the polity they were creating would be the most effective means of attaining it. Hence, they took education seriously and enshrined provisions in the constitution for its advancement. They called for the establishment of "national schools" (Article 21) and the attachment of "normal schools" to them "for the express purpose of educating and instructing the scholars as carpenters, masons, sawyers, joiners, agriculturists, smiths, architects, builders, &c." (Article 22). It is even more remarkable that Article 23 called for the establishment of schools and the procurement of schoolmistresses "to train and teach the female sex, and to instruct them in the necessary requisites." Fully cognizant of the fact that their constitutional instruments were more aspiration than reality, Article 25 mandated that "in districts where there are Wesleyan Schools at present established the kings and chiefs be requested to insist on the daily attendance of all children between the ages of eight and fourteen." Finally, Article 26 called for the construction of "main roads" to connect "the various provinces and districts with one another, and with the sea coast" and stated the standards for the construction of the roads.

The framers of the Fanti Confederation did not expect the financing for their various projects to come from the British imperial treasury; they wrote provisions into the constitution to enable them raise revenue from taxes, tolls, fines, and fees accruing from the operation of the various state agencies they proposed to create. This last factor is very important because, as we shall see presently, after their experiment had been aborted and the power of the chiefs and kings that the British colonial authorities enhanced did not include the power to tax, local governance came to be more and more dependent upon handouts from the office of the secretary of state for the colonies. That is, the aid model, by which native administration depended on purse strings controlled by British administrators, supplanted the autonomy model, in which Africans undertook the burden of financing their own governance under their own control. Some might see in such denouement the origins of the culture of dependency that has continued to afflict the former colonies in Africa to this day.

What I have tried to do in this section is to present evidence of the deployment of African agency in the sphere of constitution-making in the nineteenth century. I have refrained from commenting on the consequences of the official reaction of British imperial authorities. That is better left till the end of the chapter, where it seems more appropriate to discuss those consequences along with a consideration of similar circumstances in the other political experiment to which I now turn our attention: the Ẹ̀gbá United Board of Management and the Ẹ̀gbá United Government.

The Ẹ̀gbá United Board of Management/ Ẹgbá United Government

J. A. B. Horton, who, some have suggested, might have been the intellectual inspiration, if not instigator, of the Fanti Confederation and its constitution, committed himself to showing through scientific investigation the capability of the African for self-government and wrote extensively on the subject.[31] He was further encouraged in his task by the report of the Select Committee of the House of Commons on Africa (Western Coast) in 1865. In the section of his collection of writings devoted to the theme of self-government in West Africa, he included studies showing that some coastal West African communities were already mature enough for self-government while others would require only limited tutelage to effect a similar transition. What follows is what he had to say about some of the Yorùbá states in what is present-day Nigeria.

> The spirit of self-government seems to be taking a healthy hold on the inhabitants of the metropolis of Aku—viz., Abẹ́òkúta; the savage old native government is now undergoing a very decided change for the better, and it is modelled according to civilized constitutions, which shows the happy influence which British civilization has upon the minds otherwise disposed to improvement. . . . At present, there is established at Abẹ́òkúta a board of management for the express purpose of directing the native government, of forwarding civilization, and promoting the spread of Christianity, as well as of protecting the property of European merchants and British subjects. The Secretary and Director of this board, which is styled the Ẹ̀gbá United Board of Management, is an educated native of Sierra Leone.[32]

Horton was writing about another example of the attempts by Africans to lay hold of the torch of civilization that they inherited from the British and direct its light toward a remaking of their world in every sphere, especially in politics and economics. It was not too difficult to make the argument for a Fanti Constitution—it is written and it was formally adopted. The same is not true of the founding instruments of the Ẹ̀gbá United Board of Management (EUBM) or its successor, the Ẹ̀gbá

United Government (EUG). Some may therefore incline toward questioning the propriety of designating it a "constitutional" experiment and treating it in the same breath as our first example. Such a charge has little or no merit.

In the first place, not all constitutions follow the American or Fanti pattern of being written. Britain remains the most famous example of a nation with an unwritten constitution, and she seems to do well without one. As Walter Bagehot's *The British Constitution* reminds us, being unwritten does not detract from the identity of a constitution. In any case, usually it is when we construe a constitution merely as a legal instrument that the charge that a constitution must be written becomes more applicable. But I am more interested in the programmatic aspects of constitutions inasmuch as they are construed as blueprints or roadmaps that indicate what a society thinks of itself, where it desires to go, and what type of humans it envisions would live in it. Whether it is written and couched in formal language becomes of secondary relevance. And what would a constitution be that is bereft of guidelines about controlling and exercising power (especially violence), distributing public goods, organizing revenue collection, allocating scarce resources, and, above all, making some commitment to a certain view of human nature that forms the measure by which the other provisions are to be assessed? From the records available to us, the EUBM and its successor body, the EUG, was one such constitutional experiment. In order to make sense of what type of experiment it was, it is necessary to understand the state of Abẹ̀òkúta at the time the experiment was inaugurated.

Abẹ̀òkúta before the Ẹ̀gbá United Board of Management

In our earlier discussion, I referred to the fact that the nineteenth century witnessed a panoply of social and political experiments, many of which unfolded under the guidance of native agents. Abẹ̀òkúta was a good example. The Ẹ̀gbá, as the inhabitants of Abẹ̀òkúta are called, did not originally commence new experiments in political organization of their own will; they were forced to do so. The collapse of the old Ọ̀yọ́ Empire, a collapse accelerated by the pressures from Fulani jihadists and the subsequent loss of Ilorin, had consequences that reverberated throughout Yorùbá country. One such consequence was the Òwu War, which broke out in 1821 and became "the signal for the general disruption of the Yoruba country and the destruction of the Ẹ̀gbá towns."[33] The aftermath of the destruction of Ẹ̀gbá towns led to a new beginning around 1830 at the place that we now know as Abẹ̀òkúta. The arrival of the Ẹ̀gbá refugees in Abẹ̀òkúta did not mean that the disunity that was the bane of Ẹ̀gbá politics at their original location was no longer present. The polity was organized into different towns and quarters, each of which had a local chief, most of whom were to be found among the ranks of the "*Ológun* or war chiefs."[34]

According to Biobaku,

They reorganized themselves under Shodeke as Balogun. Apati of Kemta was promoted to the office of Seriki vice Degeshi of Ijeun, who had died. Then Lumloye of

Ilugun was appointed *Otun* or commander of the right wing, and Agbo of Gbagura the *Osi* or commander of the left wing of the Ẹ̀gbá forces. The new high command was thus made representative of all the Ẹ̀gbá and so truly *federal*. Nevertheless, the old township *Ologun* remained; for several war chiefs had no federal titles. They took township *Ologun* titles and waited for vacancies in the federal high command. The all-Ẹ̀gbá *Ologun* met at Shodeke's house and later the *Ile Ologun* Ẹ̀gbá erected nearby for their meetings.[35]

I have quoted the passage above because I would like to show that with the new settlement in Abẹ́òkúta came a different system of government led by men who did not come into office by ascription but by achievement. They were men who had distinguished themselves in war and had thereby earned the respect and allegiance of those who acquiesced in their rule. They did not completely dispense with the old institutions of governance that had been in place before the settlement at Abẹ́òkúta; they incorporated some of those positions into "the new civil authority" that Sodeke and his counterparts constituted to administer the new state once "the emergency which had given prominence to the *Ologun* was over."[36] This new civil authority, too, was organized along federal lines but it remained subordinate to the overall authority of the *ologun*.

It can be seen that Abẹ́òkúta was to a large extent a society in flux where new institutions were being put in place and whose population was wont to be equally in flux as it received new batches of refugees who had to be integrated into the society. Simultaneously, the peace that the *ologun* were able to secure for Abẹ́òkúta and its location on the Ògùn River, which flowed into the Atlantic Ocean, meant that it could take full advantage of the opportunities that coastal trade (earlier in slaves and now in "legitimate commerce") offered. As Biobaku described it:

Between 1836 and 1842 refugees poured into Abẹ́òkúta. Shodeke's fame had spread far and wide and all the Ẹ̀gbá who had hidden in the forest during the dispersal from the Ẹ̀gbá Forest began to find their way into the fortress based upon the Olumo Rock. Inhabitants of friendly towns fled before invaders and sought refuge at Abẹ́òkúta, especially from the Oke-Ogun district. Ologun chiefs, returning from successful forays, brought back Ọ̀yọ́, Ife, or Ijebu captives whom they absorbed into their households, when not sold abroad, as domestic slaves. Thus Abẹ́òkúta grew in size: the immigrants spoke many dialects and worshipped different gods.[37]

This description contains two striking characteristics. First, Abẹ́òkúta society was permeated by dynamism, much of it traceable to its expanding population. Second, the society was quite heterogeneous, a significant feature. Islam was such a presence that Biobaku spoke of a "Koranic school at Itoku" to which many Ẹ̀gbá notables sent their sons.[38] The dynamism of the society and its wealth, its openness to strangers, and its security combined to make it even more attractive to even more immigrants, many of whom were recaptives from Sierra Leone. They were soon to become the most significant component of Ègbá society.

Many of the recaptives in Sierra Leone had heard of Abéòkúta. Many of them were also Ègbá or belonged to any number of other Yorùbá ethnic groups. According to Agneta Pallinder-Law,

> By the late 1830's liberated Africans from Freetown were trading along the coast in their own ships. It would appear that it was through these traders that news of the Ègbá settlement at Abéòkúta reached Freetown, and attracted the interest of Ègbá settlers there, some of whom decided to return to their homeland and seek a future at Abéòkúta. *Saro*, as the Sierra Leone émigrés came to be called, began to arrive at Abéòkúta in c. 1839, and by 1842 500 to 600 were estimated to have come. They were received favourably by Sodeke, and many were reunited with relatives who had long regarded them as forever lost. They were not, however, fully re-absorbed into the social and judicial organization of their families and townships. Many of the early 1840's arrivals had substituted Christianity for the traditional religion and adopted elements of a European type life style.[39]

Apparently, the admiration was mutual. As Biobaku notes, "The new immigrants were impressed with the town as evidenced by the rosy account of their reaction given by Miss Tucker," who described it as "Sunrise within the Tropics."[40] In 1842, Thomas Birch Freeman, a Wesleyan missionary, arrived in Abéòkúta. It is not insignificant that Freeman was of mixed parentage, a half-caste. The Church Mission Society followed with the arrival in January 1843 of Henry Townsend, who was to play an important role in the local politics of Abéòkúta. But even "he was accompanied by two Sierra Leonians, Andrew Wilhem and John M'Cormack, who acted as interpreters."[41] With the arrival of the Europeans, the cast of essential characters in the drama of sociopolitical transformation in nineteenth-century Abéòkúta was complete. Henceforth the dynamics of politics in Abéòkúta was determined by the shifting patterns of conflict and cooperation between the Europeans, represented, on one hand, by missionaries such as Townsend and, on the other, by British administrators in Lagos, Accra, and Freetown and the Saro community and other Africans who embraced Christianity as well as the way of life it enjoined; between the indigenous political system represented by the *ologun*, the other chieftaincies, and other loci of authority and the Saro community; between indigenous rulers and their Saro cohort and the British administrators.

The tensions were not immediately obvious. Sodeke and his *ologun* welcomed the missionaries as if the latter were yet another wave of immigrants who sought to renew their lives in the bustling, heterogeneous, and secure refuge of Abéòkúta. Townsend quickly became one of Sodeke's counselors and the missionary enterprise flourished in Abéòkúta. As Pallinder-Law has pointed out:

The acceptance of both Saro and missionaries was facilitated by the character of Abẹ́òkúta political organization. Missionaries and returnees could be assimilated into the Ègbá political and social structure without losing their identity. Missionaries like Henry Townsend of the C.M.S., who spent more than twenty years in Abẹ́òkúta, held positions somewhat similar to those held by Ègbá war chiefs and lineage heads: they were responsible in the eyes of the town authorities for their own people, which in the case of Townsend meant the Saro, the converts, the resident missionaries, and visiting Europeans, be they traders, missionaries, or representatives of the British government.[42]

Townsend's prominence in Ègbá politics came with complications. But those need not detain us here. I need only note that many Saro viewed him with suspicion, others with outright hostility. In short, "not all the Saro accepted Townsend's leadership."[43] Many of them, as was the case among the Fanti, felt that they were the rightful heirs of the new civilization at which they had by then become quite adept. Their standpoint had merit. In the Methodist denomination at Abẹ́òkúta, as Pallinder-Law reports, Africans had held the leadership of the mission "for the first twelve years."[44] Even in the Anglican mission, there already was underfoot the storied rivalry between Townsend, who held clearly racist views of the ability of Africans to be missionaries, and Samuel Ajayi Crowther, the preeminent native vicar, who was clearly the preferred choice of the CMS hierarchy under the leadership of Henry Venn. In fact, Townsend exploited some of the ethnic tensions among different Yorùbá subgroups to ensure that Crowther was not a significant presence in Abẹ́òkúta; because Crowther was of Òyó extraction, it was easy for Townsend to exploit Ègbá suspicions about him.

The disagreement between Townsend and Crowther was emblematic of the antagonistic relationship between the recaptives and their erstwhile British tutors and/ or benefactors that we saw in my analysis of the Fanti Constitution. Townsend represented the segment of European missionaries who adopted a paternalistic attitude toward Africans and who believed that Africans lacked the wherewithal to be self-governing. The other component of that segment was made up of administrators in Lagos who sought to rein in the missionaries who believed in the centrality of native agency. The administrators were more concerned with establishing British political control and making the area safe for British commerce, free of competition from upstart Africans. It follows that the disagreement between the Saro in Abẹ́òkúta and the strand of opinion and attitudes Townsend represented was much deeper than differences conditioned by denominational preferences.

Neither Townsend nor the administrators in Lagos doubted that what they were dealing with in the resurgence of native agency on the West African coast in the nineteenth century was much more than protests over style. The bone of contention was the future of the peoples concerned and what they were going to make of the new forms of social living that they had been introduced to in the aftermath of slavery and Christianization. Hence, successive administrators in Lagos painted a dismal picture of the category of Africans represented by the Saro (in the present case) and the Fanti confederates (in the earlier case). What roused their ire was that many Africans believed that they were best suited, with appropriate guidance from the British, to lead their people and nations to the brave new world of modernity. The administrator and missionary detractors of these Africans saw them as fool-ish upstarts consumed by opportunism who wanted to fly before they had learned to walk. Thus, while the administrators and missionaries like Townsend were con-cerned to maintain indigenous political structures, even at the risk of freezing them where they were, some Saro and other Africans were determined that those indige-nous structures would be redesigned in light of new experiences, new needs, and new criteria of efficiency, rationality, morality, propriety, and so on. In all this, they were absolutely convinced that change or preservation was best driven by native agency with relevant help from the British and other groups as and when needed.

Historians have acknowledged the chasm between the European administra-tors and missionaries and, in the present case, the Saro in Abẹ́òkúta. For instance, Earl Phillips remarked that the "suspicion of modernizing elements that later distin-guished British administration in Africa" had been evinced by one of the first group of British administrators in Lagos, Governor Freeman, in a letter that he wrote to the Duke of Newcastle in 1864. Freeman described Abẹ́òkúta Saro as people who

> after owing their education and every farthing they possess to British philanthropy, return to their native country and then systematically endeavour to undermine Brit-ish influence and to turn the natives against the white man. With the smattering of education and the shadow of civilization they have imbibed at Sierra Leone, they would easily obtain the upper hand over the natives were the white man out of the country. . . . This class has done its best to increase our difficulties with Abẹ́òkúta, where the chiefs have been greatly guided by their advice.[45]

Henry Townsend, the arch-foe of African agency, did not fail to notice that the Saro goal was not merely a difference of emphasis; they sought a complete make-over of native society. Writing about the initiative that led to the constitution of the Ègbá United Board of Management, Townsend intimated to Henry Venn that what the men behind the board sought to accomplish was nothing short of a revo-lution. "[The Saro] will upset the native government and make it more English than white men could if they tried. . . . The great fact is that immense changes are taking place and the old chiefs, while providing as they think for the safety of the town and its institutions, are lending their power to those who, for selfish purposes, are introducing the greatest changes. . . . A great revolution is being effected in the country."[46] It is telling that Townsend used "revolution" to describe the process the Saro had initiated in Abẹ́òkúta. I would like to suggest that just as the Fanti, a dif-ferent complement of the same group of recaptives, had decided that the new way they had acquired augured best for Africa's future, the Saro desired new forms of government to make governance reflect their idea of progress. Thus, one line of fissure between Saro and their African allies and some administrators and missionaries can be traced to the divergent conceptions between these two groups of what Africa's future should be and who should direct the path to it.

A different but related line of fissure turned upon the perception by the Abéòkúta authorities, especially the *ologun* and other indigenous chiefs, that the administration in Lagos could not be trusted to do right by them and treat the Ègbá as their allies or at least refrain from doing anything that might be construed as giving comfort, material support even, to those the Ègbá regarded as their enemies. They had been discomfited by the British takeover of Lagos in 1861 and the installation there of a native authority that the Ègbá considered hostile to them. Their suspicions were confirmed in 1865 when the acting governor of Lagos, J. H. Glover, ordered the British forces to move against the Ègbá in an effort to force the Ègbá to end their siege of Ikorodu. This was done in spite of the fact that the governor "had earlier promised [the Ègbá] a free hand against Ikorodu." For the Ègbá, Glover's order amounted to a "betrayal."[47] The incident, combined with a series of other minor irritations, turned the Ègbá authorities against not only the Lagos administration but also resident Europeans in Abéòkúta, including Townsend. The Saro seized the opportunity to push to the fore their argument for the remaking of the political structure at Abéòkúta in a way that would appropriate the best of the European practices without being under the sway of Europeans or their influence. "Using this influential position to secure a niche for themselves during the period of post-war reorganization, the Saros launched their ambitions on the heels of the war in the form of the 'Ègbá United Board of Management.'"[48] Biobaku summed it up best:

> The Ègbá Government was weak. The missionary effort to obtain a strong executive at Abéòkúta by reviving the traditional kingship had been only partially successful; by electing a weak Alake, the powerful Ologun with their retainers were a law unto themselves. It would take years before the sons of chiefs who were being trained in missionary schools would have the opportunity to put into practice the concept of good government which they were learning from the mission schools. At all events, missionary influence was on the wane; difficulties with the Lagos Government and failure to obtain a settlement after the clash at Ikorodu had given the "Saro" at Abéòkúta the opportunity to gain control of the Ègbá state.[49]

The emergence of the Ègbá United Board of Management was part of the general climate of social and political experimentation that permeated much of West Africa during the nineteenth century. In the specific case of Abéòkúta, it was yet another attempt by the Ègbá elite, this time spearheaded by a new cohort of reformers made up of Saro and other returnees, to create an effective system of government for the state. The attempt that culminated in failure in 1865 had unfolded under the guidance of Townsend, who had sought to strengthen the indigenous structures as a serious option. The Saro, just like the educated Fanti, were persuaded that whatever its strengths might have been in earlier times, the system of government dominated by the *ologun* was not merely inefficient. As far as they were concerned, it might explain in part the failure of the Ègbá to counter the growing threat of imperial imposition by the British and the earlier involvement by their own folk in the iniquity that was the Atlantic slave trade. Little surprise therefore that they too were willing to grant that they were behind in the race toward civilization and that if they were to make up any ground on the Europeans, they had to get on board the train of civilization that modernity was.

THE ÈGBÁ UNITED BOARD OF MANAGEMENT

We do not have a formal declaration from the Ègbá United Board of Management. It is only in the general sense of their desire to reconfigure their polity in accordance with some philosophical principles regarding human nature and create the best society in which to realize its best possibilities that we consider theirs a constitutional experiment. As Biobaku reminds us, the board's "constitution remains obscure, though it must be recognized as an attempt to engender cooperation between the traditional chiefs and the educated elements, the Ègbá 'Saro,' with a view to establishing a stable and, in contemporary language, a 'civilized' government at Abéòkúta."[50] In fact, the announcement of its formation was understated; it came in the form of correspondence to the Lagos governor that thenceforth "all future correspondence with the Ègbá authorities was to be addressed to the EUBM."[51]

The principal inspiration behind the EUBM, the main author of its blueprint for political administration, was G. W. Johnson. For this reason, Johnson emerged as the leader of the Saro who had a preference for "civilized" government. Johnson had arrived in Lagos in 1863 and moved to Abéòkúta in 1865. According to Ajayi, he was then forty-three years old, of Òwu extraction, and a tailor by trade. "He had adventured as a foot-plateman and flutist on board a ship, and visited Britain."[52] Because Johnson was of Òwu extraction, it would have been more difficult for Townsend to undermine his legitimacy with his fellow Ègbá, as he had been able to do with Crowther. At the same time, because he had traveled the world and lived in England, he was in a position to compare the advantages of the indigenous political structure and the one that he identified with the British. And it helped that he arrived in an Abéòkúta, where "even before his arrival," there were Saro who "were advocating 'Africa for the Africans.'"[53] He and his fellow reformers did not seek to do away with the indigenous political structures; rather, they desired to move the structures along to have them absorb the best of the new and become suited to the conditions of modern administration. There is an irony here: Townsend, the stranger, pretended to be the advocate of indigeneity and the conservation of old forms of rule, whereas Johnson, the indigene, believed that indigenous institutions did not deserve to be preserved merely because they were indigenous. In Johnson's view, institutions had to pass the test of rationality, efficiency, and justice that was considered to be the metric of progress; if not, they had to be modified and whatever aspect in them militated against progress had to be extirpated. It was as if Townsend was doing his best to outgrieve the bereaved!

In order to show that their revolution did not involve the wholesale rejection of indigenous structures, the members of the EUBM put in place a creative admixture of the old and the new. As was the case with the Fanti Confederation, the educated complement was to run the affairs of the ministry and the indigenous chieftains were to be ceremonial heads in office mainly to provide legitimacy and continuity. Thus, the old had to be bathed in the ether of the new such that its continuation was justified not by ancient usage but by its function in the novel experiments in political governance. This outcome is what one might have expected. If the aim was to "combine the legitimacy of traditional rulers with the skills and the wider outlook of the educated Christian Saro to create 'an enlightened and Christian government,'"[54] then it stands to reason that those who were closer in training and temperament to Christianity and enlightenment had to take the lead. Consequently, the EUBM was a creative admixture of the old and the new: The *basorun*, Somoye, the preeminent *ologun*, was appointed the patron and president-general. But he was a ceremonial head only, for he was not even a member of the board. The real power resided in the board led by T. A. Williams as president, J. M. Turner as treasurer, and G. W. Johnson as secretary and director.[55] Johnson later modified the plan in 1871 after the death of Basorun Somoye and a notable decline in the enthusiasm of Ègbá chiefs. What remained constant throughout the period was his effort to create a federal model of governance that would allow autonomy to local constituent units within Abéòkúta. He proposed a

> reorganization of Abéòkúta government into a three-tier, federalistic structure. The supreme ruler of the town would bear the title *oba onile*. This office was a new invention. Oyekon was to be the first holder. Under the *oba onile* there would be four *oba alade*, namely the kings of the four main sections of the population of Abéòkúta, the Alake, the Osile, the Olowu, and the Agura. Ademola would remain Alake of Ake and thus subordinate to Oyekon as *oba onile*. Below the *oba alade* there would be a host of kings of townships, *oba alakete*. For himself Johnson had designed the position of *amono oba*, a kind of vizier, through whom the *oba onile* should be approached, and whose approval would be required whenever the *oba onile* took any decision or signed any document.[56]

All the designations in Johnson's proposed structure besides the traditional titles of *alake, osile, olowu,* and *agura* are his variations on themes that are commonplace in Yorùbá language and culture. *Oba alade* is simply an *oba* who wears a crown, *akete* is a type of headwear that mimics a wide-brimmed hat, and so on. It is thus easy to conclude that there was nothing new in Johnson's proposed designations. Such a conclusion is mistaken. Johnson meant the designations to signal something new. *Ilẹ̀* is the Yorùbá word for land. But it also refers to "soil," "nation," "earth," and so on. In Johnson's plan, *oba onile* is best construed as the overall ruler of Abẹ́òkúta and *ilẹ̀ Ẹgbá* would be roughly translated as the land or nation of the Ẹgbá, the geopolity upon which the federal structure was to be imposed. Sectional *oba alade* were to be responsible for the constituent units and were to be separated from the lower *oba alakete*, who were in charge of wards, by their more elevated headwear—*adé* as compared with the less regal *akete*. Perhaps the most significant of Johnson's designations and the only one that was new was that of *amono oba*. While the *oba onile* was superior to the other *oba*, that office was subordinate to that of the *amono oba*. The name is redolent with allusions from both Yorùbá culture and the new culture of Christianity and the Enlightenment. *Amono* means either "the one who knows the way" or "the one who charts the best, the most appropriate course to follow" or both. In other words, the *amono* is the savant, the one capable of seeing beyond the immediate moment to a more desirable future for the polity as a whole. He would be the high priest of progress armed with an insight into the ways of civilization and enlightenment; the guide capable of illuminating the *oba onile*'s path, which was marked, I presume, by darkness and ignorance.

It is easy to dismiss the Saro-dominated board as just an avenue for Saro jobbers to feather their own nests and fulfill their personal ambitions. And it is not enough to have Christian personnel for a polity to be Christian and enlightened. The policies that the board members sought to put in place signaled their desire to travel along the path of civilization. The board was cognizant of the importance of a well-stocked treasury to a well-run modern bureaucracy. It was equally aware that the existing system in which the *ologun* and other chieftains collected revenue by performing what equivalent of public services there was in Abẹ́òkúta was chaotic and inefficient. The board proceeded to put in place a rudimentary system for generating revenue. Much of the Abẹ́òkúta economy at that time depended on trade with the coast through the Ogun River, which empties into the Atlantic in Lagos. Up till the time that the board thought to rationalize the system, the *ologun* and other chiefs collected tolls on the river. The board imposed custom duties on the export trade on the river.[57] From being a state in which the *ologun* held sway and many chiefs literally were laws unto themselves, the board essayed to provide Abẹ́òkúta with a central authority to which all chiefs would be subordinate. Such authority would also enable the Ẹgbá to speak with one voice in their interaction with the administration in Lagos and make them better able to ward off whatever imperial designs the British in Lagos might have, especially in light of the seizure of Lagos in 1861. Finally, they reasoned, a rationalized administration would enable the Ẹgbá to create the conditions for the efflorescence of progress on their shores.

The board did not stop at the creation of the political structure. They had loftier ambitions, as Pallinder-Law notes. "They organized a postal service to Lagos, opened a secular school, and tried to persuade the mission schools to teach in English instead of the vernacular, arguing that a knowledge of English was useful in the external political and commercial relations of Abẹ́òkúta. They used the written and printed word to publicize Board decisions in addition to the traditional bell-ringing by a town crier, and they took occasional action towards sanitary improvement."[58]

As important as these steps were, they could only be the rudiments of the final product—a Christian and civilized Abẹ́òkúta—that Johnson and his cohort had in mind. In fact, were we to limit ourselves to the consideration of these steps, we would have to conclude that theirs was no more than a mere attempt to create an efficient administration for Abẹ́òkúta.[59] But Johnson meant to do more than that. He wanted to change Abẹ́òkúta society. He wanted the new way of life he and other Saro represented to be *the* way of life for Abẹ́òkúta. He wanted to bring Africans to the same level as "civilized" Europeans. He believed that Africans were best qualified to do this, assisted by Britons who wished the best for Africa and knew better how to live the best life because they had achieved it. The schools that were to be established were to be the soil in which the new life would germinate and the dissemination of the seeds from that plant would be a critical factor in the program of social transformation. In order for that program to succeed, the board needed the support of the British overlords in Lagos and London, the missionaries in both West Africa and London, and the indigenous elite in Abẹ́òkúta. The board and its principal architect, Johnson, had differing degrees of difficulties with each of these constituencies to which they looked for assistance.

The initial experiment did not survive long. The British administration in Lagos under Governor Glover was suspicious of the board's aspirations to autonomy under the British flag. There were frequent disagreements between the board and Lagos over territory, the control of trade, and sundry other items.[60] Townsend and the new breed of missionaries that was possessed of racist temperaments were not impressed by what they considered as uppity behavior on the part of Johnson and his fellow reformers, and they worked to undermine the authority of the board and shake the confidence of the chiefs in its legitimacy. In addition, the board could not always count on the support of the chiefs, some of whom regarded the board as an interloper that was wrongly taking away their sources of income and, on occasion, their access to booty. Given that the Saro architects of the board were a minority in Abẹ́òkúta society, the success of their experiment required them to enter into ever-shifting alliances with various forces at particular junctures. The upshot was that by 1874 the project had run out of options and Johnson left for Lagos. He returned to Abẹ́òkúta in 1880 and continued to work to move Abẹ́òkúta to "civilization." He never regained the preeminence that attended his original run in Ẹ̀gbá politics.

We should not judge Johnson's project as a failure because it did not survive very long. If we were to take a short-term view of the experiment, the fact that after 1874 there was not much enthusiasm for EUBM-type reform would indicate that not many in Abẹ́òkúta thought highly of it. Such a judgment would not be supported by the historical evolution of Ègbá politics. Johnson did not envisage the EUBM as a short-term fix for what was wrong with Ègbá politics. He wanted to change the course of Ègbá life in the direction of what he understood to be a "Christian and civilized" polity. In this we must judge him a success. Even Townsend, his opponent and detractor, acknowledged that the board was "pushing civilization and English customs, teaching the people the use of writing and printing and bringing about the adoption of written laws. They are doing what we cannot do, for we cannot use the means they do to accomplish their purposes."[61] Historian Pallinder-Law agreed with these sentiments in her analysis.[62] Perhaps the ultimate measure of Johnson's lasting impact is that by 1898, when the Lagos colonial government decided that Abéòkúta's politics needed to be rationalized, they copied Johnson's blueprint almost wholesale. In his quite severe assessment of what he called "demise of Ègbá independence" under Lugard, Harry N. Gailey described the EUBM thus:

> Johnson's EUBM experiment failed in practice but it indicated clearly how many of the people of Abéòkúta had an appreciation of western forms of government. There was no similar movement toward the construction of a westernized style of bureaucracy anywhere in Yorubaland in the later nineteenth century. The EUBM interlude and Johnson's concept of a central government acted as an important precedent for Governor McCallum of Lagos and progressive elements in Abéòkúta when they created the National Council of the Ègbá in 1898. Many of those who supported the bureaucracy thus created had previous personal contact with Johnson and the EUBM.[63]

The structure of Abéòkúta government eventually came to mirror Johnson's plan with two differences: first, instead of the educated elite being the leaders, the British colonial administration substituted itself; and second, the *amono* today is one of the most important chieftains in the Ègbá chieftaincy system.

The EUG

The Lagos colonial government set up the successor outfit to the EUBM in 1898, called the Ègbá United Government. In setting it up, as Ajayi notes,

> the British themselves revived the Johnson federal model of a broadly representative Ègbá United Government to include all the four Ègbá sub-groups. The Alake was the head. His advisory council included the other three obas, one senior Ogboni chief representing traditional religion, one leading war chief, the head of the trade chiefs, a representative of the Christians, and of the Muslims, each to be put in charge of an appropriate Department of Government. What is more, the legacy of Reversible Johnson survived in that the Ègbá were able to negotiate a treaty with the British that guaranteed Ègbá independence and survived under the Ègbá United Government till 1914.[64]

The new government established a central court of law; reorganized the collection of customs duties; and initiated "a considerable program of road building and the introduction of motor transport, support for mission hospitals and immunization programs, water works, and building of government offices."[65] Despite the fact that the EUG was instituted with the blessing of the British administration in Lagos, it unfolded under the direction of native agents. Its principal officers were all Ègbá, most of them Saro and their descendants, and the fact that they negotiated some measure of autonomy from direct British rule indicates the enduring impact of Johnson's revolution. The EUG reached the peak of its achievements under its storied secretary, Rev. J. H. Samuel (later Adegboyega Edun), who took over the administration of the EUG in 1902 and ran it till 1906. It is significant that throughout its life there was always tension between the EUG and the Lagos government and that much of that tension had to do with the desire of the Lagos administration to impair the EUG's autonomy and the EUG's insistence that it enjoyed under the British flag a sovereignty that was not inferior to that of the Lagos colony.

What happened after direct British rule was imposed as a result of annexation, following Frederick Lugard's amalgamation of the Northern and Southern Protectorates and the Colony of Lagos to form what is now known as Nigeria? Pallinder-Law puts it best:

> Following the British annexation, the modernization process was halted and sometimes reversed: the council lost its role of a representative, policy debating organ, and instead was given the function of an appeal court with reduced membership. The Ègbá medical officers and the E.U.G. legal advisers were dismissed, and E.U.G control over mission schools in Abéòkúta by means of grants, an inspectorate, and competitive school exhibition was abolished. A projected plan for the installation of electric streetlights was cancelled and soon the water works were reported to be out of order.[66]

Unlike the Fanti case, the issues presented in the Ègbá situation have to do with a heterogeneous polity that was being freshly reconstituted and among whom serious debates were taking place about the best direction for Abéòkúta in order to be listed among the best there was. The Saro took the European model seriously but wished to install it with sensitivity to their African historical experience and in a way that did not turn them into parodies of their European tutors. Like the Fanti, however, they too bought into the ideal of progress and presented themselves as the best candidates to lead Abéòkúta to its achievement. As in the Fanti situation, the British thought otherwise and saw those who ought to have been natural allies as enemies that had to be cut down every step of the way.

Why did Lugard deem the EUG an "eyesore" and an affront to colonial authority? Why were the leaders of the Fanti Confederation arrested and incarcerated for treason and why was their union dissolved? Why was it that instead of making common cause with those who were the best students of what the British claimed to wish to implant among West African natives the administrators chose to distort and, in that distorted state, strengthen various indigenous institutions that the natives, often under their own steam, would have discarded or changed? What were the experiments that we have examined about? Why should they command our attention at the present time? I have not asked these questions with a view to answering them in any detail in this concluding section. I hope they kindle in others a desire to extend the questions' reach to other areas of the continent during the same period. For now it suffices to point out that the two constitutional experiments considered in this chapter were part of a series unfolding across the continent during the nineteenth century. They were conducted by Africans who were doing what other humans do: trying to construct what they thought was a better way to live by combining the best of their indigenous heritage with other forms that they had become acquainted with in other cultures. Their reasons matter little. We can't always be sure that people know what is good for them or that they can always be trusted to choose rightly in any particular situation. But in the modern context, agency is a primary value and its autonomous exercise is highly prized. Indeed, John Stuart Mill insisted that considerations of an individual's good are insufficient to warrant uninvited interference with that individual's choices unless, of course, we have reason to believe that the individual concerned is out of his or her mind.

Like law, liberal politics is a practical virtue that, as Aristotle keenly reminded us, can be acquired only by practice. Africans were desirous of engaging in the practice. They debated among themselves the wisdom of particular choices about how to reorganize their societies. The colonial overlords had different ideas. Not only did they presume to know what was best for Africans—prima facie denying African agency—they were also determined that debates were unnecessary. They knew, as Africans did not, what Africans were and what they needed. It didn't matter that Africans were fully cognizant of the need for change and were willing to brave the imponderables that such processes always involve.

Again we may speculate. What if the British had facilitated the experiments rather than aborted or subverted them? There would have been debates, fights even, among the many factions, nations, and classes within the societies concerned. Even if the chiefs had won out, it could not have been on the old foundations, as the Ègbá example demonstrated. In many parts of West Africa in the nineteenth century, those foundations of indigenous authority had become so attenuated they could not survive on their own. It is instructive that in spite of the machinations of the British colonial authorities, chiefly authority never regained its original strength in the two areas where the constitutional experiments that I have examined took place. I must attribute this outcome to the pertinacious opposition of native intellectuals to the British imposition of sociocryonics. Unfortunately, colonialism generated enough distortions in the evolution of modern institutions that African appropriations of modern forms never reached the levels that they might have otherwise attained. What is important is that given the evidence that I have adduced, we can no longer take seriously the arguments of those who contend that Africa's soil and culture are hostile to liberal representative democracy. By the same token, we must beware of those who argue that liberal democracy has failed in Africa. Africa cannot have failed at something it has not had a chance to practice.

When the EUG was inaugurated with the blessing of the Lagos colonial administration, it followed very closely the plan forethought by George W. Johnson. It would not be the only time that the path charted by both the Fanti Confederation and the Ẹ̀gbá United Board of Management was trodden by others in the West African subregion. I may have given the impression that their legacy was lost to subsequent generations. Such an impression would be incorrect. On the contrary, the Fanti Confederation and the EUBM with its successor EUG left a legacy that was appropriated by succeeding generations of African intellectuals and politicians. The ranks of their successors have been no less heterogeneous and marked by contestations and conflicts than the pioneers' ranks were. However, once formal colonialism heralded the dominance of the administrator class, there were no new experiments of the nature or scale of the Fanti Confederation or the Ẹ̀gbá United Board of Management. After a racist philosophical anthropology came to dominate the colonialist mindset, Africans spent more time arguing the fact of their humanity rather than discussing what to do to ensure that their humanity kept pace with that of the rest of the world.

As the nineteenth century ended and the twentieth began and the boundaries of racist thinking increased among every class of Europeans that Africans had to deal with—missionary, trader, and administrator, some Africans adopted an extremely conservative view that sought to restore some pristine African civilization that predated the distortions brought by Christianity and colonial culture. Whatever their differences were, some Africans wanted to turn their backs on "Western civilization" and restore Africa to its past glory. But it is significant that even among the ranks of these nationalists, there were those who wanted to bring whatever African institutions and practices they desired to restore to some accommodation with contemporary realities. For instance, when some restored the *ogboni* in Yorùbá country, they distinguished it from the version that predominated among their unlettered counterparts by calling it the Reformed Ogboni Fraternity and, for a while, required its members to be Christians. Within the latter ranks we must include Edward Wilmot Blyden, the inventor of the idea of the "African personality," and William Esuman Gwira Sekyi (aka Kobina Sekyi).[67] Another group was made up of those who were closer in temperament to the modernizing tendencies I have been discussing here. Some among this group wanted to copy wholesale the ways of the European colonizers and missionaries. Their ranks were very thin indeed, in spite of the attempt by the racist European detractors to fit all Africans who took the promise and project of modernity seriously into the mode of uncreative mimics of all things Euroamerican.

By far the larger majority of African intellectuals wanted to replicate the ideas that motivated the group whose ideas have been under focus in this work. They sought to remake their world but they were not going to pretend that they had not been touched by the alien influences of Christianity, colonialism, Islam, and sundry other philosophies and religions over the centuries. Although the colonial authorities tried their best to stigmatize Africans in this category and sought to undermine their influence in their societies by promoting so-called traditional institutions, especially rule by chiefs, the Africans concerned never allowed themselves to be deterred by such machinations and damnation by their colonial overlords. In this group we must place thinkers from Herbert Macaulay to Obafemi Awolowo, Nnamdi Azikiwe to Kofi Busia. Unfortunately, they formed the class that the colonial authorities made sure never held power until the twilight of colonial rule and the imminent departure of the colonialists. It is a testament to the enduring power of the ideas canvassed by our African thinkers that the issues they identified in the nineteenth century continue to dominate the discourse of African politics and culture even at the present time. The fact that Africans are still debating what their attitudes should be toward the alien influences that have impacted African life and thought over the centuries is what makes it imperative for us to take another and closer look at their heritage.

Suppose that instead of foisting sociocryonics on West Africa, the British had taken to heart the imperative of progress, as did the Fanti confederates and their Ègbá equivalents, and adopted a view of Africans that made them worthy recipients of modernity's benefits, not merely victims of its burdens. The issues that dominate African politics and social discourse today might have been radically different. It is against this background that I think it important for us to take hold of the legacy of thought represented in the two constitutions examined in this chapter and see how we might borrow some of the confidence of our forebears in our negotiation with the legacy of modernity that, I argue, continues to confront us at the present time.

PART III

LOOKING FORWARD

_7_

Globalization
Doing It Right This Time Around

With this chapter the book comes full circle. I started out by exploring how Africa became a marked absence in the discourse of modernity even though the phenomenon has profoundly stamped Africa and made its peoples the bearers of its severest burdens but not the enjoyers of its sweetest fruits. I showed how, contrary to received wisdom, colonialism was the bulwark against the implantation of modernity in Africa. Yet I argued that this outcome was not inevitable. The key, I argued, was in isolating the specific trajectory that colonialism traversed in the African continent. In the succeeding chapters I worked through the implications of the philosophical exclusion of Africa for the career of modernity in the continent, especially in light of the introduction and unfolding of colonialism, given that people all too often believe that colonialism was the harbinger of modernity in the continent. How do things stand at the present time? I will answer this question via an excursus into two related but distinct phenomena in which the logic of modernity is worked out in the contemporary world: globalization and democratization. I shall be examining both from the perspective of that core element of modernity of which I have made a great deal in the previous chapters: subjectivity and its manifestations. How does Africa feature in the contemporary discourse of modernity, especially as it concerns globalization and transitions to democracy? In light of this declared aim, I shall be less concerned with structural processes that dominate the globalization literature and more engaged with the different ways that Africans are enabled to deploy their subjectivity in our globalizing world, both within their domestic boundaries and across the globe.[1]

Why is it important to end the book on this note? Although I have left out of our discussion the fate of Africa under the myriad forms of military and one-party rule that dominated the continent till the 1990s, this does not mean that the damage that such rule did to the political, economic, and social fortunes of African countries does not require remediation. What is more, given that I have argued in previous chapters that coming to terms with the Enlightenment project will be a significant element in an Africa resurgent in this century, it behooves us to be mindful of recent developments that supposedly move Africa along the path to that future that their nineteenth-century forebears set on before they were thwarted by colonialism.

In a sense, modernity-inflected globalization bookends the time frame of this discussion. The original inspiration for the injection of modernity into the African situation unfolded under the influence of the Atlantic slave trade and slavery. Today, scholars, African and non-African alike, continue to describe and discuss African affairs in terms that they draw from the discourse of modernity. Simultaneously, precisely because I am concerned to liberate Africa from the lockbox labeled "different," it is not out of place for me to show how the philosophical discourse of modernity enables us to see how much African countries share in common with others that are also instances of late transitions to modernity. Moreover, I would like to impress on scholars, especially African scholars, the need to situate some of the contemporary issues regarding democracy, capitalism, and globalization in the larger contexts where they rightly belong. These contexts might afford new explanatory models. This explains my choice of globalization as the anchor for this final chapter.

What is new under the globalization sun? The answer: little, if anything. It was Aristotle who said in *The Politics* that humans are political animals: *zoon politikon*. He forgot to add that we also are *zoon dunamikon*, animals that move around. And do we move around! If globalization is about anything at all, it is about movement, motion, and dynamism—the movement of peoples, ideas, services, kindness, vices, crimes, and exploitation. It should be obvious, then, that globalization is an activity. But it is not a self-actuating activity. It is always something anchored on some actor or another, be it a person, a group of persons, an institution, a country, and so on. It follows that whenever we talk about globalization, we cannot escape some reference, direct or oblique, to the issue of *who* is doing the globalizing.

In exactly the same way that globalization is not a subjectless activity, it cannot be an activity without an object. The question of what the *object* of globalization is can be posed in at least two ways. The first refers to *what* is being globalized. Here the reference turns on what is being moved from one location to another. Much of the globalization discourse focuses on this aspect. Candidates range from cultural forms to economic institutions and ideologies. The second refers to the purpose, the objective that is being sought by whomever it is that engages in the activity of globalization. Here the reference turns on the *why* of globalization. The fact that we affirm that globalization has a purpose does not mean that it always does, nor is the purpose always or even often clear, nor do the results of the activity always converge with the purpose for which it was originally initiated. Here, as elsewhere in human activity, we often fall victim to unintended consequences and are seldom clear in our minds about our reasons for acting. Yet at least one purpose runs through any and every instance of globalization: the desire to globalize, that is, the desire to cover the globe, to ensure the distribution of whatever the object is to all the nooks and crannies of the globe. Although it is easy to think of desire only in terms of real persons, it should be clear that it is idiomatic to refer to corporations and institutions as having desires to see their ideas and products globalized in variegated ways. Hence, when I speak of the desire to globalize I should not be understood to refer solely to human subjects.

There is yet another feature that is inevitably present in all forms of globalization. Given the centrality of the subject to the activity that globalization is and the additional fact that the subject is not free floating but rooted—anchored fixedly or dynamically—in some space or another, it follows that globalization is always done from a location, some locale. This fact has many implications. However global the outlook of the subject, there is no escaping the limiting role of the location—the Archimedean point from which the globe is apprehended and within which matrix global phenomena are perceived, processed, named, archived, retrieved, and disseminated. This is the truth of Empedocles's aphorism that if horses could draw, God would have four limbs and run very fast. How the globe is apprehended—indeed, how it is delimited—is always vulnerable to the limits of our location, and the latter determines, conditions, and influences how the globe is made an object of attention, reach, acculturation, representation, domination, and so on. At various times the globe—that is, the world—has been fashioned in the image of the person or group contemplating it. The world has always looked remarkably like those who have bothered to represent it to themselves or to others. Maps followed thought; geography stood no chance where imaginaries reigned supreme. For so long (from the Christian vantage point), Jerusalem was the capital of the world and the orb around which the terrestrial world was organized. At an earlier time, the boundaries of the globe were fashioned after the Greek apprehension of it; beyond that world lay the wasteland inhabited by "barbarians," for whom no act was too base. And as long as we read the history of the globe through Greek eyes, we are unlikely to come to grips with the achievements of the barbarians.

It is not just the delineation of the globe's boundaries that is captive to location; its narratives are even more so. Here is where we perforce confront the question of power. For without power, the market for narratives will feature several in contention, where the buyer will truly be at liberty to purchase the set of narratives that suits her fancy. But power intrudes. It outlaws certain narratives, renders others unattractive, denies voice to yet others, and rules others out of court. Simultaneously, it canonizes some, invests them with supremacy, and turns them into lawgivers unto those narratives it judges inferior. In our world, certain narratives have been canonized—the Greek-inspired one, for example. It is the same narrative that is often dubbed "Western" and the one that Edward Said has excoriated in his writings.[2] As a result, the putative descendants of Greeks are held to embody all that is noble in human achievement, while the descendants of "barbarians" are held not to have contributed anything worthwhile to the history of human evolution except unspeakable barbarities and execrable inhumanity.

Recall what was said above about the centrality of the subject to and the influence of location on the activity of globalization. What happens when we flip the coin and locate the descendants of barbarians in the subject position?[3] That is, we retell the story from the perspective of the descendants of the barbarians. This is not an idle proposition, for if the dominant discourse of modernity is to be believed, I, as an African, belong to the ranks of the descendants of the barbarians, and the view from our yard looks strikingly different. We may respond to the excision of our contributions to the concert of humanity by deploying irony à la Aimé Césaire.[4] Or we can claim à la Afrocentrists the *ursprünglich* authorship of all that is worthwhile in the Greek heritage.[5] Or we can proceed à la Cheikh Anta Diop, become archaeologists of truth about what our forebears did, and try as best we can to tell our stories in our own voices exercising the human prerogative of making God in our own image.[6] This, I suggest, will be the best deployment of our subjecthood and is the one that is likely to matter in the business of retelling the story of globalization. In this manner, we put in the narratives market the role of some of our forebears in constructing the ideological matrix that supplied the coagulant with which the identity and presumed cultural homogeneity of Europe was cemented: Christianity. By this I mean the role of the likes of St. Augustine and Tertullian and the Neoplatonists Philo and Origen of Alexandria.[7] We must include as well the narratives of the expansionist activities of the Almoravids in the eleventh century and the sponsorship by Mali emperors Bakary I and Bakary II of voyages of exploration to North America in the fourteenth century, which has been researched by Pathé Diagne. We would also need to include scholarship such as Lerone Bennett's *Before the Mayflower*; Ivan van Sertima's *They Came before Columbus*; Diop's *Precolonial Black Africa*; Enrique Dussel's *The Invention of the Americas*; and Jeffrey C. Gunn's *First Globalization*.[8] Nor should we forget to acknowledge the earlier movement of globalization that radiated from Arabia and encompassed huge portions of Africa and Asia starting from the seventh century under the motivation of Islam. And this must include all of the many facets of the narrative, including, especially, the trans-Saharan slave trade and the slave trade of the East African littoral.

When we retell the story of globalization in this way, we find that the current narrative represents Africa as if it has always been prostrate. In previous chapters, I noted how our prophets harked back to a more glorious history to claim respect and define their identity in the nineteenth century. I noted how Africans sought to make modernity their own by seeking to realize it in their own image. They did not try to be European; they filled European forms with African content and used African forms to frame European matter. In politics, as we saw in chapter 6, the Ègbá United Board of Management did not try to recreate the British political system. The Fanti wanted a king-president. New churches were created with liturgies that bore no resemblance to Western archetypes. These are hardly, if ever, referenced in contemporary discourse as elements of an African historical continuum. There is a simple reason why this is so. We do not often see references to these examples because the dominant narratives of the globalization that has dominated the history of the world since roughly the fifteenth century have obscured them. This globalization originated in the voyages of discovery of the fifteenth century. It remapped both the physical topography of the world and its mindscape and continues to frame the way that we talk about and apprehend the world. John Roberts's description of the transition and the new reality it inaugurated bears quoting at length:

> Europeans [in the wake of these voyages] . . . now [took] a new view of themselves and their relation to the other peoples of the globe. Maps are the best clue to this change. . . . They are always more than mere factual statements. They are translations of reality into forms we can master, they are fictions and acts of imagination communicating more than scientific data. So they reflect changes in our pictures of reality. The world is not only what exists "out there"; it is also the picture we have of it in our minds which enables us to take a grip on material actuality. In taking that grip, our apprehension of that actuality changes—and so does a wide range of our assumptions and beliefs.
>
> One crucial mental change was the final emergence of the notion of Europe from the idea of Christendom. Maps show the difference between the two. After the age of discovery, Jerusalem, where the founder of Christianity had taught and died, could no longer be treated as the centre of the world—where it appeared on many medieval maps. Soon it was Europe which stood at the centre of Europeans' maps. The final key to a new mental picture was provided by the discovery of the Americas. Somewhere about 1500 European map-makers had established the broad layout of the world map with which we are familiar. In the fifteenth century, Europe had usually been placed in the top left-hand corner of attempts to lay out the known world, with the large masses of Asia and Africa sprawled across the rest of the surface. The natural centre of such maps might be in any of several places. Then the American discoveries slowly began to effect a shift in the conventional arrangement; more and more space had to be given to the land masses of North and South America as their true extent became better known. . . .
>
> By the middle of the century the new geographical view of the world had come to be taken for granted. It was given its canonical expression in the work of Mercator. . . . Mercator's new "projection," first used in a map in 1568 . . . drove home the idea that the land surface of the globe was naturally grouped about a European centre. So Europe came to stand in some men's minds at the centre of the world. No doubt this led Europeans for centuries to absorb unconsciously from their atlases the idea that this was somehow the natural order of things. It did not often occur to them that you could have centred Mercator's projection in, say, China, or even Hawaii, and that Europeans might then have felt very different. The idea still hangs about, even today. Most people like to think of themselves at the centre of things. . . . Mercator helped his own civilisation to take what is now called a "Eurocentric" view of the world.[9]

Roberts's passage contains many analytical possibilities. But some stand out and are very germane to our discussion. First, the world that was constructed at the end of the fifteenth century—the globalization that was inaugurated then—remains the dominant picture of the world and the dominant form of globalization even as I write. The map—physical and mental—that this narrative constructed continues to structure our understanding of the world.[10] But I am jumping ahead of my discussion. I would like now to turn our attention to some of the dimensions of past globalizations to remind us of the ghosts that continue to haunt our relations across the globe even as we talk as if they have been slain or exorcised.

Exorcising the Ghosts of Globalizations Past

We need be reminded that the globalization of the fifteenth century led to a plunder of riches from the New World that had devastating consequences for its original inhabitants. It eventually led to the export of surplus populations from Europe to the Americas, Australia, New Zealand, and South Africa. In chapter 2, we saw Hegel describe the original inspiration for colonization$_2$ in our era. When Hegel spoke of a particular civil society being driven to found colonies and about the physical dispersion of huge populations to new lands, there was no hint whatsoever that the lands concerned were not uninhabited.[11] This is an illustration of the analysis that I presented earlier concerning matters of *who* is globalizing and *why* the activity is being undertaken. The philosophers of the Euroamerican tradition have not been hesitant to provide assorted justifications (some of which I have explored in preceding chapters) for why the indigenous subjects of the new lands that were being taken over were bereft of agency or why if they possessed agency it was insubstantial, inferior, or unworthy of recognition by their conquerors. John Locke, David Hume, John Stuart Mill, Immanuel Kant, Karl Marx, and others all wrote philosophical works to justify the denial of agency to and, concomitantly, respect for the native peoples of the lands that were settled by Europe's surplus population.[12] This exclusionary trend continues today. How can we proceed in our discussions of globalization in complete oblivion of the fact that the dominant narratives of globalization may not only be incomplete but false as well? They work on the assumption that the natives—whose lands were settled with Europe's surplus populations—either have no stories to tell or that their stories are not important or that entertaining their stories would add nothing to our understanding of the phenomenon under discussion. I suggest that such an approach at the present time is tantamount to continuing to labor under the cold hands of one of the ghosts that must be exorcised.

It was not just surplus populations of Europe that were exported. A different kind of export forms part of the historical evolution of the globalization we are looking at. I am talking of course of the transatlantic slave trade and slavery in the New World. Given that the defining characteristic of those who were caught in the snare of the peculiar form of slavery in the New World is that they were things, chattel, it must seem ludicrous, or at least incongruous, to speak of the subjectivity/agency of slaves. Yet once we shift our gaze from the location of slave masters to that of slaves, we confront new narratives, new maps, and new configurations of the globe. For however much the slaveholders convinced themselves of the slaves' lack of subjectivity, the slaves never once stopped affirming their humanity. And this was not limited to their accepting bondage as a condition of staying alive or merely recovering their humanity through their work on nature in the classic Hegelian narrative. On the contrary, we have evidence of the efflorescence of their subjectivity in new languages, new cultural forms, new cosmologies, and new ways of being human.[13] They rewrote the poetry of freedom in ways that could not have been anticipated by their masters. Witness the writings of David Walker, Maria Stewart, and Frederick Douglass or, in the present time, the music and ideas of Paul Robeson, Nina Simone, Gil Scott-Heron, and Wynton Marsalis.[14] I shall come back to this issue anon.

Meanwhile, Africa, from which the bulk of the slave population of the New World was taken, was called "the Barbary Coast," "the Gold Coast," "the Ivory Coast," "the Slave Coast," and so forth.[15] It was as if those lands had no people or if they were there, as if they didn't have names or they didn't matter. Nor were they considered capable of naming the world or making God. Of course, in the understanding of the colonizers, there were no people there, only subhumans. Thus there was a nauseating consistency to the colonizers' narratives. And where there was a hint of agency as Africa's globalizing conquerors understood that concept, they immediately located its provenance outside Africa. This is what has come to be known in African historiography as "the Hamitic hypothesis."[16] Where it was not possible to employ that hypothesis, the ultimate desperation got the better of one of the greatest minds in human history: Hegel denied that North Africa was or could be part of Africa even when the evidence of geography showed the idiocy of such a move. The denial was not general; the excision was peculiar to Hegel. But the mindset is pervasive, even now.[17]

The preceding examples show, first, that the dominant globalization is always presented as if it were a "view from nowhere" (apologies to Thomas Nagel).[18] It is as if globalization is invulnerable to the limitations of location that, I have argued, cannot be transcended without first acknowledging them. Sadly, Africans are no less guilty of complicity in their own subjection. Witness the dominant modes of referring to Africa in African scholarship: "Africa, south of the Sahara," "Sub-Saharan Africa," "Black Africa," and the like. These ways of referring to Africa represent an unconscious acceptance of the racist bifurcation of Africa into "Africa proper" and "European Africa," as Hegel called it. Second, only the activity engaged in by the subjects of Europe is deemed to constitute the relevant building blocks of globalization. Again, Africans have been no less guilty in this area. They speak and write as if there is only one role for Africans in the discourse of globalization: that of victim! Finally, the subjectivity of Africans and other dominated peoples who have also been participants in the drama of globalization has remained unrecognized or un-acknowledged.[19]

This is the reason for my insistence that for us to do globalization right this time around we must bring to the fore the ghosts that subvert our honest purposes pre-cisely because we think (and we are mistaken) that they have been laid to rest. I have done some of that in the earlier chapters. No doubt many of those that I iden-tified as the prophets of modernity in the nineteenth century either had their be-ginnings in the New World or were products, in part, of the exertions of returnees. The poetry of freedom they crafted and the subjectivity they deployed in making modernity's claims their own were exported to West Africa, in some way completing the dialectic.[20] Thus Africans were part of the globalizing and constitution of mo-dernity. I hope that I have gone some way toward reinscribing that part of the Black Atlantic—West Africa—that Gilroy inexplicably left out of his otherwise admi-rable book. Needless to say, what I have on offer here can only be a sampling; future work must not merely recognize but contribute to a secondary discourse of African-inflected modernity in areas beyond literature and history, the current champions.

Coming to Grips with the Specificities of Globalizations Present

The dominant globalization in the contemporary world dates from the end of the fifteenth century. The discourse through which its main forms, institutions, and practices are articulated was, if we accept Edward Said's thesis in *Orientalism*, con-structed in the aftermath of the expansion of Europe into the rest of the world. It is essentially the discourse of what Chinweizu has dubbed "The West and Rest of Us" respecting what the West has or has not done to, with, on, and about the Rest of Us and all that pertain to us, most especially our living spaces and our minds.[21] Just as in older times, contemporary discussions about globalization proceed as if all that the phenomenon entails is the radiation of people, ideas, structures, and prac-tices from the West to the Rest of the World. But if my thesis that the Rest of Us are not just passive receptors but also makers, fabricators of original ideas and strikingly different syntheses from diverse influences, exogenous as well as endogenous, is cor-rect, or at least plausible, then it behooves Euroamerican scholars to try as best they can to break their love affair with their own voices and dare to listen up to those of others whose agency they have hitherto treated with levity, contempt even.

My point is that we misapprehend contemporary globalizations when we view the process as a singular phenomenon. It is not, and I am aware that this is remarked upon a lot more at the present time. But token references will not do. Addition-ally, we are bound to misdescribe reality if we refuse to take seriously the *agency* of the Rest of the World beyond the investment in the exotic, the trivial—spices, raiment, and "world music." We must acknowledge subtle changes that the movement of peoples brings about. One now is able to savor *gbègìrì* in London restaurants, and Chinese food is easily available in Bayreuth; Seattle is home to numerous Ethiopian restaurants and Port of Spain houses a bishop of the Ethiopian Orthodox Church. Before our very eyes, new globalizations are taking place that do not represent radiations from the West. Indeed, precisely because they do not, the West has difficulties dealing with some of their mundane manifestations, especially in the area of immigration.

Despite appearances to the contrary, Europe has not been alone in exporting surplus or other portions of its populations to other parts of the world. There have been parallel globalizations all through the same period marked by European ascendancy. A former president of Peru is of Japanese descent (he conveniently restored his Japanese citizenship when he had to leave for a hurried exile); Brazil is host to the largest concentration of Japanese folk outside of Japan; Carlos Menem, a past president of Argentina, is of Lebanese extraction; and a good percentage of the population of Cape Verde is domiciled in the state of Massachusetts in the United States. Meanwhile, Italy is home to substantial populations of Eritreans and Somalis (although Canada has the largest concentration of Somalis outside of Somalia). These radiations of people out of the erstwhile receptacles of European expansion and their increasing volume represent one of the specificities of contemporary globalizations. These movements of peoples and ideas may not be as systematic or as organized as those that emanated from Europe in the past, but they represent nonetheless the deployment of agency on the part of the Rest of Us.[22] We must unearth the contradictory impulses behind this manifestation of agency.

I am arguing that globalization is not exclusively causally determined by the excesses and depredations of international finance capital. To take it only at this level is, on one hand, to restrict the relevant causality to structures and their processes and, on the other, to ascribe agency only to those who sit at the apex of the socioeconomic structure. One does not have to deny the causal efficacy of structures and their processes. Rather, what is required is to take seriously the alternative subjective causality and work out its consequences. Ordinary folk respond to the pressures they face and make of them what they will, creating in the process new social realities that are depicted on world television screens every day. It is responses of this sort that interest me in this discussion. I identify two such pressures.

(1) Africans have always been global citizens. What needs to be explained is why people move at the present time. What implications does the movement of Africans have for the issues raised in this book? The original outward movement to the new world was involuntary. The present movement, outside the harrowing experiences of trafficked women and children, is largely voluntary. This is in part associated with the phenomenon of brain drain. Again, it takes only a moment's thought to realize that there is nothing new about the so-called brain drain unless one were to assume

that the previous involuntary movement of Africans did not involve any aspects of brain drain. Such thinking will only confirm the prejudice that Africans never had any brains worth draining until they became beneficiaries of "Western" education that imparted to them the kind of expertise that is at the core of the contemporary brain drain. Yet we have evidence of such brain drain in, for example, the export of rice cultivation technology to the United States and the creation of new cultural forms in the new world.[23] Gilroy's *Black Atlantic* remains a seminal celebration of the intellectual robustness of these forms. To this must be added the pathbreaking work in the creation of British cultural studies by Stuart Hall and the theoretical exertions of W. E. B. Du Bois and Horace Mann Bond in the creation of American sociology, of Henry Sylvestre Williams and George Padmore in the emergence and articulation of Pan-Africanism, and, of course, of C. L. R. James, whose genius is yet to be acknowledged, much less celebrated by continental African thinkers and scholars. Meanwhile, in spite of the sometimes inauspicious circumstances that our immigrants find in the lands of sojourn or even the hostility of some of their hosts, they persist in their sojourn. Many others continue to move. Why do they do it?

On one hand, we have the normal, very human desire to always seek the best life possible and to go wherever there is some promise of a better life for us and our progeny. We cannot separate the current movements out of Africa into Europe and other parts of the world—there is at least one Nigerian businessman resident in Beijing[24]—from the collapse of the economies of various African countries, the legacy of economic mismanagement on a galactic scale by African "leaders," and, perhaps most important of all, the legacy of political repression, violence, and conflict. The signals from the West are heavy and unrelenting. The earlier sojourners initially did not have the benefit of the global dimension of mass culture. They set out on blind faith and a feeling that even death was preferable to what was then their lot in their homelands. They calculated that if they stayed they would rot but that if they braved the odds and survived, there was promise of regeneration in unknown lands. They do not have to be right in their calculations in order for us to admire their effort.

Meanwhile, the present is different in that the mass media and the global dimensions of mass culture ensure that even in what may be remote corners of the world people are bombarded by images of prosperity that is beyond the belief of some segments of humanity. Not only that, people have the impression that all they have to do is to get to those places and their lives will undergo a magical transformation for the better and they too will become participants in and co-enjoyers of the fabled riches of distant lands. We should not dismiss these sojourners as impossible dreamers or foolish risk-takers. The Horatio Alger motif is never too far from the surface in many of the stories of the West they read in their home countries. They may be wrong in their estimations, but it is unwarranted to dismiss their calculations as groundless. What is more, the narratives, if not the lifestyles, of those who preceded them tell them how well they can do and how quickly they can do it. In fact, in many countries, not striving to go and "make it" in the West is considered a symptom of utter madness or, at the least, sloth. We need to take this seriously. When Europeans left their homelands in the sixteenth century and later, they were shooting darts in the dark. They are not excoriated for that. Now people leave their homelands after reading books, watching television, and hearing (even if unreliable) eyewitness reports of how emigrating will lead to significant improvements in their life chances and we are slow to celebrate their gutsiness and their rationality in deciding that the adventure was warranted, maybe even worth it.

Where better to go than the places whose inhabitants have always drummed into the ears of the peoples of Asia, Africa, and South America (as well as, lately, Eastern Europe) the eminent desirability of their way of life, the infinitely brighter prospects of life for those who are fortunate to be born in their homelands, and so on? So people set sail, sometimes in the most dangerous and excruciating of conditions—cargo holds of aircraft, boiler rooms of ocean liners, and flimsy boats from the Maghreb—in search of a better life. Albanians head for Italy as a bridgehead to other points in Europe. Afghans, Iraqis, Kurds, and others head for Australia. Nigerians, Ghanaians, and Senegalese brave the Sahara and the treacherous waters off the Moroccan coast (and lately the coast of Libya) to enter Spain and then other points in Europe.[25] There are Nigerians in Germany who landed there after having traversed the breadth of Asia, starting from South Korea, then moving through Japan and Russia to the Czech Republic. This is one aspect of the impulse to emigrate. There are striking similarities between this impulse to emigrate and that identified by Hegel in the nineteenth century for both emigration and colonization on the part of Europeans. The difference is that instead of indentured contracts, we have unscrupulous people-smugglers who sometimes force their victims into lives of crime in their countries of sojourn. At the present time, there is no colonization. But there is definitely the same export of population (surplus or not), and the conditions in the home countries of our current waves of emigrants simulate the conditions of economic hardship and pauperization that Hegel said made colonization and emigration inevitable. Nor do we lack in the present the equivalents of the pirates of the past or even indenture-like conditions for many emigrants.

(2) But there is another impulse behind the current wave of immigration to (in the main) Europe and North America. This impulse, I would argue, is more effective in forcing people to relocate to other countries. At the present time, many African countries are put in the category of newly democratizing countries. This means that such countries are putting in place the mechanisms for multiparty democracy and periodic elections of their governors. Additionally, they are expected to observe the tenets of the rule of law and put in place the trappings of liberal representative government. In other words, they are called upon to deliver to their peoples the much-delayed promise of the political discourse of modernity that I have talked about in

earlier chapters: more control over their lives and more options to consider in formu-
lating their conceptions of the good life and the wherewithal to realize them. When
the focus is turned too heavily on the economic dimension of immigration, we lose
sight of the fact that many immigrants to the so-called advanced democracies cite
for motivation the greater freedom that is theirs in those lands compared to the lack
of freedom that was their lot in their homelands. In the economic sphere, either
under the tutelage of the International Monetary Fund and the World Bank or by
dint of goading by existing democratic countries such as the United States, Britain,
or Germany, African countries are busy creating free market economies where state
regulation of economic activities is reduced to a minimum and private enterprise is
given free rein to structure the economy. The political aspect of this transformation
is captured under the rubric of "democracy"; the economic dimension is represented
in the notion of "privatization."

Despite the widespread myth in scholarship about Africa about the tradition-
bound attitude of Africans, we find that the African reaction to modernity is no
less varied or complex than that of any other subjugated people. There is a sense in
which the current clamor for democracy in the continent is continuous with some
of the initial enthusiasm for experimenting with things modern in the nineteenth
century. After the abortion procured by the colonial rulers and the extreme disasters that military rule and one-party dictatorships inflicted on the African peoples,
one thing remains constant and incontrovertible: Africans never gave up on the
promise of what the Action Group in Nigeria called "freedom for all and life more
abundant."[26] They fought against military rule. They clamored for democratic rule.
And there should be no doubt that the pressures on African countries to democratize and adopt free market mechanisms can, when properly understood and executed, be assimilated to the required transition to modernity. What attenuates this
is that the good that the pressure to democratize does is diminished by the pressure
placed on African states to adopt the particular free market mechanisms of conditionalities and withholding of aid. Both mechanisms are examples of the latest version of the undermining or ignoring of African subjectivity, especially at the level of
the leadership of African countries. But ordinary people do not labor under similar
constraints: they are not vulnerable to conditionalities. While their rulers are having their collective and individual wills toyed with, the people, ordinary Africans,
are busy exercising their agency, voting with their feet. That they seek their fortunes
elsewhere via immigration is just another aspect of their insistence on having the
promise of modernity delivered for them.

It should be no surprise that this impulse has the impact that it does. Although
the promise of democracy does not feature often enough in analyses of why people
migrate, the fact that democracy promises individuals greater control over their lives
and offers some measure of freedom from the influence of groups and their tradi-

tions are two crucial reasons that people, especially those with some education, migrate to places that are touted as repositories of democratic freedoms. That is, many who emigrate from Africa do so not solely for economic reasons. Many, especially the intellectuals, emigrate because the life that they associate with their socialization into the promise of modern life is either in jeopardy or not on offer in their native lands. In fact, the truth is that many might have made better lives for themselves had they not emigrated, but they persist in their exile locations because they love the lifestyles they have come to know and cherish. When this is coupled with the disasters that result from the economic blueprint that compels countries to privatize their economies and liberalize access to them, what we have is a situation where fewer and fewer people in Africa, Asia, Latin America, and Eastern Europe believe the talk of democracy in their countries. Their reason is simple: What kind of democracy is it where the economic circumstances constrict rather than expand the possibility of the ability of individuals to control their lives and the political choices available to its denizens are a pale imitation of what democratic societies are supposed to offer?

Africans want democracy and better living. But that does not mean that they all have the same understanding of democracy or that they are unanimous about how to move their countries out of the morass of underdevelopment. Just as it happened in the nineteenth century, the principal models on offer have a lot to do with modernity. However, again African agency is not getting its deserts. Those who emigrate from the continent are facilely dismissed as "economic" refugees. Those who stay are supposedly the beneficiaries of a transition to democracy and the makings of a market economy built on free enterprise. Just as was the case with the colonial authorities who claimed to have put in place democracy and its enabling institutions on the eve of independence, Africans are again being sold a bill of goods in the contemporary period. Africans want democracy, but what they are being offered is a thin gruel of multipartyism and periodic elections.

Whatever may be going on in many African countries at the present time, only in an extremely qualified sense can they be termed a transition to democracy or to privatization. The countries of Africa, Asia, South America, and Eastern Europe have in the last two decades been offered an anemic version of democracy that falls far short of what makes the Western legacy such an alluring prospect. We are right to wonder whether intellectuals and politicians and policymakers in Europe and North America who are busy urging "democracy" and "privatization" on the rest of the world are sincere in their professions. For if they are sincere, then they must pursue policies that are sure to move African countries closer to the West. But the call to be like the West rings hollow. It may indeed be the case that some people in Africa and similar areas have seen through the insincerity that afflicts the call for Africa and the rest of the world to be like the West and realize that in their homelands they are being offered bootlegs in the name of democracy and privatization. Such individuals may decide, when able, to go to the source to enjoy the fruits of both. In what follows I explore the political and economic aspects of this conundrum.

The "Be-Like-Mike" Syndrome:
The Case for Open Borders

Let us begin by considering the following snapshots.[27] Until December 1993, the Russian president ruled by decrees. In October of that year, the president, the only elected public official in the Russian government, was faced with a recalcitrant un-elected holdover Parliament from the defunct Soviet Union. He ordered troops to march on the Parliament buildings in a deadly assault on his opponents. It should be noted that the president's actions did not fall outside the political context in Rus-sia at the time: His opponents had attempted insurrection in the streets and failed. So it is clear that this was no "democratic" struggle. But it was certainly a battle over the direction of the evolution of social processes in the country. The reaction of many analysts in the United States and of the U.S. government followed these lines: In that grim battle, the facts that the Russian president was *popularly elected* (a very important enhancer of the legitimacy of a democracy in current thinking) and that the Parliament was *not popularly elected* (a very important underminer of legitimacy in a democracy in current thinking) strengthened his hand and appeared to justify his claim that the assault was a blow for democracy.[28] President Boris Yeltsin justified his attack on Parliament thus: "In the past few months dozens of new anti-people decisions have been drafted and adopted. Many of them are deliberately de-signed to aggravate the situation. The most flagrant is the so-called economic policy of the Supreme Soviet. Its decisions on the budget, privatisation and many other areas compound the crisis and inflict huge damage on the country. . . . The inten-tional erosion of the existing and still weak legal foundations of the young Russian state is under way."[29]

The situation changed slightly after December 1993, when Russia elected a new Parliament. Needless to say, the electoral victories of Vladimir Putin do not alter the fact that only by a very generous understanding of the idea can we say that Russia is a democratic society at the present time.[30] Doubts about the current order in Russia have only been intensified by the stage-managed elections that in 2008 ushered in Dmitri Medvedev as the new president and Vladimir Putin as his prime minister. In the first place, I don't think anyone seriously considers the elections "free and fair." In the second place, the concentration of power in the presidency to the detriment of other sectors of the Russian state and society (not to mention the detriment to the capacity of ordinary Russians to control their own lives) speaks to a real lack of democracy in spite of the presence of multipartyism and periodic elections. Mean-while, with or without an elected Parliament, the Russian people, the legitimacy-embodying grantor of the president's authority (and, conversely, before December 1993, the legitimacy-embodying denier of the Parliament's authority) remained, if news reports were right, largely indifferent to the antics of the president and the Parliament. It is not that they had no interest in what was happening. Quite the contrary; the problem was that the aggravations of daily life left very little room for excitement about the perorations of politicians.

Privatization in Russia, which began under Boris Yeltsin, proceeded apace, even if not according to plan. Many industries were privatized; that is, their ownership was transferred from the state into private, *individual*, hands. Some of those hands were quite ordinary hands. Others—most, it is said—were the hands of those who happened to have run those same enterprises in the recent past.[31] What I have said applies to the privatization that took place above the table and that paid some attention to emergent and yet-to-be-consolidated procedures. A fair percentage of the privatization was less procedural, more aggressive, and, I dare say, more rewarding: It was the transfer of property executed by those who hitherto had been custodians of that property into their own hands or the hands of their friends, close associates, or family members. It is what we, in less delicate terms, would call *looting*! Regardless of how the transfer was effected, it is the end product that is of interest to us: What used to be publicly held on behalf of *all* the Russian people has now become the property of individuals—some of them oligarchs—who do not feel compelled (and are not required) to proclaim a trustee relationship. What I have just said should not be a surprise. Few laws and other regulatory mechanisms were devised to guide the process of privatization in the immediate aftermath of the collapse of communism. A little progress has been made since then. But even had such rules been in place, it is doubtful that the exercise would have included most Russians. Not much has changed in the years since. Shares in corporations are likely to be sold in public offerings to those who have disposable income to invest. This is beyond the capacity of most Russians at the moment. Thus, only those with privileged access to state resources in the past (especially as custodians) and others who operated in the underground economy were able to purchase share offerings in the process of privatization.

Here is another snapshot: Nigeria. As has been the case for the greater part of its existence as a sovereign (and I use that word with considerable hesitation) state, Nigeria was under military rule until May 1999. The military regimes that held sway in the country from 1984 to 1999, each in their own way, embarked upon the twin processes of democratization and privatization. It is not necessary to recall the lurid details of Nigeria's aborted march toward democracy under those regimes; this is a mere snapshot. But some of the moves that were made by those regimes deserve some mention, even if a cursory one, to show that whatever it was that they were committed to, democracy was not on the agenda. Given the history of false starts toward democracy in Nigeria, one of those regimes, led by General Ibrahim Babangida, in its

incomparable wisdom decided that the best democracy with the greatest chance of
success in what (according to that government) is the peculiar political terrain of the
country, was a closely supervised, extremely guarded, guided-by-the-nose democracy. The following should give the reader an idea of how closely supervised it was.[32]

To begin with, the government decreed that there would be only two parties.
Having persuaded itself that civilians could not perform the simple operation of organizing themselves into political parties, the regime proceeded to establish two
political parties: the Social Democratic Party (SDP) and the National Republican
Convention (NRC).[33] Just so that no one would be tempted to fail to see any difference between them, given their genealogies, the regime invested them with its own
versions of left and right ideologies. The SDP was "a little to the left," the NRC "a
little to the right." Finally, to fulfill the logic of this absurdity, the government wrote
the parties' manifestos! At every stage of the process the government kept intervening, and it eventually managed to secure the presidential tickets that it wanted for
both parties. Yet the government could not bring itself to accept the results of the
elections that it had brokered and controlled from start to finish. So on June 23,
1993, after what must be the most expensive political transition in the world, the
military dictator annulled the elections of June 12 of that year and plunged Nigeria
into her worst political crisis since the Civil War that ended in 1970. Babangida,
however, had misjudged the Nigerian people, who came out in tens of thousands to
protest the election annulment and eventually forced him from office in ignominy.
Although he tried to remain in power vicariously through the installation of a pup-
pet administration headed by a top Nigerian business mogul, the ploy failed when
the Nigerian Supreme Court declared that interim administration illegal.

In the aftermath, another military regime was instituted that was headed by
Babangida's erstwhile right-hand man, Sani Abacha. Abacha proceeded to un-
leash a reign of terror on Nigeria that muzzled the press and journalists and jailed,
maimed, killed, or chased into exile other opponents of the regime. The most egre-
gious example was the execution of one of the country's most accomplished writers, Ken Saro-Wiwa, along with eight other leaders of a minority rights movement,
Movement for the Salvation of the Ogoni People (MOSOP) in November 1995.
Under his draconian rule, the presumed winner of the June 12, 1993, presidential
election, Chief M. K. O. Abiola, was thrown into jail, where he eventually died
in mysterious circumstances in 1998, shortly after Abacha himself died suddenly,
supposedly of a heart attack. Abacha's reign of terror had one aim: to prepare the
ground for him to succeed himself in office as a civilian president. Abacha's successor, General Abdusalami Abubakar, hurriedly organized a transition to civilian
rule and stepped down from office in May 1999 with the installation of a popularly
elected civilian president, Olusegun Obasanjo, who went on to win a second term
that ended in 2007. For the first time in the country's history, Nigeria witnessed
the first peaceful—and so far successful—handover of power from one democrati-

cally elected regime to another. Thus, on the surface at least, Nigeria seems to have taken some giant strides on the democratic road and is, for now, judged a democratic polity. A deeper scrutiny, however, will reveal what is at best a very anemic version of democracy. I shall come back to this presently.

Privatization, too, has proceeded apace in Nigeria. The myriad forms I referred to in the Russian snapshot are to be found in Nigeria. What used to be the collective inheritance of *all* Nigerians is quickly disappearing into private individual hands. Meanwhile, the people of Nigeria, not unlike the Russians, were not exactly sitting on the sidelines: they repeatedly turned up for elections both in the aborted programs for transition to civilian rule and later on in the democratic dispensation in enough numbers to allow those who were victorious to claim legitimacy.[34] They felt that the military regime was on its way out and they were happy to play their part in the drama of democracy. Their hopes were frustrated by the annulment of the presidential elections and the successor military regimes dissolved the parliaments they elected over the course of three years from 1990 to 1993, thereby obliterating what modicum of democracy survived the previous dictator. The country witnessed periodic protests in the streets against military rule and its policies. The transition in 1999 has not meant an end to the motley aggravations of daily life that make the Nigerian people less-than-enthusiastic participants in the movement toward democracy and privatization.

Finally, let us turn to Kenya. Kenya held much-heralded presidential and parliamentary elections in December 1992.[35] The elections were remarkable in that they were held at all: At the time they were the first such elections in twenty years. Many people lost their lives to election-related violence. In the run-up to the elections, the incumbent, President Daniel arap Moi, harassed members of the opposition. Some of the latter had their papers confiscated or the prospective candidates simply disappeared until it was too late for them to file their papers for candidacy. Opposition publications were impounded in their entirety and were denied access to the electronic media. Douglas Rimmer describes these events: "More than 40 opposition candidates were prevented from delivering their nomination paper; as a consequence, KANU [the ruling party] candidates were unopposed in 15 constituencies. Another 40 candidates nominated by opposition parties defected to KANU—in return, it was generally supposed, for material rewards. The radio and television services were not impartial in their coverage of electoral campaigning, but biased in favour of the ruling party."[36] In the aftermath of the elections, which the incumbent president won with less than 37 percent of the vote but in which the opposition parties won half (100) of the contested seats, it was said that although it was not a model of what democratic elections should be, it was a worthwhile step in the movement toward democracy. Moi was eventually swept from office in the 2003 elections, an outcome that deserves recognition as a modest step in the journey to democracy.

But recent events in Kenya show that the country has a very long way to go if it is to become a democracy, richly understood. In the December 26, 2007, elections, the opposition claimed to have won but the Electoral Commission of Kenya announced the incumbent, Mwai Kibaki, as the winner of the presidential polls. The opposition took to the streets in violent protests. Although many latent issues led to the violence in Kenya, it has become clear that one reason for it was the opposition's lack of confidence (traceable to their experience in previous electoral contests) in the independence and impartiality of the Kenyan judiciary, another essential element of a proper liberal representative democracy in the modern age. As in the other two snapshots, privatization programs also took place in Kenya and the process has followed paths similar to those already identified.[37] Kenyans, too, are beset with the same aggravations of daily existence occasioned by poverty, ignorance, and ill health.

Why talk about these situations here? These are areas of the world that are not often thought about together, though I argue that thinking of them so yields much wisdom and analytical payoff.[38] To start with, the globalization under review is the one framed by modernity. The tenets of that modernity are what are now used as benchmarks for evaluating societies and the forms of social living they embody. As such, the comparative insights obtainable from so looking at them will allow scholars and social policymakers and actors alike to measure the rate of progress in the movements toward the best life for humans. We are also better placed to see how the more privileged of the world view less fortunate others in the rest of the world.

The economic and political phenomena captured in our snapshots are by no means peculiar to our three examples. They are more or less typical of developments in many other countries of Eastern Europe, Asia, Africa, and South America. In their different ways these countries are struggling to install multiparty democracies and free market economies. But what kind of democratization has taken place in the newly democratizing countries? To begin with, their elections have been hailed as steps, however unsure, toward installing democracy. Media analysts and academics alike usually tout the processes represented in our snapshots as evidence of the coming of age or the beginning of a new order for the newly democratizing countries. In minimalist analyses that barely conceal their condescension, these analysts tell us to be thankful that there are any elections at all; we are supposed to be grateful that the ruling classes in these countries are making any moves at all to satisfy Western public opinion or, more appropriately, the ideological demands of the ruling classes in Western countries.[39] My modest aim in the rest of this section is to dampen the enthusiasm that greets these developments. My skepticism is not assuaged by the fact that some of the countries concerned have had successful transitions from one dominant party to another in the course of the last fifteen years. So why am I skeptical?

A qualification is warranted. I am not opposed to democracy or even some variant of a market economy. To be opposed in any way would detract from the force of my core arguments. One cannot argue, as I have done, for the continuing relevance of modernity and fail to embrace its political discourse or some of its politico-economic presuppositions. Nor should this be read as a condemnation of the heroic efforts of the peoples of Eastern Europe, Africa, Asia, and South America to free themselves from yokes of differing weights and description. After all, the thrust of this book has been to argue for the relevance to Africa of modernity and its philosophical discourse. My skepticism is directed at my fellow analysts, especially scholars domiciled in North America and some parts of Europe, for whom the phenomena captured in the snapshots above and others like them either amount to democracy or are significant steps toward it.

The chorus of approval that greets the preceding developments is premised on what is arguably a very anemic conception of democracy.[40] It is a conception of democracy that mistakes what should be *a way of life* for a *form of government*.[41] In this conception, once there are many parties, several candidates, and elections that are (minimally) free and fair, a country is considered to be on the road to democracy. Democracy is reduced to principles of how those who govern are selected and of how rules are made to make them accountable to the ruled. Little or no attention is paid to the *general conditions of life*, some of which might have conduced to the installation of autocratic rule in the first place. Nor is any more attention paid to the temper of those who win these elections and who preside over the day-to-day running of the affairs of the polity concerned. It is as if the battle for democracy is won once a system of regular and periodic elections with many parties and a plurality of candidates is put in place.[42] The ousting of Daniel arap Moi and the installation of Mwai Kibaki in the Kenyan presidency must be judged a significant victory for democracy. But Kibaki's behavior and that of his wife, especially since his accession to office—his wife's physical assault on a journalist, his attempt to ram through a new constitution, and his continuing battles with his erstwhile comrades in the opposition—do not bespeak the implantation of a democratic temperament in today's Kenya.[43] The attitude that conflates successful electoral transitions and democracy in the "democratizing" countries, especially on the part of intellectuals in these countries and their counterparts in the extant democracies, is problematic.

The problematic character of such an attitude as I just described will become clearer when I show that in the established democracies, with all their defects, democracy means much more than multipartyism and periodic elections. The representative government that is touted as the ultimate icon of democracy is one aspect, among many others, of a complex and desirable way of life that typifies them. It is wrong to think, for example, that the United States is democratic because it has representative government and periodic elections. On the contrary, it has representative government and periodic elections because it is democratic. This is a very important distinction. If the existing democracies defined their democraticness only as multipartyism and periodic elections, they would probably not enjoy the model status they have in the contemporary situation. The elements of their democracy must include the large personal spaces within which individual preferences are supreme; the recognition and, on occasion, celebration of heterodoxy; and the very real limits they place on the power of the state to coerce the individual or frustrate her will.

Ongoing debates in the United States, Canada, and some European countries concerning the right of gay individuals to marry one another show clearly the commitment to heterodoxy. That South Africa remains the first and only country in Africa to legalize same-sex marriages speaks in favor of its democracy. That other African countries are busy looking for ways, if they don't already have them, to make it hellish to confess to homosexuality speaks to their lack of democracy, no matter how often they hold successful elections. The same can be said for the rights of women. Remember what was said about the open future and the putative preference for the merit principle under modernity. Insofar as many societies in Africa continue to operate social systems that impact individual lives and place curbs on aspirations based on ascription, we can say that democratic spaces are severely circumscribed and individuality understood as the privilege of ordering one's life howsoever one wants are not thereby recognized or provided for. The rights of women is one sphere where ascription continues to rule in many countries. Another example is the continuing accommodation of ascription-based monarchies built on heredity and primogeniture in so-called republics.

Incidentally, it would appear that the tendency to view democracy as a mere form of government is more pronounced at the present time in comparison with what used to obtain, even in Africa. As far back as 1967, Kofi A. Busia wrote: "Democracy cannot work unless those who seek to exercise these civil liberties recognize the equal rights of others to exercise them too. They must recognize the *right of others to think differently, and to choose differently.* . . . Where there are opportunities of wide contacts and of access to different ideas, there are occasions for different opinions and beliefs. Therefore, an important requirement for the success of democracy is to serve in voluntary organizations, all of which call for moral standards and good behaviour."[44]

From the requirements Busia lists, it is obvious that how the government is chosen and the kind of regime it is are functions of larger processes, derivatives of a way of life from which they draw their inspiration and to which they owe their identity and normativity. Representative government grows out of this larger democratic culture. The larger democratic culture is what attracts some immigrants, especially professionals and academics, to their lands of sojourn. Periodic elections are merely the institutionalized form of the principle that rulers may not impose themselves on the people. Once we accept the distinction between democracy and representative or whatever other forms of government may be derived from it (for example, constitutional monarchy), it must be conceded that what I have identified above as an anemic conception of democracy is inadequate.

I would like to suggest that there is a connection between modernity-inflected globalization and some of the processes that characterize social and political life in African countries at the present time. Disappointments with democratic experiments as well as frustration with forms of social living that seem to limit rather than expand spheres of personal control over individual lives explain, in part, why many make a dash for where they think the grass is greener. In the preceding discussion, I have tried to show that the ongoing processes of democratization in African countries do not rise to the level of democracy that makes the countries of the West such a magnet for assorted migrants from other parts of the world, including, especially, Africa. I know that it is not often that African immigrants are understood by both African and non-African analysts and scholars as manifesting agency or enacting their subjectivity in their boundary-crossings. Both the internal processes in their homelands and their responses to these processes can and ought to be explained in the context of the politico-philosophical discourse of modernity.

Simultaneously, instead of the current closed-door hostile response of Europeans to the immigration of desperate Africans into their borders, true globalization—a globalization that takes seriously its modern provenance—calls for (at a minimum) a recognition or (better still) a celebration of the pertinacity of these Africans in their search for better lives for themselves and their dependants. In my view, much of the current movement of surplus populations from the countries of Africa, Asia, and South and Central America is the latest replay of a similar movement in the globalization that settled the New World beginning in the fifteenth century. Indeed, the descendants of those who were welcomed by the indigenous peoples of the New World and Africa owe a duty of reciprocity to the twenty-first-century equivalents of their forebears and ought to treat them accordingly. *Open borders are an inseparable element of a globalization done right.* Recognizing the subjectivity of desperate Latin Americans braving the Arizona desert or hopping trains through Central America to make it to Mexico or that of Africans braving the Sahara and the treacherous waters of the north Atlantic is imperative if we are to put an end to a discourse of globalization in which African agency is only lamented—when it is not criminalized.

Next I examine the economic aspect of globalization. At the present time, it is normal for Western donors and aid providers and international financial institutions to insist that the emerging democracies liberalize access to their markets, privatize key public sector industries, reduce social services spending, and generally cut back on government participation in all spheres of life.[45] These requirements are now the basic conditionalities that African, Latin American, Eastern European, and Asian countries must fulfill before they can secure various types of loans and before international financial institutions, especially the International Monetary Fund and the World Bank, can approve grants for them.[46] They call on debtor countries to open their markets to goods and services from creditor countries and assume that such steps will allow the market mechanism to become the principal vehicle for allocating resources in society. Such calls disguise the real outcome desired by the donor countries and creditor agencies: *that the underdeveloped countries embrace capitalism.* The unspoken subtext for the processes and demands involved is that the countries of the former Eastern Bloc, Asia, Latin America, and Africa are called upon or, more appropriately, are being goaded into accepting that their future survival and prosperity are contingent on their willingness to develop capitalism, the ultimate emblem of Western supremacy. In other words, they should all be more like the West![47]

I wish to draw an analogy from the world of sports to show what is wrong with this manner of proceeding in the business of globalization. "Be Like Mike" was the refrain in a popular 1990s advertising jingle that featured Michael Jordan, who is widely acclaimed as the greatest basketball player ever. I assume that the writers of that jingle were being facetious in asking their audience to "Be Like Mike." The invitation hides a paradox. In the first place, it is impossible for all, most, or even many of us to "be like Mike." The world of sports is full of Michael Jordan wannabes who neglected their studies in the hope that they would attain success in professional basketball. Most are left with nothing but their dreams and much heartbreak. For every Michael Jordan, there are tens of thousands who never made it beyond their college practice teams. This point addresses only the practical impossibility of many of us being like Mike.

It may be logically impossible, too. The only reason that we are called upon to "be like Mike" is that Jordan is singular, unique, in his excellence. He is incomparable; he is inimitable. He is not just an excellent player; he is a primus inter pares in the universe of excellent sportsmen. This singularity in excellence is what makes Jordan such an icon. If we had two like him, he would not have riveted our attention the way he did on the court. If we could replicate him, that singularity would be lost and the quality that we wish to or are exhorted to emulate would be missing. The result: "be like Mike" has meaning only insofar as we cannot be like Mike. If we could be like him, there would have been no Mike to be like in the first place.

The call, in the wake of Western-inflected dominant globalization, to the rest of the world to be like the West in the economic sphere is similar to the call to "be like Mike" in sports. Though not in exactly the same way, the paradox that attaches to the call to be like Mike is present here, too. Let us focus on two aspects, one bad and the other good.[48] I take the bad one first and limit my comments to the United States. Americans consume more energy resources than any other people on earth. Most of the energy comes from nonrenewable sources. Furthermore, the sheer availability of stuff that drives the mass consumption that typifies American society creates considerable waste and incredible volumes of garbage. Suppose that Nigeria,

Brazil, India, and Russia, were to become like the United States.[49] That is, suppose the inhabitants of those countries attained the level of consumption for which the United States is notorious and the lure of which makes it the envy of the world. It is obvious that apocalypse would be upon us sooner than even the most ardent purveyors of Armageddon could predict it!

The point was made more dramatically by an eco-conscious radio broadcaster who once asked his listeners whether when the U.S. government calls for mass consumption and capitalist production in Africa and Asia it is prepared for 1 billion Indians and 1.2 billion Chinese to own or aspire to own refrigerators filled with hydrochlorofluorocarbons and automobiles that guzzle gas and emit pollutants into the atmosphere at the same rates as Americans.[50] This reality is creeping in on us. Chinese fuel consumption is rising and is putting pressure on world oil supplies. Oil-driven industrialization coupled with the emergence of the automobile as the preferred mode of transportation in China portends ill for the world's environmental well-being. The broadcaster's question might have been meant as a rhetorical gesture. But that globalizing the consumption patterns of the West cannot be part of what the Rest of Us are supposed to do when we become like the West is part of the insincerity that informs the West's exhortation that the rest of us be like it.[51] The West cannot seriously want the rest of the world to be like it because that would obliterate (or at least attenuate the impact of) the hierarchy that the West sits atop and that is a condition for the West's capacity for global dominance. It would also generate more competition for markets and give the West less access to cheap resources and fewer opportunities for diplomatic mischief-making. And the cost of being like the West will be unbearable for our planet.[52] I shall have more to say about this insincerity anon.[53]

Now I consider the good—that is, the political aspect. Without doubt, the principal appeal of the West lies in the better quality of life and higher standard of living of its inhabitants. This comparative judgment encompasses especially political life and the space it creates for individual identity and self-realization. Political life is only one aspect of this way of life. Other elements include the possibility of social mobility for individuals regardless of the circumstances of their birth, the tolerance of heterodoxy, and the accountability of rulers to the ruled. At some level, the call to be like the West includes the embrace of democracy and its political appurtenances. We have seen that access to enjoying this way of life is part of why Africans globalize. At the same time, given that most inhabitants of the continent remain homebound or stay closer to home—that is, within the continent—it becomes crucial for us to attend to their concerns too. The recommendation to liberalize the economy and democratize in the political sphere applies more to those who stay than to the émigrés.

Here is the problem. The same insincerity I alluded to above undergirds this recommendation of democracy. I contend that the democracy being recommended to the rest of the world falls radically short of what typifies democracy in the West.

The Rest of Us are being offered an anemic version of democracy that falls far short of what makes the Western legacy such an alluring prospect. That is, we may be witnessing a new version of the bait-and-switch maneuver that colonialism performed in Africa in the nineteenth century. The call to be like the West sounds increasingly like the refrain in the "Be Like Mike" jingle. Viewed from economic and political perspectives, the Be-Like-the-West syndrome sounds more like an affliction than a panacea for the rest of the world. Unfortunately, many intellectuals in Africa have embraced the twin ideas of democracy and privatization. The results in the area of democracy have been mixed. Those in the area of privatization, in the call to capitalism, have been more harrowing than ennobling.

The requirements of privatization bring in their wake a serious assault on the lives of ordinary people. Privatization has meant for most people in those countries the impoverishment of the many and the enrichment of the very few, the looting of public property, the arrival of various transnational corporations to pick the cream of the crop of state holdings in the name of debt-equity swaps, and the flooding of the local markets, subsequent to liberalization, with goods that cater to the wants of the new rich, are unaffordable for the poor, and generally sell at prices that make homemade goods less competitive.[54] Certainly some countries have done better than others, as attested by their hugely growing gross domestic products and new foreign investments. China, Poland, and Hungary readily come to mind here. Others have fared worse. Nigeria is an extreme example. It did not attract a single new penny of foreign investment outside of the oil industry through nearly thirteen years of a structural adjustment program that the International Monetary Fund mandated. Finally, in 2001, the telecommunications sector was privatized and the country reaped billions of naira from the sale of cellular licenses.[55] There are consequences for the life situations of the citizens of the countries concerned.

The halting steps toward the market have meant the enthronement of the trinity of hunger, ill health, and ignorance for millions of people.[56] Such an outcome, in turn, weakens their capacity to resist the onslaught that reduces them to subhuman existence. In fact, a principal requirement of genuine democratization—an informed electorate possessed of a robust sense of their entitlements and their duty to oppose the excesses of the governors—is one of the first victims of the processes I have described. Two paradoxes result.[57] First, the emplacement of the market mechanism supposedly requires the liberalization of access to the markets of the newly democratizing countries and reduced government spending on education and services that deliver health care. The objective is to eliminate huge government deficits and lower government participation in the economies of the countries concerned. Such policies are supposed to increase the productivity of the economy and generate prosperity for the people. What they have yielded in all cases is poorer education and limited access to health for the people.[58]

This outcome is easily explained. In most of the countries concerned, the government is usually the largest employer of labor because of the way their economies have evolved. Because the capital base is limited, the government is the only agency capable of organizing capital accumulation for large-scale economic or industrial production. The production of consumer goods is limited and because of the generally low level of production, the buying power of the populace is very limited. This, in turn, limits any possibility of quick expansion of the economy under adjustment programs. Add to all these factors the dominance of international capital headquartered in the developed countries and its ability to undercut local production, and what we have is generalized poverty and a stunted capacity for the production of goods. In such settings, reduced spending and the abandonment by government of its pivotal role in the economy in an abrupt manner can only mean unemployment and myriad forms of underemployment. The latter is aggravated by the absence of a concomitant increase in the level and rapidity of new investment that could create new jobs and absorb those who have been laid off as a result of shrinking government spending and participation in the economy.[59]

Democracy is a direct victim. Recall the reactions of ordinary Russians to the shenanigans of their politicians. Perhaps the most eloquent testimony to this is the fact that in the first elections to the Russian Parliament after the collapse of the Soviet Union, the former Communist Party and another headed by a xenophobic ultranationalist opportunist, Vladimir Zhirinovsky, won the most seats. Even though the influence of former communists has declined in Russian politics, the sham transition Putin engineered in 2008 reinforces the lack of enthusiasm for democracy on the part of Russians and their willingness to trade liberty and prosperity for security and order in the aftermath of the chaos that characterized Russia's transition from totalitarianism to a democratic rule of sorts. And in places where other opportunist rabble-rousers have been able to exploit the people's disgruntlement with their dire economic circumstances, "democracy" has restored the discredited rulers of the recent past to power: again, Poland, Hungary, and Ukraine offer convenient illustrations. I am happy to note that things have since stabilized in Poland and the country has been pulled into the European Union, a move that signaled the interest of Western Europe to make Poles the inheritors of the way of life of which representative government is merely a part, though an important part. If anyone is desirous of evidence for my contention that for Euroamericans democracy is much more than multipartyism and periodic elections, all she has to do is look at the conditions that prospective members of the European Union have to fulfill, which happen to echo much of what I have identified as a modern way of life in this work.[60]

The consequences of structural adjustment programs are devastating for all segments of the local population. They are more so for a crucial segment of the population that is needed for the success of any democratic and economic experiments: intellectuals. As a direct result of the adoption of the market mechanism (or what looks like one), the education systems in African countries (to take one desperate example) have suffered severe ravages. The requirement that governments reduce their propensity for deficit spending on social services, the bulk of which goes to education and health care services, has meant ever-decreasing allocations to the two sectors. Although I focus here on the tertiary level, primary and secondary education has fared just as badly, if not worse, given their foundational character. Many African countries are at present suffering from the ravages of a continuing brain drain by globalizing intellectuals who seek the greener pastures of Western Europe and North America. They are the same intellectuals who are needed to efficiently run the market to be created, to explain its rationale to their own people, to help their people make sense of the changes unfolding around them, to train future generations in the intricacies of democratic theory and practice and a theory of economic development, to indigenize the congeries of scholarly traditions as a result of the fluidity of boundaries in this age of information, and to work assiduously to chart new paths to an ever-more-exciting and more satisfying future for their peoples. Without this category of workers, there is little doubt that the capacity of such societies for intellectual reproduction will be seriously undermined.

Those who stay behind are not necessarily inferior thinkers. Nor is it the case that only the cream of the crop leave. The point is that of those who remain at home, many have abandoned the life of the mind to seek their fortunes in institutions in the burgeoning private sector, whose reward packages few educational institutions can match. They have become consultants with ever-dwindling knowledge bases and NGO millionaires. Of the rest who remain in educational institutions, the processes described above ensure that they hardly have the appropriate tools to work with and that the conditions of living are such that little time and energy can be devoted to the cultivation of ideas. Even as the material living conditions of this class have improved in recent times, the business of knowledge production is not being enhanced. What we have instead is a proliferation of religious fervor and both Muslim and Christian sects. In other words, in a perverse example of a self-fulfilling prophecy, Lugard's insistence that Africans did not need an education of the intellect but moral and practical education with a generous dose of religion has become the dominant model in Nigeria.

Hence the second paradox: The necessary personnel for the successful implantation of democracy and genuine economic transformation are exactly those who are being chased away into exile, internal and external, by the vagaries of fledgling markets. In an era where it is truer than at any other time in human history to say that knowledge is power, Africa is regressing in the race to create a society of knowledge. The sciences are the worst hit. Developments in the social sciences are no less dire. The humanities are bad enough. The excentricity that marks all production is more intense and infinitely more pernicious in its effects in the area of knowledge production. It is clear that African scholars who remain at home are globalizing: They send their intellectual products out to all corners of the world for the stamp of approval that an overseas-based journal supposedly brings, yet it is clear that the more Africans prefer to publish in overseas fora, including those that cannot be said to have the necessary support infrastructure for genuine critical evaluations that could improve the manuscripts, the greater the likelihood that the kind of scholarship that will help Africa will not be produced. It is the ultimate symptom of a profound underdevelopment of African agency. Globalization indeed! These paradoxes call for reflection. Resolving them is a vital component of any genuine program of democratization.

So far I have argued that the variants of democracy that people are embracing in the Rest of the World, especially Africa, are defective in certain respects. But it might be objected that if we can eliminate some of the problems I have identified and take seriously the promise of democracy and privatization (it is never called capitalism) as it has been redeemed in the West, we will do all right. The objection assumes that modernity, the movement that encompassed capitalism, liberalism, and more, is the ultimate achievement of human ingenuity concerning modes of social ordering and life. I want to attack this assumption, and I direct it at those of us who are inheritors and beneficiaries of the legacy of modernity. My rejoinder has two parts. In the first, I argue that not all of the Rest of Us can be like the West. In the second, I submit that even if we could, we should not. In what follows, I would like us to acknowledge that the task that the present calls forth is to transcend the ways of life presupposed by modernity while preserving what is best about them. An uncritical attitude toward the legacy of modernity is one reason why many intellectuals from the rest of the world think that their problems would be solved if only they could be more like the West. This is groundless optimism.

In the first place, not all states can be like the West. A few might make it, but most cannot. Just as in sports the "Be Like Mike" syndrome leaves many Michael Jordan wannabes in its wake, the "Be Like the West" version of the syndrome is sure to leave a junkyard of United States or Germany wannabes in the community of states. With limited investment dollars to go around, nation-states are already engaged in vicious bidding wars for investments that redound only to the well-entrenched power of transnational corporations.[61] And, second, even if it were possible for the rest of the world to be like the West, that would be desirable only if it is the case that the ways of life that are enjoined by modernity and realized in some parts of the West are the best life for humans or are the best possible. They are neither.

It is easy to be like the West insofar as one works with the anemic conception of democracy that I criticized above. But democracy is more than periodic elections with a plurality of candidates and regular turnovers in governments. Were we to limit ourselves to those markers, it would be difficult justifiably to call "democracies" those countries that are usually held up as shining examples for the rest of the world to follow. In them—this is definitely true of the United States—there is no plurality of opinions in electioneering. One can question how representative the elected are, given the central role of money, the proliferation of captains of consciousness, and the impact of the media's actions on the choices of many voters.[62] If we were to pay serious attention to the dwindling percentages of eligible voters who care to vote in periodic elections in, for example, the United States, we would be even less justified in calling it a "democracy." So what makes the United States and others like it "democracies" must lay somewhere beyond their method of picking those who govern periodically.

We must distinguish between "having elected governments" and "being democratic." Although being democratic must include some elective mechanisms for choosing rulers, having electoral systems in place does not a democracy make. The shortcomings in the forms of government or in the process of choosing governments in the West may make us wary of certifying them as "democratic," but they do not warrant a dismissal of the democratic nature of the societies concerned. In other words, the elements that make societies democratic are to be found in the richly textured, multidimensional ways of life that modernity inaugurated in some countries of the West. The individual who chooses not to vote has other ways of expressing her opinions about any and every issue, even if that expression involves nothing more than unprovoked, unfocused placard-carrying. The right to be different is an integral part of the promise of the many ways of life typical of democratic countries.[63] A U.S. Supreme Court justice put it nicely when he called it "the right to be let alone."[64] Other elements include the impermissibility of authority that is not consented to by those it binds. In fact, in focusing on the core tenets of modernity we are better placed to evaluate ongoing constitutional experiments in African countries and insist that those who construct and operate those institutions do so rightly and that ordinary folks who constitute the majority of the governed be educated about their entitlements and how to ensure that their governors recognize them.

Do the newly democratizing countries exhibit what I have identified as the characteristic features of the modern way of life in its rich complexity? Do they accommodate difference or heterodoxy in the requisite manner? I don't think so. In some of them, it is an offense to insult the president. This is the case in Zimbabwe and in many countries that used to be part of the former Soviet Union. Boris Yeltsin threatened to shut down the opposition press in the run-up to the parliamentary elections of December 1993. Vladimir Putin, his successor, has been trying to rein in the opposition in the name of fighting terror inspired by the war in Chechnya and at the same time squelch any oppositional moves on the part of the oligarchs through the instrumentality of selective prosecution for tax evasion. One of those oligarchs, Vladimir Khododorsky, is languishing in a Siberian jail ostensibly for tax evasion but in reality for daring to organize a political party to challenge Putin's rule. Human Rights Watch recently issued a report on extrajudicial killings in Nigeria.[65] It reported that Robert Mugabe had not only declared open warfare against his fellow citizens but that he had routinely changed the country's constitution to suit his momentary whim. Hosni Mubarak still runs a one-party "democracy" in Egypt, and the leader of the main opposition party that dared challenge him in the 2005 presidential elections was not released until February 2009 after serving five years of a fifteen-year jail sentence. Courageous man that he is, he has vowed to continue the fight for democracy in Egypt from where he left off. The Egyptian state routinely deploys violence to put down protests against constitutional reforms designed to make it impossible for genuine pluralism and heterodoxy to have a place in public discourse. One can still be charged for apostasy and blasphemy in that country. In Kenya, opposition newspapers were confiscated in the years following the first multiparty elections while Moi was still in office.[66] When the army preempted an Islamic Salvation Front victory in general elections in Algeria in 1991, Richard Rorty, a prominent postmodern democratic philosopher, remarked flippantly at a public lecture in the United States that that might not have been such a bad thing given the ideological genealogy of the front and its supporters. This is one aspect of the insincerity about democratic values I alluded to above. Would Richard Rorty have responded in that way if the annulment had taken place in France or Germany in anticipation of an electoral victory by the National Front or the Christian Social Union? I think not.

Until recently, the promise of the open future in modern states like the United States and Britain included supposedly unbounded aspirations to careers open to talent. However, the possibilities of upward mobility are now being foreclosed by economic exigencies in the developed democracies. Thus, in them too, it is becoming increasingly clear that class boundaries are hardening and that children may find that their futures will take them only as far as their parents went, if they get even that far. Ordinarily, an expanding economy such as the kind of economy that privatization is supposed to bring to the rest of the world would contribute to the fluidity of class boundaries. But if one comes from the lower classes in the newly democratizing countries, where cutbacks have been made in social services spending on educational aid, her future may well have been foretold, possibly sealed, in the circumstances of her birth. This is a throwback to the limited social mobility of the premodern era. The abiding faith in the capacity of human reason to solve all problems is under savage attack at the present time, as it should be. But variegated irrationalities remain as serious obstacles to the implantation of a genuine democratic temper or its survival: Witness the growth of different kinds of fundamentalism and other premodern or antimodern forms of particularism, especially nationalism, in putatively democratic countries. If the so-called developed democracies are chafing under the pressures just identified, how much more could one reasonably expect those who have not had the traditions of democracy to cope better?

This is a good place to go back to the issue of immigration and its implications for globalization in the present. It is partly in response to the pressures just described that we have the present movements of people from the erstwhile receptacles of European expansion. As I pointed out earlier, many in the newly democratizing countries where privatization policies are being implemented simultaneously respond to the material or empirical consequences of the paradoxes that result from structural adjustment. In place of the sham democracy on offer in their homelands, they set sail in search of the real deal. And in lieu of the immiserizing results of the neoliberal economic policies being imposed on their local economies, they brave immense odds in search of a better life for themselves and their progeny in the lands where eking out a meager existence in the margins holds out infinitely more promise in the long run than the best their homelands have to offer. I am arguing that there is a direct connection between the structure-driven globalization that is the focus of most commentators on both sides of the debate and the subjectivity-driven globalization that results from the response of ordinary folk in places such as Africa. This agency-inflected globalization is central to the phenomenon of immigration at the present time and it deserves more attention than is given to it in current literature.

Agency-inflected globalization is not without implications for how we, as scholars, analysts, and policymakers, respond to the current situation. Ordinarily, one would have thought that the apostles of open borders in trade (liberalization, it is called), a key pylon of neoliberal economics, would recognize the unintended consequences of their principles and welcome the new weary travelers in search of better lives for themselves and their posterity. That is not what we find, however. Concomitantly, one would expect to have reflected in the theoretical exertions of native thinkers in Europe and North America some openness to new ways of conceptualizing issues—new furniture of the world, as it were—brought by the new immigrants. As in older times, it is not only in the physical movement that we see globalization from Africa or Latin America but also in the corpus of theoretical reflections arising from bringing the agency of Africans and others to our understanding of the new experiences, ideas, or ways of being human that came with the earlier globalizations. These reflections have issued in the emergence of indigenous African Islamic scholars, Indian theorists of liberal democracy, African innovators in Marxism, and the like. The absence of recognition by Euroamerican scholars of the theoretical productions of African scholars is an additional specificity of the current globalization discourse.[67] Despite what I have said so far, I would like to suggest that there is no reason for despair. Indeed, I have presented the ongoing discussion in order to sensitize my readers to the exciting possibilities awaiting us once we get past inertia and a tendency to make light of the agency of the Rest of Us.

Looking Forward

When the Canadian media philosopher Marshall McLuhan introduced the phrase "the global village" into our lexicon in the early 1970s, he could not have imagined that a mere three decades later we would truly approximate the reality of the global village. But such has been the movement of history and of people in the closing decades of the twentieth century that we do indeed now inhabit what is the closest humanity has been to living in the global village. Usually when people speak of the global village at the present time, they have in mind the technologies of globalization, especially information technology, that have made it possible for us to become one another's virtual neighbors across vast expanses of space and time. The possibilities lurking in further expansion of information technologies, the much-hyped virtual global community, and the effusive (though in my humble opinion premature) celebrations of global democracy do not much interest me. My interest lies in the other possibilities that are not often apprehended but which (again in my humble opinion) present the most fecund prospects just as they promise to be the most contentious. It is to these that I now turn my attention.

I begin with a caution. In the previous section, I suggested that even if the Rest of Us could realize the best that modernity—as typified in liberal democracy and capitalism—could offer, that would be no cause for resting in our search for the best life for humans. I wish to address that issue in this concluding section. There should be no misunderstanding. I do believe that a transition to capitalism, properly carried out, would not be worse than the devil peoples in newly democratizing areas already live with. And throughout this book, I have noted the promise of modernity for many peoples, especially Africans, for whom the promise remains unredeemed. Hence, I defend not only modernity's relevance but also its necessity in the present historical conjuncture. I remain convinced that Africa should engage with modernity and move toward it. At the same time, I argue that the promise of modernity in its best realization remains inadequate for a well-rounded human life. The problem is that those who urge or (more appropriately) goad the Rest of Us toward capitalism—one manifestation, among others, of modernity—are selling the peoples concerned defective goods and those that respond enthusiastically are complicit in this historical swindle.

The collapse of communism in Eastern Europe, the overthrow of various dictators in Latin America, and the collapse of various nondescript regimes in Africa in the closing decade of the last century all converged to create a historical conjuncture of revolutionary proportions. It was and remains, in my view, a historical opportunity, especially for intellectuals, to rethink the options for humanity as it marches to that open future that is one of the fundaments of the metaphysics of modernity. The times call for a reexamination on a global scale of the ways of life that have prevailed hitherto.

The collapse of communism in particular imposed on the intellectuals of Eastern Europe who lived through its horrors a responsibility to think anew the possibility of social orderings that would realize the promise of modernity that has never been redeemed in their countries.[68] On the whole, they have pretty much made their peace with modernity.[69] They and we are called upon to go beyond, to transcend, and to rethink the limits of human flourishing presupposed by modernity and its ideological-institutional representations. That is, we should reexamine individualism as a principle of social ordering, the rule of law, liberal democracy, an abiding faith in the power of reason, the open future, and a near-obsession with novelty. A critical look at any of these representations yields only mixed blessings. For example, in spite of the centrality of law to social living in the modern state and the quantum leap that the rule of law is compared to arbitrary or monarchical rule, there is little doubt that in the normal course of life, particularly in those matters that touch us most, law is not an unqualified human good. In most cases it is an unwelcome (even if somewhat unavoidable) intrusion. Notwithstanding my unease with any absolute claims for the ideological-institutional representations of modernity, I will defend its claim to superiority over prior modes of social ordering in humanity's development from the dawn of its birth. When we smugly accept the frugal diet of democracy as multipartyism and periodic elections and privatization as wholesale looting of the common inheritance, we betray the duty to insist on securing the gains of modernity for the peoples of Africa. These gains are by no means limited to representative government. They refer to the entire way of life engendered by modernity, of which representative government is a part. They also include but are not limited to gains that involve personal freedom and economic prosperity. Additionally, we betray the duty to seek to rethink and transcend the limits of the ways of life presented by modernity. That is lamentable. My opposition arises from the fact that the dominant narratives of globalization regarding Africa hardly ever evince skepticism of the sort being canvassed here. The exceptions of course include the rump of the socialist movement, the environmental movement, and unyielding anarchists.

My skepticism is not without solid foundations in intellectual history. Karl Marx wrote: "The social revolution of the nineteenth century cannot draw its poetry from the past, but only from the future. It cannot begin with itself before it has stripped off all superstition about the past. Earlier revolutions required recollections of past world history in order to dull themselves to their own content. In order to arrive at its own content, the revolution of the nineteenth century must let the dead bury their dead. There the words went beyond the content; here the content goes beyond the words."[70] Marx was writing in the middle of the nineteenth century. He was analyzing the career of a usurper who had conned his way to power over France in a conscious but poor imitation of the original Napoleon Bonaparte. Louis Napoleon doubtless believed and acted as if he were the reincarnation of the original. But Marx recognized the epochal character of the transformations that culminated in the French Revolution and inaugurated a period of social upheavals in Europe of which the 1848 Revolutions, the immediate warrant for Louis Napoleon's rise to power, were only the latest manifestations. Marx called on his readers to realize that what the situation required was new thinking about the changed circumstances of

Europe in the aftermath of the French Revolution. He argued that the old forms of social ordering were no longer appropriate for the radically changed conditions of mid-nineteenth-century Europe. Following Marx's lead, I would like to argue that we in the contemporary world are also in a ferment that is typical of periods of epochal transformations. I too would like to caution that the social transformations inaugurated at the close of the last century "cannot draw [their] poetry from the past, but only from the future." I argue that the current responses of multipartyism and privatization to the challenge of social change in the aftermath of the Cold War, the collapse of socialism in Eastern Europe, and epochal social upheavals around the world are attempts to recollect past world history. They are, in essence, attempts to draw the poetry for the present from the past. This is the kernel of my claim that even if we could be like the West, in spite of all its obvious good sides, such an outcome will still fall far short of what would be the best life for humans.

I have already remarked that even in countries where the legacy of modernity has been realized in its best forms there are numerous tensions—social, political, and economic—that have led many to question the claim of modernity that it is the ultimate life for humans. Some of the tensions in the political sphere, for example, are forcing intellectuals and activists alike to confront the paradoxes of democracy in its modern incarnation. In the United States, to illustrate, programs to remediate past racial or sexual discrimination are likely to run counter to the promise of equal protection under the law. We see this dramatized in the ongoing onslaught against affirmative action policies all across the country. Curbing hate speech may require interference with rights that modern ideology has persuaded many are inalienable.

Nowhere are these limitations more starkly represented than in the economic sphere. Privatization has created and will continue to create a few more millionaires, billionaires even, within the newly democratizing countries but at the expense of misery for the many and of the denial of capacity of the many for democratic expression. This will be a perfectly normal outcome in a social formation in which the market mechanism is the principle of allocation of resources and individualism is the principle of reward for labor.[71] When donor countries and international financial institutions insist on cutbacks in social services spending and the emplacement of the market mechanism, there is little or no mention of the fact that in their own countries, the so-called developed democracies, there are safety nets in place for the multitude who are shafted by the market; that free market mechanisms do not guarantee a minimum standard of living for all citizens; and that much of the spending in sectors charged with social services is financed with huge government deficits.[72] On the contrary, the market is touted to the newly democratizing countries as a cure-all for their backwardness.[73]

A few other consequences follow that should give pause to those of us who want to see the promise of modernity redeemed in our countries. Given what I have described in the snapshots above, we should be more wary of any triumphalism at the present time, especially in light of the grim similarities between contemporary conditions and those of an earlier period when people thought that they were on the way to the best life for humans. I refer to the description by Alexis de Tocqueville of conditions at a time when capitalism was in its infancy and there was the same kind of gaudy optimism about human prospects under its regime as there seem to be at the present time. He remarked that his contemporaries "were driven on by a force that they [might have hoped] to regulate or curb, but [could not] overcome" and that it was a force that impelled them to the "destruction of aristocracy." What he called "despotic government" [his term for the capitalist regime] had a more deleterious impact on societies that were in turmoil, societies in which long-held values and social constraints that he associated with aristocracy in his own time had begun to fray. In communities

> in which the ties of family, of caste, of class, and craft fraternities no longer exist people are far too much disposed to think exclusively of their own interests, to become self-seekers practicing a narrow individualism and caring nothing for the public good. Far from trying to counteract such tendencies despotism encourages them, depriving the governed of any sense of solidarity and interdependence; of good-neighbourly feeling and a desire to further the welfare of the community at large. It immures them, so to speak, each in his private life and, taking advantage of the tendency they already have to keep apart, it estranges them still more. Their feelings towards each other were already growing cold; despotism freezes them.
>
> [In them, instability reigns and] each man is haunted by fear of sinking to a lower social level and by a restless urge to better his condition. And since money has not only become the sole criterion of a man's social status but has also acquired an extreme mobility—that is to say it changes hands incessantly, raising or lowering the prestige of individuals and families—everybody is feverishly intent on making money or, if already rich, on keeping his wealth intact. Love of gain, a fondness for business careers, the desire to get rich at all costs, a craving for material comfort and easy living quickly become ruling passions under a despotic government. They affect all classes, even those who hitherto have seemed allergic to them, and tend to lower the moral standards of the nation as a whole if no effort be made to check their growth. It is in the nature of despotism that it should foster such desires and propagate their havoc. Lowering as they do the national morale, they are despotism's safeguard, since they divert men's attention from public affairs and make them shudder at the mere thought of a revolution. Despotism alone can provide that atmosphere of secrecy which favors crooked dealings and enables the freebooters of finance to make illicit fortunes. Under other forms of government such propensities exist, undoubtedly; under a despotism they are given free rein.[74]

De Tocqueville's reflections enfold a deep irony. His sentiments were directed against an incipient bourgeois ruling class that had not yet become practiced at what we have come to know as liberal democracy at a time when its liberalism was real but rough at the edges and it was yet to become democratic.[75] Although de Tocqueville's fulminations were in defense of aristocracy, his description of capitalism closer to its birth aptly captures some of the processes that privatization has unleashed on many countries of Eastern Europe, Asia, Latin America, and Africa. "Love of gain, a fondness for business careers, the desire to get rich at all costs, a craving for material comfort and easy living have quickly become ruling passions" in most of the newly democratizing countries. Individualism of the worst sort has been implanted. The new moneybags feel that they are destined to rule, their making tons of money being their only badge of fitness so to do. Needless to say, this is all corrosive of true democracy. And I trace most of these consequences, in part, to the uncritical embrace of an anemic conception of democracy and a passé capitalism that cannot be the harbinger of a happier future.

That de Tocqueville's warning is relevant to the current situations in the newly democratizing countries confirms Marx's quip from the same piece from which I quoted earlier: "Hegel remarks somewhere that all facts and personages of great importance in world history occur, as it were, twice. He forgot to add: the first time as tragedy, the second as farce." We are now witnessing the farcical replay of a superseded era in the contemporary period. What we who uncritically embrace privatization and democracy at this time are doing is refusing to let the dead of the modern era bury their dead. Over 500 years of the modern age and over 200 years of its economic surrogate—capitalism—suffice to make us wary of drawing the poetry for the commencement of the twenty-first century from the past. As in the earlier case, the contemporary content goes beyond modernity's past words.

Despite the skeptical tone of the last few paragraphs, I conclude this discussion on an optimistic note. In addition to the possibilities premised on advances in information technologies, I would like to suggest that we already have the society of abundance that writers in the socialist tradition from Robert Owen to Saint Simon to Karl Marx have always regarded as the absolute sine qua non for the society of the future that they dubbed communism. This society of abundance provides the material substructure for the functioning of the global village properly conceived. An additional implication arises from the assumption of a society of abundance. It means in concrete terms that the world already produces enough stuff for its teeming inhabitants. It follows, then, that with a distribution pattern that sees the world as an integrated one, a global village in the true sense whose inhabitants' destinies are necessarily interlinked, we (humanity, that is) can afford to limit production while creating more equity in the consumption of the world's resources at their current rate of expropriation. Needless to say, such a course must involve a serious reappraisal of the consumption patterns of the inhabitants of Western countries. By so doing, we preserve the world for future generations and arrest the near-inexorable tendency toward environmental degradation. These are the possibilities that excite me and they are the ones that will make a qualitative difference in how or whether we do globalization right.

To do what I just said, open borders cannot remain at the level of rhetorical commitment: They must be truly open in both spatial and intellectual terms.[76] Seen thus, the movement of peoples becomes not the occasion for circling the *laager* but the occasion for opening up to new experiences; endeavoring to learn new tongues; cultivating new tastes in food, fashion, and loving; and generally absorbing fresh productive energies while discovering the essential oneness of humanity in its infinite presentations. New forms of nativism lead away from this brave new world; seeing Africa, for example, as a continent of blighted peoples who will always need help leads away from this brave new world; seeking to keep current advantages in the distribution and consumption of the world's resources leads away from this brave new world. It requires the commitment of substantial resources to other parts of the world in order to enable them not merely to live as humans but also, more importantly, to free up their energies for common survival, even flourishing. That is the challenge of globalization done right.

Conclusion

This book has raised and, I hope, answered many questions regarding the nature of the relation between Africa and modernity. I have argued that at least in its Western part Africans had begun a transition to modernity in the first three quarters of the nineteenth century and that that transition was aborted when formal empire foisted a peculiar variety of colonialism on much of the continent. Ever since, the history of the continent has been one of what colonialism did to the continent and African scholars have demonstrated a remarkable amnesia regarding what their forebears did when they first engaged the phenomenon of modernity. Given that at the present time African countries without exception are challenged once again to prosecute what is now a late transition to modernity, it is incumbent on us scholars to ensure that the continent is not led down blind alleys and into ineffective strategies. A primary aim of this book is to contribute to that effort.

Although there has been a renewed interest in the subject of modernity and Africa, discussions of its philosophical discourse have been few and far between. Even philosophers such as Kwame Gyekye, Tsenay Serequeberhan, Kwame Anthony Appiah, Kwasi Wiredu, and Valentin Mudimbe have not been too interested in isolating and exploring the tenets of modernity such as I have in this book. I do not point this out to take any special credit. As anyone familiar with the works of the authors just iterated will readily attest, they all have addressed the theme of modernity, especially Serequeberhan, Gyekye, and Appiah. If by isolating the core tenets of the politico-philosophical discourse of modernity, I point our scholars to the possibilities inherent in claiming this inventory of concepts for our endeavors to make sense of African events and processes, one aspect of my objective for this book will have been met.

Moreover, I can only hope that in introducing to my readers the modest but trailblazing ambitions of African genius in one area of the continent at the beginning of the nineteenth century, others might be challenged to use the lens thus provided to look at goings on in other parts of the continent for similar products. Who knows, similar archeological digs might unearth better, more informative and, I dare say, more original contributions of African intellectuals to the evolution of the discourse and institutionalization of modernity in the continent. If nothing else, weaning African scholars away from their required elemental hostility to modernity will free up space for real debates among us on the desirability or otherwise of modernity and its institutional appurtenances. We shall move away from the current inchoate engagement to a deliberate and robust debate about the place of and what ought to be our reaction to individualism, the centrality of reason, the open future, the idea of progress, the rule of law, and liberal democracy.

I have also elected in this book to make African agency front, back, and center in the discussion. This explains the cast of characters and themes that dominate it. Subjectivity is central to the constitution of modernity. This takes off the table the misunderstanding abroad in African scholarship that to be modern is to be misshapen in a Western mode. Part of what modernity requires or at least presupposes is that the self that is at its heart will be made by the individual. So even if an African wishes to be "Western" she must do so in *her own way* or, failing that, suffer the stigma of inauthenticity. We have seen that one of the most profound subversions of modernity orchestrated by colonialism in the continent was to deny the African the prerogative of choosing how to be human. When we directly engage the discourse of modernity and make our peace with it, we shall find that a whole lot of the specialness—DIFFERENCE—that African and Africanist scholars love to claim for all things African is bogus and is a lean-to that Africans, especially African scholars, can and should do without. I have highlighted the writings of the apostles discussed in this book, the constitutional experiments that I considered, and the battles that Africans who have always chosen to be modern fought with their detractors who wanted to wall them in with difference to show the current generation that we are not sentenced permanently to the false binary of being either a resister or a victim of modernity. I identify with those who sought to make it their own and by so doing offered both their immediate communities and the wider world lessons in African radical subjectivity. I know that many African scholars think along similar lines. Only Anthony Appiah, Abiola Irele, and Paulin Hountondji have professed their belief in the worth of modernity directly. Should the discussion here provide others with the conceptual wherewithal to domesticate modernity without alibis, a substantial part of my aim shall have been attained.

In future work, I expect to delve more deeply into the record of reflections by African thinkers, especially in the areas of social and political philosophy, and this in as comprehensive a manner as their exertions will accommodate. What did Africans think of and say about freedom, the principles for the moral distribution of power in the state, the question of citizenship, the grounds of political obligation, and so on? In short, this book is best read as the opening salvo in an intellectual quest that promises abundant yield and excitement. Everyone is invited.

NOTES

Introduction

1. The Commonwealth is the group of former British colonies and dominions that are still nominally headed by the British queen. It used to be all Anglophone until Mozambique joined. In this book, the term refers only to the former British colonies in Africa.

2. Nigeria passed under military rule six years into independence. Kenya and Tanzania did not experience military rule, although Tanzania had an unsuccessful mutiny in 1964 that, ironically, Nigeria helped thwart. Nigeria was a mixed economy and Kenya embraced what is generously characterized as a free enterprise economy, while Tanzania was a socialist state.

3. There is renewed interest in the career of modernity in Africa. The following titles are noteworthy: J. and J. L. Comaroff, *Of Revelation and Revolution*, vol. 1, *Christianity, Colonialism, and Consciousness in South Africa* (Chicago: University of Chicago Press, 1991); J. and J. L. Comaroff, *Of Revelation and Revolution*, vol. 2, *The Dialectics of Modernity* (Chicago: University of Chicago Press, 1997); Frederick Cooper and Ann Laura Stoler, eds., *Tensions of Empire: Colonial Cultures in a Bourgeois World* (Berkeley: University of California Press, 1997); Jean Copans, "No Shortcuts to Democracy: The Long March towards Modernity," *Review of African Political Economy*, no. 50 (March 1991); Gaurav Desai, *Subject to Colonialism: African Self-Fashioning and the Colonial Library* (Durham, N.C.: Duke University Press, 2001); Jan-Georg Deutsch, Peter Probst, and Heike Schmidt, eds., *African Modernities: Entangled Meanings in Current Debate* (Oxford and Portsmouth, N.H.: James Currey and Heinemann, 2002); and Olakunle George, *Relocating Agency: Modernity and African Letters* (Albany: State University of New York Press, 2003). The literature on the politico-philosophical discourse of modernity is much smaller. Titles include Valentin Mudimbe, *The Invention of Africa: Gnosis, Philosophy, and the Order of Knowledge* (Bloomington: Indiana University Press, 1988); Kwame Anthony Appiah, *In My Father's House* (New York: Oxford University Press, 1991); Simon Gikandi, *Maps of Englishness: Writing Identity in the Culture of Colonialism* (New York: Columbia University Press, 1996); Kwame Gyekye, *Tradition and Modernity* (New York: Oxford University Press, 1997); and Elísio Salvado Macamo, ed., *Negotiating Modernity: Africa's Ambivalent Experience* (Dakar, London, Pretoria: Codesria Books/Zed Books/University of South Africa Press, 2005).

4. Martin Kilson, "African Political Change and the Modernisation Process," *Journal of Modern African Studies* 1, no. 4 (December 1963): 425–440; Biodun Jeyifo, "In the Wake of Modernity," *Anglophonia/Caliban* 7 (2000): 73.

5. As far as I know, no one has examined these elements of modernity and their career in Africa in the aftermath of their introduction on the continent in the nineteenth century. This book makes a start in that direction.

6. See Jeyifo, "In the Wake of Colonialism and Modernity," 73; and Frederick Cooper, "Conflict and Connection: Rethinking Colonial African History," *American Historical Review* 99, no. 5 (December 1994): 1516–1545.

7. See Philip D. Curtin, ed., *Africa and the West: Intellectual Responses to European Culture* (Madison: University of Wisconsin Press, 1972); J. F. Ade Ajayi, *Christian Missions in Nigeria, 1841–1891: The Making of a New Elite* (Ibadan: Ibadan University Press, 1965); Adu Boahen, *African Perspectives on Colonialism* (Baltimore, Md., and London: Johns Hopkins University Press, 1987); Albert Memmi, *The Colonizer and the Colonized* (Boston: Beacon Press, 1967); Mudimbe, *The Invention of Africa*; A. J. Christopher, *Colonial Africa* (London: Croom Helm, 1984); A. D. Roberts, ed., *The Colonial Moment in Africa* (Cambridge: Cambridge University Press, 1990).

8. Contra Mudimbe, *The Invention of Africa*. But Jean Comaroff and John L. Comaroff, in the works cited in note 3 above, made a related case for Southern Africa, although their political economy approach and class analysis of the process limited the attention they paid to one of the core elements of modernity: the principle of subjectivity. This point has been seized upon by some of their critics. See Elizabeth Elbourne, "Word Made Flesh: Christianity, Modernity, and Cultural Colonialism in the Work of Jean and John Comaroff," *American Historical Review* 108, no. 2 (April 2003): 435–459; Paul S. Landau, "Hegemony and History in Jean and John L. Comaroff's *Of Revelation and Revolution*," *Africa* 70, no. 3 (2000): 501–519; and Isabel Hofmeyr, "Studying Missionaries in a Post-National World," *African Studies* 63, no. 1 (July 2004): 119–129. See also Brian Stanley, "Enlightenment and Mission: A Re-Evaluation," Currents in World Christianity, Position Paper No. 11, Centre for Advanced Religious and Theological Studies, Faculty of Divinity, University of Cambridge, Cambridge, 1996; Jehu Hanciles, "Conversion and Social Change: A Review of the Unfinished Task in West Africa," Currents in World Christianity, Position Paper No. 119, Centre for Advanced Religious and Theological Studies, Faculty of Divinity, University of Cambridge, Cambridge, 1999.

9. See Boahen, *African Perspectives on Colonialism*; Emmanuel A. Ayandele, *The Missionary Impact on Modern Nigeria* (London: Longman, 1966); P. F. de Moraes Farias and Karin Barber, eds., *Self-Assertion and Brokerage: Early Cultural Nationalism in West Africa*, Birmingham University African Studies Series 2 (Birmingham: Centre of West African Studies, 1990); and Lamine Sanneh, *Abolitionists Abroad: American Blacks and the Making of Modern West Africa* (Cambridge, Mass.: Harvard University Press, 1999). Recaptives were Africans taken as slaves who were freed by the British Navy on the high seas before they made it to the Americas and were returned to Sierra Leone and, eventually, to points in West Africa, including, in some cases, their original homes. Returnees were Africans who repatriated from the New World to West Africa.

10. See Peter C. Williams, *The Ideal of the Self-Governing Church: A Study in Victorian Missionary Strategy* (Leiden: E. J. Brill, 1990); Peter C. Williams, "'Not Transplanting': Henry Venn's Strategic Vision," in *The Church Mission Society and World Christianity, 1799–1999*, ed. Kevin Ward and Brian Stanley (Grand Rapids, Mich.: Eerdmans, 2000), 147–172; and Lamine Sanneh, "The CMS and the African Transformation: Samuel Ajayi Crowther and the Opening of Nigeria," in Ward and Stanley, *The Church Mission Society and World Christianity*, 173–197.

11. Ajayi, *Christian Missions in Nigeria*; J. F. Ade Ajayi, "Henry Venn and the Policy of Development," in *The History of Christianity in West Africa*, ed. Ogbu Kalu (London: Longman, 1980); Wilbert R. Shenk, *Henry Venn: Missionary Statesman* (Maryknoll: Orbis, 1983); Max Warren, ed., *To Apply the Gospel: Selections from the Writings of Henry Venn* (Grand Rapids, Mich.: Eerdmans, 1971); Williams, *The Ideal of the Self-Governing Church*.

12. The issue of the role that difference and its treatment played in the constitution of the discourse of modernity and colonialism in Africa has been treated in Mudimbe, *The Invention of Africa*; Jean and John L. Comaroff, *Of Revelation and Revolution*, vol. 1; and Cooper and Stoler, *Tensions of Empire*.

13. This is fully explicated in chapter 2.

14. Philosophical anthropology has not received the attention it deserves in the scholarship on colonialism in Africa when compared to that of India, for example. See Christopher Fyfe, "Race, Empire and the Historians," *Race & Class* 33, no. 4 (1992): 15–30; and Uday Singh Mehta, *Liberalism and Empire* (Chicago: University of Chicago Press, 1996).

15. The French called a similar policy "association." See Alice L. Conklin, *A Mission to Civilize: The Republican Idea of Empire in France and West Africa, 1895–1930* (Stanford, Calif.: Stanford University Press, 1997); and A. I. Asiwaju, *West African Transformations: Comparative Impacts of French and British Colonialism* (Lagos: Malthouse Press, 2001).

16. See Mahmood Mamdani, *Citizen and Subject* (Princeton, N.J.: Princeton University Press, 1996).

17. See Fred Dallmayr and G. N. Devy, "Introduction," in *Between Tradition and Modernity*, ed. Fred Dallmayr and G. N. Devy (New Delhi: Sage Publications, 1998), 21.

18. Philip D. Curtin, "African Reactions in Perspective," in *Africa and the West: Intellectual Responses to European Culture*, ed. Philip D. Curtin (Madison: University of Wisconsin Press, 1972), 234–238. Curtin's identification of "modern" with "any of the variety of different kinds of societies that are capable of using industrial technology to create a high-production and high-consumption economy" (232) is emblematic of the absence of serious engagement with the politico-philosophical discourse of modernity.

19. The refusal to valorize this manifestation of African agency is a glaring shortcoming in the work of a thinker like Achille Mbembe, for whom, it appears, there are only two possible responses to modernity open to Africans: resisting or assuming the role of victim. The thinkers whose responses occupy me in this book did not neatly fall into either of these categories. They were agents who exhibited the entire range of responses

found in other climes to the challenges of modernity. See Achille Mbembe, "African Modes of Self-Writing" and the debate it generated in *Public Culture* 14, no. 1 (2002): 239–273 and 14, no. 3 (2002). I am indebted to Akin Adesokan for bringing this debate to my attention.

20. Anne Phillips, *The Enigma of Colonialism: British Policy in West Africa* (London and Bloomington: James Currey and Indiana University Press, 1989).

21. Boahen, *African Perspectives on Colonialism*; David Kimble, A *Political History of Ghana* (Oxford: Clarendon Press, 1963); Francis Agbodeka, "The Fanti Confederacy 1865–69," *Transactions of the Historical Society of Ghana* 7 (1964): 82–123; Toyin Falola, ed., *Tradition and Change in Africa: The Essays of J. F. Ade Ajayi* (Trenton, N.J.: Africa World Press, 2000); Omoniyi Adewoye, *The Judicial System in Southern Nigeria, 1854–1954* (Atlantic Highlands, N.J.: Humanities Press, 1977).

22. Such works will complement analyses by Simone Weil, Jean-Paul Sartre, Jean and John Comaroff, Mahmood Mamdani, V. Y. Mudimbe, Aimé Césaire, Frantz Fanon, and Amilcar Cabral.

23. See Olúfẹ́mi Táíwò, "What Is 'African Studies'? African Scholars, Africanist Scholars and the Production of Knowledge," in *Reclaiming the Human Sciences and Humanities through African Perspectives,* ed. Helen Lauer and Kofi Anyidoho, vol. 2 (Accra: Sahara Press, forthcoming).

24. There is some movement in this direction in the works of Achille Mbembe, Nkiru Nzegwu, Kwame Anthony Appiah, Tsenay Serequeberhan, and Kwame Gyekye.

25. I have purposely omitted the issue of Italian colonialism in the Horn of Africa.

26. G. W. F. Hegel, *The Philosophy of Right* (Oxford: Clarendon Press, 1958); Jürgen Habermas, *The Philosophical Discourse of Modernity* (Cambridge, Mass.: MIT Press, 1990); Charles Taylor, *Sources of the Self: The Making of the Modern Identity* (Cambridge, Mass.: Harvard University Press, 1989); Enrique Dussel, *The Invention of the Americas* (New York: Continuum Books, 1995); Samir Amin, *Eurocentrism* (New York: Monthly Review Press, 1989); David Harvey, *The Condition of Postmodernity* (Oxford: Polity Press, 1990).

1. Colonialism

The original version of this chapter was presented to the Thirteenth Annual Conference of the International Society for African Philosophy and Studies, held at Rhodes University, Grahamstown, South Africa, 2–4 April 2007. Another version was presented at the colloquium of the Philosophy Department, Occidental College, Los Angeles, California, on 31 October 2007. I would like to thank Kory Schaff for inviting me to Occidental College and to all who attended the different sessions for giving me the benefit of their comments and criticisms.

1. Colonialism reached its apogee in theories of dependency that posited that the so-called peripheries could not develop capitalism and that the best they could attain was a kind of *compradoral* development that would make them forever beholden to the capitalist centers.

2. Malaysia, Singapore, and South Korea easily come to mind in this respect.

3. The newly industrializing countries of Asia, especially South Korea, Singapore, and Malaysia, have all become principal sources of foreign direct investment in Africa. India now has a program of foreign aid for African countries. See Ernest Harsch, "Africa and Asia Forge Strong Alliances," *Africa Recovery* 18, no. 1 (April 2004): 1. In August 2006, news came out that Chad was kicking out two oil companies, Chevron and Petronas of Malaysia, from its oil industry. Now Malaysia is a direct exploiter of African labor. While I celebrate Malaysia's success, I must lament Africa's continuing failure.

4. See in general Samir Amin, *Neocolonialism in West Africa* (London: Penguin, 1973); Anne Phillips, *The Enigma of Colonialism: British Policy in West Africa* (London/Bloomington: James Currey/Indiana University Press, 1989); Walter Rodney, *How Europe Underdeveloped Africa* (London: Bogle L'Ouverture, 1972); Mahmood Mamdani, *Citizen and Subject* (Princeton, N.J.: Princeton University Press, 1996); and Geoffrey Kay, *Development and Underdevelopment: A Marxist Analysis* (London: Macmillan, 1976).

5. Elísio Macamo talks of the ambivalence that marks the African experience of modernity and traces it to the fact that "colonialism was the historical form through which modernity became a real social project on the African continent. Colonialism, however, was premised on the denial of that same modernity to Africans." Macamo, "Introduction," in *Negotiating Modernity: Africa's Ambivalent Experience*, ed. Elísio Salvado Macamo (Dakar, London, Pretoria: Codesria Books/Zed Books/University of South Africa Press, 2005), 8. His second claim converges with my position. He is, however, wrong in locating colonialism as the form through which modernity became a real social project in Africa. That may be true of southern African countries, but it is definitely not applicable to the West African situation that anchors the case I make in this book.

6. Robert Delavignette, *Christianity and Colonialism*, trans. J. R. Foster (New York: Hawthorn Books, 1964), 8.

7. V. Y. Mudimbe, *The Invention of Africa* (Bloomington: Indiana University Press, 1988), 1.

8. Frederick Cooper has criticized African historians for neglecting local colonialisms and other forms of oppression in their discussion of colonialism. See Cooper, "Conflict and Connection: Rethinking Colonial African History," *American Historical Review* 99, no. 5 (December 1994): 1521.

9. A discussion of the philosophical justification for this will be presented in the next chapter.

10. Delavignette, *Christianity and Colonialism*, 8.

11. Tsenay Serequeberhan makes the same point thus: "It is clear, then, that colonialism arises from the internal dynamics of European modernity." Serequeberhan, "The Idea of Colonialism in Hegel's *Philosophy of Right*," *International Philosophical Quarterly* 29, no. 3 (1989): 312. The next five paragraphs have been excerpted from my "Reading the Colonizer's Mind: Lord Lugard and the Philosophical Foundations of British Colonialism," in *Philosophy and Racism*, ed. Susan Babbitt and Sue Campbell (Ithaca, N.Y.: Cornell University Press, 1999), 157–186.

12. Serequeberhan's article works out in great detail how colonialism is derived from Hegel's discourse in the *Philosophy of Right*. My discussion adopts a much more limited approach. My interest is in showing that given the intimate connection between colonialism and modernity, it might have operated differently in Africa. That it did not do so may not wholly be attributable to modernity, as Serequeberhan's piece appears to suggest. In fact, it may be that, as I argue in this work, colonialism may be responsible for the subversion of modernity in Africa.

13. G. W. F. Hegel, *Philosophy of Right*, trans. and intro. T. M. Knox (Oxford: Clarendon, 1958), 149.

14. Ibid., 150.

15. Ibid.

16. Ibid., 151.

17. See ibid., 151.

18. Ibid.

19. Ibid., 151–152, my italics.

20. See, in general, Bhikhu Parekh, "Liberalism and Colonialism: A Critique of Locke and Mill," in *The Decolonization of Imagination*, ed. Jan Nederveen Pieterse and Bhikhu Parekh (London: Zed, 1995), 81–98; Uday Singh Mehta, *Liberalism and Empire: A Study in Nineteenth-Century British Liberal Thought* (Chicago: University of Chicago Press, 1996); Edward Said, "Zionism from the Standpoint of Its Victims," in *Anatomy of Racism*, ed. David Theo Goldberg (Minneapolis: University of Minnesota Press, 1990); John Locke, *Two Treatises on Government*, 2nd ed., ed. Peter Laslett (Cambridge: Cambridge University Press, 1967); John Stuart Mill, "Considerations on Representative Government," in J. S. Mill, *Three Essays* (Oxford: Oxford University Press, 1985); and Karl Marx, "On Imperialism in India," in *The Marx-Engels Reader*, 2nd ed., ed. Robert C. Tucker (New York: Norton, 1978).

21. Hegel, *Philosophy of Right*, Addition, 278. This passage contains some fecund and acute observations. The most important is that dealing with the comparative advantages of independence and decolonization.

22. Albert Memmi, *The Colonizer and the Colonized* (Boston: Beacon Press, 1991), chapters 1 and 2.

23. For a critical analysis of Hegel's philosophy of history and its treatment of Africa, see Olúfẹ́mi Táíwò, "Exorcising Hegel's Ghost: Africa's Challenge to Philosophy," *African Studies Quarterly* 1, no. 4 (1998), available at www.Africa.ufl.edu/asq/v1/v1_i4.htm.

24. On the export of culture, see Serequeberhan, "The Idea of Colonialism in Hegel's *Philosophy of Right*," 312.

25. The list of important philosophers who accepted this point of view is long. John Locke justified the seizure of Native American land in the name of moving the Indians to modernity. Mill did the same thing, calling for "parental despotism" for backward peoples. See Parekh, "Liberalism and Colonialism: A Critique of Locke and Mill," 85, 87, 94–96; and John Stuart Mill, "On Liberty," in J. S. Mill, *Three Essays* (Oxford:

Oxford University Press, 1985). According to Mill, "Despotism is a legitimate mode of government in dealing with barbarians, provided the end be their improvement, and the means justified by actually effecting that end. Liberty, as a principle, has no application to any state of things anterior to the time when mankind have become capable of being improved by free and equal discussion" ("On Liberty," 16). Even Karl Marx and Frederick Engels accepted colonialism in India and Algeria on the same premises. See Karl Marx, "The British Rule in India," and "The Future Results of British Rule in India," in Karl Marx and Frederick Engels, *Selected Works*, vol. 1 (Moscow: Progress Publishers, 1969).

26. In the rest of this book I shall restrict my remarks to English-speaking Africa. I am not alone in taking an internalist stance in my evaluation of modernity's career in Africa. James Africanus Horton, J. E. Casely Hayford, Aimé Césaire, Frantz Fanon, and Amilcar Cabral all adopted an internalist view of modernity and used it to indict colonialism for not delivering on its promise of moving Africans and their societies along the path to progress. When we look at the writings of European critics of colonialism, too, we find a similar standpoint in critiques by Jean-Paul Sartre and Simone Weil.

27. Delavignette, *Christianity and Colonialism*, 19.

28. See Atul Kohli, "Where Do High-Growth Political Economies Come From? The Japanese Lineage of Korea's 'Developmental State,'" in *The Developmental State*, ed. Meredith Woo-Cumings (Ithaca, N.Y.: Cornell University Press, 1999), 93–136.

29. Frederick D. Lugard, *The Rise of Our East African Empire*, 2 vols. (London: Frank Cass & Co., 1968), 75.

30. Albert Demangeon, *The British Empire: A Study in Colonial Geography*, trans. Ernest F. Row (London: George C. Harrap & Co., 1923), 123, my italics.

31. Ibid., 123–124. See also M. Semakula Kiwanuka, "Colonial Policies and Administrations in Africa: The Myths of the Contrasts," *African Historical Studies* 3, no. 2 (1970): 295–315; reprinted in Gregory Maddox, ed. and intro., *The Colonial Epoch in Africa* (New York and London: Garland Publishing, 1993).

32. Demangeon, *The British Empire*, 124.

33. Ibid., 135.

34. See Jean-Paul Sartre, *Colonialism and Neocolonialism* (London and New York: Routledge, 2001); J. P. Little, ed. and trans., *Simone Weil on Colonialism: An Ethic of the Other* (Lanham, Md.: Rowman & Littlefield, 2003).

35. This section is excerpted from my "Colonialism and Its Aftermath: The Crisis of Knowledge Production," *Callaloo: A Journal of African American and African Arts and Letters* 16, no. 4 (1993): 891–908.

36. Cooper's piece, which makes so much of African agency, could not cite any of the earlier attempts to domesticate modernity by Africans in the nineteenth century, even though he correctly apprehended the revolutionary nature of some missionaries' work on the African mindscape. Cooper, "Conflict and Connection: Rethinking African Colonial History."

37. See Lamine Sanneh, *Abolitionists Abroad* (Cambridge: Harvard University Press,

1999); and James D. Graham, "Indirect Rule: The Establishment of 'Chiefs' and 'Tribes' in Cameron's Tangayika," *Tanzania Notes and Records,* nos. 77 and 78 (1976), 1–9; reprinted in Maddox, *The Colonial Epoch in Africa.*

38. Elísio Macamo has indicated that it may even have been more complex in the Portuguese colonial possessions. See his "Denying Modernity: The Regulation of Native Labour in Colonial Mozambique and Its Postcolonial Aftermath," in *Negotiating Modernity: Africa's Ambivalent Experience,* ed. Elísio Salvado Macamo (Dakar, London, Pretoria: Codesria Books/Zed Books/University of South Africa Press, 2005), chapter 3.

39. "An examination of the imprint of the various groups of Europeans interacting with Africans and with the African environment, offers a means of disentangling the complex changes which took place in the geography of Africa in the colonial period. It must be remembered that Africa was peripheral to European interests and that the numbers involved were small compared with those engaged in penetrating the other continents on the Great Frontier. Furthermore, many of the social and political ideas associated with the Turner thesis, such as the growth of democracy and private enterprise, did not apply in an environment where state control was so pervasive. . . . In this Africa followed the Latin American, not the Anglo-American prototype, unfettered by the laws and representative assemblies which characterised the metropoles. It was the distinctive colonial state which emerged, not a developed frontier state." A. J. Christopher, *Colonial Africa* (London: Croom Helm, 1984), 2.

40. Ibid., 55–56. It should be noted that the period when schools and clinics symbolized colonial policy coincided with the period of the struggle for independence.

41. See Richard Roberts and Kristin Mann, "Law in Colonial Africa," in *Law in Colonial Africa,* ed. Kristin Mann and Richard Roberts (Portsmouth, N.H., and London: Heinemann and James Currey, 1991), especially 19–23.

42. It continued in Tanzania until 1975.

43. See chapter 5 below.

44. See chapters 2 and 3 below.

45. D. A. Low, *Eclipse of Empire* (Cambridge: Cambridge University Press, 1993), chapter 7. See also Iheanyi J. Samuel-Mbaekwe, "Colonialism and Social Structure," *Transafrican Journal of History* 15 (1986), 81–95; reprinted in Maddox, *The Colonial Epoch in Africa.*

46. (Boston: Beacon Press, 1970).

47. (New York: Grove Press, 1967).

48. As opposed to this, the acknowledgement of the humanity of Indians warranted the many knots with which the philosophers of the modern age were tied up when they proclaimed the universal humanity of all while proclaiming the inferior humanity of Indians.

49. Trans. J. Sibree, intro. C. J. Friedrich (New York: Dover Publications, 1956).

50. For a critical discussion of Hegel's submissions, see Táíwò, "Exorcising Hegel's Ghost." Of course, Hegel was not alone. For the similar views of other philosophers, see Emmanuel C. Eze, ed., *Race and the Enlightenment Reader* (Malden: Blackwell, 1997).

51. This has begun to change. See recent works by Olakunle George, Simon Gikandi, Tsenay Serequeberhan, Kwame Gyekye, and Elísio Macamo.

2. Running Aground on Colonial Shores

The original version of this chapter was delivered as a public lecture during my tenure as a Visiting Distinguished Minority Scholar at the University of Wisconsin–Eau Claire in November 1996. A version was presented to the Conference to Celebrate the Centenary of the Philosophy Doctoral Programme at the University of Toronto, Toronto, Canada in October 1997. Another version was read before the seminar series on "The Black Atlantic: Race, Nation, and Gender" at the Center for Historical Analysis at Rutgers University, New Brunswick, New Jersey, in March 1998. The first complete version was done during my tenure as a Visiting Professor at the Institut für Afrikastudien, Universität Bayreuth, Bayreuth, Germany, in 1999. It was presented to a Colloquium at the Carter G. Woodson Center for African–American and African Studies at the University of Virginia. I would like to thank the many participants at these various fora, whose sometimes spirited, even vehement, reactions to the thesis of the essay have forced me to think more carefully about its development. I am grateful to Loyola University, Chicago, which granted me a research leave in the spring semester of 1996. The University of Wisconsin–Eau Claire, the Universität Bayreuth, and the University of Virginia, which have hosted me and provided the appropriate setting for me to develop these ideas and write them up, have materially supported the research that went into the essay.

1. Consider this analogy that I hope will help illuminate the omissions illustrative of colonialism in the African context. Let us dilate on the fate and significance of an object that many readers know quite intimately and is a fixture in the furniture of their world: the sofa bed. It was a few years ago that I came upon the significance of the lowly sofa bed for the movement that has typified our age and after which global history, at least as told by the Western tradition, is named: modernity. I discovered that the sofa bed is an icon of modernity. Think of it: it is a bed, it is a sofa. Now you see the bed, now you don't. It enables the kinds of transformation that typify everyday life; it gives ordinary folks some quiet confidence that "there's always a place to stay." It embodies some of the promise of modernity and its metaphysical template: economy of space, ease of use, huge returns on minimum expense, and great functionality. Ultimately, it illustrates the permanence of impermanence. Growing up in Ibadan, one of Nigeria's largest cities, I never saw a sofa bed. It wasn't because people did not need it—quite the contrary. I knew many families, besides my own, for whom the sofa bed would have filled a real and pressing need. It was not uncommon for six-member families to shack up in one room or sometimes two rooms. But the sofa bed was nowhere in sight. My recent discovery has enabled me to make sense of this remarkable absence. For in some profound sense, the absence of the sofa bed offers a metaphor for the failings of colonialism that are usually not represented in the dominant narratives of the career of colonialism or of modernity. The parallels are intriguing. All the elements that serve as the ideational

underpinning of the sofa bed bespeak a state of mind, an attitude, a symbol of a way of life. This was what was not made available to Africans by colonialism. I shall argue in the rest of this discussion that the ideational underpinnings of colonialism were denied Africans and that when they sought to make such ideas their own they were thwarted and quite often punished for so aspiring.

2. For a different characterization, see Albert Memmi, *The Colonizer and the Colonized* (Boston: Beacon Press, 1972), 10. See also V. Y. Mudimbe, *The Invention of Africa* (Bloomington: Indiana University Press, 1988), 46–47.

3. Margaret Strobel, *European Women and the Second British Empire* (Bloomington: Indiana University Press, 1991).

4. For example, see Frederick D. Lugard, *The Rise of Our East African Empire*, 2 vols. (London: Frank Cass & Co., 1968).

5. This is an important caveat. Indeed, it was my apprehension of the optimism and enthusiasm of the early missionary efforts that first piqued my curiosity about what might have been had they remained the dominant force in the colonies and why their program was never adopted by their administrator and trader successors. Furthermore, as time went on, the mindset of the missionaries became increasingly like those of their administrator and trader counterparts, and they, too, became complicit in the subversion of social transformation in the colonies. I cite historical evidence later to support this contention in the relevant sections of this chapter.

6. I am aware that some may consider speculation to be wrongheaded. But given that this is not an attempt to retell history, it cannot be easily dismissed. On the contrary, I have been led down the road to speculation because the historical data allude in several ways to the possibility that colonialism might have unfolded differently in Africa. Hence it becomes important to make sense of why certain available roads were not taken. Additionally, because the exigencies that have necessitated a continuous engagement with the period of colonialism in Africa have not been definitely taken care of in the present, it is imperative that we try to figure out how we might proceed differently in light of our understanding of what took place in the past.

7. This is the colonialism that I am referring to throughout this discussion, unless otherwise stated.

8. Elísio Salvado Macamo, "Introduction," in *Negotiating Modernity: Africa's Ambivalent Experience*, ed. Elísio Salvado Macamo (Dakar, London, Pretoria: Codesria Books/Zed Books/University of South Africa Press, 2005), 1.

9. Mudimbe, *The Invention of Africa*, 45.

10. Ibid., 45.

11. Ibid., 46.

12. Ibid., 47.

13. Ibid., 46.

14. Ibid., 47.

15. Delavignette, *Christianity and Colonialism*, 50.

16. Ibid., 66.

17. Ibid., 72.

18. Ibid., 74.

19. Ibid., 57. This injunction was contained in a 1659 document titled "Instructions for the Use of Vicars Apostolic Leaving for the Chinese Kingdoms of Tonkin and Cochin China"; cited in ibid., 57.

20. Ibid., 58.

21. William Knight, *The Missionary Secretariat of Henry Venn, B.D.* (London: Longmans, Green, and Co., 1880), 283.

22. Ibid., 285.

23. Ibid., 284.

24. Ibid., 285.

25. Ibid., 307.

26. J. F. Ade Ajayi, *Christian Missions in Nigeria 1841–1891: The Making of a New Elite* (Ibadan: University of Ibadan Press, 1965), 17. One must not discount the importance of the American missionary's observation. The absence of middle classes, of a regime of private property, and so on, was used by different writers, including John Locke, and Hegel, to justify the expropriation of other people's lands—especially in North America—by European colonizers. Incidentally, the Baptist-sponsored university in Ìwó, Òsun State, Nigeria, is named after the missionary from whom Ajayi quoted, Thomas Bowen. It is an index of what qualitative distinctions native agency is capable of that it would not extend the same consideration to any of the British administrators who served in Nigeria.

27. Lamine Sanneh, *Abolitionists Abroad* (Cambridge: Harvard University Press, 1999); Mudimbe, *The Invention of Africa*; A. J. Christopher, *Colonial Africa* (London: Croom Helm, 1984), 83.

28. From this point on, unless specified, this is the class I am interested in.

29. Ajayi, *Christian Missions in Nigeria*; Ayandele, *The Missionary Impact on Modern Nigeria*; A. Adu Boahen, *African Perspectives on Colonialism* (Baltimore, Md.: Johns Hopkins University Press, 1987); Christopher, *Colonial Africa*; Roberts, *The Colonial Moment in Africa*.

30. Lamine Sanneh, *West African Christianity: The Religious Impact* (London: C. Hurst & Co., 1983), chapter 2; Ajayi, *Christian Missions in Nigeria*, chapter 1.

31. Ayandele, *The Missionary Impact on Modern Nigeria*, 4.

32. Ibid., 5.

33. Ibid., 4–5, my italics. See also O. U. Kalu, "General Introduction: The Task," in *The History of Christianity in West Africa*, ed. O. U. Kalu (London: Longman, 1980), 7.

34. Although my sympathy lies with Ajayi in his more positive assessment of the missionary impact, I do not think that Ayandele's view is any less compelling or is in any way flawed. By their very nature, revolutions always occasion wide divergences of interpretation regarding their positive or negative outcomes. The same French Revolution

that gave us the Declaration of the Rights of Man and Citizen also gave us Robespierre. What is important in this discussion is the ontological character of the processes that I am describing, not their evaluation.

35. This must be qualified because evangelicals did not share this attitude. But their views did not prevail in the missionary enterprise, even though the debate among the various Christian sects regarding the relation between spirituality and material success was intense and occasioned severe tensions among the groups.

36. Although I focus on Buxton in much of the discussion to follow, he was by no means alone in his views. Rev. Henry Venn, Crowther's mentor, was a stout theorist of native agency–driven mission and the redemption of the promise of civilization for his African wards. See especially Max Warren, ed., *To Apply the Gospel: Selections from the Writings of Henry Venn*, intro. Max Warren (Grand Rapids, Mich.: William B. Eerdmans, 1971); Knight, *The Missionary Secretariat of Henry Venn*; C. Peter Williams, *The Ideal of the Self-Governing Church: A Study in Victorian Missionary Strategy* (Leiden: E. J. Brill, 1990); Jehu Hanciles, *Euthanasia of a Mission: African Church Autonomy in a Colonial Context* (Westport, Conn.: Praeger, 2002); and T. E. Yates, *Venn and Victorian Bishops Abroad* (Uppsala: Swedish Institute of Missionary Research/London: SPCK, 1978).

37. Buxton's book was published in 1840. It is cited in Ajayi, *Christian Missions in Nigeria*, 10–11. Ajayi offers a full discussion of Buxton's plan.

38. Ibid., 12.

39. "Prospectus of the Society for the Extinction of the Slave Trade and for the Civilization of Africa, Instituted June 1839," in Thomas Fowell Buxton, *The African Slave Trade and Its Remedy*, intro. G. E. Metcalfe (London: Dawsons of Pall Mall, 1968), 1–10. For ease of presentation I have adopted the schematization in Ajayi, *Christian Missions in Nigeria*, 16–17.

40. Ajayi, *Christian Missions in Nigeria*, 18. T. J. Bowen, *Adventures and Missionary Labours in Several Countries in the Interior of Africa*, 2nd ed., intro. E. A. Ayandele (London: Frank Cass, 1968), 339–340.

41. Bowen, *Adventures and Missionary Labours in Several Countries in the Interior of Africa*, 338.

42. Ibid.

43. Ibid., 342.

44. Ibid., 339. One must remark on the prescience of Bowen's arguments and their continuing relevance in our day.

45. It is very easy to misread this desire to learn from Europe as an attempt to recreate or mimic Europe. Yes, educated Africans wished to be like Europe in their quality of life insofar as knowledge could guarantee such an outcome. They did not want to become black Europeans; they just wanted the freedom to be whatever they chose. This argument about subjectivity and choice would lead to schisms in the religious communities later on.

46. Additionally, the idea of Africans as equal but unfortunate children of God who are adjudged capable of exercising agency and working like Europeans for their own sal-

vation may have presaged a radical theology akin to liberation theology that the contemporary church in Africa may wish to recover. Segun Ilesanmi made this suggestion to me.

47. For a running indictment of the colonial authorities for not borrowing a page from the books of the missionaries in the task of developing native agency, see Henry Venn, *West African Colonies: Notices of the British Colonies on the West Coast of Africa* (London: Dalton and Lucy, 1865).

48. For a discussion of how Buxton was able to prevail on the British government to share part of the cost of the enterprise, see J. Gallagher, "Fowell Buxton and the New African Policy, 1838–1842," *Cambridge Historical Journal* 10, no. 1 (1950): 38–58.

49. C. C. Ifemesia, "The 'Civilising' Mission of 1841: Aspects of an Episode in Anglo-Nigerian Relations," *Journal of the Historical Society of Nigeria* 2, no. 3 (1962): 291–310; reprinted in *The History of Christianity in West Africa*, ed. Ogbu Kalu (London: Longman, 1980), 81–102, 100.

50. Ibid., 98.

51. See C. C. Wrigley, "Aspects of Economic History," in *The Colonial Moment in Africa*, ed. A. D. Roberts (Cambridge: Cambridge University Press, 1990), 77–139, 133–134.

52. Hence the caveat at the beginning of this discussion concerning the importance of recognizing phases in the evolution of missionary activities and differences over policies and methods among missionaries.

53. The views of Henry Townsend, who was of a similar disposition among the earlier complement of missionaries, did not become dominant until the demographic and ideological shifts of the third quarter of the nineteenth century.

54. That this was the case is overwhelmingly supported by historians of the African independent churches. See J. B. Webster, *The African Churches among the Yoruba* (Oxford: Oxford University Press, 1964); J. D. Y. Peel, *Aladura: A Religious Movement among the Yoruba* (Oxford: Oxford University Press, 1968); J. Akin Omoyajowo, *Cherubim and Seraphim: The History of an African Independent Church* (New York: Nok Publishers International, 1982); and Francis Kimani Githieya, *The Freedom of the Spirit: African Indigenous Churches in Kenya* (Atlanta: Scholars Press, 1997).

55. For a very illuminating discussion, see Henrika Kuklick, *The Savage Within: The Social History of British Anthropology, 1885–1945* (Cambridge: Cambridge University Press, 1993), especially chapter 5. Kuklick notes: "If the history of colonial anthropology shows us little about the development of anthropology as a discipline, it illuminates colonial social history—a matter of considerable significance in the general scheme of things. Colonial anthropology rationalized systematic policies of colonial officials that had long lasting consequences. In the postcolonial era, new nations have faced various problems fostered by colonialism. . . . Their political problems were in no small part engendered during the colonial era by officials who believed that their decisions were dictated by evolutionist social science" (183). See also Christine Bolt, *Victorian Attitudes to Race* (London: Routledge & Kegan Paul, 1971), chapter 4.

56. According to Ajayi, "in the Yoruba Mission in 1887, there were 6 European Mis-

sionaries, 51 African Pastors and Catechists, 41 African teachers, 7,111 members and 1,941 school children." Quoted in E. A. Ayandele, *Holy Johnson: Pioneer of African Nationalism, 1836–1911* (New York: Humanities Press, 1970), 138.

57. The trend continues at the present time. Missionaries continue to be the principal agents for rendering various African languages into written forms. In Nigeria, for instance, there is not a single example of the secular authorities ever having spearheaded the creation of scripts for any of its numerous languages. We are not even in a position to determine how many have become or are in danger of becoming extinct. The Bible Society of Nigeria continues, with foreign help, the task of creating scripts for local languages.

58. A good proportion of the debate engendered by E. Bolaji Idowu's *Olodumare: God in Yoruba Belief* (London: Longmans, 1962) and some of the severest criticisms of the book revolve around the charge that Idowu had hellenized Olodumare, a direct consequence of his accepting unwittingly the biblical register that framed the original rendering of Yoruba into writing. For the latest consideration of this issue, see J. A. I. Bewaji, "Olodumare: God in Yoruba Belief and the Theistic Problem of Evil," *African Studies Quarterly* 2, no. 1 (1998), available at web.africa.ufl.edu/asq/v2/v2i1.htm. See also A. D. Roberts, "African Cross-Currents," in *The Colonial Moment in Africa*, ed. A. D. Roberts (Cambridge: Cambridge University Press, 1990), 237.

59. J. F. Ade Ajayi, "Native Agency in Nineteenth Century West Africa," in *Tradition and Change in Africa: The Essays of J. F. Ade Ajayi*, ed. Toyin Falọla (Trenton, N.J.: Africa World Press, 2000), 109.

60. Bowen, *Adventures and Missionary Labours*, 321–322. There is no suggestion in this quote that the Africans could not profit from learning to make and read the Bible or that their use of this skill would be limited to spiritual ends.

61. Ajayi, *Christian Missions in Nigeria*, 126.

62. In this respect, see Roberts, "African Cross-Currents," 237–241; Boahen, *African Perspectives on Colonialism*, chapter 1; Michel Rene Doortmont, "Recapturing the Past: Samuel Johnson and the Construction of Yoruba History" (Ph.D. diss., Erasmus University of Rotterdam, The Netherlands, 1994); and J. D. Y. Peel, *Religious Encounter and the Making of the Yoruba* (Bloomington: Indiana University Press, 2001).

63. This judgment is widely diffused throughout the historical literature. But of course, historians do not build upon it the kind of speculative structure that I do here. This is one speculation that takes off from solid empirical grounds.

64. For records, figures, and contributions by various missions, see Sanneh, *West African Christianity*, chapter 6.

65. Boahen, *African Perspectives on Colonialism*, 16.

66. Sanneh writes, "One of the richest Nigerian businessmen, R. B. Blaize, donated £1,000 to the Anglican Native Pastorate in 1895 to set up an industrial school in Lagos. When that did not materialise, he bequeathed £3,000 in his will to the Egba United Government, with which the Abẹòkúta Industrial Institute was opened in 1908." Sanneh, *West African Christianity*, 153. The career of the Ẹgbá United Board of Management is discussed in chapter 6 below.

67. Barely twenty-five years later, some of the graduates of these native-founded institutions were spreading the joy and fruits of education by becoming proprietors of their own secondary schools. One example is Ibadan Boys' High School, Ibadan, founded in 1938 by an old student of Ibadan Grammar School.

68. For details, especially on the crucial role Fourah Bay College played throughout West Africa, see Sanneh, *West African Christianity*.

69. Boahen, *African Perspectives on Colonialism*, 16. For the situation in Nigeria, see Ajayi, *Christian Missions in Nigeria*; and Ayandele, *The Missionary Impact on Modern Nigeria*.

70. See Ajayi, *Christian Missions in Nigeria*, 156–162.

71. Ibid., 159.

72. M. J. C. Echeruo, *Victorian Lagos* (London: Macmillan, 1977); Patrick Dele Cole, *Modern and Traditional Elites in the Politics of Lagos* (London: Cambridge University Press, 1975); Pauline Baker, *Urbanization and Political Change: The Politics of Lagos 1917–1967* (Berkeley: University of California Press, 1974).

73. See W. Murry Jack, "Old Houses of Lagos," *Nigeria Magazine*, no. 46 (1955): 96–117; A. B. Laotan, "Brazilian Influence on Lagos," *Nigeria Magazine*, no. 69 (August 1961): 156–165; Ikemefuna Stanley Ifejika Okoye, "Good News for Modern Man: Architecture as Evangelical Mission in Southern Nigeria," *Passages*, no. 6 (1993): 13–15.

74. Omojola writes: "The greatest challenge to European power took place, naturally, in the Church, since it was the most important focal point for educated Africans in nineteenth century Nigeria. Within the Church itself, African Christians agitated for missionary policies more sympathetic to African customs and beliefs. One of the significant results of this agitation was the emergence, by the beginning of [the twentieth] century, of Nigerian hymnody. In addition to being the bedrock of the growth of modern Nigerian music, the new indigenous church music constituted the most significant artistic symbol of the nineteenth century Nigerian challenge to European hegemony." Bode Omojola, "Historical Background of Modern Nigerian Art Music," *Nigerian Art Music* (Ibadan and Bayreuth: IFRA and Bayreuth African Studies, 1995), 9–10.

75. On theatre generally, see Ebun Clark, *Hubert Ogunde: The Making of Nigerian Theatre* (London: Oxford University Press, 1979); and Biodun Jeyifo, *The Yoruba Travelling Theatre of Nigeria* (Lagos: Nigeria Magazine Publications, 1984).

76. See Christopher Alan Waterman, *Jùjú: A Social History and Ethnography of an African Popular Music* (Chicago: University of Chicago Press, 1990).

77. For details, see Omoniyi Adewoye, *The Judicial System in Southern Nigeria, 1854–1954* (Atlantic Highlands, N.J.: Humanities Press, 1977).

78. Writing on using film as a way of preserving Africa's oral traditions, Mbye Chan made the following observation: "It was in reference to the urgency of recovering and deploying the knowledge and wisdom of this last generation of great depositories, this living memory of Africa [its old persons], that Hampathe Ba made his now canonical statement that in Africa an old person who dies is a library that burns." Mbye Chan, "Official History, Popular Memory: Reconfiguration of the African Past in the Films of Ousmane Sembene," in *Ousmane Sembene: Dialogues with Critics and Writers*, ed.

Samba Gadjigo, Ralph H. Faulkingham, Thomas Cassirer, and Reinhard Sander (Amherst: University of Massachusetts Press, 1993), 24. On the importance of finding other media—writing, film—to preserve local languages, witness Sembene's justification for incorporating original dialogue in Diola in his film *Emitai*: "It is unfortunate that today, in 1990, Diola is slowly disintegrating. It is at risk of disappearing and other, more dominant cultures are taking over" (40). Because we are not keeping track, we do not even know how many African languages are already extinct and how many more are in danger of disappearing. Additionally, we do not even know how many languages there are in Nigeria alone, much less in Africa.

79. See Ayo Bamgbose, ed., *Yorùbá Metalanguage (Èdè-Ìperí Yorùbá)*, vol. 1, 2nd ed. (Ibadan: University Press, 1992); Oladele Awobuluyi, *Yorùbá Metalanguage (Èdè-Ìperí Yorùbá)*, vol. 2 (Ibadan: University Press, 1990); and Ayo Bamgbose, *Yorùbá: A Language in Transition* (Lagos: J. F. Odunjo Memorial Lectures Organising Committee, 1986).

80. See Christopher, "Introduction" in Christopher, *Colonial Africa*.

81. Confusion about modernization and modernity explains Agneta Pallinder-Law's analysis of the Ègbá United Government's career. See Agneta Pallinder-Law, "Aborted Modernization in West Africa? The Case of Abeokuta," *Journal of African History* 15, no. 1 (1974): 65–82.

82. Ajayi, *Christian Missions in Nigeria*, 140.

83. Ibid., 140.

84. Ibid., 103.

85. Ibid., 108–109, my italics.

86. I do not in any way suggest that the missionaries thought that they were apostles of modernity. Indeed, I would not be surprised to find that some of them might have preached against what they considered to be the excesses of their age. Nor am I presenting what the missionaries might have given as their own understanding of what they were doing. My point is that there is much merit in reinserting the processes that were taking place during this period in the more complex matrix of modernity and that doing so promises much more productive explanations of the historical processes concerned and of their continuing reverberations in our own day.

87. For a historical account, see Sanneh, *West African Christianity*, chapter 1.

88. G. W. F. Hegel, *The Philosophy of Right* (Oxford: Clarendon Press, 1958), 286.

89. Ibid., 84.

90. See in general Charles Taylor, *Sources of the Self: The Making of the Modern Identity* (Cambridge: Harvard University Press, 1989), parts III and V.

91. See, for example, the story of Joseph Boston May in Leo Spitzer, *Lives in Between: Assimilation and Marginality in Austria, Brazil, West Africa, 1780–1945* (Cambridge: Cambridge University Press, 1989), chapter 2; and P. F. de Moraes Farias and Karin Barber, "Introduction," in *Self-Assertion and Brokerage: Early Cultural Nationalism in West Africa*, ed. P. F. de Moraes Farias and Karin Barber (Birmingham: Centre for West African Studies, 1990).

92. Ajayi, *Christian Missions in Nigeria*, 108.

93. For an account of how these same principles led to the creation of African

churches, sometimes as a consequence of schisms in the mother churches headquartered
in Europe and North America, see Olúfémi Táíwò, "African-Instituted Churches," in
Encyclopedia of Protestantism, ed. Hans J. Hillerbrand (New York: Taylor and Francis,
2003).

94. Ajayi, *Christian Missions in Nigeria*, 106.

95. Ibid., 108.

96. That this idea was not lost on their African converts, even if they could or would
not fully model their lives on it, is reflected in a song that could serve as an epigram to
this discussion:

> *Bóò lọ èmi ó lọ*
> > *Bóò lọ èmi ó lọ*
> *Ìgbàgbọ́ bàbá kò le gbọmọ là*
> > *Bóò lọ èmi ó lọ*
> *Ìgbàgbọ́ ègbọ́n kò le gbàbúrò*
> > *Bóò lọ èmi ó lọ.*

> If you don't go, I will go
> > If you don't go, I will go
> A father's faith cannot save his offspring
> > If you don't go, I will go
> An older sibling's faith cannot save the younger
> > If you don't go, I will go.

Of course, it is one thing to understand an idea at the cognitive level; it is another
to follow what it entails at the behavioral level.

97. J. F. Ade Ajayi, "Nineteenth Century Origins of Nigerian Nationalism," in *Tradition and Change in Africa: The Essays of J. F. Ade Ajayi*, ed. Toyin Falola (Trenton: Africa World Press, 2000), 69–83.

98. Lamine Sanneh considers this to be the distinctive trait of Liberia and Sierra
Leone before the formal imposition of colonialism in Sierra Leone aborted the commitment to the formal equality of all in a polity guided by the merit principle and substituted the rule of chiefs based on ascription. See Sanneh, *Abolitionists Abroad*.

99. Boahen, *African Perspectives on Colonialism*, 23.

100. For a full discussion, see chapter 4 below. But for an extended exploration of the
dominant racial template that shaped Victorian England's views of Africans and what
was appropriate for them, see Bolt, *Victorian Attitudes to Race*, especially chapter 4.

101. Ajayi, "Colonialism: An Episode in African History," in *Tradition and Change
in Africa: The Essays of J. F. Ade Ajayi*, ed. Toyin Falola (Trenton: Africa World Press,
2000), 171.

102. Samir Amin, *Eurocentrism* (New York: Monthly Review Press, 1989), 100–101.

103. Ibid., 100–101. A similar mythical equivalent to the "Dark Continent" for Africa is found in George W. F. Hegel's *Philosophy of History*, trans. J. Sibree, intro. C. J.
Friedrich (New York: Dover Publications, 1956).

104. For an opposite view, see Enrique Dussel, *The Invention of the Americas* (New

York: Continuum, 1995); and Enrique Dussel, *The Underside of Modernity: Apel, Ricoeur, Rorty, Taylor, and the Philosophy of Liberation* (Atlantic Highlands, N.J.: Humanities, 1996). Dussel argues that modernity was constructed against the Other, originally construed as Latin America. I do not think that both positions are mutually exclusive. For other views that combine both positions, see Edward Said, *Orientalism* (New York: Pantheon, 1978); and James Blaut, *1492: The Debate on Colonialism, Eurocentrism and History* (Trenton, N.J.: Africa World Press, 1992).

105. For an attempt to trace the differentiated paths of historical transformation in some parts of Europe that did not make the transition to modernity and its immediate precursors, see Perry Anderson, *Passages from Antiquity to Feudalism* (London: Verso, 1979).

106. See. in general, Peter McDonough, Samuel H. Barnes, and Antonio López Pina, *The Cultural Dynamics of Democratization in Spain* (Ithaca, N.Y.: Cornell University Press, 1998). I shall be making more of this commonality in chapter 7 below.

107. Jürgen Habermas, *The Philosophical Discourse of Modernity*, trans. Frederick G. Lawrence (Cambridge: MIT Press, 1990), 4.

108. Ibid., 5.

109. Ibid. The emphasis on secularism is also to be found in Samir Amin's "Modernité et interprétations religieuses," *Afrique et Développement* 29, no. 1 (2004): 7–53, especially the section on "La modernité."

110. Habermas, *The Philosophical Discourse of Modernity*, 12.

111. Ibid., 17, italics in original.

112. Amin, *Eurocentrism*, 81–82.

113. Hegel, *Philosophy of Right*, 266–267.

114. Olúfẹ́mi Táíwò, "Cabral," in *A Companion to the Philosophers*, ed. Robert Arrington (Oxford: Blackwell, 1999), 9.

115. Amilcar Cabral, *Unity and Struggle*, trans. Michael Wolfers (London: Heinemann, 1980), 127.

116. Frantz Fanon, *The Wretched of the Earth* (New York: Grove Weidenfeld, 1968), chapter 1.

117. See, in general, Edward W. Blyden, *Black Spokesman: Selected Published Writings of Edward Wilmot Blyden*, ed. Hollis R. Lynch (London: Frank Cass, 1971); Nnamdi Azikiwe, *Renascent Africa* (London: Frank Cass, 1968); Kwame Nkrumah, *I Speak of Freedom* (London: Panaf, 1961); and American Society of African Culture, ed., *Pan-Africanism Reconsidered* (Berkeley: University of California Press, 1962).

118. J. F. A. Ajayi, "Henry Venn and the Policy of Development," in *The History of Christianity in West Africa*, ed. Ogbu Kalu (London: Longman, 1980), 65. See also Henry Venn, "The Coming into Being of a Church," in Henry Venn, *To Apply the Gospel*, ed. Max Warren (Grand Rapids, Mich.: Eerdmans, 1971), 51–83; Knight, *The Missionary Secretariat of Henry Venn*, especially the chapters titled "On Nationality," and "The Native Pastorate."

119. For a particularly significant episode that illustrates the changing conditions

under which native agency had to work at this time, see Hollis R. Lynch, "The Native Pastorate Controversy and Cultural Ethnocentrism in Sierra Leone 1871–4," in *The History of Christianity in West Africa*, ed. Ogbu Kalu (London: Longman, 1980), 285–86.

120. See J. F. A. Ajayi, *A Patriot to the Core: Bishop Ajayi Crowther* (Ibadan: Spectrum, 2001), chapter 3.

121. It is possible to date the onset of the dominance of this way of thinking about Africans. I have found a remarkable convergence in the historical literature on the third quarter of the nineteenth century as the time this latter view began to enjoy dominance. See Boahen, *African Perspectives on Colonialism*; Kuklick, *The Savage Within*; and Christopher Fyfe, "Race, Empire and the Historians," *Race & Class* 33, no. 4 (1992): 15–30. According to Fyfe, "Before the European partition of Africa, a white skin did not in itself confer authority. Over most of the continent, white people had no authority. Those white people who ventured inland had to pay respect to African authority. If they suffered indignities or death, their home governments remained unmoved. Even as late as 1885, Kabaka Mwanga of Buganda could have a white bishop of the Church of England put to death without impunity" (15).

122. This complaint was central to the critiques of colonialism and modernity undertaken by Fanon in *The Wretched of the Earth* and *Black Skin, White Masks* (New York: Grove, 1967); in Mannoni, *Prospero and Caliban* (Ann Arbor: University of Michigan Press, 1990); in Aimé Césaire, *Discourse on Colonialism* (New York: Monthly Review Press, 1972); and in Memmi, *The Colonizer and the Colonized*.

123. See Philip D. Curtin, "African Reactions in Perspective," in *Africa and the West*, ed. Philip D. Curtin (Madison: University of Wisconsin Press, 1972), 242.

124. See Agneta Pallinder, "Adegboyega Edun: Black Englishman and Yoruba Cultural Patriot," in *Self-Assertion and Brokerage: Early Cultural Nationalism in West Africa*, ed. P. F. de Moraes Farias and Karin Barber, (Birmingham: Centre of West African Studies, 1990), 11–34; Spitzer, *Lives in Between*, chapter 6.

125. P. R. McKenzie, "Samuel Crowther's Attitudes to Other Faiths: The Early Period," in *The History of Christianity in West Africa*, ed. Ogbu Kalu (London: Longman, 1980), 250–265; P. R. McKenzie, *Inter-Religious Encounters in West Africa: Samuel Ajayi Crowther's Attitude to Traditional Religion and Islam* (Leicester: University of Leicester, 1976).

126. The following excerpt from Knight's memoir of Henry Venn is illustrative of how much African converts cherished responsibility and supplying the proverbial elbow grease to further their own advancement. "We will end this paper by recording one instance of the important results which sometimes arose from his friendly confidential intercourse with Africans visiting England. In the year 1855 a negro merchant from Sierra Leone had brought his wife and family to visit England. After his usual kindly custom, Mr. Venn invited them all to his house and asked them about their travels. The merchant had traveled all about England, and had also visited Paris, and talked in a manner which showed that he must have spent a considerable sum of money. After some conversation Mr. Venn said, 'Well now, if you can spend so much money on your travels, you

ought surely to be able to do more towards the support of your own clergymen in Sierra Leone.' The African sprang to his feet and said, 'Of course we could, Mr. Venn; but so long as you treat us like children, we shall behave like children. Treat us like men and we shall behave like men. We spend our money upon ourselves because you don't invite us to support our clergy. Whilst the Church Missionary Society pays for everything in Sierra Leone, there is nothing for us to do. Let us have a share in managing our own Church affairs, and you will see that we shall soon be able to meet our own expenses.' To this conversation Mr. Venn often afterwards referred as having proved to him that the colony of Sierra Leone had then become ready to pass from the elementary stage of missions to the settled state of a native African Church, self-supported and self-governed." Knight, *The Missionary Secretariat of Henry Venn*, 545–546. By the time under discussion, the confidence that would later be shown in the appointment of Crowther to a bishopric had become attenuated, if not extirpated, both for the temporal and spiritual segments of the colonial regime. The view of the African as a child who could not be trusted to run her own affairs, I am afraid, continues to dominate Africa's relations with its erstwhile colonial rulers.

127. The administrators were not alone. But the focus turns on them because they called the shots in the colonies. Missionaries at this time shared the same view of Africans. Their position, however, continued to be ambiguous. As Bolt puts it, "Though the missionary might be caught up in the extension of British rule in Africa, and while his support for 'legitimate' commerce as an aid to Christian civilization and attack on one vital aspect of African culture might seem to invite this extension, as we have seen, the evangelist could also find himself in conflict with the trader and official, assuming the role of defender of people he had come to convert." Bolt, *Victorian Attitudes to Race*, 213–214.

128. Fyfe, "Race, Empire and the Historians," 15.

129. See Andrew Roberts, "The Imperial Mind," in *The Colonial Moment in Africa*, ed. A. D. Roberts (Cambridge: Cambridge University Press, 1990), 33–34.

130. Michael Crowder attributed this view to Sir Harry Johnston. Michael Crowder, *West Africa under Colonial Rule* (Evanston, Ill.: Northwestern University Press, 1968), 397. James Africanus Horton refuted this claim in the nineteenth century. See Horton, *West African Countries and Peoples*, intro. George Shepperson (1868; Edinburgh: Edinburgh University Press, 1969), 32–33.

131. Fyfe, "Race, Empire and the Historians," 22. There is no need to speculate on the latter point about punishment, at least in the case of Nigeria. That was Lugard's justification for insisting on the preservation of caning in the colony even when it had fallen into disfavor in England. See chapter 4 below.

132. The subversion of this principle in the United States was one of the key motivations for the founding of the Republic of Liberia and the willingness of many accomplished Black Americans to relocate to a territory that they barely knew and whose conditions would tax the patience and energies of many of them to their utmost limits. See Edward Wilmot Blyden, "Our Origin, Dangers and Duties," in *Origins of West Af-*

rican Nationalism, ed. Henry S. Wilson (London: Macmillan, 1969), 94–95; James Africanus Horton, *West African Countries and Peoples*, intro. George Shepperson (1868; Edinburgh: Edinburgh University Press, 1969), 15.

133. Crowder, *West Africa under Colonial Rule*, 393–394. For the exclusion of Africans from the colonial service, see Roberts, "The Imperial Mind," 33; for the caliber of recruits to the colonial civil service in West Africa, see page 48. See also Robert Heussler, *Yesterday's Rulers: The Making of the British Colonial Service* (Syracuse: Syracuse University Press, 1963) for a rich compendium of evidence that what Heussler called the "Colonial Service" was based solely on British imperialism in Africa and how its selection procedures were unapologetically opposed to the merit principle.

134. Fyfe, "Race, Empire and the Historians," 16.

135. Heussler, *Yesterday's Rulers*, 8–9.

136. For an excellent treatment of this theme from a historical standpoint, see Christopher Lasch, *The True and Only Heaven: Progress and Its Critics* (New York: Norton, 1991); and Marshall Berman, *All That Is Solid Melts into Air: The Experience of Modernity* (New York: Simon and Schuster, 1982).

137. Echeruo, *Victorian Lagos*.

138. See Kristin Mann, *Marrying Well* (Cambridge: Cambridge University Press, 1990).

139. See chapter 6 below.

140. I discuss this in chapter 5 below.

141. Curtin, "African Reactions in Perspective," 231–244.

142. The school I attended, Ibadan Grammar School, was founded in 1913 by a parson who later became the Anglican bishop of Ibadan. His school's motto was a juxtaposition of Latin and Yorùbá on the school crest.

143. Karl Marx and Frederick Engels, *Collected Works*, vol. 8 (New York: International Publishers, 1975), 335, italics in the original.

144. Frederick D. Lugard, *The Dual Mandate in Tropical Africa* (London: Frank Cass, 1965), 426.

145. Ibid., 426.

146. Ibid., 427.

147. Ironies abound here. India of the "literary education" and "arrested industrial development" is today a nuclear power and boasts the second largest software industry in the world. Nigeria of the moral education is consistently led by some of the most morally degenerate humans to walk the face of the earth and remains distinctly backward in the race for development.

148. Lugard, *The Dual Mandate*, 427.

149. Ibid., 428. By the way, the object of scorn here was missionary education.

150. Ibid., 460. It is a mark of Lugard's influence on colonial thinking that an Advisory Committee on Native Education in the British Tropical African Dependencies in 1925 recommended the following: "The central difficulty in the problem lies in finding ways to improve what is sound in indigenous tradition. Education should strengthen

the feeling of responsibility to the tribal community, and, at the same time, should strengthen will power; should make the conscience sensitive both to moral and intellectual truth; and should impart some power of discriminating between good and evil, between reality and superstition. . . . The greatest importance must therefore be attached to religious teaching and moral instruction." *Education Policy in British Tropical Africa* (London: 1925), quoted in Bruce Fetter, ed., *Colonial Rule in Africa: Readings from Primary Sources*, intro. Bruce Fetter (Madison: University of Wisconsin Press, 1979), 131.

3. Prophets without Honor

This chapter is the written version of a presentation of the same title to a special panel on Politics and Prophecy in Africa at the Annual Conference of the American Academy of Religion, Nashville, Tennessee, in November 1999. I am grateful to Simeon Ilesanmi, who invited me to participate on the panel. A different version of the paper was presented to the conference Henry Sylvestre Williams and Pan-Africanism: A Retrospection and Projection, held at the University of the West Indies, St. Augustine, Trinidad & Tobago, 7–12 January 2001. It was also presented to the conference Hegel and Africa, held at Northwestern University, Evanston, Illinois, in March 2001. I would like to thank John McCumber and Robert Gooding-Williams, who invited me to contribute to that conference. Finally, I did the research for and wrote the original draft of the paper during my tenure as a Visiting Postdoctoral Research and Teaching Fellow at the Carter G. Woodson Institute for Afro-American and African Studies, University of Virginia, Charlottesville, Virginia, in the 2000–2001 academic year. I gratefully acknowledge the financial support of the Ford Foundation for my stay there. And I thank Reginald Butler and Scot French, Director and Associate Director, respectively, of the Woodson Institute for facilitating my work there during my tenure. Originally published in *West Africa Review* 3, no. 1 (2002).

1. Of course, this is by no means the first assessment of the prophets' contributions. For a similar analysis, see Lamine Sanneh in *Abolitionists Abroad: American Blacks and the Making of Modern West Africa* (Cambridge: Harvard University Press, 1999). But V. Y. Mudimbe has a different view; see *The Invention of Africa* (Bloomington: Indiana University Press, 1988). Ajayi beat a different path among historians; see Ajayi, *A Patriot to the Core: Bishop Ajayi Crowther* (Ibadan: Spectrum Books, 2001). There is renewed interest in the activities of the prophets even if that interest does not go to the extent articulated in this chapter. For example, the Church of Nigeria of the Anglican Church Worldwide Communion has recently named its new university after Samuel Ajayi Crowther. Both James Africanus Beale Horton and S. R. B. Attoh-Ahuma have recently been discussed in Kwaku Larbi Korang, *Writing Ghana, Imagining Africa* (Rochester, N.Y.: Rochester University Press, 2003), and in Robert W. July, *The Origins of Modern African Thought* (1967; Trenton, N.J.: Africa World Press, 2004). Unfortunately, the analysis of the philosophical dimensions of the heritage of the prophets has been slim to none.

2. Olúfẹ́mi Táíwò, "On the Misadventures of National Consciousness: A Retrospect on Frantz Fanon's Gift of Prophecy," in *Frantz Fanon: A Critical Reader*, ed. Lewis Gordon, T. Sharpley-Whiting, and Renée White (Oxford: Blackwell, 1996), 256.

3. Representative literature includes David E. Apter, *The Politics of Modernization* (Chicago: University of Chicago Press, 1965); David E. Apter and Carl G. Rosberg, eds., *Political Development and the New Realism in Sub-Saharan Africa* (Charlottesville and London: University of Virginia Press, 1994); and Henry Bienen, ed., *The Military and Modernization* (Chicago: Aldine, Atherton, 1971).

4. On the failure of modernization in a specific African country and a general review of the literature on this supposed failure, see Jeremiah I. Dibua, *Modernization and the Crisis of Development in Africa* (London: Ashgate, 2006).

5. The literature on the career of modernity in Asia is growing. For samples relevant to our discussion, see Tani E. Barlow, ed., *Formations of Colonial Modernity in East Asia* (Durham, N.C.: Duke University Press, 1997); Gi-Wook Shin and Michael Robinson, eds., *Colonial Modernity in Korea* (Cambridge, Mass.: Harvard University Asia Center, 1999); and Tu Wei-Ming, "Multiple Modernities: A Preliminary Inquiry into the Implications of East Asian Modernity," in *Culture Matters*, ed. Lawrence E. Harrison and Samuel P. Huntington (New York: Basic Books, 2000).

6. In the last chapter I focused on the teachers and the processes that set the transition in motion. Here the searchlight is turned on the products, both biographical and ideational, of those teachers and processes.

7. See Francis Fukuyama, *The End of History and the Last Man* (New York: Free Press, 1992); and Samuel Huntington, "The Clash of Civilizations?" *Foreign Affairs* 72, no. 3 (Summer 1993): 22–49; the ensuing responses in "Comments," *Foreign Affairs* 72, no. 4 (September/October 1993): 2–26; and Huntington's reply, "If Not Civilizations, What?" *Foreign Affairs* 72, no. 5 (November/December 1993): 186–194.

8. Henry Venn, *West-African Colonies: Notices of the British Colonies on the West Coast of Africa* (London: Dalton and Lucy, 1865), 5. Eighty-one years later, another CMS missionary indicted the British colonial authorities on almost the same terms of not recognizing, deepening, and working with native talents that the church had nurtured to shape the future of indigenous societies. See Walter R. Miller, *Have We Failed in Nigeria?* (London: United Society for Christian Literature, 1947).

9. Venn, *West-African Colonies*, 5.

10. Ibid., 16–17.

11. Ibid., 27–28.

12. Ibid., 28.

13. Ibid., 30.

14. Quoted in Henry S. Wilson, ed., *Origins of West African Nationalism* (London: Macmillan, 1969), 127.

15. "Resolutions of the Select Committee of the House of Commons, 26 June 1865," *Parliamentary Papers, 1865*, quoted in Wilson, *Origins of West African Nationalism*, 151.

16. Ajayi, "Nineteenth Century Origins of Nigerian Nationalism," in *Tradition and Change in Africa: The Essays of J. F. Ade Ajayi*, ed. Toyin Falola (Trenton, N.J.: Africa World Press, 2000), 73.

17. I think that Wole Soyinka succumbed to this temptation when he wrote: "There is nothing to choose ultimately between the colonial mentality of an Ajayi Crowther, West Africa's first black bishop, who groveled before his white missionary superiors in a plea for patience and understanding of his 'backward, heathen, brutish' brothers, and the new black ideologues who are embarrassed by statements of self-apprehension by the new 'ideologically backward' African." Wole Soyinka, *Myth, Literature and the African World* (Cambridge: Cambridge University Press, 1976), xii. I think Soyinka's judgment is too harsh. I am gratified that recent developments indicate a welcome shift toward a more balanced judgment of the bishop among scholars in Nigeria. The Anglican Communion in Nigeria has named its recently chartered university after him. Femi Osofisan has recently written and directed the production of a play on Crowther's life, commissioned by the Nigeria Province of the Anglican Church Communion. J. F. Ade Ajayi recently published his biography of the bishop, *A Patriot to the Core: Bishop Samuel Ajayi Crowther* (Ibadan: Spectrum, 2002). A new Crowther Centre for Mission Education has just been set up in Oxford, England, in his memory.

18. Davidson Nicol, "Introduction," in *Black Nationalism in Africa 1867: Extracts from the Political, Educational, Scientific and Medical Writings of Africanus Horton*, ed. Davidson Nicol (New York: Africana, 1969), 14.

19. J. F. A. Ajayi, *A Patriot to the Core: Bishop Ajayi Crowther* (Ibadan: Spectrum Books, 2001), 4.

20. I once described his achievements to an interviewer. What my interviewer concluded from my iteration of his accomplishments was that Crowther "sounds to me [the interviewer, that is] like one of those Victorian era overachievers." I couldn't agree more.

21. Ajayi, *A Patriot to the Core*, 128.

22. Samuel Ajayi Crowther, *Omode Eru-kunrin ti o di Bisopu tabi Itan Samuel Ajayi Crowther*, 7th ed. (Lagos: Church Missionary Society Bookshop, 1940).

23. James Frederick Schön and Samuel Crowther, *Journals of the Rev. James Frederick Schön and Mr. Samuel Crowther: Who, with the Sanction of Her Majesty's Government, Accompanied the Expedition up the Niger in 1841 on Behalf of the Church Missionary Society*, 2nd ed. (London: Frank Cass, 1970).

24. Lamine Sanneh, "The CMS and the African Transformation: Samuel Ajayi Crowther and the Opening of Nigeria," in *The Church Mission Society and World Christianity, 1799–1999*, ed. Kevin Ward and Brian Stanley (Grand Rapids, Mich.: William B. Eerdmans, 2000), 180.

25. Sanneh, "The CMS and the African Transformation," 181. Soyinka was, therefore, wrong in his judgment of Crowther. Even if he had chosen to grovel—which I don't think he did—he still would have been within his rights as a subject to so do.

26. Andrew F. Walls, "The Legacy of Samuel Ajayi Crowther," *International Bulletin of Missionary Research* 16, no. 1 (January 1992): 20.

27. Ajayi, A *Patriot to the Core*, 128.

28. Ibid., 7–8.

29. Walls, "The Legacy of Samuel Ajayi Crowther," 18.

30. See especially J. F. A. Ajayi, *Christian Missions in Nigeria, 1841–1891: The Making of a New Elite* (London: Longmans, 1965), 253–264; and Walls, "The Legacy of Samuel Ajayi Crowther," 19. Walls's evaluation further buttresses the time line that I identified in the previous chapter for the triumph of the racist attitudes that substituted the aid model for the erstwhile autonomy model.

31. Nicol, "Introduction," 3.

32. Ibid., 4.

33. Ibid., 1.

34. E. A. Ayandele, "James Africanus Beale Horton, 1835–1883: Prophet of Modernization in Africa," *African Historical Studies* 4, no. 3 (1971): 691–707. Contrast this with Christopher Fyfe, *Africanus Horton, 1835–1883: West African Scientist and Patriot* (New York: Oxford University Press, 1972).

35. Ayandele, "James Africanus Beale Horton, 694.

36. Ibid., 695.

37. Ibid., 696.

38. Ibid.

39. Ibid., 701.

40. Nicol, *Black Nationalism in Africa*, 25; Horton, *West African Countries and Peoples*, 40.

41. This is a peculiarly modern phenomenon. It is a metaphysics of separation that zeroes in on the knowing rather than the doing of the good or the right. Horton was indifferent to whether or not his interlocutors were good or bad people; it was enough that they were ignoramuses.

42. Ayandele, "James Africanus Beale Horton," 703.

43. Dr. Knox, quoted in Horton, *West African Countries and Peoples*, 32.

44. Quoted in ibid., 32–33.

45. Ayandele was simply wrong when he accused Horton of not studying the customs.

46. Horton, *West African Countries and Peoples*, 59.

47. Ibid., 60.

48. See David Kimble, A *Political History of Ghana: The Rise of Gold Coast Nationalism, 1850–1928* (Oxford: Clarendon Press, 1963).

49. Horton, *West African Countries and Peoples*, 114. Fyfe misread him here as an advocate of authoritarianism. See *Africanus Horton*, 81.

50. Horton, *West African Countries and Peoples*, 125

51. I offer a full discussion of these experiments in chapter 6.

52. Horton, "Letter No. IX, to the Right Hon. Earl Granville, K. G., D. C. L., Secretary of State for the Colonies," reprinted in Henry S. Wilson, ed., *Origins of West African Nationalism* (London: Macmillan, 1969), 205.

53. S. R. B. Attoh-Ahuma, *The Gold Coast Nation and National Consciousness* (Lon-

don: Frank Cass, 1971), vii–viii. This may be one of the earliest articulations by a modern-era African thinker of the philosophical orientation that seeks a principle of forward movement in an indigenous heritage.

54. For a different approach to Ahuma's discussion of the idea of the nation, see Korang, *Writing Ghana*, chapter 4.

55. Here Ahuma was no different from other similarly located intellectuals in the colonial world. See Fred Dallmayr and G. N. Devy, eds., *Between Tradition and Modernity* (New Delhi and London: Sage Publications, 1998).

56. Ahuma, *The Gold Coast Nation and National Consciousness*, 22.

57. Ibid., italics in original.

58. James Africanus Horton, *West African Countries and Peoples*, intro. George Shepperson (Edinburgh: Edinburgh University Press, 1969), 248.

59. Ahuma, *The Gold Coast Nation and National Consciousness*, 23, italics in original.

60. Ibid., 2–3.

61. Ibid., 35.

62. Ibid., 8.

63. Ibid., 9. One is struck by the contemporary resonance of these ideas. It holds great promise when applied to contemporary discussions of "tribalism" and the so-called nation-building problematic that is often referred to in debates about Africa's situation in the world. I have no doubt that the play of sociocryonics that managed to steer even African eyes away from seeing the complexity of their own societies helps explain why African scholars and political leaders and policymakers think that what should be processed as a problem of creating a supranational citizenship to overlay the many traditions of particularism found in most African countries should be understood instead as a problem of welding together the disparate "tribes" into a nation. The situation in Africa is typical of that of most countries in the world in the modern era.

64. I have limited myself to West African scholars because the contributions of fellow freedmen, freemen, and recaptives and their descendents in the United States, the Caribbean, and the United Kingdom have been the object of scholarly attention in recent times, the most important being the work of Paul Gilroy in *The Black Atlantic* (Cambridge: Harvard University Press, 1993).

4. Reading the Colonizer's Mind

This is a revised version of an essay with the same title published in Susan Babbitt and Sue Campbell, eds., *Racism and Philosophy* (Ithaca, N.Y.: Cornell University Press, 1999), 157–186.

1. See Albert Memmi, *The Colonizer and the Colonized* (Boston: Beacon Press, 1972); Aimé Césaire, *Discourse on Colonialism* (New York: Monthly Review Press, 1972); Frantz Fanon, *The Wretched of the Earth* (New York: Grove Press, 1968).

2. Memmi, *The Colonizer and the Colonized*, 10.

3. Christianity of the second wave. The earlier wave in the sixteenth century evangelized rulers.

4. Lamine Sanneh, *Abolitionists Abroad: American Blacks and the Making of Modern West Africa* (Cambridge: Harvard University Press, 1999).

5. My concern here is not with the evaluation of the activities of the missionaries. While it may appear that I applaud their revolutionary goals, I do not wish to suggest that revolution is essentially good or that all revolutionary movements are good. My limited purpose here is to contrast their attitude with that of their administrator colleagues.

6. A. H. M. Kirk-Greene, "New Introduction," in Frederick D. Lugard, *Political Memoranda*, 3rd ed. (London: Frank Cass, 1970), xx.

7. Frederick D. Lugard, *The Dual Mandate in British Tropical Africa* (Edinburgh and London: William Blackwood and Sons, 1922), b.

8. Lugard, *The Dual Mandate,* 615.

9. Ibid., 618.

10. Frederick D. Lugard, *The Rise of Our East African Empire*, 2 vols. (London: Frank Cass & Co., 1968), 1:2. Although Lugard did not let on in the text the nature of his illness, his biographer, Margery Perham, had no reticence about disclosing it. He had been jilted in love and this had led to illness, she said. His mental illness puts in context his claim that what he needed was "active hard work—rather than rest." See Margery Perham, "Introduction," in *The Diaries of Lord Lugard*, 4 vols., ed. Margery Perham (Evanston, Ill.: Northwestern University Press, 1959), 1:18.

11. Lugard, *The Rise of Our East African Empire,* 2.

12. Ibid., 11.

13. Ibid., 20, italics in the original.

14. Ibid., 19–20.

15. Ibid., 27.

16. Ibid., 27–28.

17. Ibid., 309–310.

18. Ibid., 40, italics in the original.

19. Ibid., 75.

20. Ibid., 191.

21. Ibid., 73–74.

22. Lugard, *Political Memoranda,* 6.

23. Ibid., 9, my italics.

24. Ibid., 11–12.

25. Ibid., 11.

26. Ibid., 296.

27. Of course, what I just pointed out relies on the evidence provided in the last two chapters about the availability of indigenous personnel to create a modern bureaucracy.

28. Lugard, 297.

29. Ibid.

30. Ibid., 298.

31. See Harry A. Gailey, *Lugard and the Abeokuta Uprising: The Demise of Egba Independence* (London: Frank Cass & Co., 1982), 48–53.

32. Lugard, *Political Memoranda*, 83.

33. Ibid., 84.

34. Ibid., 93.

35. See Omoniyi Adewoye, *The Judicial System in Southern Nigeria, 1854–1954* (Atlantic Highlands: Humanities Press, 1977).

36. Lugard, *Political Memoranda*, 89, my italics.

37. Ibid., 275, my italics.

38. Lugard contended: "The procedure of the Supreme Court is too elaborate, the rules by which it is bound are too rigid, for adaptation to a society such as exists among the primitive tribes" of the interior of Nigeria. Quoted in Adewoye, *The Judicial System in Southern Nigeria*, 141.

39. Adewoye, *The Judicial System in Southern Nigeria*, especially chapter 5. "The judicial reorganization was thus in the nature of a response to what was considered a serious political or administrative problem: how to curtail the influence of the African lawyer" (137).

40. Lugard, *Political Memoranda*, 275.

41. Ibid., 130.

42. Ibid., 125.

43. Ibid., 135.

44. Ibid., 9.

45. (London: Macmillan, 1977).

46. M. J. C. Echeruo, *Victorian Lagos* (London: Macmillan, 1977), 1.

47. Ibid., 30.

48. Ibid.

49. Ibid., 35. See also P. F. de Moraes Farias and Karin Barber, eds., *Self-Assertion and Brokerage: Early Cultural Nationalism in West Africa* (Birmingham: Centre of West African Studies, 1990).

50. Echeruo, *Victorian Lagos*, 35.

51. Ibid., 50.

52. Ibid., 41.

53. See, in general, Akintola Wyse, *The Krio of Sierra Leone* (London: C. Hurst & Co., 1989), chapter 3; Leo Spitzer, "The Sierra Leone Creoles, 1870–1900," in *Africa and the West*, ed. Philip Curtin (Madison: University of Wisconsin Press, 1972), 99–138; A. J. H. Latham, *Old Calabar, 1600–1891* (Oxford: Clarendon Press, 1973), chapter 6; Kwabena O. Akurang-Parry, "'We Shall Rejoice to See the Day When Slavery Shall Cease to Exist': The Gold Coast Times, the African Intelligentsia, and Abolition in the Gold Coast," *History in Africa* 31 (2004): 19–42.

54. *The Mirror*, 17 March 1888, quoted in ibid., 29.

55. Lugard, *The Dual Mandate*, 76, my italics.

56. Ibid., 79–80.
57. Ibid., 81–82.
58. Ibid., 85.

5. The Legal Legacy

The initial research for this chapter was supported by the Rockefeller Foundation in 1991. More recent work has been supported by a Henry Phillips Research Grant in Jurisprudence from the American Philosophical Society in 1996 and a research leave from Loyola University in the spring of 1996. This version was completed during my tenure as a Visiting Professor at the Institut für Afrikastudien, Universität Bayreuth, Bayreuth, Germany, in the summer of 1999. I gratefully acknowledge the support. I would like to thank Susan Babbitt, who organized the original seminar at the Department of Philosophy, Queen's University, Kingston, Ontario, Canada, where I first articulated the ideas that formed the basis of this chapter. A different version was presented to the colloquium on The Re-Emergence of African Civilisation at the 3rd Pan-African Historical Theatre Festival (PANAFEST '97) in Cape Coast. I am grateful for the invitation from Professor Kofi Anyidoho to participate in the event.

1. In the rest of this discussion, unless otherwise specified, all references to Africa are to Anglophone African countries.

2. E. P. Thompson, *Whigs and Hunters: The Origins of the Black Acts* (London: Allen Lane, 1975). Although the main focus of this chapter turns on the first decade after independence and, as much as possible, leaves out the situations under conditions of military rule, the fact that some of the same problems continue to ravage Africa even in these times of transition to democracy is the best evidence we have of the recalcitrance of the colonial legacy in the area of law. Current examples include Robert Mugabe's undeclared war on Zimbabwe's white citizens and opposition party members; Bakili Miluzi's and Frederick Chiluba's failed attempts in Malawi and Zambia, respectively; and Yoweri Museveni's successful effort in Uganda to rewrite their countries' constitutions to enable each one of them to run for unconstitutional third presidential terms.

3. Justice Louis D. Brandeis in *Olmstead v. United States*, 277 U.S. 438 (1928).

4. See Taslim O. Elias, *Judicial Process in the Newer Commonwealth* (Lagos: University of Lagos Press, 1990), 158; B. O. Nwabueze, *Judicialism in Commonwealth Africa* (London and Enugu: Hurst/Nwamife, 1977), 201.

5. The idea of abolishing the legal profession was mooted in Tanzania. See Fauz Twaib, *The Legal Profession in Tanzania*, Bayreuth African Studies 46 (Bayreuth: Bayreuth African Studies Series, 1997), 80–81.

6. For an exploration of the contemporary situation, see Olufemi Taiwo, "The Legal Subject in Modern African Law: A Nigerian Report," *Human Rights Review* 7, no. 2 (January–March 2006): 17–34.

7. See generally B. O. Nwabueze, *Constitutionalism in the Emergent States* (London: Hurst, 1973); Elias, *Judicial Process in the Newer Commonwealth*; and J. P. W. B. McAus-

lan and Y. P. Ghai, *Public Law and Political Change in Kenya* (Oxford: Oxford University Press, 1970).

8. Kenya, Nigeria, Ghana, and Uganda all inserted bills of rights into their independence constitutions.

9. Nwabueze, *Constitutionalism in the Emergent States*, 1.

10. Ibid., 16.

11. Nwabueze, *Judicialism in Commonwealth Africa*, 1–2. I leave for another discussion many questions raised by this characterization. Do all the conditions have to be met before we can say that we have judicial power? For example, it is problematic to put point 7 here because the enforcement of judicial decisions lies beyond the scope and exercise of judicial power.

12. Kayode Eso, "The Court as the Guardian of the Constitution," paper presented at the All-Nigeria Judges' Conference, Abuja, 1988, 8.

13. See generally Githu Muigai, "The Judiciary in Kenya and the Search for a Philosophy of Law: The Case of Constitutional Adjudication," *Human Rights Law and Practice* 1, no. 1 (May 1991): 8–44; and M. K. B. Wambali and C. M. Peter, "The Judiciary in Context: The Case of Tanzania," in *The Role of the Judiciary in Plural Societies*, ed. Neelan Tiruchelvan and Radhika Coomaraswamy (New York: St. Martin's Press, 1987), 131–145.

14. This has intensified in recent times in light of the ongoing transitions to democracy in various African countries, the growing strength and sophistication of civil society, and the adoption and ratification of the African Charter of Human and Peoples' Rights.

15. I can easily update the bibliography in this section. But I am careful not to encourage the impression that my model works in all time frames. Even if it does, the reasons will differ from one period to another. Now that we have had military rule in some of the countries referred to in the discussion, one might use the ravages of military rule to explain the collapse in the postmilitary era of judiciaries in, say, Nigeria, Ghana, Sierra Leone, Liberia, Sudan, or Uganda. I limit myself to the immediate post-independence period here because it is closer to the abortion that is of moment in this chapter and more intimately causally tied to it.

16. Gaius Ezejiofor, "A Judicial Interpretation of Constitution: The Nigerian Experience during the First Republic," in *The Supreme Court of Nigeria 1956–1970*, ed. A. B. Kasunmu (Ibadan: Heinemann, 1977), 67.

17. Ibid., 87. A lack of confidence in the judiciary helps explain, in part, why the aftermath of the inconclusive presidential elections in Kenya in December 2007 led to people making their case on the streets with violence in 2008.

18. Indeed, to the extent that the explanations offered in this book are adequate or correct, we can more successfully explain some of the recent developments that have been excluded from coverage here. It is quite consistent in tone with the rest of this book, where attention is directed at abortions that were enacted during the colonial period that, I argue, help us to understand the career of some core tenets of modernity in Af-

rican countries. Furthermore, the country from which I have drawn most of my exemplars, Nigeria, fell victim to military rule barely six years into its independence. Thus, it is easy for one to conclude that the current problems regarding the noninstitutionalization of the rule of law may be traceable to the distortions to the democratic system occasioned by decades of military rule. But this cannot be a promising tack to take. Kenya and Tanzania, which offer us sources for comparative experience, have never been under military rule. Attempted coups in both countries failed, for different reasons. That these two countries manifest similar problems with the rule-of-law regime as those of Nigeria is my evidence for the claim that the situation under review may not easily be explained as the isolated consequences of post-independence historical contingencies. What is more, as long as we do not isolate the deeper causes of the problems in the legal system that I have traced to the abortion of the transition to modernity procured by colonial administrators, it is unlikely that we will identify the appropriate remedies for what ails our modern institutions.

19. Alexander Hamilton, "Number 78," in *The Federalist Papers*, ed. Clinton Rossiter (New York: New American Library, 1961), 532.

20. Although the constitution referred to here is the 1989 Nigerian constitution, no Nigerian constitution has departed from this pattern.

21. P. Nnaemeka-Agu, "Judicial Powers: *Quo Tendimus*," in *Nigerian Essays in Jurisprudence*, ed. T. O. Elias and M. I. Jegede (Lagos: MIJ Professional Publishers, 1993), 290, my italics.

22. Michael Oakeshott, *Rationalism in Politics* (New York: Basic Books, 1962), 124. See Olufemi Taiwo, *Legal Naturalism* (Ithaca, N.Y.: Cornell University Press, 1996), chapter 3, for an account of how judges perform their law-making function.

23. Nwabueze, *Judicialism in Commonwealth Africa*, 308. One cannot deny that some progress has been made in recent times. But that we continue to celebrate what, given the enabling principles of our municipal legal systems, ought to be taken for granted is a sign that things are not what they ought to be under the current dispensation. How limited is the progress that has been made is evidenced by the fact that none of the countries referred to here can be called a rule-of-law regime without serious qualification.

24. Ibid., 242–243. The situation Nwabueze described was by no means limited to Nigeria. For similar opinions regarding Kenya, see Y. P. Ghai and J. P. W. B. McAuslan, *Public Law and Political Change in Kenya*, chapter XI, especially 455. For Tanzania, see Wambali and Peter, "The Judiciary in Context," 134–141.

25. When the opposite is the case and the judiciary's moral authority is intact, we have a situation like that of Roosevelt's court-packing scheme in 1937, which he had to abandon hastily when the populace cried foul. See Robert G. McCloskey, *The American Supreme Court* (Chicago: University of Chicago Press, 1960), chapter 6.

26. The resulting delegitimation was cited by coup makers as one of their excuses for Nigeria's first coup d'etat in January 1966. See Olufemi Taiwo, "Political Obligation and Military Rule," *Philosophical Forum* 27, no. 2 (Winter 1996): 161–193.

27. Elias, *Judicial Process in the Newer Commonwealth*, 92.

28. Ibid.

29. Aguda, "The Challenge of Nigerian Law and the Nigerian Lawyer in the Twenty-First Century," Nigerian National Merit Award Winner's Lecture, delivered at Abẹ̀òkúta on 14 September 1988, 16; quoted in C. N. Okeke, "Judges and the Politics of Jurisprudence," in *Nigerian Essays in Jurisprudence*, ed. T. O. Elias and M. I. Jegede (Lagos: MIJ Professional Publishers, 1993), 101.

30. See Kayode Eso, *The Court as Guardian of the Constitution* (Lagos: Federal Government Printer, 1988); B. Obinna Okere, "Judicial Activism or Passivity in Interpreting Nigerian Constitution," and P. G. E. Umeadi, "Judicial Activism: A Nigerian Experience," both in *Current Legal Problems in Nigeria*, ed. E. I. Nwogugu (Enugu: Fourth Dimension Publishers, 1988), 43–70 and 71–87, respectively; C. C. Nweze, "A Survey of the Shifting Trends in Judicial Attitudes to Fundamental Rights in Nigeria," and Osita C. Eze, "The Rule of Law and the Bench," both in *Perspectives in Law and Justice: Essays in Honour of Hon. Justice Eze Ozobu*, ed. I. A. Umezulike and C. C. Nweze (Enugu: Fourth Dimension Publishers, 1996), 30–86 and 135–152, respectively.

31. Nwabueze, *Judicialism in Commonwealth Africa*, 309–310. F. U. Okafor has argued that legal positivism is incompatible with the African legal tradition. See F. U. Okafor, "Legal Positivism and the African Legal Tradition," *International Philosophical Quarterly*, 24 (1984): 157–164. For a comprehensive discussion of the debate about the appropriateness of legal positivism in the African context, see Jare Oladosu, "Choosing a Legal Theory on Cultural Grounds: An African Case for Legal Positivism," *West Africa Review* 2, no. 2 (2001), available at www.westafricareview.com/vol2.2/oladosu.html.

32. It is remarkable how little African jurists and scholars evidence any awareness of this simple fact in their fulminations against positivism. The truth, though, is that legal positivism is not monolithic. There is H. L. A. Hart's version, which accommodates "a minimum content of natural law"; Hans Kelsen's "pure theory of law"; and Joseph Raz's writing on "the morality of freedom." See Hart, *The Concept of Law* (Oxford: Clarendon Press, 1961); Hans Kelsen, *The Pure Theory of Law*, trans. Max Knight (Berkeley: University of California Press, 1967); Joseph Raz, *The Morality of Freedom* (Oxford: Clarendon Press, 1984).

33. What is often lost on many contemporary critics of positivism is that the original inspiration of its founder, John Austin, was to open the window, even if slightly, to legal reform against what he saw as the mummifying tendencies of the then-dominant natural law theory. The window on change that is a crucial part of Hart's reformulation of analytical positivism remains a fundamental part of its appeal in our own time. An earlier paper of mine might have given the impression that I think that legal positivism is essentially conservative or predisposed to complicity with executive misbehavior; Jare Oladosu has read the paper in this way. See Olúfémi Táíwò, "Legal Positivism and the African Legal Tradition: A Reply," *International Philosophical Quarterly* 25, no. 2 (1985): 197–200; P. C. Nwakeze, "A Critique of Olúfémi Táíwò's Criticism of 'Legal Positivism and African Legal Tradition,'" *International Philosophical Quarterly* 27, no. 1 (1987): 101–105; and Oladosu, "Choosing a Legal Theory on Cultural Grounds."

34. See M. I. Jegede, "Problem of *Locus Standi* (Standing to Sue) in the Administration of Justice," in *Nigerian Essays in Jurisprudence*, ed. T. O. Elias and M. I. Jegede (Lagos: MIJ Professional Publishers, 1993), chapter 10; Niki Tobi, "Special Jurisdiction for the Preservation of Fundamental Rights under the Nigerian Constitution," in *Individual Rights under the 1989 Constitution*, ed. M. A. Ajomo and Bolaji Owasanoye (Lagos: Nigerian Institute of Advanced Legal Studies, 1993), 44–67.

35. This view is well supported in the history of the evolution of judicial review of legislative and executive actions in the United States. Indeed, the Nigerian independence constitution provided for judicial review of legislative and executive actions, whereas the U.S. constitution does not.

36. Justices Eso and Aguda seem to think that activism is obviously right or unproblematic. However, it can be problematic. It raises issues of fidelity to law, duty to uphold law as it is, the problem of moral pluralism, and so on that I cannot go into here. A good source of insights into the complex issues raised by positivism and fidelity to law is Robert Cover, *Justice Accused: Antislavery and the Judicial Process* (New Haven, Conn.: Yale University Press, 1975).

37. The careers of Hugo Black and Felix Frankfurter in the U.S. Supreme Court are quite instructive in this respect. See Mark Silverstein, *Constitutional Faiths: Felix Frankfurter, Hugo Black, and the Process of Judicial Decision Making* (Ithaca, N.Y.: Cornell University Press, 1984).

38. On the importance of institutional history as a limit on judicial discretion, see Ronald Dworkin, *Taking Rights Seriously* (Cambridge, Mass.: Harvard University Press, 1977).

39. See P. N. Bhagwati, "Social Action Litigation: The Indian Experience," and Upendra Baxi, "Taking Suffering Seriously: Social Action Litigation in the Supreme Court of India," both in *The Role of the Judiciary in Plural Societies*, ed. Neelan Tiruchelvan and Radhika Coomaraswamy (New York: St. Martin's Press, 1987), 20–31 and 32–60 respectively.

40. Cyclosporin is the anti-rejection drug that is reported to have revolutionized organ transplant surgery.

41. Mahmood Mamdani has advanced a similar argument for failure in the political sphere. See his *Citizen and Subject: Contemporary Africa and the Legacy of Late Colonialism* (Princeton, N.J.: Princeton University Press, 1996). This is not to ignore the efforts at law reform and the institution of a body such as the Nigerian Institute for Advanced Legal Studies, Lagos, Nigeria, which is dedicated to research into the law and its operations. What was called for in light of what happened in the colonial period was a social transformation that would have included the recovery of the soul of the legal system, the shell of which was left as a colonial legacy by the departing British.

42. Habermas, *The Philosophical Discourse of Modernity: Twelve Lectures*, trans. Frederick Lawrence (Cambridge, Mass.: MIT Press, 1987), 17, italics in original.

43. See Harry Beran, *The Consent Theory of Obligation* (London and New York: Croom Helm, 1987).

44. See Thomas Hobbes, *Leviathan*, ed. and intro. C. B. Macpherson (Harmonds-worth: Penguin, 1968); John Locke, *Two Treatises on Government*, ed. Peter Laslett (Cambridge: Cambridge University Press, 1967); Jean-Jacques Rousseau, *The Social Contract and Discourses*, trans. and intro. G. D. H. Cole (London: Dent, 1979); John Rawls, *A Theory of Justice* (Cambridge, Mass.: Harvard University Press, 1971); and Robert Nozick, *Anarchy, State, and Utopia* (New York: Basic, 1972).

45. See Colin Morris, *The Discovery of the Individual: 1050–1200* (New York: Harper & Row, 1972) for an even longer genealogy.

46. Habermas, *The Philosophical Discourse of Modernity*, 22.

47. Baron de Montesquieu, *The Spirit of the Laws* (New York: Hafner, 1949).

48. See Clinton Rossiter, ed., *The Federalist Papers* (New York: New American Library, 1961), especially No. 51 by James Madison.

49. Akintunde Obilade and Akinola Aguda are rare exceptions.

50. Witness how frequently constitutions are altered or the powers that be seek to alter them in the continent.

51. Suspicion of government is definitely not absent among the people.

52. For readers interested in the gory details of how bad this can be, see M. Ayo Ojomo and I. E. Okagbue, eds., *Human Rights and the Administration of Criminal Justice in Nigeria* (Lagos: Nigerian Institute of Advanced Legal Studies, 1991).

53. And in any case the history of the rule of law can be traced only tenuously to the Magna Carta.

54. Ironically, law may be the principal sphere in which African intellectuals bother to talk about the protection of the individual. In politics, sociology, and, most embarrassing of all, philosophy, because of the dominance of the so-called collectivist/communalist "nature" of Africans, there is hardly any treatise devoted to the deep understanding of individualism as a principle of social ordering and all that that entails for both the individual and the society of which he or she is a part.

55. This has been changing in Nigeria with the growth of human rights organizations such as the Civil Liberties Organisation, the Committee for the Defence of Human Rights, the Campaign for Democracy, and so forth. But the ideas that animate such activism have yet to permeate the wider society, and therein lies the problem.

56. See, in general, Mamdani, *Citizen and Subject*.

57. The French and Portuguese colonies were not without their own tensions and contradictions. What I just said is not intended as a positive appraisal of French and Portuguese colonialisms; I am merely pointing to a descriptive difference.

58. I pointed out the contradiction in this approach in chapter 4. A similar transition took place in the French West African territories from the initial policy of "assimilation" to one of "association," or what was essentially a Gallic system for indirect rule. See Alice L. Conklin, *A Mission to Civilize: The Republican Idea of Empire in France and West Africa, 1895–1930* (Stanford, Calif.: Stanford University Press, 1997), chapters 5 and 6, especially 187–202.

59. Of course, I have made extensive use of the exceptions in this work, but even they have not focused on the individual the way that I have here.

60. Ghai and McAuslan, *Public Law and Political Change in Kenya*, 18. The only difference is that the protectorate does not conduct its own foreign affairs and is not considered a sovereign country in diplomatic terms.

61. Ajomo, "The Development of Individual Rights in Nigeria's Constitutional History," in *Individual Rights under the 1989 Constitution*, ed. M. A. Ajomo and Bolaji Owasanoye (Lagos: Nigerian Institute of Advanced Legal Studies, 1993), 3.

62. Nwabueze, *Judicialism in Commonwealth Africa*, 144.

63. Twaib, *The Legal Profession in Tanzania*, 26.

64. Ibid., 26–27.

65. Lord Hailey, *An African Survey*, 1938 ed., quoted in A. G. Karibi-Whyte, *The Relevance of the Judiciary in the Polity—in Historical Perspective* (Lagos: Nigerian Institute of Advanced Legal Studies, 1987), 50.

66. Ghai and McAuslan, *Public Law and Political Change in Kenya*, 34.

67. It is interesting to juxtapose the domestication of Christianity, in spite of its "Western" inflection and the nondomestication of, say, democracy, again in its "Western" inflection in Africa.

68. Quoted in Ghai and McAuslan, *Public Law and Political Change in Kenya*, 144; also Wambali and Peter, "The Judiciary in Context," 133.

69. Ibid., 144.

70. Ibid., 144–145.

71. Ibid., 145.

72. Ibid.

73. Ibid., 146.

74. Ibid.

75. The Commission of Inquiry into the Administration of Justice in Kenya, Uganda and the Tanganyika Territory in Criminal Matters, held in May 1933 and chaired by H. Grattan Bushe.

76. Ghai and McAuslan, *Public Law and Political Change in Kenya*, 146.

77. Omoniyi Adewoye, *The Judicial System in Southern Nigeria: 1854–1954* (Atlantic Highlands, N.J.: Humanities Press, 1977), 159.

78. Here Adewoye collapses modernity and colonialism and the groups and processes that I argue must be separated both empirically and conceptually. Adewoye, *The Judicial System in Southern Nigeria*, 146–147.

79. A. E. Afigbo, *The Warrant Chiefs* (London: Longman, 1972).

80. Omoniyi Adewoye, "One Hundred Years of the Legal Profession in Nigeria," seminar paper presented to the History Department, University of Ibadan, Ibadan, Nigeria, 1986, 5.

81. Ibid., 4–5.

82. Ibid., 5.

83. A. G. Irikefe, "Keynote Address," in *Current Legal Problems in Nigeria*, ed. E. I. Nwogugu (Enugu: Fourth Dimension Publishers, 1988), 26.

84. Karibi-Whyte, *The Relevance of the Judiciary in the Polity*, 53.

85. Ghai and McAuslan, *Public Law and Political Change in Kenya*, 407.

86. For ouster clauses, see ibid., 38;on the administrator as Leviathan, 37; on wide discretion, 409; on collective punishment, 410. On retroactive legislation, see Nwabueze, *Judicialism in Commonwealth Africa*, 214; and on the consequences of colonial practices, 267, 274–275. See also Twaib, *The Legal Profession in Tanzania*, 29.

87. Oputa, "The Independence of the Judiciary in a Democratic Society—Its Need, Its Positive and Negative Aspects," in *Nigerian Essays in Jurisprudence*, ed. T. O. Elias and M. I. Jegede (Lagos: MIJ Professional Publishers, 1993), 226, my italics.

88. Ibid., 227.

89. For similar views, see Nwabueze, *Judicialism in the Commonwealth*, 267; and Twaib, *The Legal Profession in Tanzania*, 94–96.

90. Twaib, *The Legal Profession in Tanzania*, 97.

91. Karibi-Whyte, *The Relevance of the Judiciary in the Polity*, 58–59, my italics.

92. Ghai and McAuslan, *Public Law and Political Change in Kenya*, 508.

93. Ibid., 509.

94. Variants of these explanations can be found in Nwabueze, *Judicialism in Commonwealth Africa*; and Ghai and McAuslan, *Public Law and Political Change in Kenya*.

95. Adetokunbo Ademola was Nigeria's first indigenous chief justice after independence. Taslim Elias, who is probably Africa's preeminent jurist and foremost legal scholar, was the successor to Adetokunbo Ademola as chief justice. He ended his career on the World Court bench at The Hague.

96. See Alan Barth, *Prophets with Honor: Great Dissents and Great Dissenters in the Supreme Court* (New York: Vintage, 1975).

6. Two Modern African Constitutions

This chapter is based on a presentation to the Sixth Annual Conference of the International Society for African Philosophy and Studies (ISAPS) at the University of Nairobi, Nairobi, Kenya, 10–12 March 2000. A revised version was read to a colloquium at the Department of Philosophy, Queen's University, Kingston, Ontario, Canada, on 9 February 2003. I would like to express my gratitude to those who attended those presentations and gave the benefit of their critical reactions. My thanks go to Professor Susan Babbitt for inviting me to Queen's University.

1. For a discussion, see C. B. Macpherson, *The Life and Times of Liberal Democracy* (Oxford: Oxford University Press, 1977).

2. Much of the resistance to the kind of direction taken in this collection of essays can be traced to the same reactive nationalism.

3. James Africanus Horton, *West African Countries and Peoples* (1868; Edinburgh:

Edinburgh University Press, 1968); Edward Wilmot Blyden, *Christianity, Islam and the Negro Race* (1887; Edinburgh: Edinburgh University Press, 1967); John Mensah Sarbah, *Fanti Customary Laws*, 3rd ed., intro. Hollis Lynch (1897; London: Frank Cass, 1968); S. R. B. Attoh-Ahuma, *The Gold Coast Nation and National Consciousness* (London: Frank Cass, 1971); Joseph Ephraim Casely Hayford, *Gold Coast Native Institutions* (London: Frank Cass, 1970).

4. David Kimble, *A Political History of Ghana: The Rise of Gold Coast Nationalism, 1850–1928* (Oxford: Clarendon Press, 1963), 220.

5. Ibid., 224.

6. Ibid. See also Horton, *West African Countries and Peoples*, 256.

7. *Report from the Select Committee on Africa (Western Coast); Together with the Proceedings of the Committee, Minutes of Evidence, and Appendix* (London: HMSO, 1865).

8. J. F. Ade Ajayi, "A New Christian Politics? The Challenge of the Mission-Educated Elite," in *Tradition and Change in Africa: The Essays of J. F. Ade Ajayi*, ed. Toyin Falola (Trenton, N.J.: Africa World Press, 2000), 133.

9. Ibid.

10. Francis Agbodeka, "The Fanti Confederacy 1865–69," *Transactions of the Historical Society of Ghana* 7 (1964): 82.

11. Ibid.

12. Ibid., 84.

13. Ibid., 85.

14. The works by Ajayi, Agbodeka, and Kimble already cited contain copious references to such efforts on the part of the British and Dutch administrations.

15. See chapter 2.

16. *Parliamentary Papers, 1865*, quoted in Henry S. Wilson, *Origins of West African Nationalism* (London: Macmillan, 1969), 151.

17. See Christine Bolt, *Victorian Attitudes to Race* (London: Routledge & Kegan Paul, 1971).

18. For some insightful discussions, see Philip C. Curtin, ed., *Africa and the West: Intellectual Responses to European Culture* (Madison: University of Wisconsin Press, 1972).

19. Quoted in Wilson, *Origins of West African Nationalism*, 212–213.

20. John Mensah Sarbah, *Fanti National Constitution*, 2nd ed., intro. Hollis R. Lynch (London: Frank Cass & Co, 1968), Appendix C, 327.

21. Kimble, *A Political History of Ghana*, 231.

22. Agbodeka, "The Fanti Confederacy 1865–69," 106.

23. Ibid., 88.

24. Kimble, *A Political History of Ghana*, 229–230.

25. Sarbah, *Fanti National Constitution*, 327, my italics.

26. Agbodeka, "The Fanti Confederacy," 117.

27. Kimble, *A Political History of Ghana*, 254.

28. For a twentieth-century version of this attitude, see Obafemi Awolowo, *Path to*

Nigerian Freedom (London: Faber and Faber, 1947); and *The People's Republic* (Ibadan: Oxford University Press, 1968).

29. Quoted in Kimble, *A Political History of Ghana*, 247.

30. Awolowo would later use the same metric to rank the national groups in Nigeria. See *Path to Nigerian Freedom*, chapter 5.

31. See Horton, *West African Countries and Peoples* (1868; Edinburgh: Edinburgh University Press, 1969), especially Part II on "African Nationality."

32. Horton, *West African Countries and Peoples*, 151.

33. Saburi O. Biobaku, *The Egba and Their Neighbours: 1842–1872* (Oxford: Clarendon Press, 1957), 13.

34. Ibid., 21.

35. Ibid. My emphasis.

36. Ibid.

37. Ibid., 24–25.

38. Ibid., 25.

39. Agneta Pallinder-Law, "Government in Abeokuta 1830–1914: With Special Reference to the Egba United Government 1898–1914" (Ph.D. diss., Department of History, University of Gothenborg, Sweden, 1973), 21.

40. Biobaku, *The Egba and Their Neighbours*, 26.

41. Ibid., 31. It is important to take specific notice of the presence of native agents in important roles because of the excessive emphasis on European agency in the business of social transformation in West Africa during the period in question.

42. Pallinder-Law, "Aborted Modernization in West Africa? The Case of Abeokuta," *Journal of African History* 15, no. 1 (1974): 68.

43. Ibid.

44. Ibid.

45. Freeman to Duke of Newcastle, Lagos, 9 April 1864, CO 147/6, quoted in Earl Phillips, "The Egba at Abeokuta: Acculturation and Political Change, 1830–1870," *Journal of African History* 10, no. 1 (1969): 126.

46. Townsend to Venn, Abẹ̀òkúta, 1 November 1866, CMS CA2/085, quoted in Phillips, "The Egba at Abeokuta," 128.

47. Pallinder-Law, "Government in Abeokuta," 34. See also Phillips, "The Egba at Abeokuta," 126.

48. Phillips, "The Egba at Abeokuta," 126.

49. Biobaku, *The Egba and Their Neighbours*, 79.

50. Ibid., 79.

51. Pallinder-Law, "Government in Abeokuta," 35.

52. Ajayi, "A New Christian Politics?" 139. See also Phillips, who reported that Johnson "had lived in England"; "The Egba at Abeokuta," 127.

53. Phillips, "The Egba at Abeokuta," 127. It is significant to note that the demand that Africa be for Africans was not shared by all Saro or by many recaptives. For a contrary view, consider the following from Samuel Ajayi Crowther:

If we have any regard for the elevation of Africa . . . our wisdom would be to cry to those Christian nations which have been so long labouring for our conversion, to re-double their Christian efforts for the evangelization of this continent. . . . We can act as rough quarry-mends, who hew out blocks of marble from the quarried, which are conveyed to the workshop, to be shaped and finished into perfect figures by the hands of the skillful artists. In like manner native teachers can do, having the acquaintance with the language in their favour, to induce their heathen countrymen to come within the reach of the means of grace and hear the word of God. What is lacking in good training and sound evangelical teaching, the more experienced foreign missionaries will supply, and thus give shape to new churches in heathen countries. . . . Africa has neither knowledge nor skill to devise plans to bring out her vast resources for her own improvement; and for want of Christian enlightenment, cruelty and barbarity over-spread the land to an incredible degree. Therefor to claim Africa for the Africans alone, is to claim for the right of a continued ignorance to practice cruelty and acts of bar-barity as her perpetual inheritance. For it is certain, unless help come from without, a nation can never rise much above its present state.

"Bishop Crowther's Charge at Lokoja," 13 September 1869, CMS CA3/04A, quoted in Wilson, *Origins of West African Nationalism*, 150. This quote illustrates that even as the African modernizers were all agreed that Africa was backward and that the civilization that they had been socialized into, with its inspiration from Europe and the New World, was superior and worthy of emulation, they disagreed among themselves as to the role of Europeans in their forward march as African world-makers. They also agreed that Af-rican agency needed to remain pivotal in any process of social transformation.

54. Ajayi, "A New Christian Politics?" 139.

55. Ibid.

56. Pallinder-Law, "Government in Abeokuta," 43–44.

57. The full text of the declaration is reprinted in Horton, *West African Countries and Peoples*, 152–153.

58. Pallinder-Law, "Aborted Modernization in West Africa?" 70.

59. Harry Gailey's statement that "Johnson's idea was to provide a more efficient bu-reaucratic mechanism which could be controlled by the Saros" supports this impression. *Lugard and the Abeokuta Uprising: The Demise of Egba Independence* (London: Frank Cass & Co, 1982), 18.

60. See Biobaku, *The Egba and Their Neighbours*.

61. Quoted in Ajayi, "A New Christian Politics?" 139.

62. Pallinder-Law, "Government in Abeokuta," 44.

63. Gailey, *Lugard and the Abeokuta Uprising*, 20.

64. Ajayi, "A New Christian Politics?" 141.

65. Pallinder-Law, "Aborted Modernization in West Africa?" 77. See Pallinder-Law, "Government in Abeokuta," for an extended discussion of the programs and activities of the Ẹgbá United Government. See also Gailey, *Lugard and the Abeokuta Uprising*, chapter 3.

66. Pallinder-Law, "Aborted Modernization in West Africa?" 79.

67. See the excellent anthology edited and introduced by the late J. Ayodele Langley, *Ideologies of Liberation in Black Africa 1856–1970* (London: Rex Collings, 1979).

7. Globalization

This is the revised version of a public lecture delivered as a Visiting Professor at the Institute of African Studies, Universität Bayreuth, Bayreuth, Germany, in July 1999. A remote ancestor of this paper, "'They Call It Democracy': Reflections on the Current Situation," was presented to a conference Challenges for Democracy: Rethinking Political Philosophy, sponsored by the Guelph-McMaster Joint Doctoral Programme in Philosophy and the Guelph Political Studies Department, University of Guelph, Guelph, Ontario, Canada, March 1993. A previous version was presented to the conference Contemporary Transformations in Africa and the Discourses of Transnationalism and Diaspora, African Studies Workshop, University of Chicago, Chicago, Illinois, June 1995. Yet another version was read before the Faculty Seminar in the Department of Philosophy at Seattle University in 2003. I would like to thank those present at the various sessions and my former colleagues, Andrew Cutrofello of the Philosophy Department at Loyola University and Jennifer Lisa Vest, then of the Philosophy Department of Seattle University, for reactions and comments that have helped in the revision of this essay. My thanks go to Hugh Miller, another former Loyola University colleague, for bringing a crucial passage to my notice at a most opportune time.

1. It may be pointless to list the many texts in which the concern with structural processes dominates in the discourse of globalization. A fairly representative and popular sample is Frank J. Lechner and John Boli, eds., *The Globalization Reader* (Malden: Blackwell, 2003). See also Jan Aart Scholte, *Globalization: A Critical Introduction* (New York: Palgrave, 2000), chapter 2.

2. Especially *Orientalism* (New York: Vintage, 1978). In this discussion, "Greeks" and "Barbarians" are tropes. I hope they make the points that the world is divided and that power is unevenly distributed, especially the power of naming the real world.

3. Consonant with the specific focus of this book, for the most part I eschew the usual focus on structures and processes, especially economic processes. Of course, I will address the power imbalance in the world and the fact that this imbalance does have an impact on the lineaments of subjectivity around the world at the present time. To the extent that the focus on the philosophical discourse of modernity enables Africans to demand a different quality of relationship between them and the rest of the world, especially Europe and North America, I can regard my job as done. It may even be that such a different understanding of and attitude toward modernity is what is needed to enable Africans to take on the monster as other parts of the erstwhile so-called Third World have done.

4. Aimé Césaire, *Discourse on Colonialism* (New York: Monthly Review Press, 1972).

5. Molefi K. Asante, *The Afrocentric Idea* (Philadelphia, Pa.: Temple University Press,

1998); George G. M. James, *Stolen Legacy* (New York: Philosophical Library, 1954); Théophile Obenga, *A Lost Tradition: African Philosophy in World History* (Philadelphia: The Source Editions, 1995); Innocent C. Onyewuenyi, *The African Origin of Greek Philosophy: An Exercise in Afrocentrism* (Nsukka: University of Nigeria Press, 1994).

6. Cheikh Anta Diop, *The African Origins of Civilization: Myth or Reality*, trans. Mercer Cook (Westport, Conn.: Lawrence Hill, 1974); Martin J. Bernal, *The Afro-Asiatic Roots of Classical Civilization* (London: Free Association Books, 1987).

7. See especially Thomas C. Oden, *How Africa Shaped the Christian Mind: Rediscovering the African Seedbed of Western Christianity* (Downers Grove, Ill.: IVP Books, 2007).

8. Personal communication, L'Université Cheikh Anta Diop, Dakar, Senegal; Lerone Bennett, *Before the Mayflower: A History of Black America*, 5th rev. ed. (Harmondsworth: Penguin, 1984); Ivan van Sertima, *They Came before Columbus: The African Presence in Ancient America* (New York: Random House, 1977); Cheikh Anta Diop, *Precolonial Black Africa: A Comparative Study of the Political and Social Systems of Europe and Black Africa, from Antiquity to the Formation of Modern States* (Westport, Conn.: Lawrence Hill, 1987); Enrique Dussel, *The Invention of the Americas: The Eclipse of "the Other" and the Myth of Modernity* (New York: Continuum Books, 1995); Jeffrey C. Gunn, *First Globalization: The Eurasian Exchange, 1500 to 1800* (Lanham, Md.: Rowman & Littlefield, 2003).

9. J. M. Roberts, *The Triumph of the West*, quoted in Stuart Hall, "The West and the Rest: Discourse and Power," in *Modernity: An Introduction to Modern Societies*, ed. Stuart Hall, David Held, Don Hubert, and Kenneth Thompson (Cambridge: Blackwell, 1996), 200.

10. Arno Peters's projection map, which seeks to draw the map of the world to scale so that the respective mass of each continent is accurately depicted, has not caught on. It turns out that the northern hemisphere is not as dominant as is represented on almost all non-Peters maps. It is interesting to speculate on why this map has not become the world standard, since it was first published in 1974 in German and in English for the first time in 1983.

11. On the significance and implication of this presumed emptiness of the occupied lands in the Palestinian case, see Edward Said, "Zionism from the Standpoint of Its Victims," in *Anatomy of Racism*, ed. David Theo Goldberg (Minneapolis: University of Minnesota Press, 1992), 210–246.

12. See Bhikhu Parekh, "Liberalism and Colonialism: A Critique of Locke and Mill," in *The Decolonization of Imagination*, ed. Jan Nederveen Pieterse and Bhikhu Parekh (London: Zed, 1995), 81–98. See also Uday Singh Mehta, *Liberalism and Empire: A Study in Nineteenth-Century British Liberal Thought* (Chicago: University of Chicago Press, 1996). Recall what was said earlier about Lugard and how Africans had no entitlement to their portion of the globe. It was claimed for some nebulous humanity in whose name the land was being exploited even as Africans were carefully defined out of this common humanity.

13. John Thornton, *Africa and Africans in the Making of the Atlantic World, 1400–1680* (Cambridge: Cambridge University Press, 1992); and Paul Gilroy, *The Black Atlantic* (Cambridge, Mass.: Harvard University Press, 1993) are examples of earlier scholarly attempts to reinscribe the evidence of African agency into the narratives of modernity.

14. David Walker, *One Continual Cry: David Walker's Appeal, Its Setting, and Its Meaning*, ed. Herbert Aptheker (New York: Humanities Press, 1965); Maria Stewart, *Maria W. Stewart: America's First Black Woman Political Writer*, ed. Marilyn Richardson (Bloomington: Indiana University Press, 1987); Frederick Douglass, *My Bondage and My Freedom*, ed. and intro. William L. Andrews (Urbana and Chicago: University of Illinois Press, 1987); Paul Robeson, *Here I Stand* (Boston: Beacon Press, 1971); Paul Robeson, "Ballad for Americans" and "Statement—We Are Climbing Jacob's Ladder," on *Scandalize My Name*, Book of the Month Club Record 30-5647, 33 rpm recording, 1980; Nina Simone, "Mississippi Goddamn," on *Saga of the Good Life and Hard Times*, BMG Music, CD, 1997; *The Mind of Gil Scott-Heron: A Collection of Poetry and Music*, Arista Records, 33 rpm recording, 1978; Wynton Marsalis, "Premature Autopsies (Sermon)," on *The Majesty of the Blues*, CBS, CD, 1989.

15. The point here is apt to be misunderstood. I am not suggesting that Africa exported its surplus population in the same fashion as Europe did. I am merely saying that however we look at it, those slaves managed to globalize if not whole cultures they embodied, at least significant parts of them. Thanks to this factor, Yorùbá is a global language, whereas Greek or Swedish is not.

16. The Hamitic hypothesis is the view that ascribes African achievements in the areas designated "Black," "Sub-Saharan," or "proper" Africa—from statecraft to artistic expressions to grand physical structures—to light-skinned "Hamitic" peoples and denies any achievements attributable to Africa's Negroid populations.

17. See Olufemi Taiwo, "Exorcising Hegel's Ghost: Africa's Challenge to Philosophy," *African Studies Quarterly* 1, no. 4 (1998), available at www.Africa.ufl.edu/asq/v1/v1_i4.htm.

18. The key pieces of globalization that are standard fare in the discussion start out, albeit on occasion unwittingly, from the fact of capitalism, modern mass culture, and politico-ideological structures that all epitomize the hegemony of "Western" ideas. Whatever is focused on is "Western" by default or it is what the West does or does not do and the reactive responses of the Rest of Us who are victimized by it.

19. Recently there have been some developments in the direction of recognizing the agency of Africans. See for example Paul E. Idahosa, "A Tale of Three Images: Globalization, Marginalization, and the Sovereignty of the African Nation-State," in *Africa at the Crossroads: Between Regionalism and Globalization*, ed. John Mbaku and S. C. Saxena (Westport: Praeger, 2004), chapter 4; Wim van Binsbergen, Rijk van Dijk, and Jan-Bart Gewald, eds., *Situating Globality: African Agency in the Appropriation of Global Culture* (Leiden: Brill, 2004).

20. I think that this is what makes Lamine Sanneh's *Abolitionists Abroad: African*

Americans in the Making of Modern West Africa such an important work (Cambridge: Harvard University Press, 1999).

21. Chinweizu, *The West and Rest of Us: White Predators, Black Slavers, and the African Elite* (New York: NOK Publishers, 1978).

22. On the other hand, those who are familiar with the criminal enterprise of people-smuggling in different parts of the globe might object. People-smuggling is a very well-organized undertaking, and it seems to share some of the characteristics of the earlier patterns of indentured servants and their principals. Exploring these similarities is beyond the ken of the present discussion. But see Bhargavi Ramamurthy, *International Labour Migrants: Unsung Heroes of Globalisation*, SIDA Studies no. 8 (Stockholm: Swedish International Development Cooperation Agency, 2003).

23. See for example Judith A. Carney, *Black Rice: The African Origins of Rice Cultivation in the Americas* (Cambridge: Harvard University Press, 2002); Harry Belafonte, *The Long Road to Freedom: An Anthology of Black Music*, Buddha Records, CD, 2000.

24. He was interviewed in a radio program on BBC World Service in 1999 in a discussion of globalization. From the lone caller to a global broadcast in 1999, we now have a distinctive African community in another part of China. See Evan Osnos, "The Promised Land: Guangzhou's Canaan Market and the Rise of an African Merchant Class," *The New Yorker*, 9 February 2009.

25. Ironically, parts of the ancient Barbary Coast.

26. The Action Group was the first mass party in Nigeria and was in power from 1952 till well into the post-independence period in what was then called Western Nigeria. It adopted a version of socialism as its platform and has a reputation for running the most progressive administration in Africa, save for Kwame Nkrumah's Convention People's Party in Ghana. I find it significant that it placed freedom before abundance in its party slogan.

27. Again, I use the examples in this section not as a report of ongoing activities but as a foil for the argument that I am trying to build. Of course, if it turns out that the incidents reported in what follows are exceptions, then the force of the argument will be impaired. Fortunately, the case I make here remains relevant to the situation in the different parts of the world that I refer to, especially the African continent.

28. At that time, the U.S. administration pursued a nobody-but-Yeltsin policy. He was anointed as the sole hope for the survival of democracy in Russia.

29. "Russia Turns Its Back on Parliament," *The Economist*, 9 October 1993, 57, quoted in Maxwell A. Cameron, *Democracy and Authoritarianism in Peru* (New York: St. Martin's Press, 1994), 165.

30. See Joseph R. Blasi, Maya Kroumova, and Douglas Kruse, *Kremlin Capitalism: Privatizing the Russian Economy* (Ithaca, N.Y.: ILR Press, 1997).

31. The outcome of the privatization process has been the emergence of the so-called Russian oligarchs, with whom the president is now locked in mortal combat. He is prepared to clip their wings if they do as much as indicate interest in determining how Russia should be run. One of the oligarchs, Boris Berezovsky, escaped to a well-appointed

exile in the United Kingdom, and another, Mikhail Khodorkovsky, is languishing in a Siberian jail, ostensibly on tax evasion charges but some might say for daring to contemplate standing for election for president.

32. For analyses of the aborted transition program, see Julius Ihonvbere, *Nigeria: The Politics of Adjustment and Democracy* (New Brunswick, N.J.: Transaction, 1994), especially chapter 5; Pita Agbese, "The Impending Demise of Nigeria's Third Republic," *Africa Today* 37, no. 3 (1990): 23–44; Eghosa E. Osaghae, *Crippled Giant: Nigeria since Independence* (Bloomington: Indiana University Press, 1998).

33. Actually, the politicians did form various political organizations to vie for recognition as political parties. But the government chose not to register any of them, even though the National Electoral Commission had presented a list of nine associations it considered viable for purposes of recognition. Even so, Richard Joseph referred to the process as "guided democratization"; see Richard Joseph, "Africa: The Rebirth of Political Freedom," in *The Global Resurgence of Democracy*, ed. Larry Diamond and Marc F. Plattner (Baltimore, Md., and London: Johns Hopkins University Press, 1993), 311. It will become obvious from what follows that I do not share the celebratory tone of the book.

34. The elections in April 2007 were of a different order, though. Many of the results were nullified by tribunals, and the findings of the tribunals were upheld on appeal. The invalidations have been mostly because they did not meet minimum thresholds of democracy.

35. See Stephen Ellis, "Democracy in Africa: Achievements and Prospects," and Roger Tomkys, "Implementing Africa's Second Liberation: The Case of Kenya," both in *Action in Africa*, ed. Douglas Rimmer (London: The Royal African Society in association with James Currey and Portsmouth, N.H.: Heinemann, 1993).

36. "Kenya: Editorial Addendum," in *Action in Africa*, ed. Douglas Rimmer (London: The Royal African Society in association with James Currey and Portsmouth, N.H.: Heinemann, 1993), 151.

37. Major scandals over privatization in Kenya have claimed a vice president and a finance minister since 2003.

38. For a similar effort at thinking Africa and Eastern Europe together in the matter of transitions to democracy, see Mihaela Serban Rosen, ed., *Constitutionalism in Transition: Africa and Eastern Europe* (Warsaw: The Helsinki Foundation for Human Rights, 2003).

39. Witness the rapidity with which a market has mushroomed in the business of election monitoring. See especially Giuseppe Di Palma, "Why Democracy Can Work in Eastern Europe," in *The Global Resurgence of Democracy*, ed. Larry Diamond and Marc F. Plattner (Baltimore, Md., and London: Johns Hopkins University Press, 1993), 257–267.

40. Of course there are dissenters. But the fact that they are all regarded as ongoing transitions to democracy (with a few bumps on the road here and there) is the general foil for the argument I offer here.

41. For an instance of this mistake, see Philippe C. Schmitter and Terry Lynn Karl,

"What Democracy Is . . . and Is Not," in *The Global Resurgence of Democracy*, ed. Larry Diamond and Marc F. Plattner (Baltimore, Md., and London: Johns Hopkins University Press, 1993), 40–41.

42. See Issa G. Shivji, "Three Generations of Constitutions and Constitution-Making in Africa: An Overview and Assessment in Social and Economic Context," in *Constitutionalism in Transition: Africa and Eastern Europe*, ed. Mihaela Serban Rosen, (Warsaw: The Helsinki Foundation for Human Rights, 2003), 74–92.

43. I wrote those words before the December 2007 elections. The elections merely confirm my contention that there is and ought to be more to democracy than multipartyism and elections.

44. Kofi A. Busia, *Africa in Search of Democracy* (New York: Praeger, 1967), 107, my italics. Similar sentiments were expressed even earlier by Sylvanus Olympio, the late president of Togo: "The test of a democratic regime in Africa might not necessarily be the actual presence of a second party or several parties, so much as whether or not the regime tolerated individualists. This is the crucial point, for societies are not built or improved by conformists." James Duffy and Robert Manners, *Africa Speaks* (Princeton, N.J.: Van Nostrand, 1961), 76–77.

45. See Joseph Stiglitz, *Globalization and Its Discontents* (New York: Norton, 2003), for a critique of the operation of these conditionalities by someone who worked within the structures that usually impose them. I have been pleasantly surprised by the convergence of the conclusions drawn by an authority like Stiglitz and the speculative analyses that I originally formulated in the period 1993 to 1997.

46. For information on the impact of structural adjustment programs on various African countries, see Ihonvbere, *Nigeria*, chapter 4; Ishrat Hussain, "Trade, Aid, and Investment in Sub-Saharan Africa," in *Action in Africa*, ed. Douglas Rimmer (London: The Royal African Society in association with James Currey and Portsmouth, N.H.: Heinemann, 1993), 75–106; World Bank Policy Research Report, *Adjustment in Africa* (Oxford: Oxford University Press, 1994); G. O. Olusanya, R. O. A. Akindele, and Adebayo Olukoshi, eds., *The African Debt* (Lagos: NIIA, 1989); and Claude Ake, "Rethinking African Democracy," in *The Global Resurgence of Democracy*, ed. Larry Diamond and Marc F. Plattner (Baltimore, Md., and London: Johns Hopkins University Press, 1993), 70–82.

47. The theme of the creeping homogenization of life forms across the globe is a recurrent one in the discourse on globalization. As will be clear in what follows, I do not believe that the danger is as great as is often portrayed. The problem I find instead is that many in the West do not seriously intend that the rest of us become like them.

48. The analogy can be extended. Mike loves to gamble: are we to emulate him in this, too?

49. When earlier versions of this chapter were written, China was in the initial stages of its mammoth economic expansion and India was putting in place the pivots of its recent phenomenal economic development. What originally was a rhetorical speculation—I have purposely left it that way in the text—has become lived experi-

ence and we already are seeing the makings of the disaster that awaits our planet and its inhabitants, arising from industrialization strategies built on nonrenewable fossil fuels. For some sobering analyses and prognostication, see Jacques Leslie, "The Last Empire: China's Pollution Problem Goes Global," *Mother Jones*, November/December 2007; and Richard Behar, "Special Report: China in Africa," *Fast Company*, 9 May 2008, available at www.fastcompany.com.

50. I heard the eco-conscious broadcaster on National Public Radio's "All Things Considered," I think in 1995. The fact that much of Africa has become the graveyard for Euroamerica's hand-me-down appliances means that many appliances with chlorofluorocarbons are still wreaking havoc with the world's atmosphere from the obscure parts of the globe, where they are shiny emblems of newly minted social mobility for teeming populations. Because of the massive inflow of capital by General Motors, Ford, Fiat, and Volkswagen into the automobile industries in China, Argentina, and Brazil, we are now witnessing in the field of energy consumption, especially oil, the pressures that will result if and when the world's centers of population begin to replicate the consumption patterns of Euroamerica. A good source for tracing the news on this front is www.automotiveindustrynews.com.

51. When the leaders of the West call for the rest of us to be like the West, they understand globalization in terms of the univocal narrative that I alluded to earlier. They want to be able to go in to Asia, Latin American, and African countries and have their pick of national treasures to pick up for nothing. They also want to continue to beggar those countries in order to sustain their economies and benefit their own people.

52. This raises the question of the irresponsible patterns of consumption in the West itself. It is a global issue because the rest of us pay for this profligacy.

53. There are other aspects of this insincerity. Serious productive investments are not made in Africa. The imposition of the market is meant to make the countries concerned buy more from the West. Thus, they may be markets for Western goods, but they are not market economies.

54. A BBC report on 11 November 1994 cited the Chinese government's alarm at the wholesale pilfering of or fire sale of state property to party officials. See the special issue of *World Press Review* (March 1996) on China.

55. World Bank reports routinely show the glaring neglect of Africa in foreign direct investment as capital moves across the globe.

56. Stiglitz, *Globalization and Its Discontents*.

57. For another analysis that isolates a different kind of paradox in the process of globalization in Africa, see David E. Apter, "Globalization and Its Discontents: An African Tragedy," *Dissent* (Spring 2002): 13–18.

58. Writings about Africa are replete with references to the growing immiserization of African peoples and the declining indices of well-being in all areas of life even as other parts of the so-called underdeveloped world are scoring impressive reductions in poverty rates.

59. I am refraining in this discussion from considerations of internal conditions that

might discourage the influx of foreign direct investment in some countries and what I think is the racialization of capitalism under late modernity, which makes international capital less than enthusiastic about investing in African countries even when there is evidence that some of them, for example Mozambique, actually have higher-than-average returns on investment.

60. Conversely, there is a lesson in contrasting this with how Turkey is being kept out.

61. We now have countries fighting to have factories relocated to them from other countries; American cities are giving automobile and other companies free rides to keep them. The reluctance of industrialized countries to come up with codes of conduct for transnational corporations regarding their behavior in less-industrialized countries is a case in point. Indians are still suffering from the effects of the disaster at a Dow Chemical Company plant in Bhopal back in 1984.

62. Witness the popularity of term limits in the United States, which is explained in part by voter frustration at their inability to unseat incumbents whose coffers are bulging with special-interest money.

63. See John Stuart Mill, *On Liberty*, chapter 3, "Of Individuality As One of the Elements of Well-Being," excerpted in Jene M. Porter, ed., *Classics in Political Philosophy* (Englewood Cliffs: Prentice-Hall, 1997), 514–538.

64. Louis D. Brandeis, dissenting in *Olmstead v United States*, 277 U.S. 438 (1928). Recall Busia's suggestion that democracy "must recognize the right of others to think differently, and to choose differently." And Olympio wants a democratic regime to be judged "by whether or not it tolerated individualists." (See note 44 above.)

65. *"Rest in Pieces": Police Torture and Deaths in Custody in Nigeria*, Human Rights Watch Reports 17, no. 11 (July 2005).

66. When Louis Leakey announced in the nineties that he and other Kenyans were forming a new opposition party, he was denounced by Mr. Moi as a racist who does not understand Kenyans. The problem, though, is that Mr. Leakey is a native-born "white" Kenyan. The UN Commission on Human Rights has recently accused the Kenyan police of having committed large-scale extrajudicial killings of members of an outlawed group in 2007.

67. For a specific indictment of continental European scholars on this score, I refer to Enrique Dussell's *The Underside of Modernity* (Buffalo: Prometheus Books, 1996). Paul Gilroy's *The Black Atlantic: Modernity and Double Consciousness* (Cambridge: Harvard University Press, 1993) is a significant attempt to document the contributions of what he identified as "the Black Atlantic" to the construction of the discourse of modernity that are not recognized in the canons of the discourse.

68. William Leon McBride, *Philosophical Reflections on the Changes in Eastern Europe* (Lanham, Md.: Rowman & Littlefield, 1999).

69. Of course, I am leaving the postmodern critics out of my account.

70. Karl Marx, "The Eighteenth Brumaire of Louis Bonaparte," in Karl Marx and Frederick Engels, *Collected Works*, vol. 11 (New York: International Publishers, 1975).

71. The mechanism for remediation in the advanced countries—the welfare state—is

unavailable and (given current neoliberal pressures) cannot be created in the newly democratizing countries.

72. For supporting philosophical arguments for this viewpoint, see Ronald Dworkin, *A Matter of Principle* (Cambridge: Harvard University Press, 1985), part 3.

73. See for criticism Robert H. Bates, "Governments and Agricultural Markets in Africa," in *Toward a Political Economy of Development: A Rational Choice Perspective*, ed. Robert H. Bates (Berkeley: University of California Press, 1988), 331–358.

74. Alexis de Tocqueville, *The Old Regime and the French Revolution*, trans. Stuart Gilbert (New York: Doubleday, 1955), xii–xiv.

75. See C. B. Macpherson, *The Life and Times of Liberal Democracy* (Oxford: Oxford University Press, 1977).

76. Jason Riley's *Let Them In: The Case for Open Borders* (New York: Gotham Books, 2008) came out too late to be addressed here. But it is interesting that a free trader like him is willing to bite the bullet and let the law of supply and demand determine immigration policy in the United States. My case for open borders is built on different foundations.

SELECTED BIBLIOGRAPHY

Adewoye, Omoniyi. *The Judicial System in Southern Nigeria 1854–1954*. Atlantic Highlands, N.J.: Humanities Press, 1977.

Agbodeka, Francis. "The Fanti Confederacy 1865–69." *Transactions of the Historical Society of Ghana* 7 (1964): 82–123.

Ajayi, J. F. A. *Christian Missions in Nigeria 1841–1891: The Making of a New Elite*. Ibadan: University of Ibadan Press, 1965.

———. *A Patriot to the Core: Bishop Samuel Ajayi Crowther*. Ibadan: Spectrum, 2002.

Amin, Samir. *Eurocentrism*. New York: Monthly Review Press, 1989.

———. "Modernité et interprétations religieuses." *Afrique et Développement* 29, no. 1 (2004): 7–53.

Appiah, Kwame Anthony. *In My Father's House*. New York: Oxford University Press, 1991.

Asiwaju, A. I. *West African Transformations: Comparative Impacts of French and British Colonialism*. Lagos: Malthouse Press, 2001.

Attoh-Ahuma, S. R. B. *The Gold Coast Nation and National Consciousness*. London: Frank Cass, 1971.

Ayandele, Emmanuel A. *The Missionary Impact on Modern Nigeria 1842–1914*. London: Longman, 1966.

Biobaku, Saburi O. *The Ègbá and Their Neighbours: 1842–1872*. Oxford: Clarendon Press, 1957.

Blyden, Edward Wilmot. *Christianity, Islam and the Negro Race*. 1887; Edinburgh: Edinburgh University Press, 1967.

Boahen, Adu. *African Perspectives on Colonialism*. Baltimore, Md.: Johns Hopkins University Press, 1987.

Bolt, Christine. *Victorian Attitudes to Race*. London: Routledge & Kegan Paul, 1971.

Bowen, T. J. *Adventures and Missionary Labours in Several Countries in the Interior of Africa*. 2nd ed. Intro. E. A. Ayandele. London: Frank Cass, 1968.

Busia, Kofi A. *Africa in Search of Democracy*. New York: Praeger, 1967.

Buxton, Thomas Fowell. *The African Slave Trade and Its Remedy*. Intro. G. E. Metcalfe. London: Dawsons of Pall Mall, 1968.

Césaire, Aimé. *Discourse on Colonialism*. New York: Monthly Review Press, 1972.

Christopher, A. J. *Colonial Africa*. London: Croom Helm, 1984.

Comaroff, J., and J. L. Comaroff. *Of Revelation and Revolution.* Vol. 1, *Christianity, Colonialism, and Consciousness in South Africa.* Chicago: University of Chicago Press, 1991.

———. *Of Revelation and Revolution.* vol. 2, *The Dialectics of Modernity.* Chicago: University of Chicago Press, 1997.

Conklin, Alice. *A Mission to Civilize: The Republican Idea of Empire in France and West Africa, 1895–1930.* Stanford, Calif.: Stanford University Press, 1997.

Cooper, Frederick, and Ann Laura Stoler, eds. *Tensions of Empire: Colonial Cultures in a Bourgeois World.* Berkeley: University of California Press, 1997.

Curtin, Philip. *Africa and the West: Intellectual Responses to European Culture.* Madison: University of Wisconsin Press, 1972.

Dallmayr, Fred, and G. N. Devy, eds. *Between Tradition and Modernity.* New Delhi: Sage Publications, 1998.

Delavignette, Robert. *Christianity and Colonialism.* Trans. J. R. Foster. New York: Hawthorn Books, 1964.

Demangeon, Albert. *The British Empire: A Study in Colonial Geography.* Trans. Ernest F. Row. London: George C. Harrap & Co., 1923.

Desai, Gaurav. *Subject to Colonialism: African Self-fashioning and the Colonial Library.* Durham, N.C.: Duke University Press, 2001.

Deutsch, Jan-Georg, Peter Probst, and Heike Schmidt, eds. *African Modernities: Entangled Meanings in Current Debate.* Oxford and Portsmouth, N.H.: James Currey and Heinemann, 2002.

Dussel, Enrique. *The Invention of the Americas.* New York: Continuum, 1995.

Echeruo, M. J. C. *Victorian Lagos.* London: Macmillan, 1977.

Elias, T. O., and M. I. Jegede, eds. *Nigerian Essays in Jurisprudence.* Lagos: MIJ Professional Publishers, 1993.

Eze, Emmanuel C., ed. *Race and the Enlightenment Reader.* Malden: Blackwell, 1997.

Falola, Toyin, ed. *Tradition and Change in Africa: The Essays of J. F. Ade Ajayi.* Trenton, N.J.: Africa World Press, 2000.

Fanon, Frantz. *The Wretched of the Earth.* New York: Grove, 1968.

Farias, P. F. de Moraes, and Karin Barber, eds. *Self-Assertion and Brokerage: Early Cultural Nationalism in West Africa.* Birmingham University African Studies Series 2. Birmingham: Centre of West African Studies, 1990.

Fyfe, Christopher. "Race, Empire and the Historians." *Race & Class* 33, no. 4 (1992): 15–30.

George, Olakunle. *Relocating Agency: Modernity and African Letters.* Buffalo: State University of New York Press, 2002.

Gikandi, Simon. *Maps of Englishness: Writing Identity in the Culture of Colonialism.* New York: Columbia University Press, 1996.

Gilroy, Paul. *The Black Atlantic.* Cambridge, Mass.: Harvard University Press, 1993.

Gyekye, Kwame. *Tradition and Modernity.* New York: Oxford University Press, 1997.

Habermas, Jürgen. *The Philosophical Discourse of Modernity*. Cambridge: Massachusetts Institute of Technology Press, 1990.

Hall, Stuart, David Held, Don Hubert, and Kenneth Thompson, eds. *Modernity: An Introduction to Modern Societies*. Cambridge: Blackwell, 1996.

Harvey, David. *The Condition of Postmodernity*. Oxford: Polity Press, 1990.

Hegel, G. W. F. *The Philosophy of Right*. Oxford: Clarendon Press, 1958.

Heussler, Robert. *Yesterday's Rulers: The Making of the British Colonial Service*. Syracuse, N.Y.: Syracuse University Press, 1963.

Horton, James Africanus. *West African Countries and Peoples*. Intro. George Shepperson. Edinburgh: Edinburgh University Press, 1969.

Jeyifo, Biodun. "In the Wake of Modernity." *Anglophonia/Caliban* 7 (2000): 71–84.

Kalu, Ogbu, ed. *The History of Christianity in West Africa*. London: Longman, 1980.

Karibi-Whyte, A. G. *The Relevance of the Judiciary in the Polity—In Historical Perspective*. Lagos: Nigerian Institute of Advanced Legal Studies, 1987.

Kimble, David. *A Political History of Ghana: The Rise of Gold Coast Nationalism, 1850–1928*. Oxford: Clarendon Press, 1963.

Kuklick, Henrika. *The Savage Within: The Social History of British Anthropology, 1885–1945*. Cambridge: Cambridge University Press, 1993.

Langley, J. Ayo. *Ideologies of Liberation in Black Africa: 1856–1970*. London: Rex Collings, 1979.

Little, J. P., ed. and trans. *Simone Weil on Colonialism: An Ethic of the Other*. Lanham, Md.: Rowman & Littlefield, 2003.

Lugard, Frederick D. *The Dual Mandate in Tropical Africa*. London: Frank Cass, 1965.

———. *The Rise of Our East African Empire*. 2 vols. London: Frank Cass, 1968.

Macamo, Elísio Salvado, ed. *Negotiating Modernity: Africa's Ambivalent Experience*. Dakar, London, Pretoria: Codesria Books/Zed Books/University of South Africa Press, 2005.

Maddox, Gregory, ed. *The Colonial Epoch in Africa*. Intro. Gregory Maddox. New York and London: Garland Publishing, 1993.

Mamdani, Mahmood. *Citizen and Subject*. Princeton, N.J.: Princeton University Press, 1996.

McAuslan, J. P. W. B., and Y. P. Ghai. *Public Law and Political Change in Kenya*. Oxford: Oxford University Press, 1970.

Mehta, Uday Singh. *Liberalism and Empire*. Chicago: University of Chicago Press, 1997.

Memmi, Albert. *The Colonized and the Colonized*. Boston: Beacon, 1967.

Mernissi, Fatima. *Islam and Democracy: The Fear of the Modern World*. Trans. Mary Jo Lakeland. Reading, Mass.: Addison-Wesley, 1992.

Mudimbe, V. Y. *The Invention of Africa: Gnosis, Philosophy, and the Order of Knowledge*. Bloomington and London: Indiana University Press and James Currey, 1988.

Nwabueze, B. O. *Judicialism in Commonwealth Africa*. London and Enugu: Hurst/Nwamife, 1977.

Ojomo, M. Ayo, and I. E. Okagbue, eds. *Human Rights and the Administration of Criminal Justice in Nigeria*. Lagos: Nigerian Institute of Advanced Legal Studies, 1991.

Pallinder-Law, Agneta. "Government in Abéòkúta, 1830–1914: With Special Reference to the Ègbá United Government 1898–1914." Ph.D. diss., University of Gothenborg, Sweden, 1973.

Phillips, Anne. *The Enigma of Colonialism: British Policy in West Africa*. London and Bloomington: James Currey and Indiana University Press, 1989.

Pieterse, Jan Nederveen, and Bhikhu Parekh, eds. *The Decolonization of Imagination*. London: Zed, 1995.

Roberts, A. D., ed. *The Colonial Moment in Africa*. Cambridge: Cambridge University Press, 1990.

Said, Edward. *Orientalism*. New York: Vintage, 1978.

Sanneh, Lamine. *West African Christianity: The Religious Impact*. London: C. Hurst & Co., 1983.

——. *Abolitionists Abroad: American Blacks and the Making of Modern West Africa*. Cambridge: Harvard University Press, 1999.

Sarbah, John Mensah. *Fanti Customary Laws*. 3rd ed. Intro. Hollis Lynch. 1897; London: Frank Cass, 1968.

——. *Fanti National Constitution*. 2nd ed. Intro. Hollis R. Lynch. London: Frank Cass & Co, 1968.

Sartre, Jean-Paul. *Colonialism and Neocolonialism*. London and New York: Routledge, 2001.

Serequeberhan, Tsenay. "The Idea of Colonialism in Hegel's *Philosophy of Right*." *International Philosophical Quarterly* 29, no. 3 (1989): 301–318.

Shenk, Wilbert R. *Henry Venn: Missionary Statesman*. Maryknoll: Orbis, 1983.

Spitzer, Leo. *Lives in Between: Assimilation and Marginality in Austria, Brazil, West Africa, 1780–1945*. Cambridge: Cambridge University Press, 1989.

Stiglitz, Joseph. *Globalization and Its Discontents*. New York: Norton, 2003.

Taylor, Charles. *Sources of the Self*. Cambridge: Harvard University Press, 1989.

Thornton, John. *Africa and Africans in the Making of the Atlantic World, 1400–1680*. Cambridge: Cambridge University Press, 1992.

Tiruchelvan, Neelan, and Radhika Coomaraswamy, eds. *The Role of the Judiciary in Plural Societies*. New York: St. Martin's Press, 1987.

Twaib, Fauz. *The Legal Profession in Tanzania*. Bayreuth African Studies 46. Bayreuth: Bayreuth African Studies Series, 1997.

Van Hensbroek, Pieter Boele. *Political Discourses in African Thought: 1860 to the Present*. New York: Praeger, 1999.

Venn, Henry. *West African Colonies: Notices of the British Colonies on the West Coast of Africa*. London: Dalton and Lucy, 1865.

Wambali, M. K. B., and C. M. Peter. "The Judiciary in Context: The Case of Tanzania." In *The Role of the Judiciary in Plural Societies*, ed. Neelan Tiruchelvan and Radhika Coomaraswamy, 131–145. New York: St. Martin's Press, 1987.

Ward, Kevin, and Brian Stanley, eds. *The Church Mission Society and World Christianity, 1799–1999*. Grand Rapids, Mich.: Eerdmans, 2000.

Warren, Max, ed. *To Apply the Gospel: Selections from the Writings of Henry Venn*. Grand Rapids, Mich.: Eerdmans, 1971

Williams, C. Peter. *The Ideal of the Self-Governing Church: A Study in Victorian Missionary Strategy*. Leiden: E. J. Brill, 1990.

Wilson, Henry S., ed. *Origins of West African Nationalism*. London: Macmillan, 1969.

INDEX

OLÚFẸ́MI TÁÍWÒ is Professor of Philosophy and Global African Studies and Director of the Global African Studies Program at Seattle University. He is author of *Legal Naturalism: A Marxist Theory of Law*.

CPSIA information can be obtained
at www.ICGtesting.com
Printed in the USA
BVHW030302202322
63207SBV00005B/182

9 780253 221308